A Multimodal Language Faculty

Also available from Bloomsbury

The Semiotics of Emoji, Marcel Danesi
Circus as Multimodal Discourse, Paul Bouissac
The Visual Narrative Reader, edited by Neil Cohn
The Visual Language of Comics, Neil Cohn
Who Understands Comics?, Neil Cohn
The Patterns of Comics, Neil Cohn

A Multimodal Language Faculty

A Cognitive Framework for Human Communication

Neil Cohn and Joost Schilperoord

BLOOMSBURY ACADEMIC
LONDON • NEW YORK • OXFORD • NEW DELHI • SYDNEY

BLOOMSBURY ACADEMIC
Bloomsbury Publishing Plc, 50 Bedford Square, London, WC1B 3DP, UK
Bloomsbury Publishing Inc, 1359 Broadway, New York, NY 10018, USA
Bloomsbury Publishing Ireland, 29 Earlsfort Terrace, Dublin 2, D02 AY28, Ireland

BLOOMSBURY, BLOOMSBURY ACADEMIC and the Diana logo are
trademarks of Bloomsbury Publishing Plc

First published in Great Britain 2024
Paperback edition published 2026

Copyright © Neil Cohn and Joost Schilperoord, 2024, 2025

Neil Cohn and Joost Schilperoord have asserted their right under the Copyright,
Designs and Patents Act, 1988, to be identified as Authors of this work.

Cover design: Jade Barnett
Cover image © Daniel Bosma

All rights reserved. No part of this publication may be: i) reproduced or transmitted in any form, electronic or mechanical, including photocopying, recording or by means of any information storage or retrieval system without prior permission in writing from the publishers; or ii) used or reproduced in any way for the training, development or operation of artificial intelligence (AI) technologies, including generative AI technologies. The rights holders expressly reserve this publication from the text and data mining exception as per Article 4(3) of the Digital Single Market Directive (EU) 2019/790.

Bloomsbury Publishing Plc does not have any control over, or responsibility for, any third-party websites referred to or in this book. All internet addresses given in this book were correct at the time of going to press. The author and publisher regret any inconvenience caused if addresses have changed or sites have ceased to exist, but can accept no responsibility for any such changes.

A catalogue record for this book is available from the British Library.

A catalog record for this book is available from the Library of Congress.

ISBN: HB: 978-1-3504-0241-6
PB: 978-1-3504-0245-4
ePDF: 978-1-3504-0242-3
eBook: 978-1-3504-0243-0

Typeset by Integra Software Services Pvt. Ltd.

For product safety related questions contact productsafety@bloomsbury.com.

To find out more about our authors and books visit www.bloomsbury.com
and sign up for our newsletters.

For Ray

Contents

List of Figures	ix
List of Tables	xiii
Preface	xiv

Part One Foundations

1	Reimagining Language	3

Part Two Modalities

2	What Is a Modality?	41
3	Interfacing between Modalities	73

Part Three Meaning

4	Conceptual Structures for Multiple Modalities	93
5	Multimodal Semantic Interactions	113

Part Four Grammar

6	The Complexity Hierarchy	147
7	Interactions between Combinatorial Schemas	185

Part Five Multimodality

8	Unimodal Expressions in a Multimodal Model	197
9	Independent Multimodal Interactions	207
10	Substitutive Multimodal Interactions	225

Part Six A Multimodal Language Faculty

11	Consequences of a Multimodal Language Faculty	245
12	Evolution of a Multimodal Language Faculty	263
13	Toward a Multimodal Linguistics	277

Notes	295
References	299
Index	325

Figures

1.1	Various T-shirts which all use a picture substituted for a verb	11
1.2	Tripartite structures of language distributed in a Parallel Architecture, along with emergent states of omnia, semia, sequentia, and modalia	20
1.3	Multimodal Parallel Architecture	28
1.4	Lexical items for the word heart, and the heart shape	29
2.1	Idiosyncratic and regularized sensory signals and their types, along with their interface with meaning	49
2.2	Tiers of phonological structure for *Emlen gives his loveliest smile*	51
2.3	Formology of the bodily modality	53
2.4	Formemes of the graphic modality	55
2.5	Graphological structure	57
2.6	Different correspondences between graphological and phonological structures	63
3.1	Four types of co-durative interfaces between a sentence and a gesture across time	76
3.2	Five types of mixed-durative interfaces between a sentence and a picture	78
3.3	Interfaces used in non-durative relationships	80
3.4	Types of carriers involved in Emergent relationships depending on their Root and Adjacent Awareness	83
3.5	Representational and Framing Planes in a panel from *JA!*	86
4.1	Schematization of a supramodal conceptual structure	95
4.2	Scene depicting a woman watching a man running into a tree	98
4.3	Motion events compared across an English sentence and a graphic depiction	99
4.4	Signification arising from the components of the Parallel Architecture	102
4.5	Formalization of idiosyncratic and regularized and graphics iconic of people, and the American Sign Language sign for a tree	104
4.6	Lexical entries for indexical signs of deictic pointing gesture	107
5.1	Multimodal relationships with complete and absent co-reference between pictures and text	114
5.2	Optimal innovation of the phrase *in the garbage of Eden* in reference to "in the garden of Eden"	118
5.3	Sentences involving background knowledge from auxiliary domains	120

5.4	Sequence of a juggler tossing pins, and tossing an anvil	122
5.5	Structure of visual representations using a visual optimal innovation, and integration of an auxiliary domain	124
5.6	Upfix which requires a metaphor to be understood	126
5.7	Examples of complete coreference for text-image and co-speech gesture relations	128
5.8	Examples of included coreference for text-image relationships, co-speech gesture, and co-speech gesture with further modulation of phonology	131
5.9	Examples of partial coreference in co-speech gesture, and text-image relations	132
5.10	Absent co-reference using an emergent satellite carrier, an emergent private carrier, and an inherent text-image relationship	134
5.11	Absent coreference in text-image relationships with face emoji	136
5.12	Absent coreference in text-image relationships with thumbs up/down emoji	137
5.13	Absent co-reference between text and an emoji, and co-speech gesture with a pinching gesture, and a metaphoric gesture	139
5.14	Multimodal *I want you* Uncle Sam recruitment poster, and optimal innovation of the poster with Darth Vader	140
6.1	One-unit schemas in expressions in onomatopoeia, two-word speech, gestures, and visual signs	151
6.2	Two-unit child utterance *Mommy cookie* meaning *Mommy eats a cookie, Give me a cookie Mommy, Do you want a cookie Mommy?*	153
6.3	Two-unit visual arrays using a Before-After Construction and a Comparison Construction	155
6.4	Two-unit schemas in the graphic modality including an emoji rebus, visual affixes of heart upfixes and a motion line, a negation affix	157
6.5	Unordered linear arrays	159
6.6	Ordered and unordered arrays for the same visual units of U.S. Holidays	161
6.7	Linear arrays that are ordered and unordered from airplane safety manuals	162
6.8	Instructional manual that uses a simple phrase schema	165
6.9	Structural categories in three sentences and three visual narratives	167
6.10	Embedding in the narrative grammar of visual languages	172
6.11	Structurally ambiguous visual narrative sequence with two interpretations	174
6.12	Formalization of a motion gesture	177

6.13	Hierarchic structure of a panel from *That Deaf Guy*	178
6.14	Graphic depictions of a "person running"	179
6.15	Semiotic properties of the Parallel Architecture	182
7.1	Multimodal interactions of Independent and Substitutive allocations	188
7.2	Substitution in a linear array	191
7.3	Co-speech gesture interactions using Independent and Substitutive allocations	193
7.4	Visual narrative sequence with Asymmetrical and Symmetrical Complex substitutive allocation	193
8.1	Multimodal Parallel Architecture	198
8.2	Emergent semia in each modality	200
8.3	Omnia in various modalities	203
9.1	Symmetrical Simple interactions in the Parallel Architecture	208
9.2	Symmetrical Simple interactions between text and image	209
9.3	Simple Symmetrical interactions of a deictic pointing gesture	210
9.4	Multimodal Before-After Construction	211
9.5	Symmetrical Simple interaction using a single picture and a linear written array	212
9.6	Symmetrical Simple interaction in a street sign from Nara Japan using linear arrays of image and words, and in an abstract schema for street signs	214
9.7	Asymmetrical interactions in the Parallel Architecture	215
9.8	Asymmetrical co-speech gesture interaction	216
9.9	Asymmetrical interactions between complex text and simple image sequences	217
9.10	Short boxing sequence with an ideophone and single words depicting thoughts	219
9.11	Symmetrical Complex interactions in the Parallel Architecture	221
9.12	Symmetrical Complex relations between a visual sequence and text	221
9.13	A multimodal *That Deaf Guy* comic strip, and the interactions diagrammed in the Parallel Architecture	224
10.1	Substitutions of images for verbs	228
10.2	Substitutive allocation in co-speech gestures	231
10.3	Substitutive allocation in a visual narrative sequence	233
10.4	Substitutive allocation within a language with an ideophone	235
10.5	Switching in visual register	237
10.6	Substitutions of graphics into sentences with varying degrees of acceptability	239

11.1	Multimodal Parallel Architecture	246
11.2	Relationships between an abstract Language and cross-linguistic diversity	250
11.3	Modality-general universals manifesting in the Parallel Architecture	253
11.4	Parallel Architecture with interfaces	255
11.5	Parallel Architecture with permeable relations between communicative systems, and relativistic relations of those systems to other cognitive systems	261
12.1	Various parts of the Parallel Architecture that require explaining in an evolutionary theory	269
12.2	Graphemic qualities of animal tracks, etchings from ochre and shells up to 100,000 years ago and diagram of a sand drawing scene from Central Australian Aboriginals	271

Tables

1.1	Distribution of structures of modality, grammar, and meaning across different classes of behaviors	24
2.1	Sensory and cognitive components of natural and other modalities	66
2.2	Characterization of multisensory, multimodal, cross-sensory, and cross-modal mappings	68
2.3	Diagrammed correspondences in the McGurk effect, sound-color synesthesia, and writing systems	70
3.1	Component parts of modalities, with duration as the primary characteristic of modality interactions	74
3.2	Characteristics across modality interfaces	88
6.1	The Complexity Hierarchy	148
7.1	Possibilities for multimodal interactions between combinatorial schemas of two expressions	186
13.1	Contrasting assumptions between the amodal and multimodal conceptions of language	289

Preface

We can probably mark the genesis of this book in 2016, but the ideas presented within it actually began much earlier. In 2003, Neil had recently completed his undergraduate degree at UC Berkeley and was in the early development of his ideas about visual languages. While developing a linguistic account of the structure of sequential images, he recognized that visual narrative sequencing often changed its complexity depending on its interaction with text, such as in contexts like comics. In addition, he had discovered work by David Wilkins discussing how Australian Aboriginals combined speaking, signing, and drawing in trimodal expressions, in both narratives and daily communication. He combined these threads in a paper with the seeds of the model presented in this book, originally posted as a preprint on Neil's website in 2003 as "Interfaces and interactions: A study of bimodality."

A few years later, Neil entered graduate school at Tufts University where he further developed his theories of visual language, and better situated his theories of multimodality into the Parallel Architecture model of his mentor, Ray Jackendoff. His earlier ideas were thus retooled into a paper in 2010, which was rejected following review from the journal *Cognitive Science*. The project sat until Neil was a postdoctoral fellow at UC San Diego, and was finally reworked further and published in 2016 as "A multimodal parallel architecture: A cognitive framework for multimodal interactions" in *Cognition*.

Meanwhile, in 1999 in the Netherlands, Joost joined Leo Noordman's Text Linguistics group at Tilburg University, and was invited by new colleague Fons Maes to co-teach a course called Tekst en Beeld (*Text and Image*). This enabled him to combine his long-standing interests in the cognition of written text production and understanding with this new and fascinating research area: the semantics of expressive systems beyond vocal language. His research interests shifted to exploring how visual language evokes conceptual categories like metaphor, hyperbole, irony, optimal innovation, negation, and argumentation, and how these expressions interact with the use of text in multimodal messages. He developed these ideas of visual meaning-making in his 2018 paper "Ways with pictures: Visual incongruities and metaphor." Meanwhile, the Tekst en Beeld course evolved into Multimodal Communication, concerned with multimodal interactions in informative, instructive, and persuasive genres like advertising, political cartooning, comic strips, and instruction manuals.

Shortly after the publication of Neil's 2016 *Cognition* paper, he joined Joost in the faculty at Tilburg University, and then "they" became "we." We began co-teaching the Multimodal Communication master's class in the Fall of 2016, which we structured around Neil's multimodal model, and taught it to students who also used it in their empirical course projects. Through this experience, we noticed both how well the model accounted for a wide range of phenomena, but also where it had problems.

Across several years of teaching, we together iteratively revised the model until on a bus ride back from a departmental retreat in January of 2018, we realized a book needed to be written.

Over 5 years later, with an interlude of a pandemic pushing us to do most collaborative writing online (which turned out to be a good method), we now present to you the results of our efforts. One of the traits that we share is an interest in the intellectual history of the study of language and cognition, which hopefully is reflected throughout our book. To situate our own work within this history, we see this book as focusing on the topic that seems to be rising as a central question of our own era. That is, what is the relationship between language and our other expressive behaviors, and how do they all combine in multimodal expressions? We are certainly not the first to broach this topic, but we believe that our approach not only provides an accounting for these phenomena, but heralds a new paradigm for considering all the fundamental questions pervading the linguistic and cognitive sciences.

We have several people to thank who contributed to this work. Neil is especially grateful for several formative scholarly influences, the foremost being the influence of his graduate mentors, Ray Jackendoff, Gina Kuperberg, Phil Holcomb, and postdoctoral mentors Marta Kutas and Jeff Elman. He is also thankful for his time studying with Susan Goldin-Meadow as a master's student, and previously with his "foster-advisor" Dan Slobin, who both fundamentally helped shape his ideas. Joost would like to thank his mentor Arie Verhagen, and senior colleague Fons Maes who introduced him to issues of multimodality.

We both would like to thank a number of our colleagues. We have benefited from colleagues at Tilburg University past and present, Rein Cozijn, Jan Engelen, Renske van Enschot, Paul van den Hoven, Emiel Krahmer, Fons Maes, Leonoor Oversteegen, Lisanne van Weelden. We are also grateful to our collaborators and colleagues within and outside our Visual Language Lab, including Naomi Caselli, Emily Coderre, Marie Coppola, Myrthe Faber, Tom Foulsham, Sharitha van der Gouw, Irmak Hacımusaoğlu, Harry van der Hulst, Bien Klomberg, Lenneke Lichtenberg, Les Loschky, Joe Magliano, Mirella Manfredi, Morgan Patrick, Michał Szawerna, and Aditya Upadhyayula.

We would also like to acknowledge the valuable insights that have come from scholarly discourse in feedback to our papers and presentations, particularly from our colleagues John Bateman, Charles Forceville, Hans Hoeken, Emar Maier, Margot van Mulken, Asli Özyürek, Wilbert Spooren, Gerard Steen, Janina Wildfeuer, Eva Wittenberg, and Jeff Zacks, and from our anonymous reviewer of our initial book manuscript.

We should also thank our hundreds of students over the years of our classes on Multimodal Communication who were subject to the development of our theoretical framework, along with dozens of thesis students who applied it.

Finally, Neil would like to thank Maaike and Emlen, and Joost would like to thank Henrieke, both for who they are, and for their putting up with our loud and excited voices through the doors and floors of our offices every time we met online for our writing sessions.

Our original title for this book was "Reimagining Language" and the sentiment of that original title remains in the spirit of this work. We hope it can provide an impetus and invitation for further questioning the foundations of what language is and how it fits within our communicative capacities.

Neil Cohn and Joost Schilperoord
Tilburg, The Netherlands
September 2023

Part One

Foundations

1

Reimagining Language

The study of language has persisted across millennia, but the past 200 years have seen significant strides for understanding language as a serious topic of scientific inquiry. Thinking about language has gone from observations about the similarities and differences between the languages of the world, to an acknowledgment that this diversity has its basis in an abstract linguistic system, and that this system is instantiated in human cognition (Chomsky 1965, Goldsmith and Laks 2019, Levelt 2013). These insights have given way to various theories guiding the assumptions of what language is and models of how it works, yielding highly successful research programs across the language sciences.

Despite this, the theories leak.

The foundations of contemporary understandings of language have largely persisted since the beginning and middle of the 20th century. This research has yielded several primary assumptions about the nature of language and its study, whether explicitly stated or implicitly embedded in the models proliferating across linguistic research (Smith 2003). Let's now turn to characterizing what we see as these guiding assumptions.

The foundational assumption is that speech is the prototypical channel for language (Goldsmith and Laks 2019, Levelt 2013). While speech may not be considered as the only channel for language, it has remained a primary focus. This emphasis comes clearly in the widely cited design features of language from linguist Charles Hockett (1960), who prominently includes the "vocal channel" as a criterion for behaviors to be considered as "language." Hockett's list has been disputed in the last decades (Kegl 2020, Smith 2003), but primacy of speech has endured within linguistic models. For example, though many of the prominent theories of language competence have been extended beyond speech, all directly focus on accounting for the structures of spoken language (Chomsky 1965, 1995, Goldberg 1995, Jackendoff 2002, Kaplan and Bresnan 1981, Lakoff 1971, Langacker 1987, Pollard and Sag 1994, Sadock 1991).

This focus on speech as prototypical leads to two contrasting consequences, with research either focusing or not focusing specifically on speech sounds as interesting phenomena. In the first case, speech as a primary locus of language gives way to research on how speech sounds are structured, a primary topic of debates in the study of language from the 1800s through the middle of the 1900s (Goldsmith and Laks 2019, Levelt 2013). By emphasizing speech as the primary channel for linguistic expression, it renders other channels as auxiliary or peripheral. For example, writing is then simply a tertiary extension of speech, while gestures or pictures would be considered as paralinguistic, extralinguistic, or auxiliary to the primary linguistic expressions. Such an orientation also reinforces a **unimodal** view of language, where linguistic expressions in other channels are perceived to arise only when the primary vocal channel is unavailable or impaired.

Acknowledging speech as the prototypical instance of language can also lead, somewhat paradoxically, to an orientation that ignores the contributions of speech sounds themselves. With the understanding that linguistic systems are guided by abstract principles, the variability of speech sounds across systems can be viewed as tertiary to the more fundamental properties of the language system that persist regardless of this diversity. Indeed, many of the primary debates about linguistic structure in the latter part of the 20th century had little to say about the substance of linguistic form, instead debating the relative contributions of syntax and semantics (Culicover and Jackendoff 2005, Harris 1993, 2021, Huck and Goldsmith 1995). This orientation reinforces what we call an **amodal** or modality-independent view of language, where the true nature of language persists regardless of its channel of expression (i.e., vocal, bodily, graphic, etc.). An amodal view is furthered by the perceived mutability of language, since the representations of speech can also manifest in writing or braille, and sign languages also proliferate as linguistic systems. This amodal view ultimately arrives at a position where the "sensorimotor output" of linguistic expressions is viewed as separate from the core language faculty (Hauser, Chomsky, and Fitch 2002).

Both a unimodal and an amodal view of language are also implicated by the foundational notion that the relation between form and meaning is **arbitrary**. Though there were precedents (Levelt 2013), this idea is largely attributed to the linguistic theories of Genevan linguist Ferdinand de Saussure (1972 [1916]). Arbitrariness is the observation that the properties of the linguistic form—i.e., speech sounds—are not reflected in their paired meanings. Thus, the sounds of a word are ultimately only conventionally related to the meanings they express. Arbitrariness has been taken as a fundamental defining trait of language, codified by Hockett's (1960) design features. An arbitrary relationship between form and meaning reinforces the split view of treatment about linguistic form. Since the formal properties of the signal have little suggestion about their meaning, it may be interesting to study such diverse forms (i.e., research on phonology), while a view that arbitrariness renders form as unimportant in the face of the meaning that it signals leads to ignore such forms (i.e., an amodal view).

1.1 Challenges to an Amodal Language Faculty

To summarize, linguistic research has characterized language as an amodal system of arbitrary signs primarily expressed by the vocal-auditory channel, embedded in human cognition. While these ideas originate from the beginning and middle of the 20th century, various recent threads of research pose challenges for these assumptions, but have largely not consolidated into an alternative conceptual frame for the understanding of language. We now turn to some of these lines of research and the challenges they pose to unimodal and/or amodal assumptions about the nature of language.

1.1.1 Sign Language

Sign languages are linguistic systems that manifest through bodily movements rather than speech sounds, and proliferate in diverse systems around the world independent of speech. The study of sign language has been part of debates about the nature of language since the 1800s (Levelt 2013), but contemporary research on sign language has grown in the latter half of the 20th century (Brentari and Crossley 2002, de Vos and Pfau 2015, Emmorey 2021, Stokoe 1960). At this point, it should be widely accepted that sign languages are natural linguistic systems with the full range of complexity and diversity as spoken languages. On the surface, sign languages support an amodal notion of language, since they instantiate linguistic structure in a modality outside of speech (Kegl 2020). Yet, though signed languages demonstrate abstract features like any other linguistic system, they also enact those structures in ways that are unique to bodily expressions (Emmorey 2023, Liddell 2003, Sandler 2017). Indeed, attempts to simply transfer the lexical and grammatical components of speech directly into the body, like in Manually Coded English, often result in forms that lack the naturalness of naturally developing sign languages (Supalla 1991, Wilbur, Marschark, and Spencer 2003).

Consider the ways that sign languages encode their form. Like spoken languages, sign languages combine bodily primitives into segmental structures, yet unlike speech, sign languages have multiple articulators (Fenlon, Cormier, and Brentari 2017, Sandler 2017). Hands can make multiple handshapes and orientations across various movements, and are articulated in various positions of the body, and which may also be accompanied by conventionalized facial expressions. Because of these multiple articulators, simultaneous production of signs is an inherent part of sign languages, not just linear sequencing like in the acoustic speech signal.

In addition, though early research on sign language emphasized the arbitrariness of signs to reinforce its linguistic status, contemporary research has more widely acknowledged the proliferation of iconicity and indexicality in signed lexicons (Emmorey 2023, Goldin-Meadow and Brentari 2017, Liddell 2003, Lillo-Martin and Gajewski 2014, Sandler 2017). Iconicity and indexicality also extend to sign language grammars, such as in the indexical treatment of anaphoric relations. Though the principles guiding anaphoric relations are consistent with those in spoken languages, instead of just using lexicalized pronominals, sign languages can also signal anaphoricity by pointing to established spaces set in front of a signer's body (Frederiksen and Mayberry 2022).

Under one interpretation, these distinctive traits might be taken as a challenge to the linguistic status of sign languages. Such a perspective sets the properties of speech as a baseline, with the expectation that any other linguistic system must conform to those properties to be considered linguistic. Yet, if the equal status of sign language is to be taken seriously, such differences should be an indication that these speech-centric criteria may be faulty to begin with. Rather, the assumptions about "what language is" should be changed to better accommodate these unique properties.

Moreover, despite the rightful recognition of sign language as a natural language, various linguistic theories maintain speech as the prototypical form of language, and implicitly reinforce the idea of the bodily modality as secondary or auxiliary. Such ideas permeate the stereotype that sign languages are reflective of alternate linguistic systems that arise when the primary speech system is inaccessible, such as through disability. While deaf communities (and sometimes deafblind communities) are the predominant users and creators of sign languages, they are used by both hearing and deaf individuals. Sign languages also persist in some hearing communities which use them in multimodal interactions and/or contexts like times of bereavement (Green 2014, Wilkins 2016) or vows of silence (Umiker-Sebeok and Sebeok 1987). In addition, the capacity for sign languages is adjacent to those of spoken languages, particularly evident in expressions by bimodal bilinguals who simultaneously speak and sign rather than simply codeswitching between languages (Emmorey 2023).

An implied secondary status to the bodily modality also arises within linguistic theories. While some theoretical frameworks of the language faculty have been used to describe sign languages, they all first model speech (Chomsky 1965, 1995, Goldberg 1995, Jackendoff 2002, Kaplan and Bresnan 1981, Lakoff 1971, Langacker 1987, Pollard and Sag 1994, Sadock 1991). At most, these approaches are conceptualized as amodal, with allusions that they also account for the properties of sign language, but without explicit detail of it. Yet, this also creates some confusion: by invoking "phonology" as an amodal structure to account for the generalizable properties of both speech sounds and bodily expressions, this then obscures the properties unique to each expressive system (Emmorey 2023, Fenlon, Cormier, and Brentari 2017, Sandler 2017). This amodal notion also prevents an accounting for their relative roles within a language architecture: is there only one phonology in the architecture of language that indiscriminately subsumes both spoken and signed phonology, or does each modality have its own phonology represented in the linguistic architecture (unlike all prominent linguistic models), and if so, what is their relationship?

This lack of representation extends to many studies which purport to analyze the typological or "universal" features of language, but fail to include sign languages within their corpora or experimental stimuli (e.g., Skirgård et al. 2023). Consider also the widespread "gesture first" theories of linguistic evolution, which posit the bodily channel as a first place for "language" to evolve, before adapting to the vocal channel (Armstrong 2002, Corballis 2002, Givón 1995, Hewes 1973, Tomasello 2010). These theories reinforce an assumption of amodality, since "language" is then separate from both the vocal and bodily channels. Yet, whether intentional or not, this gesture-first conception implicitly places the bodily modality as more primitive and secondary to the more "evolved" modality of speech.

All of this is to say that, if sign language is to be accepted as a true natural language (which it is), it needs to be treated as such directly within theories about what the language faculty is and how it works. This includes accounting for both the commonalities of spoken and signed languages and for each modality's distinctive characteristics, with the features of both systems being given equal weight in determining the assumptions of how languages are built.

1.1.2 Gesture

The past several decades have also seen proliferation in the study of gestures, expressive bodily movements that can be produced both independently and alongside speech (Goldin-Meadow and Brentari 2017, Kendon 1972, McNeill 1992). They range in their systematicity from highly conventionalized gestural isolates (e.g. thumbs up or down, nodding, waving) to the fully novel gesticulations that accompany speech (Kendon 1988, McNeill 1992). They also span various types of meaning-making: some are arbitrary, while others are iconic and/or indexical, and still others use more complex mappings like metaphors. Gestures also vary systematically across cultures (Cooperrider, Slotta, and Núñez 2018, Kita 2009).

In addition, when they are simultaneously produced, gestures are inextricably tied to the structure of speech. Gestures are tightly coordinated with phonological and syntactic structures (Holler and Levinson 2019, Rasenberg, Özyürek, and Dingemanse 2020). Speech and gesture also share a common "growth point" of semantics, with gestures sometimes conveying concepts that elaborate on or are absent entirely from those expressed in speech (McNeill 1992). The integration of speech and gesture is further highlighted by "component" or "language-like" gestures (Clark 1996, McNeill 1992), where gestures may fill the role of an otherwise unexpressed syntactic unit (Ladewig 2020), such as in *I caught a* <small pinching gesture> *fish*. In addition, the way that concepts are encoded in the typological patterns of spoken languages often appears in the gestures of those speakers (Gu et al. 2017, Haviland 1993, Núñez and Sweetser 2006).

Given that speech and gesture are so intertwined, it has led to questions about their status in relation to each other: are gestures *part* of language? Are they *separate* from language? Despite their intimate relationship, predominant models of language competence have not explained the multimodal relationship between speech and gesture (Chomsky 1965, Jackendoff 2002, Langacker 1987), though some have been extended for such purposes (Ladewig 2020). In addition, such models have also not typically described the relationship between gesture and sign languages, or why people still gesture, whether or not they have developed a full sign language (Emmorey 2023).

1.1.3 Homesign

A central emphasis in the language sciences since the 1960s has also focused on the degree to which language is **innate**. Early advocates for language as a human "instinct" point to its critical learning period (Lenneberg 1967), and the rapid acquisition of linguistic competence by children relative to the stimulus in their environments (Chomsky 1968), while counterarguments have highlighted the role of social learning in language development, among others (Tomasello 2010). While debates continue about the balance of nature and nurture, there is general agreement that some capacity of language competence is an innate and natural capacity of human beings. Given these debates, one natural question is: what happens when a learner is deprived of the "nurture" of language exposure?

While the idea of language impoverishment cannot be ethically experimentally tested, this "forbidden experiment" has occurred due to various circumstances. Some documented cases have arisen due to parental neglect or abuse (e.g., the famous case of Genie), but language deprivation is a persisting risk to deaf children who have no access to a spoken language, but are also not taught a sign language. It should be stressed that language deprivation can be detrimental for children's ability to learn language, and such impoverishment has been shown to affect brain structures associated with language processing (Cheng et al. 2023, Mayberry et al. 2011), and the later the exposure to any language, the harder it is for children to learn (Lillo-Martin and Henner 2021).

When deaf children have no access to spoken or signed languages, they invent their own bodily communication systems called "homesigns," which have been studied since the 1970s by psycholinguists like Susan Goldin-Meadow (Goldin-Meadow 2003b). Since they receive no language input, homesigns are largely created by the children themselves, and which need to be learned by caregivers. Yet, homesigns generally use a more constrained lexicon than externally acquired languages, and their combinatorial structure is typically limited to short sequences motivated by the semantic structure of the signs rather than distributional grammatical roles (i.e., parts of speech). For example, homesigns often use heuristics like a default order of *agent-patient-act*, which appears to persist no matter the (inaccessible) languages in the children's environments (Gershoff-Stowe and Goldin-Meadow 2002, Goldin-Meadow et al. 2008).

Based on research about homesign and other cases of impoverished language learning, Goldin-Meadow has proposed that linguistic systems can be characterized into two classes. Resilient systems persist in the absence of learning an external language, and are characterized by a constrained lexical inventory and limited combinatorics motivated by semantics. In contrast, fragile systems must be learned via an external linguistic system. These include the potential for a lexicon of unlimited length, and for combinatorial systems that are not characterized by semantics alone, but also use traits like grammatical roles and phrase structures.

These distinctions again raise important questions for modeling the language faculty: If homesigns do not rise to the complexity of being considered full "languages," how should they be categorized? Moreover, how are such resilient and fragile systems reflected within cognitive architectures of linguistic competence?

1.1.4 Writing

Additional questions arise from consideration of the structure and neurocognition of written language. Though writing is an invention, it plays a fundamental role in the experience and comprehension of language, especially in contemporary literate societies. Yet, many languages have no corresponding written language, and throughout most of history the majority of people were not literate. For these latter reasons, theories of linguistic competence have typically not included writing in their scope.

Writing systems on the surface would also appear to support an amodal view of language, since expressions that are naturally vocal are conveyed instead as visual marks. This is reinforced by the categories used to differentiate writing systems, which often imply a clean mapping into particular linguistic structures. All writing systems use a mapping of speech sounds onto graphic representations, but they are typically categorized as whether the graphic units distinctly depict speech sounds (phonographic), depict morphemes (logographic), or directly depict semantics (ideographic or pictographic).

Nevertheless, writing systems of the world involve more complexity than these categories suggest (Sproat 2000). Despite their mapping of speech sounds to graphics, most writing systems also invoke traces of meaning at some granularity, whether it is in the overt pictorial depictions of meaning (as in some components in Chinese characters or Egyptian hieroglyphics) or in the differentiation of homophones by means of alternative spellings (ex. *I*, *aye*, *eye*). Thus, in addition to the correspondences between speech sounds and graphics, there is variation in the degree to which the graphics themselves convey meaning, and combinations of both meaning and sound components are possible.

The connection between speech sounds and graphic marks also comes with consequences. In terms of neurocognition, writing has been described as "recycling" neural machinery innately dedicated to other purposes (Dehaene 2011). To this end, literacy alters the structures of the brain (Carreiras et al. 2009, Dehaene 2011, Wolf 2008), which is why learning to read and write requires explicit and substantial instruction. Thus, the adaptation of speech to writing is not a result of a natural amodal quality of language, but rather because graphics have been forcefully pushed to correspond with speech sounds in a way that is unnatural to innate neurobiological predispositions.

In addition, though theories of the language faculty have often excluded characterizations of writing, linguistics research itself has been heavily influenced by the conventions of written languages rather than speech. For example, the notions of *words* and *sentences* derive from written norms, rather than reflecting the more dynamic segmentation and productive creativity of spoken utterances (Chafe 1994, Coulmas 1989). This written origin is one reason such categories come into question when confronted with the complexity of typologically diverse languages (Haspelmath 2017).

Furthermore, a substantial amount of the psycholinguistic literature on language processing comes from studies using written language, not speech. While this is not necessarily problematic, if literacy changes the structures of the brain (Carreiras et al. 2009, Dehaene 2011, Wolf 2008), then such experiments are characterizing an "altered" language competence compared to what is theorized by speech-centric linguistic models. This implies that models should identify what changes in the language faculty due to literacy, and in doing so should include the basic structures that allow for writing. This again raises the question: what is the "phonology" of writing, such that it involves a mapping between both vocal and graphic signals?

1.1.5 Graphic Systems

While writing may be an unnatural use of graphic representations, the production of actual pictures is not. The capacity for creating pictures—i.e., drawing—is unique to human beings. While writing needs to be explicitly taught, drawing development occurs spontaneously across developmental stages through exposure and practice across a critical learning period (Cohn 2012, Davis and Gardner 1992, Read 1958, Rosenblatt and Winner 1988). In addition, though the oldest writing systems were invented around 10 to 12,000 years ago (Coulmas 1989), archeological evidence of deliberate mark-making is among the oldest records of human intelligence from at least 250,000 years ago (García-Diez and Ochoa 2019), while cave paintings have been dated to 45,000 years ago, providing some of the oldest evidence of human meaning-making (Aubert et al. 2019).

1.1.5.1 Text-Image Relationships

Like the multimodal combinations of gestures and speech, pictures have been integrated with language for thousands of years in integral ways. The practice of *picture recitation*, where storytellers guide an audience through sequential pictures, dates back to at least 400 BC in India and spread all over the world (Kaminishi 2006, Mair 2019, Petersen 2011). Similar multimodal interactions between speech, sign language, and narrative sand drawings persist in practices used by Australian Aboriginals (Green 2014, Wilkins 2016). Pictures have also been combined with writing for millennia, whether in Egyptian hieroglyphics which accompany wall carvings, the text-image relationships in Mayan pottery and Aztec codices, or the illustrations that accompany biblical texts, to name just a few (Kunzle 1973, Petersen 2011).

In contemporary society, speech combines with pictures in slide-show presentations or videos, while text-image relationships appear in virtually all types of media: comics, cartoons, advertisements, websites, memes, etc. (Bateman 2014). This integration is particularly apparent in the frequent use of emoji alongside text in online digital communication, which has led to comparisons between emoji and gestures (Gawne and McCulloch 2019, McCulloch and Gawne 2018), along with a growing body of research questioning their linguistic status (Cohn, Engelen, and Schilperoord 2019, Ferrari 2023, Homann et al. 2022, Paggio and Tse 2022).

Like gestures, the independence of modalities is challenged by the integration of simple pictures into the syntactic structure of text. Consider the well-known slogan *I* ♥ *NY*, created by designer Milton Glaser, as seen on T-shirts, mugs, posters, and other paraphernalia. Here, the heart-shape plays the role of a verb in a canonical *subject-verb-object* sentence structure. Specifically, it means LOVE and is pronounced as *love*. Now consider the following sentences, all taken from real-world contexts:

(1)

a) I ♥ Papa (Baby romper)
b) I ♥ making new friends (Twitter post)
c) Please drive slowly. We ♥ our children. (Street sign)
d) They ♥ weddings (Twitter post)
e) I ♥ transitive pictograph verbalizations (T-shirt)

Across these examples, the heart plays a role in the uninflected verb position carrying the consistent meaning (and possibly pronunciation) of *love*. Repeated exposure to these kinds of expressions may lead one to generalize the heart in different sentences to create a construction in the form of *subject-♥$_{Verb}$-object*, a pattern even self-referentially appearing in (1e). This use of the heart for *love* in English has extended to many other languages using this construction, including those with different words orders.

Now consider the sentences in Figure 1.1, all appearing on T-shirts. Each sentence uses a picture in the verb position where the semantics of the pictures-as-verbs either maintain the meaning of LOVE and/or invoke association to the direct object of the sentence. Following the original construction which used the place of New York, direct objects with a location use a verb-picture related to that place, like for Tokyo with a sport played there (sumo) or a monster that destroys it (Godzilla). However, this pattern can be used beyond places. For example, *Nyuk* is an utterance typically made by Curly from The Three Stooges, whose face appears in the verb position of that sentence, while the skull-and-crossbones comes from an activist T-shirt reflecting a displeasure with a former U.S. president.

These examples imply a more general construction of *subject-picture$_{Verb}$-object* where the verb slot must be filled by a picture, not a written word, and also one that semantically connects to the direct object. This forms an abstract grammatical pattern, but with slots *mandatorily* filled by different modalities, and in fact these patterns form a taxonomy from general (S-Picture$_V$-O) to constrained (S-♥$_V$-O) to specific (I ♥ NY).

Figure 1.1 Various T-shirts which all use a picture substituted for a verb.

Such examples again raise questions for the nature of the language faculty: How can models of the language faculty account for multimodal interactions? How can there be lexical constructions defined by multiple "phonologies" (i.e., both speech/writing and graphics)? How can units of one channel (like pictures or gestures) play syntactic roles in the grammar of another channel (like speech/writing)?

1.1.5.2 Visual Languages

While the integration of pictures with writing has motivated questions about their relationship to language, another line of research has demonstrated that graphic representations also have linguistic features. The stereotype of pictures is that they reflect what people see, whether by vision or mental imagery (e.g., Fan et al. 2023). This perceptual viewpoint renders pictures as highly variable and lacking any internal structure (due to the unstable nature of natural percepts), and this tie to vision renders pictures as a reflection of how a drawer sees the world. While this perceptual viewpoint may reflect the phenomenological experience of what it feels like to draw, this idea has only arisen in the last few hundred years (Cohn 2014a, Willats 2005, Wilson 1988), and it does not accurately characterize how pictures are structured, how they are processed, or how people learn to draw.

Both theoretical and empirical research has shown that pictures are composed of systematic patterns at numerous levels of structure, both for small component parts—like how people draw hands, noses, or eyes—for whole figures, for systematic scenes, and also for non-perceptible elements—like hearts, motion lines, or speech balloons (Cohn 2013b, 2024, Forceville 2011, McCloud 1993, Schilperoord 2013, Schilperoord and Cohn 2023, Weissman et al. 2023, Wilkins 2016, Wilson 1988, 1999). These "visual lexical items" use hierarchic combinatorial structures both for the organization of the graphic forms themselves (Willats 1997) and for the composition of their more abstract morphological components (Cohn 2018a, Forceville 2011, Schilperoord and Cohn 2023).

In addition, sequences of images are guided by a range of combinatorial schemas. In the most complex sequencing, visual narratives use images that play categorical roles determined by distributional tendencies, which embed within recursive combinatorial structures, and are modified by a range of additional constructional schemas (Cohn 2013c, 2015b, 2024). These combinatorics result in distance dependencies, structural ambiguities, coordination constraints, and anaphoric relations between units. All of these structural features are typically associated with syntax, and their manipulation in visual narratives also results in neural responses similar to those observed to manipulation of syntax in sentences (Cohn 2020b, Coopmans and Cohn 2022).

Both visual lexical items and their sequential combination differ between particular communities of users. On the surface these differences are reflected in stable visual "styles" which are not indicative just of individual people, but rather recognizable as varying across cultures and time periods. In addition, patterns in sequencing differ across populations, suggestive of varying grammars that follow regularities observed in linguistic typology (Cohn 2024). Like spoken and signed languages, variations between graphic systems also provide defining characteristics of people's identities and social bonds to communities (Green 2014, Pimienta 2022).

Learning to draw also resembles characteristics of language development. Children instinctively and spontaneously produce graphics if given the chance, and early representations appear to be consistent across very young children (Willats 1997), implying universal tendencies prior to acquisition of cross-system diversity. Drawing development progresses across developmental benchmarks from a scribbling (i.e., babbling) stage, to the mapping of basic units to spatial conceptual primitives, and on to the refinement of those units (Kindler and Darras 1997, Willats 2005). They also extend known visual lexical items to fill gaps (such as using human faces on animal bodies or suns for hands) similar to children's extension of words to superordinate categories or to cover lexical gaps (Wilson and Wilson 2009).

This developmental process occurs through imitation and natural production, unlike the explicit instruction required of literacy. In addition, drawing development progresses across a critical learning period that apexes at puberty, after which drawing ability stagnates throughout life without dedicated learning (Cohn 2012, Davis and Gardner 1992, Read 1958, Rosenblatt and Winner 1988). Yet, no such stagnation occurs for people who acquire graphic representations from imitating an external conventionalized system (Wilkins 2016, Wilson 1988, 1999). This contrast between the proficiency of drawers with and without influence of an external system aligns with the distinction between fragile and resilient systems in language learning (Cohn 2012). In other words, drawing development is not a process of learning how to articulate perception, but of building up a "visual vocabulary."

The comprehension of visual sequences also follows a developmental trajectory. Children start with understanding the objects and events within individual pictures (ages 2-3), before recognizing the coreference between objects across images (ages 4-6), and further recognition of structural patterns and inferencing. Sequential image understanding also does not come for free with perception and event cognition: substantial research indicates that people need exposure and practice with visual narrative systems across development, and without such exposure they cannot construe the sequence *as a sequence* (Cohn 2020a). In addition, comprehenders' proficiency with visual narratives and their "age of acquisition" modulate both behavioral and neural responses to sequential image processing (Coderre and Cohn 2023, Cohn 2020a). Moreover, sequential image processing varies based on the patterns of which diverse visual narrative systems comprehenders are exposed to (Cohn and Foulsham 2020, Cohn and Kutas 2017), suggesting not just general proficiency, but also system-specific proficiency.

These features of the structure, cognition, and development of pictures have motivated Visual Language Theory (Cohn 2013b, 2020a, 2024), which argues that the graphic channel instantiates linguistic features independent of its relations to speech. **Visual languages** are the representational systems that people use to draw, just as they use spoken languages to speak and signed languages to sign. Consistent with other linguistic systems, visual languages are decomposable into sub-structures of lexicons and grammars, vary in diverse systems across populations which give a sense of identity to users, are learned through exposure and practice across a critical learning period, and are processed with the same neural responses as other languages.

None of these aspects of graphics have been integrated into models of the language faculty—be it the structure of graphics themselves, their extension to writing, or their multimodal interactions with writing. The current exclusion of graphics from the language faculty should again consider writing: What is "recycled" by extending speech sounds to graphics is the natural systems that are used to draw. Why should such a mapping lie outside the language faculty, rather than being an adaptation within previously unconnected sub-parts of an existing architecture? Similarly, how can multimodal interactions and lexical entrenchment between speech/writing and pictures persist when pictures are assumed to lie outside the linguistic system?

1.1.5.3 Unique Features

One of the reasons that lines have been drawn between certain behaviors qualifying as "language" compared to others is the invocation of particular design features as criteria for defining language (Hockett 1960, Smith 2003, Zuidema and Verhagen 2010). Some of these features aim to be inclusionary, to extend the notion of "language" across behaviors, and thereby give them a sense of value because of that label. At other times, these features are constructed with exclusionary intent to restrict "language" to particular behaviors in contrast to either other human communicative behaviors, or in contrast to animal communication systems. Here we highlight two design features that have been particularly persistent for defining uniquely "linguistic" structure: arbitrariness and recursion.

As described at the start, **arbitrariness** is one of the most invoked features used to define language (Hockett 1960). This is canonically characterized within the binary "Saussurean Sign" which divides into two linked components: a sensory signal (signifier) coupled to its referent (signified). These components are said to maintain an arbitrary relationship, meaning that the sensory signal has no indication of its meaning, and instead is understood solely through conventionality—i.e., that the meaning attributed to the signifier is through agreement between interlocutors. Though arbitrariness is a mapping, the signifier and signified are often viewed as inextricably linked, forming a singular sign, and arbitrariness is often then intermixed with the notion of conventionality.

Despite being central to many claims about language for a century, cracks have emerged in the armor of arbitrariness. First, though early work on sign language was pushed to deny non-arbitrary features (Goldin-Meadow and Brentari 2017, Lillo-Martin and Gajewski 2014, Sandler 2017), contemporary research has acknowledged that it is rich in other types of reference, including indexicality (i.e., signification through indication) and iconicity (i.e., signification through resemblance). These latter notions come from the semiotic theories of the American philosopher Charles Sanders Peirce (1940), though in linguistics research they are often understood through the lens of a Saussurean Sign (a point we will return to in Chapter 4).

Second, substantial work has shown that iconicity and indexicality are also widespread in speech (Clark 1996, Ferrara and Hodge 2018). Iconicity in lexical items has received substantial study, both for overt iconicity like ideophones (Dingemanse 2017), and for its more subtle functioning throughout lexicons (Perlman and Woodin 2021, Winter et al. 2023). Grammatical patterns also use iconicity such as in direct quotes, serial event constructions, and others (Marx and Wittenberg 2022, Schlenker et al. 2022, Zwaan and Radvansky 1998), while iconicity facilitated by phonology occurs when people imitate other people's voices, raise the volume of their voice to imply size, or extend vowels to imply length (Clark 1996, 2016), as in *looooooooong*.

Thus, though arbitrariness pervades language, multiple types of signification are intrinsic and important functional parts of the system. Not only should this full range of signification be part of the "design features" for understanding what language is, but it should also be accounted for directly within models of the linguistic architecture itself (Perlman and Woodin 2021).

A more recently considered design feature is **recursion**, particularly as it pertains to syntactic structure. Recursion is a formal property where units or constituents of one type can embed in constituents of that same type. In the context of syntax, recursion allows for the embedding of phrases within phrases and substantial syntactic complexity. Within generative grammar, syntax is assumed as the only source of combinatoriality for language, and over time recursion has been taken as the sole function for this generative engine (Chomsky 1995). Recursion has been a part of syntactic theories for decades, but it was codified as a design feature when this sole recursive engine was claimed as the primary innovation in language evolution (Hauser, Chomsky, and Fitch 2002).

Like arbitrariness, syntactic recursion as the only source of generativity also reinforces an amodal view of language. Recursion as a design feature is placed in the "narrow" faculty of what makes language special, while the "sensorimotor aspects" of the system (i.e., those related to the expressive channel) are considered part of the "broad" faculty of language (Hauser, Chomsky, and Fitch 2002). By excluding aspects of the channel from the core properties of language, what is important and generative about language is necessarily amodal.

Yet, against this "syntacto-centric" view of recursion (Culicover and Jackendoff 2005), combinatoriality also persists in phonology, semantics, and morphology (Booij 2010, Goldsmith 1976, Jackendoff 2002, Langacker 1987, Sadock 1991). In other words, all structures of the linguistic system use combinatoriality, often with recursion (Jackendoff 2002). In addition, syntax itself may not be solely characterized by recursion, as syntactic systems involve a range of complexity (Jackendoff and Wittenberg 2014, 2017).

Recursion also characterizes the structure of other expressive behaviors. In the early 1980s, linguist Ray Jackendoff and composer Fred Lerdahl decomposed musical structure into several recursive components (Lerdahl and Jackendoff 1982), some of which have been posited to overlap with language (Jackendoff 2009b). In addition, as described above, individual images use recursive combinations of graphic components (Cohn 2018a, Willats 1997, 2005), while visual sequencing can involve recursive combinatoriality showing traits considered typical of syntax, including distance dependencies, structural ambiguities, anaphoric relations, and constraints on coordination (Cohn 2013c, 2018b, 2024, Coopmans and Cohn 2022). In addition, recursive structures are involved in numerous other cognitive systems, such as the mental representation of visual objects (Biederman 1987, Marr 1982) and visual scenes (Võ 2021), and the structure of events (Jackendoff 2007, Zacks and Tversky 2001). Indeed, proposals of domain-general processing of hierarchic structure go back to the 1950s (Lashley 1951).

Altogether, design features that have been proposed to distinguish language as unique result in a restricted view that both fails to capture the complexity of language itself and/or does not acknowledge how such features appear in other behaviors. That is, design features often provide poor criteria for accurately assessing what is linguistic, and when they are described in models restricted only to language, it reduces the explanatory power of accounting for such features across cognitive domains (Corballis 1991, Fitch and Martins 2014, Pinker and Jackendoff 2005). While both arbitrariness and recursion should be incorporated into models of language, they should not be looked at as exclusive defining features and the broader perspective on such features should also be acknowledged.

1.1.6 Neurocognition

While the classification of distinctive features typically comes from linguistic theories, a similar thread of uniqueness comes from empirical research on the neurocognition of language. Early research on the psychology of language identified specific "language areas" (ex. Broca's and Wernicke's areas) which were thought to characterize language production and comprehension specifically (Levelt 2013), and the idea of a "language network" in the brain persists in contemporary research (Fedorenko and Blank 2020). Yet, the neurobiology of sign language shares many areas with speech; it also involves those that do not overlap (Emmorey 2023, 2021). In addition, many neural mechanisms thought to be language-specific have since been shown to involve more general functions.

Consider Broca's area (the left inferior frontal gyrus, BA44 and BA45), which was traditionally associated with language production or the processing of syntax specifically (Levelt 2013). Yet, Broca's area is activated not only for syntax, but for phonology and semantic processing as well (Hagoort 2014). In addition, it is also activated in the processing of music, actions, pictures, and visual narrative sequencing (Cohn 2020a, Fadiga, Craighero, and D'Ausilio 2009, Fazio et al. 2009, Koechlin and Jubault 2006, Maess et al. 2001, Willems, Özyürek, and Hagoort 2008). All of this has suggested that these areas subserve a more general function associated with linearization and hierarchic processing across behaviors, whether as a whole (Corballis 1991) or subdivided across behavioral types (Fedorenko and Blank 2020, Hagoort 2014, Hagoort and Indefrey 2014).

A similar shift occurred in the study of semantic processing. In 1980, cognitive neuroscientists Marta Kutas and Steve Hillyard identified a distinctive brainwave associated with semantic processing in language (Kutas and Hillyard 1980), which they named the "N400" because of its electrical polarity ("N" for Negative) and its timing (peaking 400 milliseconds after the onset of the words). Over the next several decades, additional research showed that N400s were evinced not only by words, but also by pictures, photos, math problems, and virtually all meaningful stimuli (Kutas and Federmeier 2011). This suggested that the N400 indexed a default brain response to the processing of meaning, and its associated brain area (the anterior temporal lobe) has since been argued as reflecting a supramodal hub of semantic memory (Calzavarini 2023, Kutas and Federmeier 2011, Kuhnke et al. 2023, Ralph et al. 2016, Xu et al. 2009).

Other brainwave responses have similarly shifted from being interpreted as language specific to general. Neural responses originally associated with grammatical processing (P600, LAN) (Hagoort, Brown, and Groothusen 1993, Neville et al. 1991, Osterhout and Holcomb 1992) have also been evoked by music (Koelsch 2011a, Patel 2003, 2008), visual narrative sequencing (Cohn 2020b), scene processing (Võ 2021), and event processing (Sitnikova, Holcomb, and Kuperberg 2008). Meanwhile, brainwaves associated with processing anaphoric relationships (Nref) (van Berkum 2012) have been evoked by anaphoric relations in wordless visual narratives (Coopmans and Cohn 2022). In addition, certain neural responses have reliable relationships to each other (N400 and P600), modulated by both language proficiency and age of acquisition (Tanner, Goldshtein, and Weissman 2018). Yet, this same interaction appears to the processing of visual narrative sequences, which are similarly modulated by proficiency and the age at which participants began reading visual narratives (Coderre and Cohn 2023).

All of these findings suggest that the neurobiological basis of language processing is not partitioned from that of other behaviors, and that language processing itself taps into more general functional mechanisms. So, why are these connections not reflected in the cognitive architectures posited for the language faculty itself?

1.1.7 What to Do?

While many of these aspects of language and communication are recognized and acknowledged within the study of language, they have not been directly incorporated into the models that characterize the structure of language, nor have they changed the assumptions about what language is. Rather, they are typically subsumed within a general amodal view of language (sign language) or otherwise viewed as auxiliary or marginalia (writing, iconicity, gesture, graphics, etc.) that need not be represented in the core of linguistic competence.

This book is based on the idea that such treatment is not reflective of the actual substance of these phenomena. Rather, these phenomena are relegated to the periphery because they do not fit cleanly within the prevailing paradigms and models of language. The solution then is not to exclude or ignore such phenomena as inconvenient outliers, but rather to propose new models and paradigms that better account for the full richness of human beings' communicative competence.

1.2 Decomposing and Recomposing "Language"

A prerequisite to proposing a new model and paradigm of language is that of categorization. How do we categorize phenomena that have limited linguistic features in relation to full languages? How do we categorize multimodal interactions that integrate expressions that are "not language" (i.e., gestures, pictures) with language in inseparable ways? What are phenomena that display all the structural and cognitive traits of languages, but are not typically called "language"?

All of these questions tap into a more fundamental issue: *What is language?* Indeed, despite language being the object of much research across numerous disciplines, what it *is* persists as a question which in many cases remains inadequately addressed. As discussed, language often is defined by a list of criteria by what language does, by how it is used, or by its various descriptive features. Yet, many of these lists of descriptors or design features maintain a speech bias, including overextension or implied exclusivity of certain features (like arbitrariness) and/or excluding features from other channels, like sign languages.

Calling something "language" is often also a matter of stating its value. For many people, elevating or acknowledging their communication system as "language" justifies its worth. Defining "language" is further complicated because the term is colloquially used in metaphorical or semi-metaphorical ways. For example, the "language of music" possibly describes structural and/or behavioral consistencies between music and language, despite their clear differences (Jackendoff 2009b, Patel 2008). In addition, computer codes are called "programming languages," despite betraying substantially different properties than natural languages (for example, their "syntax" and its rules are overt, rather than an underlying system where the constraints may be unconscious and unknown to a user). Similar metaphoric or extended usages persist in describing the communication systems by other animals.

Here, we seek a more descriptive basis for the question of *What is language?* We begin by addressing where we need to look to find such a definition. Language is a social and cultural phenomenon, and hence the term carries social and cultural value. However, language has been recognized as a psychological phenomenon ever since the progressive consolidation of the linguistic sciences in the 1800s (Goldsmith and Laks 2019, Levelt 2013). If language originates in the mind, we need to look to its cognitive correlates—its component parts—in order to understand what it is. The parts of language are not found in the culturally manifested expressions "out there" in the world, but instead in the minds that construct and comprehend those expressions. This means that the identifying ingredients of language itself are not the "features" or "characteristics" that one can describe about the messages, but in the mental structures that coalesce to allow those expressions. We argue that three core cognitive components comprise these ingredients for language, but they also persist across other behaviors.

First, languages (and other communicative systems) use a **modality**, which is the channel by which a message is expressed and conveyed. As will be detailed in Chapter 2, we define a modality as a certain channel's *sensory signals* together with their *cognitive correlates*. For example, speech uses the *vocal modality*, which is produced through oral articulation, and perceived via the auditory system, with codified phonemics combined using phonological structures. Gestures and sign languages use the *bodily modality*, produced through articulation of the body (hands, torso, face, etc.) in different positions and movements, while perceived through the visual and/or haptic system, with corresponding cognitive correlates (Fenlon, Cormier, and Brentari 2017, Sandler 2017). Finally, pictures manifest in the *graphic modality*, which is produced through bodily motions that leave traces to make marks, which are perceived through the visual system, and have corresponding primitives and combinatorial structures (Cohn 2012, Willats 1997). Modalities are how we produce and experience our expressions.

A second component is the capacity to convey **meaning**. We follow Jackendoff (1983, 1987, 2002) in calling this Conceptual Structure. As described above, research has shown that meaning is encoded in a supramodal "hub" of semantic memory which aggregates conceptual information from across sensory and cognitive systems (Calzavarini 2023, Kuhnke et al. 2023, Kutas and Federmeier 2011, Ralph et al. 2016, Xu et al. 2009). Conceptual Structure is fundamentally combinatorial and constitutes an independent cognitive system, though how this meaning is packaged depends on the modality (i.e., vocal and graphic expressions access meaning in different ways), or on the representational systems within a modality (i.e., English and Swahili access meaning through different lexical and grammatical patterns).

The final linguistic component is that of **grammar**, a combinatorial system for organizing information, particularly for packaging meaning in order to be expressed. Taxonomies of these combinatorial principles have been posited to describe a range of grammatical complexity for different types of expressions (Chomsky 1956, Jackendoff and Wittenberg 2014), and similar taxonomies have been posited for sequence processing in neurocognition (Dehaene et al. 2015).

These three components of modality, meaning, and grammar are recognized by nearly all models of the structure of language, albeit mostly under different names (i.e., phonology, semantics, morphosyntax). We here invoke these more generalized terms which can ultimately extend beyond what is typically considered "language," which will become clear below. Debates throughout the language sciences largely have focused on the relative distributions and relationships of these components within the architecture of the language faculty (Culicover and Jackendoff 2005, Harris 1993, 2021, Huck and Goldsmith 1995), but not their existence within the system.

To resolve these debates, Jackendoff (2002) proposed that these components maintain an equal status within a **Parallel Architecture** of the language faculty. We depict this architecture in Figure 1.2 using our generalized terminology, where a modality, meaning, and grammar persist as independent structures, but with interfaces between these components. Within this model combinatoriality is not placed in just one structure (such as grammar alone), but rather each structure allows for combinatoriality using the operation of Unification, a principle of assembling schematic structures.

Because these components are independent, expressions can use all or only some of the structures in the Parallel Architecture. That is, some may express meaning without using grammar, and others may use grammar without meaning. These relative distributions motivate us to introduce new terms for specific *emergent interactions* between the cognitive components of a modality, meaning, and grammar. This will allow us to sidestep whether any specific behavior that uses those emergent states qualifies as a "language." We call these emergent interactions **omnia**, **semia**, **sequentia**, and **modalia**, which are diagrammed in Figure 1.2b–e. Each term highlights the primary component that defines its structural makeup. We describe each of these in turn below.

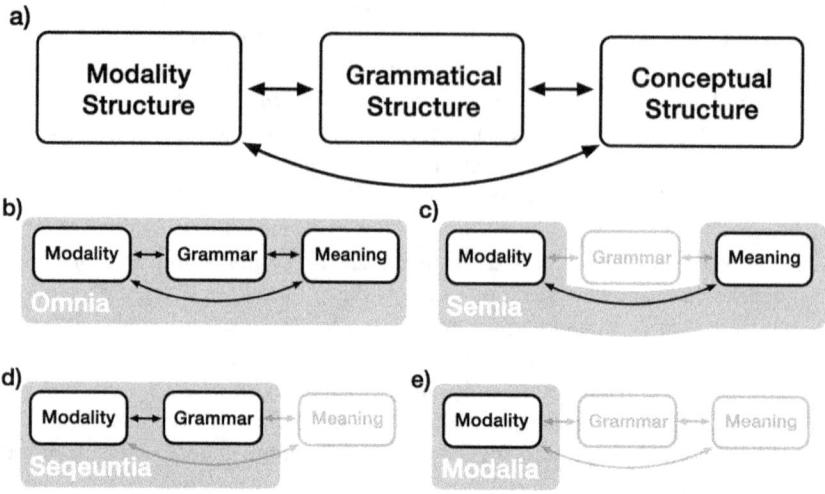

Figure 1.2 The tripartite structures of language distributed in a) a Parallel Architecture, along with emergent states of b) omnia, c) semia, d) sequentia, and e) modalia.

1.2.1 Omnia

Our first class involves an interaction between all three components of modality, meaning, and grammar. When all components are present, we refer to it as ***omnia***. Omnia systems therefore use a modality to express meaning that is organized with a complex combinatorial system (Figure 1.2b). The complexity of the combinatoriality in omnia systems may manifest in their units (morphology) and/or in their sequencing (syntax). In addition, they also have a rich lexicon, giving rise to productivity that uses this entrenched knowledge. Users therefore need to be exposed to omnia systems to acquire proficiency. Omnia systems align with Goldin-Meadow's (2003b) notion of a fragile system, which requires exposure to gain fluency in its open-ended lexicon and complex grammar.

In that they use all three structural components of modality, meaning, and grammar, omnia systems are prototypical of full languages. In the case of *spoken languages*, meaning is expressed using a grammar with the vocal modality. This combination of elements reflects Jackendoff's (2002) original Parallel Architecture, composed of phonological structures (modality), syntactic structures (grammar), and conceptual structures (meaning). This same combination of structures occurs in the bodily modality for *sign languages*, another omnia system that uses robust lexicons and complex combinatoriality acquired through exposure across a developmental trajectory. These bodily omnia systems are thus structurally equivalent to the vocal omnia systems, just manifesting in a different modality.

In addition to the vocal and bodily modalities, as described, graphic representations also use systematic patterns characterizable as a lexicon, which are organized using complex combinatorial systems. In other words, meaning is expressed using a grammar through the graphic modality, in line with other omnia systems. Such structural similarities with the omnia of spoken and sign languages have motivated us to call such systems *visual languages*, and, as discussed, these consistencies also persist in their (neuro)cognitive processing (Coderre and Cohn 2023, Cohn 2020b, a, Loschky et al. 2020, Robertson 2000) and in their development (Cohn 2012, Kindler and Darras 1997, Panesi and Morra 2021, Willats 2005, Wilson 1988).

1.2.2 Semia

The second structural class characterizes utterances and/or whole systems which use a modality that expresses meaning, but without a grammar (Figure 1.2c). We call these *semia*, to emphasize their capacity for meaning-making as their primary characteristic, thus drawing on the root "sem-" consistent with *sem*antics and *sem*iotics. Though we here characterize semia as lacking grammar, in future chapters we will provide a more nuanced treatment of this status, where it is not so much the absence of a grammatical system, but a particular structurally simple combinatoriality. This will be addressed later on.

Semia have the potential to use lexicalized forms, which are entrenched correspondences between form and meaning, but they also may manifest as non-lexicalized "idiosyncratic" forms. For example, gesture systems use both idiosyncratic gesticulations and lexicalized emblems (like thumbs up or waving). Semia systems are consistent with Goldin-Meadow's (2003b) notion of resilient systems which persist regardless of a comprehender's level of exposure to and practice with an external system. As such, semia typically use more limited lexicons and do not display the type of complex combinatoriality as in fragile (i.e., omnia) systems.

In the vocal modality, semia arise in isolated meaningful expressions, such as vocal gestures (Dingemanse 2017). Vocal semia therefore include idiosyncratic forms like yelling and laughing. However, lexicalized semia may be embedded within omnia systems, just lacking the grammatical specifications found in the broader omnia lexicon. For example, lexicalized semia include ideophones (*boom*, *meow*), interjections (*shhh*, *aha!*), or exclamations (*wow!*, *ouch!*), which all appear within the omnia system of English.

The bodily modality also uses semia in gestures, including both lexicalized bodily semia like gestural emblems (thumbs up, the middle finger) and more idiosyncratic gesticulations (Gawne and Cooperrider 2022, McNeill 1992). More elaborate semia systems might include the homesigns (Goldin-Meadow 2003b) created by deaf children who do not have access to a signed or spoken language, and thus have constrained vocabularies and limited combinatoriality.

Semia also appear within the graphic modality for meaningful pictorial representations without complex combinatorial sequencing. Prominent graphic semia include emoji, which use an explicit lexicon (Częstochowska et al. 2022, Weissman et al. 2023), but seem to exhibit only simple combinatoriality in their sequencing (Cohn, Engelen, and Schilperoord 2019, Gawne and McCulloch 2019). Other graphic semia include the conventional images that appear as street signs, iconography, and logos, and the conventionalized ways that most people draw stick figures, houses, flowers, mountains, etc. (Cohn 2012, Long, Fan, and Frank 2018). More complex graphic semia manifest as paintings, drawings, single panel cartoons, and other graphics appearing as single-unit representations. As semia persist in the absence of acquiring an omnia system, graphic semia often characterize the resilient level proficiency of people who "can't draw" (Cohn 2012), and therefore lack the robust visual lexicon and grammar of a fragile omnia system.

1.2.3 Sequentia

Another type of emergent interaction occurs in the combination of a modality with a grammar, but without correspondence to meaning (Figure 1.2d). We call these ***sequentia***, to emphasize their primary characteristic of using complex combinatoriality, most often in a sequence. Like all emergent interactions, sequentia can involve entrenched lexicalized patterns in addition to idiosyncratic sequencing. Though complex combinatoriality is sequentia's primary characteristic, they crucially lack robust correspondences to meaning.

Music is an auditory sequentia system, which has been posited to involve combinatorial structures comparable to those of language (Lerdahl and Jackendoff 1982). Learning to play different "styles" of music involves acquiring varieties of entrenched patterns, and this expertise in varied musical sequentia is subject to developmental constraints (Penhune 2011, Trainor 2005). Despite music's structured combinatoriality, it does not seem to correspond to meaning like omnia or semia. Music can certainly evoke emotive or affective meaning, and has at least some capacity for conventionalized correspondences to specific meanings, such as leitmotifs. For example, a clear "lexicalized" correspondence exists between the famous music from the soundtrack of the movie *Jaws* and a sense of impending doom. However, instrumental music has limited capacity to express concepts and categories, unless also interacting with a meaning-making expression like semia or omnia (Koelsch 2011a).

Similarly, sequentia persist in the bodily modality in a variety of ways. Complex combinatoriality occurs in dancing such as salsa, waltzing, or tango, which do not overtly convey conceptual expression (Charnavel 2019). Some forms of dance do convey conventionalized meaningful information (i.e., they contain semia), such as aspects of ballet or Indian dance which express specific meanings from their movements (Patel-Grosz et al. 2022). In addition to dance, other bodily sequentia would include the structured patterns of martial art forms, which exhibit complex patterning and combinatorics in fairly lengthy sequences which vary depending on the "style" (e.g., karate vs. kung fu), but which do not correspond to any conceptual structures other than the moves they convey (Stadler et al. 2021). We might similarly include the patterns from other athletic activities into bodily sequentia, which can involve fairly complicated combinatorics, such as gymnastics routines or synchronized swimming.

Sequentia can also persist in the graphic modality. In recent years, experimentation with "abstract comics" (Molotiu 2009) has yielded expressive sequences of images, arguably many with complex combinatoriality, but which use pictorial representations that lack content corresponding to recognizable concepts. These sequences often display the shifting and changing aspects of visual forms, like blobs or lines, but do not convey representations in ways that could be construed as meaningful.

1.2.4 Modalia

Our final class of emergent interactions concerns expressions that have only a modality, without correspondence to meaning or a grammar (Figure 1.2e). Since the presence of only a modality is the outstanding feature of these expressions, we call them **modalia**. Once again, modalia can be entrenched as lexicalized forms, or persist as fully idiosyncratic expressions. For example, vocal modalia include the "vocables" often used in singing which lack meaning, such as the entrenched utterances of *sha-la-la*, *bi-bop-a-lu-bop*, or the canonical scale (*do-re-mi-fa-so-la-ti-do*, or in Indian music, *sa-re-ga-ma-pa-dha-ni*). These are all conventionalized vocal modalia. However, idiosyncratic vocal modalia also occur, such as the vocables arising during scat singing, which is a form of improvisational jazz singing that borders on sequentia for its musical properties.

Bodily modalia occur in contexts of abstract dance, where movements are made purely for movement's sake, without explicit meaning, but also without displaying complex combinatoriality. Similarly, abstract art would be a form of graphic modalia, where pictorial forms play with the sensory aspects of the graphic modality, but which do not overtly correspond to meaning. Experiencers of modalia may feel compelled to construe meaning out of their sensory experience, even if it is not directly encoded in an explicit way.

1.2.5 Reimagining Language

By decomposing the primary components of language and other expressive systems, we end up with four primary classes that distinguish the relative presence of a modality, grammar, and meaning. These are summarized in Table 1.1. All of these classes involve the presence of modality, possibly with some distribution of meaning and/or grammar. We acknowledge the additional possibility where a modality is *not* present, but it remains meaningful, like, for example, silence that is loaded with intent or meaning. We might posit these as **absentia**, but as they appear in such pointed and constrained contexts, and have little possibility for diverse encoded forms, we find them difficult to generalize beyond individual tokens.

We should reiterate that our presentation of these classes is somewhat simplified. Our characterization here of the complete absence of certain structures is a bit more extreme than the architecture specifies. To foreshadow this, our shorthand here of an "absence" of a grammar characterizes the presence of a structurally simple grammar within a range of combinatorial complexity. We will elaborate on this in later chapters.

Beyond the contributions of these three primary components of a modality, grammar, and meaning, research of these various systems has found considerable overlap across their *structure*, *processing*, and *development*. A first common structural trait of these systems is their capacity for lexicons. By this, we mean that various

Table 1.1 The distribution of structures of modality, grammar, and meaning across different classes of behaviors.

	Modality	Grammar	Meaning	
Spoken language	X	X	X	
Sign language	X	X	X	Omnia
Visual language	X	X	X	
Vocal gestures	X		X	
Bodily gestures	X		X	Semia
Single pictures	X		X	
Music	X	X		
Dance	X	X		Sequentia
Visual sequencing	X	X		
Vocables	X			
Bodily motions	X			Modalia
Abstract art	X			

behaviors establish fixed correspondences between component structures which are stored in memory as "lexicalized" forms beyond purely idiosyncratic expressions. Lexical items proliferate in spoken and signed omnia (stereotypically as words), while regularized bodily semia persist in gestural emblems (Gawne and Cooperrider 2022). The ability to draw, whether as omnia or semia, requires a "visual lexicon" of graphic patterns (Cohn 2013b, 2012, Schilperoord and Cohn 2023). In addition, systematic patterns of musical sequentia vary across musical styles, as do bodily sequentia in styles of dancing, martial arts, and other athletic pursuits. We see this widespread entrenchment of lexicalized forms as the interaction of *memory* with the cognitive expressive system, and will elaborate on this in Chapter 2.

Within systems that express meaning like omnia or semia, the units also can convey rich mappings between semantic domains or mental spaces, such as in conceptual metaphors, analogies, or blending. Such conceptual integration has been extensively studied in the verbal domain (Fauconnier and Turner 1998, Lakoff and Johnson 1980), but it also appears in bodily movements like gesture or sign languages (Cienki and Müller 2008, McNeill 1992), and in pictorial representations (Forceville 2016, Kennedy 1982, Schilperoord 2017). In addition, conceptual integration arises through multimodal interactions between speech, writing, gesture, and/or pictures (Cienki and Müller 2008, Forceville and Urios-Aparisi 2009, Tasić and Stamenković 2015). The consistency across unimodal and multimodal conceptual integration is also corroborated by findings supporting that the processing of meaning in all expressions taps into a supramodal hub for semantic memory (Calzavarini 2023, Kuhnke et al. 2023, Kutas and Federmeier 2011, Ralph et al. 2016, Xu et al. 2009). We will further discuss these correspondences in Chapters 4 and 5.

Similarities between omnia and sequentia persist in their combinatorial systems. This includes categorical roles played by units (i.e., parts-of-speech) and/or hierarchic constituent structures displaying recursive embedding. These structural properties give rise to the possibility of, for example, center-embedding, long-distance dependencies, ellipses, and coordination. When interacting with conceptual structures, these combinatorial systems also may yield structural ambiguities or anaphoric relations. While these features of combinatorial systems have been acknowledged in the vocal and bodily modalities for omnia systems (i.e., spoken and signed languages), similar structural properties appear in the sequencing of images graphic omnia (Cohn 2013b, 2020a). In addition, widespread recognition has emerged for these features in the sequentia of music (Jackendoff and Lerdahl 2006, Lerdahl and Jackendoff 1982). Again, the similarities across these behaviors are supported by consistent neural responses observed to the processing of syntax in sentences in vocal and bodily omnia (Emmorey 2021, Hagoort, Brown, and Groothusen 1993, Neville et al. 1991, Osterhout and Holcomb 1992), of sequencing in graphic omnia (Cohn 2020b, Coopmans and Cohn 2022), and syntax of musical sequentia (Koelsch 2011a, Patel 2003). These findings align with neurocognitive theories of sequence processing mechanisms spanning across behaviors (Dehaene et al. 2015) that are facilitated by neural areas devoted to linearization and hierarchic assemblage (Corballis 1991, Fedorenko and Blank 2020, Zaccarella and Friederici 2017). We address these combinatorial schemas and their features more in Chapter 6.

Similarities also exist in development and proficiency of these systems. In general, systems that involve entrenched lexicalized forms have developmental trajectories that benefit from early exposure and acquisition. With age, people become less able to achieve full proficiency in a given system. This optimized learning before puberty has been widely acknowledged for the spoken and signed omnia, where a lack of exposure may render a person with only a semia system (Goldin-Meadow 2003b). For example, with no access to a spoken or signed omnia, deaf children create semia systems of homesign, yet both deaf and hearing individuals retain a semia system of gestures whether or not they learn a sign language (Emmorey 2023). As discussed above, similar developmental patterns persist for the ability to draw and to comprehend and produce visual sequences (Cohn 2020a, Wilson 1988, 2016), including a critical learning period apexing around puberty, sensitive to exposure and practice with external systems (Cohn 2012). Similar developmental constraints on proficiency persist for learning sequentia like music and various athletics (Ford et al. 2012, Penhune 2011, Trainor 2005).

In addition to developmental similarities, all of these systems often display asymmetries in productive and comprehensive proficiency. It is possible to understand an omnia system of a spoken language, but not be able to produce it, as occurs with cases of receptive multilingualism, where people are often capable of understanding typologically similar second language without being able to produce it (Gooskens 2019). Likewise, many people have comprehensive fluency in understanding pictures or visual narrative sequences, even though they may not be able to proficiently draw. Similarly, people may be able to appreciate and be moved by music, even if they have little ability to produce it. In all of these cases, a person may gain comprehensive fluency of a system through exposure, but with reduced productive fluency by degrees of practice.

The consistency across these aspects of structure, processing, and development reinforces the similarities between omnia, semia, sequentia, or modalia. These similarities have buttressed comparisons with language for most all of these phenomena, while at the same time making their categorization difficult when the choice is only "language" versus "not-language." These behavioral classes can thus provide distinctions between systems, whether or not you call them "languages."

We offer this then as our answer to the question of "what is language?" and also to our goal of "reimagining language." By decomposing the elements of language and various human expressive systems, we show how those component structures interact in a variety of ways across human behaviors. These behaviors thus fall into systematic identifiable classes of omnia, semia, sequentia, and modalia, all of which are sometimes referred to as "language." Often, the term "language" is applied to these different systems because of prescriptive social or cultural persuasions or intentions rather than because of their descriptive structural components. Whether or not people wish to maintain the term "language" for all or some behaviors is up to them, so long as they acknowledge the differences between omnia, semia, sequentia, and modalia as distinct structural categories.

1.3 From Amodal to Multimodal

The categories of omnia, semia, sequentia, and modalia provide a way to classify the range of expressive systems without defaulting to a binary of "language" or "not language." However, this still does not address the challenges posed by expressions outside of speech, whether produced by the body (sign language, co-speech gestures, homesign) or through graphics (drawing, writing, text-image interactions). How does a communicative architecture accommodate the range of modalities used in both unimodal and multimodal expressions?

Most all models of language have only posited a single "phonology" as the system for organizing the productive and sensory aspects of speech sounds or the body (Chomsky 1965, 1995, Goldberg 1995, Jackendoff 2002, Langacker 1987). As discussed, while an amodal notion of phonology has the benefits of equally subsuming multiple modalities, it also obscures the unique characteristics of each modality. Writing poses another problem, since writing requires *both* phonological and visual-graphic representations. Yet, these graphic properties are not represented in linguistic architectures, whether for writing or for naturalistic pictures. An amodal phonology is further challenged by multimodality, where singular meaningful expressions may manifest simultaneously in different modalities (ex. omnia of speech co-occurring with semia of gestures).

A helpful alternative categorization comes from the phonologist Harry van der Hulst (in prep), who proposed the term ***formology*** to describe the cognitive systems which span across all modalities and make them perceivable and producible. Formology then includes modality-specific systems of *phonology* for the vocal modality, *cherology* for the bodily modality, and *graphology* for the graphic modality. The benefit of this classification is that it acknowledges both the unique properties of each modality and their general functional and structural similarities.

With both the modality-independent (formology) and modality-specific (phonology, cherology, graphology) aspects of expression, a new challenge arises: if there are three separate formologies, the language faculty cannot simply have one generalized "module" for all three components. This again becomes apparent where multiple formologies might be necessary, whether as a unimodal expression (ex. writing needs a phonology mapped to a graphology), or multimodal interactions (ex. both a cherology and phonology for co-speech gesture). So, what would a language faculty look like if it included multiple formologies?

1.4 The Multimodal Parallel Architecture

We propose a *multimodal language faculty* which makes explicit that all three formologies are present *at once*. We depict this multimodal Parallel Architecture in Figure 1.3a. In this model, phonology, cherology, and graphology all persist in parallel as part of our communicative and expressive competence. All formologies can manifest in omnia, semia, sequentia, and modalia as different **emergent states** through the interactions of the structures within the multimodal Parallel Architecture. The important implication is that "language," or any of our distinguished behavioral classes, is not an amodal representation that "flows out" of different formologies, but rather that all are present and persisting as part of a larger holistic communicative faculty.

Out of this multimodal architecture, spoken language arises as an interaction of the phonology with a grammar and a meaning, without other formologies being engaged (Figure 1.3b). This interaction reflects Jackendoff's (2002) original Parallel Architecture. Vocal semia are similar (Figure 1.3c), involving phonology but without a complex grammar. Expressions using cherology maintain similar interactions, with bodily omnia (sign language) involving all three structures (Figure 1.3d) and bodily semia (like gestures) using no complex grammar. Graphic expression maintains similar structures, whether as omnia (visual languages) using all structures (Figure 1.3f) or as semia (single images) without robust grammars (Figure 1.3g). We can now also account for writing, as in Figure 1.3h, which includes a correspondence between phonology and graphology. Thus, all of these behaviors emerge through different interactions of the component parts of a single broader architecture.

Importantly, this architecture does not view the body or graphics as alternative "options" to phonology, but rather all formologies persist equally alongside each other. As all behaviors are emergent states arising from this holistic architecture, *multimodal* expressions arise as the combinations of these states. For example, co-speech gesture is schematized in Figure 1.3i, where the vocal omnia of speech now persists alongside the bodily semia of gestures, both converging on the same conceptual structure.

Where in this architecture might we find the lexicon? Within the Parallel Architecture, the lexicon is not a separate structure of stored representations, but rather the stored structures manifest in their interfaces (Jackendoff and Audring 2020). Lexical items are thus encoded as declarative schemas, which can range across single morphemes, words, idioms, grammatical constructions, and purely syntactic schemas.

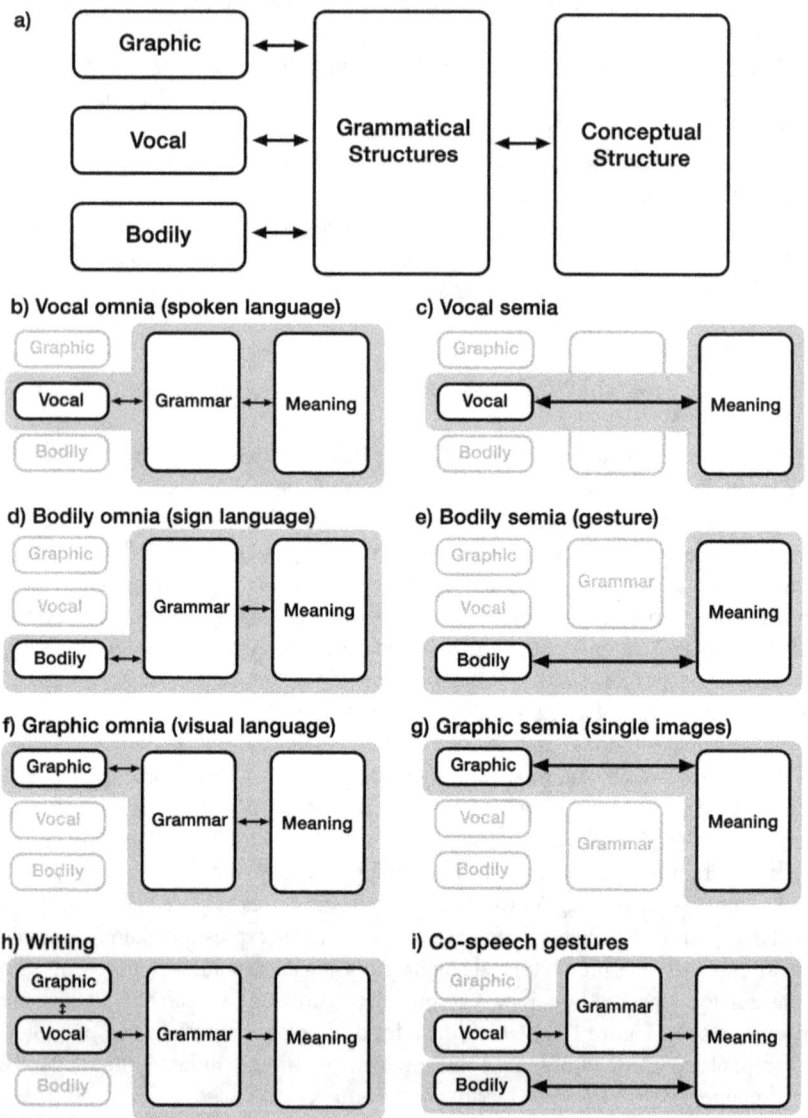

Figure 1.3 The multimodal Parallel Architecture. Note: the diagram leaves out the arrow between Modality and Meaning for simplicity, although it also has an interface.

This position is consistent with theories of construction grammar and constructional morphology (Booij 2010, Goldberg 1995).

Consider the vocal word *heart*, for which we provide the lexical entry in Figure 1.4a, which includes some formal notation that we will explain in subsequent chapters. As a spoken word, it is encoded with phonological structures (PS) of /hɑrt/, and this also

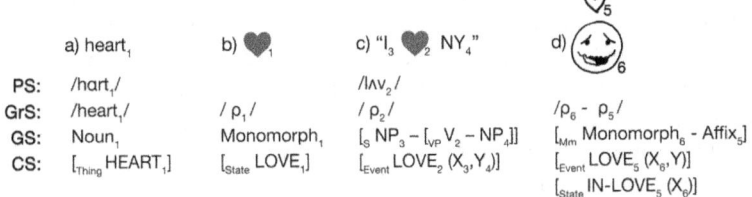

Figure 1.4 Lexical items for a) the word heart, and the heart shape, b) in isolation, c) as a verb, and d) as an upfix.

corresponds to a graphological spelling (GrS) of /heart/. This word additionally has a morphosyntactic encoding (Grammatical Structure; GS) as a noun, corresponding to a meaning (Conceptual Structure; CS) as a thing HEART. The correspondences across levels of structure are marked in Figure 1.4a by subscripted indices, here "1."

We can similarly specify a lexical encoding for the graphic heart-shape, which in fact has multiple entries. First, a simple heart-shape in Figure 1.4b has the graphology of its pictorial form. This shape constitutes an entire visual region, which we notate with "rho" (ρ), discussed further in the next chapter. Also anticipating the discussion in subsequent chapters, we consider the heart morphogrammatically as a *monomorph*—a isolatable visual form that can stand alone (Cohn 2018a, Schilperoord and Cohn 2023)—while its conceptual specification is the state LOVE. Because the word "heart" provides a label for the heart-shape, the word (Figure 1.4a) and base image (Figure 1.4b) are **sister schemas** (Jackendoff and Audring 2020). This is expressed by the similar indices ("1") shared across levels and formologies in Figure 1.4a and Figure 1.4b.

The heart-shape has at least two additional entries. First, as discussed, the heart can be used as a verb in a construction (i.e., *I ♥ NY*), as characterized in Figure 1.4c. Here, the heart-shape carries the phonology /lʌv/ and plays the role of a verb in a canonical SVO English sentence schema, which has the conceptual structure of an event of LOVE with arguments corresponding to the noun phrases. This example shows that there are not only words in a lexicon, but also grammatical constructions with open slots that can be filled by other lexical items. It also shows that lexical items can be multimodal, i.e., encoded across multiple formologies.

An additional heart-shape lexical entry concerns its usage as a visual affix in graphic representations, as in Figure 1.4d, such as an *upfix*, a bound graphic morpheme that floats "up" above a character's head to indicate a cognitive or emotional state (Cohn 2013b, 2018a). The graphology places a heart-shape above or near a character's head, again notated as a region (ρ_5) that acts as a visual variable. At the level of the morphogrammar, the heart-shape corresponds to an affix, which cannot stand alone, attaching to the monomorph of a character to then form a larger monomorph (Cohn 2018a, Schilperoord and Cohn 2023). This corresponds to two potential meanings: a transitive *event* LOVE with arguments for its morphological stem and some other entity (i.e., the person loves something), or, alternatively, a *state* of an argument corresponding to the morphological stem as being IN-LOVE (i.e., the person is in love).

Expressions using any formology thus make use of, and can combine, these encoded lexical items which include information from all three components of the Parallel Architecture. Stored lexical items range in size from bound form-meaning mappings (like affixes), to whole isolable forms (words, monomorphs), and to grammatical constructions. Because this range of complexity occurs across all formologies, their combination within the model allows for multimodal constructions (as in Figure 1.4c).

As described above, our model posits that all formologies persist within the Parallel Architecture simultaneously. There is no "flow" of an "amodal" language into one modality or another (setting aside writing, to be discussed in Chapter 2), because all formologies are co-present and functional as part of a holistic system. This renders our heart examples as different emerging interactions of structures within the architecture. The word *heart* involves the interaction between the phonology, grammar, and meaning, while the heart-shape involves the interaction between the graphology, grammar, and meaning. The *I ♥ NY* construction thus involves an emergent interaction characterized by multiple formologies.

As this architecture encodes multiple formologies in parallel, no principled boundaries exist between the encoded lexical items of each modality. Rather, interconnected features persist within and across lexical items, which converge into networks of schemas that maintain common characteristics, not divided by the modalities specifically, per se. This treatment is comparable to theories of the encoding of different languages of the same modality, as in unimodal multilingualism (Goldrick, Putnam, and Schwarz 2016, Jackendoff and Audring 2020). In fact, cross-modal correspondences arise in instances of writing, where the graphology is also recruited in connection with the phonology. In addition, formologies may interact and intersect to create multimodal lexical items.

The byproduct of this architecture is that both unimodal and multimodal expressions arise out of different emergent interactions between structures within an overarching language faculty. Out of these emergent states we thus have what look like different behaviors. Terms like *language, gesturing, signing, drawing, writing, speaking,* and others create a sense of autonomy to behaviors that is unwarranted given an "inside-out" cognitive perspective, especially in relation to each other. In light of the Parallel Architecture, all of these behaviors are *byproducts* of interactions manifesting from a single system, undermining this supposed behavioral autonomy. As will be demonstrated, complex cognitive interactions are potentially so multiplicitous that it makes discrete categorization difficult to describe the full range of human expressive behaviors.

Multimodality is thus not necessarily the combination of omnia, semia, sequentia, or modalia, but rather, it arises out of interactions between their component parts, i.e., between formologies, between grammars, and between meanings. Sometimes this renders interactions between seemingly independent behaviors, but characterization of multimodality must occur at the descriptive level of their *components*, not at level of the whole systems. This treatment differs from theories of multimodality as interactions between whole indivisible expressions, i.e., speech *plus* gesture, drawing *plus* writing (Bateman 2014, Bateman, Wildfeuer, and Hiippala 2017, Forceville 2020, Kress 2009).

Within the Parallel Architecture, the question of whether co-speech gestures are "a part" of language or not simply vanishes. Co-speech gesture combines a vocal omnia (speech) with a bodily semia (gesture), but as co-emergent parts of a single architecture, making them intrinsically linked as a holistic expression, as in Figure 1.3i. This holism is reflected in the shared Conceptual Structure, or "growth point," for both modalities (McNeill 1992). That is, gesture is not "part of language" but rather the *spoken* language and gesture are externalized through different formologies, but belong as parts of a greater whole that as yet has gone unnamed.

Naming each and every *multimodal emergent interaction* is unwieldy, because there are so many possible combinations of omnia, semia, sequentia, and modalia. We will demonstrate that such multiplicity occurs because interactions are not best described between indivisible expressions, but within each of the structures of the Parallel Architecture, i.e., between modalities (Chapter 3), between grammars (Chapter 7), and between conceptual structures (Chapter 5).

1.5 A Multimodal Paradigm

Models of linguistic competence frame conceptions of language as a whole. We have earlier described how prevailing ideas about language carry assumptions that it is an amodal system of arbitrary signs primarily expressed by the vocal-auditory channel, embedded in human cognition. A multimodal language faculty plugs the "leaks" in this amodal conception of language, but with it requires a reconsideration of the fundamental principles of this faculty. We call this set of assumptions the **Multimodal Paradigm**.

1.5.1 Multimodal by Default

A first assumption of a multimodal model is that the language faculty is not amodal or unimodal, but rather is multimodal. Expressions use multiple formologies, and these structures persist in parallel with no implied ranking between them. Within a truly multimodal understanding of language and communication, there are *no primary versus auxiliary* distinctions. Terms implying peripheral status like extralinguistic, paralinguistic, secondary modalities, or non-verbal communication all cease to be useful descriptors of expressive behaviors.

When one modality is used as a predominant communicative system, this omnia may give the appearance of a unimodal linguistic faculty. Just because hearing communities primarily use spoken omnia and deaf communities primarily use bodily omnia, it does not mean that these are alternative unimodal options for an amodal system. All formologies are available to all humans, but development will determine the complexity of how they develop and are used (a point we will return to below). Some cultures maintain fully developed omnia in vocal, bodily, *and* graphic expressions (Green 2014, Wilkins 2016), and bimodal bilinguals simultaneously express spoken and signed omnia (Emmorey et al. 2008), while a similar co-occurrence happens in co-speech gestures between spoken omnia and bodily semia (Goldin-Meadow 2003a,

McNeill 1992). The acquisition of sign and spoken language does not hinder each other (Pontecorvo et al. 2023), while infants also elicit responses across modalities, further implying a multimodal system (van der Klis, Adriaans, and Kager 2023).

Indeed, maintaining an assumption of unimodal primacy will make a multimodal system look like an amodal system, but dissolving such rankings allows for accounting for the full range of human expressive capacities.

1.5.2 Common Components

A multimodal architecture also changes assumptions about the relative autonomy of language and other behaviors. A system with multiple equal formologies accounts for why similar structure, processing, and development persist across what are otherwise labeled as autonomous behaviors with unique design features. As discussed, similar structural components are maintained across vocal, bodily, and graphic expressions, and these similarities are embedded overtly within a multimodal model. Rather than being autonomous, all human communicative behaviors arise as emergent interactions of shared components within a holistic architecture. Such a holistic model accounts for why we observe similar neurocognitive processing, developmental trajectories, and critical learning periods across these behaviors.

1.5.3 Semiotic Proliferation and Optimality

Arbitrariness has been taken as a fundamental design feature of language, yet, as discussed, extensive findings have shown that iconicity and indexicality also proliferate within speech, and all three types of signification persist in all modalities. While arbitrariness may be *one* feature of signification in expressions across modalities, it is not the *only* feature or even a defining feature. Rather, symbolicity, indexicality, and iconicity all play complementary roles within expressive systems, and this semiotic proliferation is what should be taken as a fundamental design feature of language. Just like how an assumption of unimodality will make a multimodal system look amodal, an assumption of arbitrariness will make a multi-semiotic system look like a symbolic system.

In order to fully account for how expressive systems operate, a focus on arbitrariness should give way to accounts of the full range of signification and the functional properties of that variety. We will show in Chapter 4 that iconicity, indexicality, and symbolicity all arise directly from the structural organization of the multimodal Parallel Architecture.

Although all types of signification are available to all modalities, modalities may be optimized for different signification. That is, the relative properties of a sensory signal—such as speech sounds, bodily movements, or mark-making—may provide relative advantages and disadvantages for different types of meaning-making. Rather than an amodal focus on arbitrariness which ignores the properties of modalities, the Multimodal Paradigm focuses instead on the relative features of each modality and how they allow for meaning-making both on their own and in complement with other modalities.

1.5.4 Affordances

In contrast with a view that the form of expressions contributes little to the substance of their meaning, expressions are bound to the *affordances* of their modalities. The notion of affordances originally comes from Gibson (2014 [1979]), but here we mean that, though abstract structures may persist throughout expressive systems, the varying sensory traits of modalities will render distinctive ways for those structures to manifest. Consider again the case of anaphoric relations: because the bodily modality affords the use of physical space, anaphoric relations can be conveyed by pointing to different positions in front of a signer (Frederiksen and Mayberry 2022). Because the vocal modality is confined to temporally sequential expressions, it affords encoding of anaphora in conventionalized pronouns. Indeed, as was discussed, similar neurocognitive responses have been observed to the processing of meaning across all modalities (Calzavarini 2023, Kuhnke et al. 2023, Kutas and Federmeier 2011, Ralph et al. 2016, Xu et al. 2009), suggesting that the differences in meaning-making capacities of modalities are less about the meanings themselves, and more about the affordances by which each modality accesses meaning.

With this view of a multimodal system, modalities persist in parallel and can—and should—operate in different ways. This contrasts with the amodal notion of intertranslatability, i.e., that the same meanings should be expressible or translatable in the same ways. For example, an amodal intranslatability would expect that abstract concepts, negation, and hypotheticals, expressed as units (like words) in one modality, should also be expressible as units in another modality. However, if the unique affordances of modalities are taken seriously, then the assumption of complete intertranslatability disappears, and we can acknowledge that some modalities may do a better job in accessing certain conceptual structures than others. Indeed, this view holds that modalities exist as complementary pathways to the expression and access of meaning, with each modality considered as part of a broader whole, not as competing alternatives.

1.5.5 Innateness

A multimodal model of the language faculty has consequences for how we conceive of innateness. Because modalities persist in parallel within the architecture, such a model predicts similar developmental trajectories for different expressive systems, and for what happens when such exposure and practice is not attained. We posit that for all modalities, exposure and practice determine which parts develop greater complexity.

Semia are innate. As will be discussed at length in Chapter 11, by this we mean that the vocal, bodily, and graphic formologies along with their correspondences to conceptual structure are genetically endowed as natural channels for human meaning-making. These innate states are reflected in Figure 1.3c,e,g. Evidence for what is innate can be inferred from what persists in the absence of learning an external system, what Goldin-Meadow (2003b) has called the resilient system of language. When deaf children lack exposure to spoken or signed languages, they create homesigns, which convey meaning through the bodily modality but without a complex grammar—i.e., a bodily semia. In addition, whether or not a person learns a sign language, they still maintain the bodily semia of gesture. Similarly, even when people do not acquire the patterns of a graphic omnia, they retain the ability to produce doodles and basic drawings as graphic semia, a state that is often referred to as "I can't draw."

While semia persist regardless of exposure and practice, interaction with an external system is required to learn omnia. Omnia are fragile systems in Goldin-Meadow's (2003b) terms, reflected in Figure 1.3b,d,f. Although exposure and practice are needed to acquire omnia, what is innate is the potential to acquire such systems. Specifically, we posit that the capacity for complex combinatoriality is genetically endowed, but this needs to be activated with exposure and practice to a system that has those properties.

This view of innateness holds that there is a cognitive language faculty with innate properties. But rather than being an "all or nothing" matter, interaction with external systems (vocal, bodily, or graphic) will determine which aspects of that system will develop into greater complexity and which will persist as basic meaning-making capacities. In terms of architectural development, this renders a person who speaks only a spoken language but does not sign or draw omnia (but retains bodily and graphic semia) as similar to a person who only signs a language but does not speak or draw an omnia system (but retains vocal or graphic semia). In both cases, only one modality is developed as a full omnia, while others persist as semia.

An amodal perspective on language has framed what is innate (or not) as divorced from the expressive modalities themselves. The multimodal view instead incorporates human expressive modalities as components of an innate faculty, and this view thereby explains not only what allows for the learning of mature languages, but also what happens in the absence of external system, and why various expressive behaviors persist regardless.

1.6 What's Next?

In order to "plug the leaks" of theories of language, we have proposed a multimodal Parallel Architecture and corresponding principles that offer an integrated view of language and multimodality to account for the full range of human communicative expression with a basis in cognition. To fully flesh out this theoretical framework, the rest of the book will first describe the component parts of the Parallel Architecture and the interactions that occur within each of its structures. We then turn to the multimodal interactions that arise from this architecture, and finally consider the consequences of this model.

We begin in Chapter 2 by addressing the question of *What is a modality?* We decompose modalities into two primary parts: their sensory signals, which are the physical properties of sound, light, and the body, and cognitive representations, which are the formological structures corresponding to these sensory signals. Our theory delineates the differences between multi-modal, cross-modal, multi-sensory, and cross-sensory experiences. This approach clarifies what natural modalities are, and how they differ from media produced by tools.

Having established modalities and their parts, we turn in Chapter 3 to how they combine in multi-modal interactions. We argue that modalities combine through their featural components, foremost through the sensory feature of *durativity*: whether they are capable of extending across a temporal span. If modalities do not involve a duration, such as in the spatial representations of text and pictures, various spatial integrations serve to "bundle" modalities into cohesive units.

Chapter 4 turns to characterizing what role modalities play in the organization of Conceptual Structure. On both theoretical and empirical grounds, we argue that modalities do not differ in encoding meaning, but rather in how they correspond to the algebraic and geometric aspects of meaning. Thus, the unique sensory properties of different modalities provide them with affordances for how they access meanings. Interfaces between these structures therefore characterize types of signification, which allows us to situate Peircean semiotics within a cognitive communicative architecture.

Chapter 5 then explores how meanings combine by explicitly formalizing how varying sources of meaning integrate into a holistic semantic representation. We show how coreference provides a binding semantic mechanism for uniting and integrating meaning across multiple inputs. This gives rise to a range of coreference types which operate in similar ways in both unimodal and multimodal expressions.

All theories of linguistic structure must contend with the nature and role of grammar, and this challenge becomes even more salient when grammars persist across multiple modalities. We take up this task in Chapter 6 by elaborating on recent work by Jackendoff and Wittenberg (2014, 2017) which has provided an ecologically valid hierarchy of grammars, *The Complexity Hierarchy*, based on schematic constructions used to express meaning. We argue that this approach reflects the basic cognitive principles of processing sequences, which allows us to provide formal grounding to our categories of omnia, semia, and sequentia, along with explaining how combinatoriality operates across different structural levels (morphology, syntax, narrative) and across modalities.

Based on this combinatorial taxonomy, Chapter 7 identifies two core dimensions of interactions between grammars. *Symmetry* characterizes interactions between grammars with varying complexity, and *Allocation* characterizes whether the grammars operate on their own (independent) or play roles as units inside each other (substitutive). These dimensions of grammatical interactions not only account for simultaneous combinatorial systems in different modalities, but they also explain the grammatical structuring of codeswitching, how ideophones integrate into sentence structures, and features of other complex unimodal expressions.

Having established the components of the Parallel Architecture, we then turn to their emergent interactions. We begin in Chapter 8 by detailing the unimodal emergence of both omnia and semia within each modality. Chapter 9 then surveys various multimodal interactions where expressions remain independent of each other. We show how our model can account for complex expressions including, for example, co-speech gesture, memes, advertisements, street signs, political cartoons, comics, and others, while highlighting how much of this information is entrenched in a multimodal lexicon. Chapter 10 then focuses on interactions where expressions play roles within each other's grammars, exemplified by our *I* ♥ *NY* example. We show that substitution arises between all modalities, demonstrating a naturally occurring instance of linguistic complementary distribution, thereby providing a diagnostic for whether different expressions belong integrated into a holistic architecture.

If speech is not a privileged modality, and our communicative capacities are actually multimodal by default, then the question arises: Why do we have a multimodal language faculty and what are its consequences? In Chapter 11, we argue first that multimodality offers *multiplicity*, for providing multiple options for expressing meaning, and *utility*, for optimizing modalities' affordances for communication. We then consider various ways that modalities might interact within a multimodal system, requiring a reconceptualization of issues of cross-linguistic variation, linguistic universals, innateness, and linguistic relativity.

We further explore the consequences of a multimodal language faculty for its implications on theories of language evolution in Chapter 12. We contend that primary theories of language evolution have wrongly diagnosed the contemporary end-state of our language faculty (i.e., as an amodal, unimodal, arbitrary, and recursive speech-based language faculty), and as such have also proposed untenable theories of how it evolved by allocating any properties of language that fall outside that presumed end-state to being evolutionary precursors. First, we address the pitfalls in primary domains of research about the evolution of modalities, meaning, and grammar, and then outline the implications of language evolution for a multimodal language faculty.

Finally, in Chapter 13 we further interrogate the contrasts between amodal assumptions of language and the Multimodal Paradigm. We close by reflecting on the consequences of this reimagining of our linguistic and communicative capacity for an inclusive vision of language and human expression across all its modalities.

We close this chapter with two final caveats. First, in our extended discussion about the component parts of the multimodal Parallel Architecture, we do a lot of formalization. This allows us to show in great detail how the system works. By laying bare our model in a formalized way, it provides a maximally explicit exposition of our claims and also invites the opportunity for critique. That said, we realize that such formalization is not to everyone's tastes, and we hope that our argumentation is understandable even if such formalisms are glossed over. Readers less interested in these technical nuances can also skip ahead to a more philosophical treatment if they want to explore the consequences of such a multimodal model (Chapter 11), its implications for evolution (Chapter 12), and/ or the contrasts between assumptions of a multimodal and amodal conception of language (Chapter 13).

Second, often established terminology can carry loaded expectations, can be misleading, or can carry baggage built up over decades of research and debate. We dealt with this already in this chapter, where we created terms of omnia, semia, sequentia, and modalia to sidestep an all-or-nothing use of the term "language." We also did this by reframing "formology" as the modality-independent cognitive organization of expressive channels. In line with this, readers should be prepared for us to further alter existing terms or propose new terminology throughout this book. In some cases, we find it necessary to "rebuild" our understanding of a multimodal language faculty in the wake of the categorization offered by traditional linguistic research, while in other cases, we are guided by the intents of creating a model of language and communication that openly acknowledges diversity and inclusivity as part of its terminology.

Part Two

Modalities

2

What Is a Modality?

We begin detailing the component parts of the multimodal Parallel Architecture by addressing **modalities**. Specifically, *what is a modality?* This question has been less of interest within studies of unimodal linguistics, where contrasts between spoken and signed languages maintain the predominant amodal view of language (Kegl 2020). Under this view, language happens to flow into the vocal or bodily modalities in equal ways, and while their affordances have been acknowledged and studied (Sandler 2017), an assumption of an amodal system requires little meditation on the nature of what is a modality in the first place.

In contrast, this "What is a modality?" question has been debated by many approaches to *multi*modality, where it is crucial to identify just what is "multi" in these interactions. These theories agree that defining a modality is a challenge and, in their attempts to do so, have often appealed to a variety of elements involved in the meaning-making and componential qualities of modalities, and/or their sensorial forms (Bateman, Wildfeuer, and Hiippala 2017, Bateman 2012, Forceville 2009, 2021, Kress 2009, Kress and van Leeuwen 1996, 2001). Typically, modalities are described as different expressive systems themselves (like speech, gesture, pictures), and only sometimes are distinctions made between natural representational capacities (like drawing and speaking), sensory experiences (like sound or taste), and unnatural—i.e., non-biological—media (like photography, film, braille). Other work has distinguished between modalities as sensory signals that differ across "codalities" of varying patterned representations, such as that both writing and drawing use the graphic modality (Clark and Salomon 1986).

Many approaches include criteria of meaning-making inherent to the characterization of a modality. This combines two separable aspects of the system: the structure of the form (or "mode" or "channel") and the conceptual structure. In usage, the term "modality" may take on two senses, as either the sensory form or metonymically as referring to a whole meaningful behavior by referring to its sensory form (e.g., the term "gesture" is sometimes used to refer to cherology and sometimes to the behavior that uses a combination of cherology and meaning). Complicating this further, while spoken languages are readily acknowledged as having separate components of a form (phonological structure) and a meaning (conceptual structure), this division is often undertheorized in modalities outside of vocal or bodily expressions (e.g., graphic representations).

Our approach overlaps with the intuitions of these precursors, but maintains a distinctly biological/cognitive perspective. Let us begin by arguing for three fundamental qualities that a theory of modality should account for:

1. Modalities are *perceivable*, meaning that they must be accessed by biological sensory systems, and thus be characterizable by representational systems that are mediated by those sensory systems. In addition, those sensory systems create affordances that constrain the modalities' expressions (for example, we can primarily produce sounds in sequences across time).
2. Modalities are *producible*, meaning that they must emerge from the biological capacities of the human body, sometimes combined with a mediating technology. For example, drawing, speaking, and gesticulating are all natural ways that humans use to express internal cognitive representations, while film, perfumes, and braille all require technology that is external to human biology.
3. Modalities are *independent*, meaning that they exist as representational systems (formologies) separate from conceptual structures, and manipulatable in their own right. This renders modalities as capable of expressing both meaningful signals (when interfacing with conceptual structure) and non-meaningful signals (without such interfaces). Thus, in line with the Parallel Architecture we can also specify that modalities are ...
    i. ... able to interface with conceptual structure in a non-idiosyncratic way,
    ii. ... able to interface with combinatorial structures.

We view these qualities as fundamental to modalities' identification. They intersect with an orthogonal property of *intentionality*: signals are produced with communicative or expressive purpose at will and under control of the producer. While inadvertent expressions also often use modalities, in the context of human communication, the intent and control of modalities are inherent to their use.

Given these characteristics, we view modalities as an *aggregation* of various features across both 1) sensorial and 2) cognitive dimensions (Clark and Salomon 1986, Kiefer, Kuhnke, and Hartwigsen 2023). Sensorial dimensions characterize a modality's perceptual primitives, its sense experience, how that sensory experience affords juxtaposition, and the systems involved with perceiving (input) and producing (output) those signals. Cognitive dimensions relate to the mental formological structures corresponding with those sensory signals that constrain their detection and production.

By decomposing the parts that make up modalities into their sensorial and cognitive dimensions, we offer a way to clarify and make explicit their identification and the relationships within and between them. Understanding multimodal communication requires us to decompose them into their parts and explain how they relate to each other, rather than taking modalities as whole behaviors (speech, drawing, gesture) or media (film, music). Just like how phonology and phonetics are an independent part of any theory of speech, so too should the parts of any other expressive systems be disentangled and characterized separately.

2.1 Sensory Signals

In all theories of modalities, sensorial phenomena play a central role as we produce and perceive signals as particular sensory experiences, each characterized by their own unique properties. In fact, these sensory phenomena are the only part of a communicative signal that we consciously experience (Jackendoff 1987, 2007, Prinz 2017). For example, what we consciously experience when we perceive speech is a continuous wave of sounds interacting with our auditory system. Below this surface of awareness, our cognitive apparatus decomposes those waveforms into discrete speech sounds that in turn interface with meaning. The process of decoding and interpreting is entirely an internal, mental process, which is set in motion by certain sensory phenomena: the signal of a modality. Thus, we first address the various facets that make up the sensory experience of a modality.

2.1.1 Sensory Stimulus

First, we address the ***sensory stimulus*** itself, by which we mean the properties of a given stimulus, or its physics. Such stimuli span across our senses of vision, hearing, touch, taste, and smell (at the least), of which our modalities make use. Music and speech are sounds, which travel along soundwaves, while visual stimuli are light and the properties of such stimuli modulate our sensory experience. Sounds vary across dimensions of volume, pitch, amplitude, etc., while light varies in its spectrum, giving rise to different colors and brightness, among others.

2.1.2 Perception (Input)

We interact with a given sensory stimulus through dedicated biological systems that have developed over the course of human evolution. These ***perceptual input*** systems use specialized receptors which allow us to become aware of an outside stimulus, and which serve as gateways between what's "out in the world" and what's "inside our body/mind." For example, light is received by our retinas and processed through our visual system, while sound is received by our ears, and processed by our auditory system. These sensory systems decode corresponding sensory stimuli, of which the signals of expressive modalities are merely a part (i.e., the processing of speech is not auditory processing alone), and we make subsequent connections to conceptual structures (i.e., semantic memory).

2.1.3 Production (Output)

Though we might receive sensory signals from a range of sources, communicative modalities are more constrained in how they are produced by humans. Evolution has endowed us with dedicated physical ***production (output)*** systems we use to produce sensory stimuli ourselves using our organs and muscles. For example, in order to produce speech sounds (and singing and whistling), we use the vocal tract which involves muscles (throat, tongue) interacting with our oral cavity and lungs. Gestures, sign languages, and dancing involve the muscles throughout some or all of the body. Drawing involves moving the muscles of specific body parts, usually hands and arms, often in combination with external materials (sand, paint, etc.).

Production can also involve the use of *external tools*. Instruments have been developed to create further sounds, while brushes, pencils, and pens facilitate more precise markings for the drawing system than just the hands. Contemporary technology allows for film, using a camera, to capture both static and moving images of actual percepts, disconnected from or interfacing with our biological production systems. Computer technology facilitates production across nearly all sensory systems. For example, computer graphics (especially 3D modeling) and electronic sounds involve the creation of representations that would not be possible using only humans' natural capacities.

We thus can characterize two separate types of output systems, those that are natural to our biology, and those that are mediated by tools. This distinction is important for distinguishing between 1) modalities that are a reflection of what is natural to the human species, and thus endowed as part of our evolved heritage, and 2) modalities that arise from the ingenuity of our species, often as byproducts of the natural modalities themselves. That is, the vocal system for producing sounds, the bodily system for producing gesticulations, and the graphic system for producing drawings are humans' **natural** modalities. Other technologically mediated modalities have only become possible because of the expressions within our natural modalities, i.e., a camera could never have been invented without humans first being able to speak or draw. However, the lasting impact of such technologies has created an adaptation to a technological extension of human expression that extends beyond our natural modalities (Clark and Chalmers 1998).

Related to tools, additional distinctions have also been made about the **media** and **materiality** of modalities' expressions (Bateman 2012). We conceive of media as the carriers of a modality, but not bearing features of it. The graphic modality may manifest as marks created by drawing in sand or as ink on paper, but these are differences in the media that are employed, not in the modality. In addition, media differ in their materiality, i.e., their make-up and substance. For example, marks made with ink on paper may be precise but may bleed with pressure, while marks made in sand are grainy and often imprecise. These properties relate to the materiality of the media, again not to the modality itself, as would the distinction between speaking in air versus underwater. However, such materiality may have ramifications on the use and structures of the modality, such as how the precision of drawing with ink allows for substantial detail in the contents of what is drawn, while drawing in sand requires simpler marks with less detail.

2.1.4 Primitives

With our production systems we are able to output the sensory signal that in turn can be detected by the perceptual systems. These outputs involve their own structure, which is made up of **sensory primitives**, or building-blocks, of a given stimulus.

These primitives reflect the properties of the stimulus (e.g., sound) constrained by the production system (e.g., sounds able to be produced by the mouth). Thus, the sensory primitives are not merely aspects of the sensory signal (such as soundwaves comprising sound), but describe the properties of a produced signal. For example, the spoken word "dog" is composed of vocal primitives /d/, /ɔ/, and /g/ even though they emerge in an inseparable continuous sound stream (Selkirk 1984). So, the aggregation /dɔg/ is not a primitive on its own. These sounds only exist as part of the sensory experience of speech.

In the bodily modality, the expressive primitives constitute the shape or posture of body parts, their position in space, and their motions. For example, gestures and sign languages combine specific handshapes and movements into signals (Fenlon, Cormier, and Brentari 2017, Sandler 2017). Bodily expressions are received through visual perception, but because they exist as manifested through the body, they can also be detected through our sense of touch, as in cases where people understand sign language through the tactile system (Edwards and Brentari 2020, Willoughby et al. 2018, 2020).

Graphic pictures use articulated signals of marks made of dots, circles, curves, splatters, and other physical graphic units. However, aggregations of such marks (i.e., to make a face, letters, or other representations) are not primitives unto themselves. For example, a smiley face ☺ is made up of two dots, a curve, and a circle, which provide the physical, sensory primitives for this visual utterance, but the face as a whole is not a primitive. The temporal nature of producing graphic marks constrains them to be produced one at a time through our articulatory system (most likely, but not always, our hands), though in perception they may all appear as a single analog whole.

Like signals from the bodily modality, marks are received through the visual senses, but can be imbued with tactile features for those with visual impairments, such as with raised dots, as in Braille, or raised lines, as in adapted graphics. These sensory primitives are no longer just visual units, but also operate as tactile primitives to function with a different perception (input) system. Thus, even though sensory primitives may be produced with the intents as a single sensory signal, their multisensory nature allows them to be perceived across multiple sensory systems (e.g., bodily movements may be stereotypically expected to be seen, but can also be felt; sounds are typically meant to be heard, but their vibrations could also be felt).

2.1.5 Duration

The physical properties of the primitives constrain how they can be organized. For example, producing a signal with the primitives /d/, /ɔ/, and /g/ requires an articulatory system that results in each sound successively manifesting across a temporal duration. In contrast, the graphic marks that make up a smiley face ☺ impose no duration, but instead exist as a spatial whole with no constraints of time. These modulations of **duration** follow from the affordances of the sensory signals.

Here we find an asymmetry between the constraints imposed between auditory and visual signals. Auditory signals have a more constrained duration. Speech sounds impose a duration on the experience of the signal because of the properties of soundwaves, and the articulatory system of the mouth. In music, instruments produce sound one at a time across a duration, but multiple instruments can coalesce in a simultaneous expression, still bound by temporality. This inherent temporality thus requires that both production and perception occur across whatever limited duration that the sensory signal appears in. This results in a signal that is "rapidly fading" (Hockett 1960) because the produced sound leaves no remnant in the environment, again, which is a byproduct of the sensory stimulus.

The duration of visual signals is more complicated than with sound. If visual signals unfurl across time, such as viewing bodily motions or seeing a film on a screen, they impose a duration, although they remain "rapidly fading" and leave no remnant behind. However, other visual signals do persist, despite their durativity. Graphic marks are most often produced in time as each line or dot is produced by a drawer, but the remnants of that process constitute a spatial representation that exists all at once, hiding the temporality of its production. Thus, although the process of drawing is rapidly fading, the aftermath of that process persists, given the materiality of the substance that is drawn into (for example, we know paint on cave walls persists across millennia, but drawings in sand do not).

Nevertheless, graphic representations are perceived in time with the persistence of the signal constrained by our perceptual system—i.e., how much of a signal can the fovea fixate at once. For relatively small representations, like a smiley face or many words, a single fixation may capture the entire signal at once, but to capture larger representations, such as a drawing or painting of a scene, the eye must fixate its different parts, which can only unfurl in saccades across time. Thus, visual signals using marks may be produced and perceived in succession but the material substance persists "all at once."

The affordances of a signal's inherent duration or persistence beyond a duration will have ramifications on how modalities interact with each other. To foreshadow our later discussion, modalities that both have durativity, such as speech and gesture, can interact using temporal correspondences that make use of that duration. Interfacing between modalities that lack inherent durativity, such as text and pictures, requires other methods of non-temporal interacting, such as spatial configurations using proximity or particular visual cues. We will elaborate on these relationships in the next chapter.

2.2 Cognitive Representations

So far, we have discussed the properties and processing systems related to perceiving and producing the sensory stimuli of an expressive modality. However, these properties and systems cannot alone account for the representations involved in modalities. For example, we cannot attribute all of speech perception to general auditory processing, and similarly we cannot attribute all processing of line drawings to basic visual processing. Therefore, perceiving these natural modalities is not merely a matter of basic perception because in order to recognize them we first must have *knowledge* of them. If we hear the sounds /d/, /ɔ/, and /g/, we connect those physical stimuli with our knowledge of them, and this is what enables us to recognize the stimuli in a particular way. In addition, in order to create such signals, we must have cognitive representations that form the basis of the sensory signals that we produce using our articulatory apparatuses. Thus, in order to account for modalities, we need to characterize the cognitive correlates of their sensory stimuli.

These correlates fall into two associated categories. Cognitive primitives or *formemes* characterize the mental instantiation of modality units, while a combinatorial system or *formology* characterizes how these primitives connect with each other.

2.2.1 Formemes

Formemes are the cognitive primitives that correspond to sensory primitives. All natural modalities have such primitives, but their properties are modality-specific, each with their own affordances (Fenlon, Cormier, and Brentari 2017, Sandler 2017), and stored as independent neural substrates (Pa et al. 2008). Thus, the primitives for speech sounds are **phonemes**, bodily primitives are **cheremes**, and the graphic primitives are **graphemes**. Formemes in each modality are also decomposable into numerous sub-features. For example, features of phonemes characterize their articulation (plosive, labial, fricative, etc.), while cheremes involve contrastive dimensions of handshapes, location of articulation, movement, and orientation (Fenlon, Cormier, and Brentari 2017, Sandler 2017). Graphemes have been posited to use features of direction, orientation, curvature, and others, also related to their articulation (Krampen 1984, Olivier 1974, Willats 1997).

2.2.2 Formological Structures

In addition to recognition of the units of a modality, we must also know what units can go together to constitute a sensory experience. While formology describes the modality-general mental representations governing expressive systems, each modality has its own encoding of combinatorics: **phonology** for vocalizations, **cherology** for bodily expressions, and **graphology** for graphics. Modality-specific formologies constrain what combinations of primitives qualify as "well-formed" and how they organize into larger groupings. Such structures involve the segmentation of a modality, but the specific manner in which this occurs differs based on the structural properties of the sensory signals.

2.3 Semiotics of Modalities

We have now established that modalities decompose into sensory signals and corresponding cognitive representations. Sensory signals may manifest in two characterizable ways, in interactions with cognitive representations. Following the semiotic theory of C.S. Peirce (1940), we can characterize sensory signals as either being **idiosyncratic** (Peirce: sinsigns) or **regularized** (legisigns).

Idiosyncratic signals are unique and different each time they appear. They are fully distinctive instances. For example, a footprint in the sand looks like a foot and shows the direction of a walker, but each impression creates a unique and distinctive imprint, without regularity. Similarly, clouds that are perceived to be in the shape of a person may whisk away momentarily, and no two cloud-people will ever be the same. If someone utters a word you've never heard before, such as Neil's grandfather's word "nur," it would be idiosyncratic until this phonemic string becomes entrenched within your mental lexicon. All of these are sensory percepts that may establish links to meaning to a particular observer, but the percepts themselves are idiosyncratic instances. Idiosyncratic signals are purely *tokens*, which have no associated type.

In contrast, regularized signals are patterned, repeatable, and systematic. For example, the words on this page are all stored representations that are lexicalized and repeatable. A smiley face is a regularized and patterned way of depicting an abstracted face. Regularized signals reflect a *type* encoded in memory within the cognitive representations that we posit above. An idiosyncratic signal would thus use the same perceptual mechanisms, but would lack such typified cognitive representations. Because types manifest distinctly, each manifestation is thus a *replica* (in Peirce's terms): an idiosyncratic appearance of a regularized sensory signal. Such a distinction in linguistic terms would be a type (a regularized signal) and token (the idiosyncratic appearance of a type, i.e., a replica). These distinctions between regularity and idiosyncrasy are represented in Figure 2.1 related to their encoded formology (or lack thereof), along with their correspondences to conceptual and spatial structures of meaning (discussed in Chapter 4).

Technically, a manifested sensory signal is always idiosyncratic, because sensory experiences will vary per instance by their contexts. What matters then is whether this sensory signal corresponds to a regularized cognitive representation. For a vocal string of a regularized word (like *person*), each replica will vary in its volume, pitch, voice, and other productive dimensions, along with the constraints of context such as time of day, social setting, or a speaker's mood and emotion. A stored regularized type persists across all these dimensions and infinite possible contexts for replicas. A "pure" idiosyncratic signal has no such underlying regularization (i.e., no type), and each contextual instance remains unique, such as the cloud-people.

Thus, regularized signals are forms stored in memory, i.e., the formological component of lexical items, which in the Parallel Architecture also carries indices to stored representations in other structures, such as to conceptual structure which encodes its meaning. A regularized vocal signal, like *person*, maintains corresponding phonemes stored in memory, with additional links to meaning. Similarly, a smiley face ☺ is lexicalized with a regularized configuration of a circle, dots, and a curve stored in memory, again with links to meaning. These regularized representations (types) give rise to the "replicas" (tokens) in production.

The representations corresponding to regularized signals are stored for each particular comprehender. However, regularized representations shared between people are **conventional**. For example, Neil's grandfather made up the sound string "nur" as a regularized word for himself, but upon teaching his family this word, they created a conventionalized sound string for their small language community.

What Is a Modality?

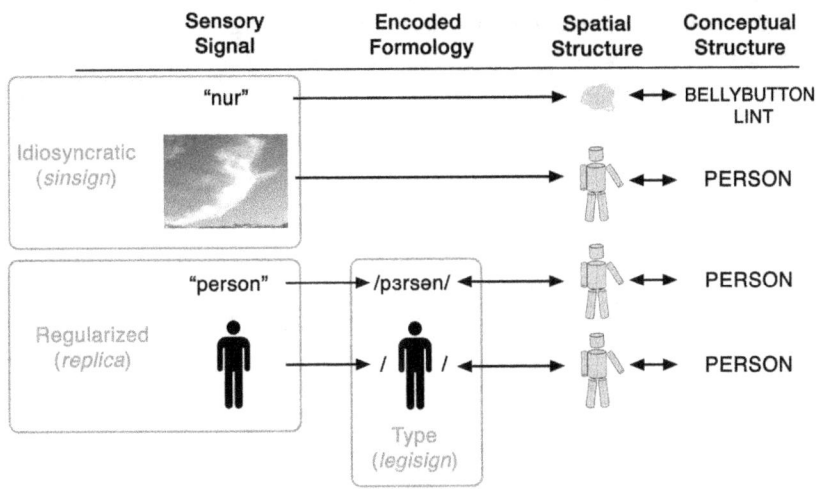

Figure 2.1 Idiosyncratic and regularized sensory signals and their types, along with their interface with meaning (spatial and conceptual structures). Peircean terminology is in italics.

Extending such regularity across larger populations leads to broader conventionalized vocabularies (Raviv, Meyer, and Lev-Ari 2019), no matter the modality.

These distinctions between idiosyncratic and regularized signals, and their corresponding replicas and/or conventions, are all characterizations of the modality itself. Nowhere in this distinction do we yet make connections to meaning, even if the signals may invite such construal. In this sense, we directly contrast from the traditional Saussurean Sign, where a signifier (i.e., modality) and signified (i.e., meaning) are said to maintain an arbitrary relationship and are thus only understood through conventionality. However, when arbitrariness and conventionality are equated, it attributes a sensory signal's connection to meaning (arbitrariness) as a property of the signal itself (conventionality).

This conflation renders a view where the signal has the property of how it signifies. For example, theories that posit "iconic phonology" (e.g., Sandler 2017) attribute the property of iconicity (a way a signal connects to meaning) to the signal (i.e., phonology). Yet, the manifestation of the modality as idiosyncratic or regularized (or by extension, conventional) has no intrinsic meaningful qualities, in line with the independence of structures in the Parallel Architecture. Indeed, expressive systems often contain conventionalized *modalia* without correspondence to meaning, such as vocables like *sha-la-la-la* or *bee-bop-a-lu-bop*.

All sensory signals are technically arbitrary, regardless of how they connect to meaning. Produced sensory signals are just manifestations of sound, light, etc. and are just acoustic or visual experiences. The characterizations of such experiences as idiosyncratic or regularized (or subsequently, conventional) are *properties of the sensory signal itself* (and/or its corresponding formology). On the other hand, all characterizations of meaning-making (symbolicity, indexicality, iconicity) are aspects of the *correspondences* of these signals to conceptual structures, and as such, we will detail them further in Chapter 4.

2.4 Human Expressive Modalities

We have now established a range of sensory and cognitive aggregates of the organization of modalities. Based on these characterizations we can distinguish modalities from each other, and further classify natural and mediated modalities. Teasing out these distinctions illustrates the ways modalities manifest and contrast. We will take various types of modalities in turn, but these distinctions overall are provided at the end of this section, in Table 2.1.

2.4.1 Natural Modalities

A first classification is that of humans' natural expressive modalities. By "natural" we here mean modalities that humans have an innate predisposition for using, even without external motivation or instruction, or instantiation in an external tool. The innateness of these systems is evidential because even in the absence of an acquired representational system, they retain their ability to convey meaning. That is, even if someone does not acquire a sign language, they still retain the "resilient" ability (Goldin-Meadow 2003b) to use their hands to create meanings with gestures. Similarly, even if someone does not learn a full visual language (i.e., an established graphic representational system), they still retain the ability to doodle and make basic graphic expressions (Cohn 2012). Expressive systems of a given modality are acquired across a particular developmental trajectory (optimally prior to puberty), often passively through exposure and imitation rather than explicit instruction, but they build on innate predispositions to express meaning by producing sounds, bodily movements, or graphic marks.

2.4.1.1 The Vocal Modality

Each natural modality involves all the components that we have outlined above. For example, the *vocal modality* uses a sensory stimulus of sound, which is perceived through our auditory system (input through our ears). Speech sounds are produced by the vocal tract, with primitives of articulated sound, which are durative, and correspond to cognitive primitives of phonemes that are organized through phonological structures. These characteristics together constitute what we experience as a single vocal modality.

The dimensions of this vocal modality have been thoroughly researched for over a hundred years, resulting in sophisticated theories of the formology of speech. This work has shown that phonological structure uses several parallel tiers that encode speech sounds at different levels (Bolinger 1989, Ewen and van der Hulst 2001, Goldsmith 1976, Selkirk 1984). We merely provide a sketch of this research to highlight the organization of the formology of the vocal modality.

As has been well established, speech sounds are a sensory signal that are produced at articulation points within the vocal tract. Speech sounds are produced and perceived as a continuous signal, but we parse this signal into a sequence of discrete segments called **phonemes**, a minimal primitive of sound that is contrastive between expressed forms (i.e., minimal units of sound that can distinguish words from each other). Phonemes can be distinguished in terms of a set of distinctive features related to their physical realization, like for example vocality, sonority, voice, and so on.

Because phonemes are abstract cognitive representations, they correspond to speech sounds which may vary greatly in their physical realizations as replicas: whispering, shouting, in noise, etc. Despite the variety of physical realizations which differ on a token-by-token basis, a common type for the cognitive primitive allows us to perceive such tokens as the same thing. Experiences can also modulate those representations. For example, the sensory stimulus of /lɔr/ (*lore*) and /rɔr/ (*roar*) will be recognized as separate words by English speakers, who distinguish the primitives of {l} and {r}, but they may not be recognized as separate words by Japanese speakers, who lack this distinction.

A phonological structure organizes phonemes into coherent groupings of syllables. As depicted in the sentence *Emlen gives his loveliest smile* in Figure 2.2, some words consist of only one syllable (like *his, gives,* and *smile*), while others contain multiple syllables (*Emlen* and *loveliest*). Syllables are structured around a nucleus, which is usually a vowel. The nucleus may be followed by a coda (typically a consonant), which together are called a rime, which can be preceded by an onset (also typically a consonant). The name *Emlen* consists of two syllables, the first which has only a rime with /ɛ/ as nucleus and /m/ as coda, the second with the onset of /l/ and a rime with the nucleus of /ɛ/ and a coda of /n/.

Multiple syllables group into **prosodic structures**, which specify a level of sound structure at the word level or above. Prosodic structures first combine syllables into **intonation units**, possibly signaled by the phonotactic relationships between phonemes. For example, the consonant cluster /ml/ in *Emlen* cannot form a grouping of its own, and thus signals the break between syllables *Em-len*. In addition, the **metrical grid** of prosody specifies the relative stress of the syllables. For example, this arises in the difference between the pronunciation of *permit* as either a noun (*a PERmit*) or a verb

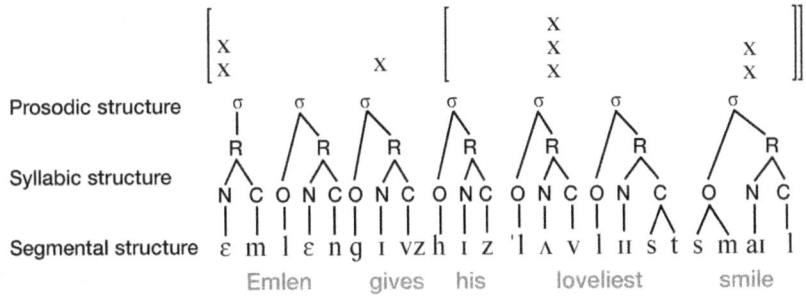

Figure 2.2 Tiers of phonological structure for the English sentence *Emlen gives his loveliest smile*.

(*to perMIT*). Whole utterances may also invoke correspondences to meaning from intonation, based on relative stress assignment which marks focus, which may also indicate a pragmatic stance, like the intentionality signaled by where stress may fall. For example, a difference in focus arises between *Emlen gives his loveliest SMILE* (*smile* is focus) versus *EMLEN gives his loveliest smile* (*Emlen* is focus).

2.4.1.2 The Bodily Modality

The *bodily modality* manifests in gestures and sign languages (Fenlon, Cormier, and Brentari 2017, Sandler 2017, Stokoe 1960), along with sequentia like dance. It uses visual and tactile sensory stimuli, which are perceived through our visual system (input through our eyes) and our haptic system (input through our skin), and produced by the body (particularly hands and faces), with primitives of hand shapes and other body parts, movements, and orientations, which are durative. These sensory experiences correspond to bodily cognitive primitives of cheremes that are organized through cherological structures. Similar to sound experiences, these characteristics coalesce to constitute what we experience as a holistic modality of the body.

The cognitive primitives of **cheremes** vary across dimensions of handshape, location of articulation, movement, and orientation (Fenlon, Cormier, and Brentari 2017, Sandler 2017). Like phonemes and graphemes, cheremes are meaningless, sub-sign units, used in sign languages and gesturing to build larger expressions which correspond to meaning. These dimensions motivate contrasts, similar to how phonemes differ in contrastive ways. For example, the British Sign Language handshapes of signs for *gay* and *unsure* (Figure 2.3a) differ in terms of the shape of the fingers (closed versus extended), while signs for *brother* and *paper* (Figure 2.3b) contrast in horizontal and vertical movement (Fenlon, Cormier, and Brentari 2017). Other signs may differ in the orientation of the hand (Figure 2.3c), which is contrastive even in the difference between thumbs-up and thumbs-down gestures. It is also worth noting that the haptic qualities of handshapes also factor into the tactile use of sign languages, where deafblind individuals do not have access to the visual features of the signal, but do have access to their touch (Edwards and Brentari 2020, Willoughby et al. 2018, 2020).

Non-manual articulators are also involved in the bodily modality. The **place of articulation** of signs provides a contrastive dimension (Figure 2.3d), with signs appearing in particular body regions (body, head, torso, arm) across different planes of space (vertical, horizontal, sagittal). Body positioning is contrastive as well, such as torso leans, while facial gestures (mouth, eyelids, eyebrows) play integral roles in signs (Brentari and Crossley 2002).

Cherological structures organize cheremes into larger constituents that allow correspondence to meaning. Since the bodily modality uses multiple articulators (two hands), it allows both simultaneous and sequential production of primitives. This distinction appears in cherology as **inherent features** (simultaneous hand shapes and positions to produce signs) and **prosodic features** (sequential movements to produce signs). For example, sequential hand movement (with hands differing in both shape and location of articulation) is employed to produce signs evoking events like *see* and

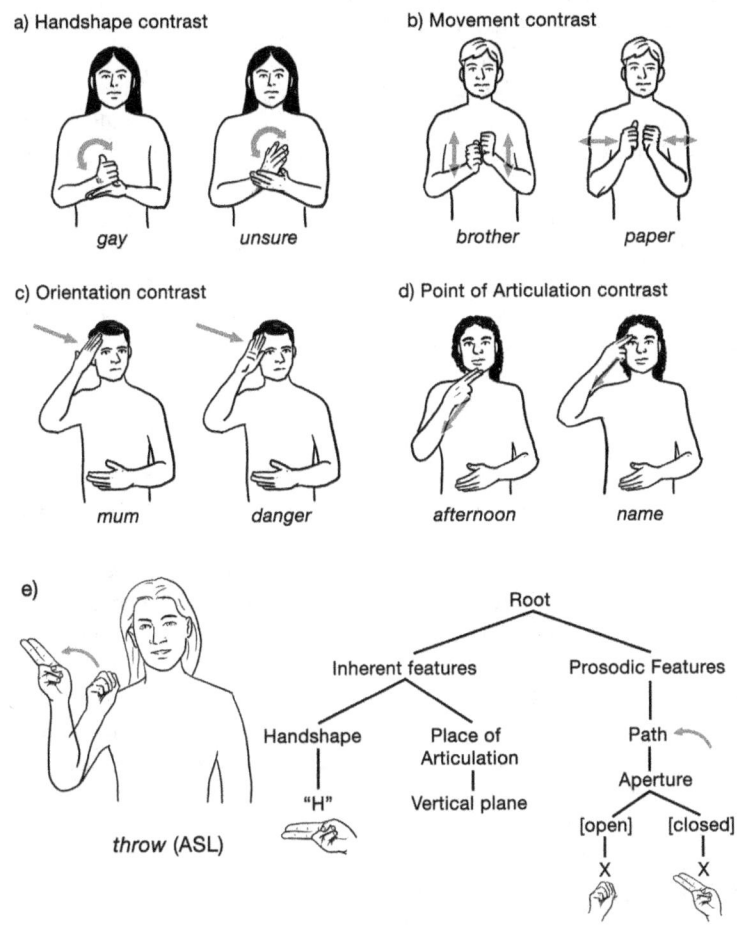

Figure 2.3 The formology of the bodily modality: a–d) signs from British Sign Language distinguished by contrastive cheremic features, adapted from Fenlon, Cormier, and Brentari (2017), and e) the structure of the American Sign Language word *throw* (Brentari 2011).

throw in American Sign Language, consisting both of a path with two slots separated across a duration of time, as depicted in Figure 2.3e.

Movements provide the most salient cherological properties to make signs *perceivable*, and they play a primary role for organizing units similar to a syllable nucleus (Fenlon, Cormier, and Brentari 2017, Sandler 2017, 2010). In sign languages, movement characterizes the well-formedness and intelligibility of signs, providing an analogous function to the sonority provided by vowels. Syllables can be characterized by a single movement, but multiple simultaneous movements can also constitute more sonorous single syllable than one with only a single movement. Cherological principles (also called *parameters*) in the bodily modality constrain possible combinations of primitives (or *features*), yet signs often have a strong tendency to be monosyllabic as segmental units, even when being multimorphemic.

A **prosodic structure** provides a suprasegmental organization of cherology, with the compositionality of intonational arrays often spanning whole prosodic constituents that include the multiple articulators of the body (Brentari and Crossley 2002, Nespor and Sandler 1999, Sandler 2010). For example, facial articulations often play a fundamental role at the intonational level of prosodic structure, taking on both emotional and grammatical functions (Nespor and Sandler 1999, Sandler 2010). Like in the vocal modality, prosody in the bodily modality involves intonational units which can interface with aspects of syntax, and which can provide illocutionary force and pragmatic meaning to utterances.

2.4.1.3 The Graphic Modality

Finally, our third natural modality is the *graphic modality*. Compared to the formologies of the vocal and bodily modalities, the structure of the graphic modality is relatively less theorized. The graphic modality uses visual (and possibly tactile) sensory stimuli, which are perceived through our visual system (input through our eyes) and possibly our haptic system (input through our skin). Graphic production may be a substance left on the surface of a material (a *mark* or *stroke*) or can be an imprint into a material (an *impression*). They are produced by the body moving (particularly our hands) on a substance (such as paper or sand), with primitives that are durative in production but non-durative in their potential for persisting (i.e., we produce them in time, but they may last). Durative graphics (aided by tools) become *animation*. These sensory experiences correspond to cognitive primitives of graphemes that are organized through graphological structures.

Marks are the physical manifestation of graphic production made on top of a surface, while impressions are physical imprints made into a surface. They might vary in numerous features of length, width, thickness, texture, and other dimensions, often modulated by the materiality of the substance they are created in (e.g., ink versus sand). However, these physical marks correspond to **graphemes**, which are meaningless non-compositional cognitive representations that correspond with those marks (Willats 1997). Various approaches have posited inventories of graphemes including dots, lines, curves, swirls, and blobs, as depicted in Figure 2.4a, along with underlying features like symmetry, extendibility, enclosure, or rotation (Krampen 1984, Olivier 1974). Graphemes relate to each other based on their orientation, proximity, alignment, and other dimensions (not notated here).

Like all formemes, graphemes provide contrastive distinctions between visual forms. The lowercase letters "c" and "e" are both composed of a curve, but the "e" includes an additional line (or extension of the curve, depending on the font) to distinguish it from a "c." The letters "d" and "b" use the same graphemes of a curve and a line, but their lateral orientation differs, as does the vertical orientation of "W" compared to "M." These graphemes are straightforward in writing systems, such as those you are reading right now, but they are repurposed from *natural* graphology for creating drawings.

Consider the pictorial shapes in Figure 2.4b–g, which differ only in their bottom graphemic components of curves, lines, and angles. The well-formedness of the shapes as cylinders or cubes depends on using the appropriate graphemes, which are again contrastive: (b) is a well-formed cylinder, but not (c) with a line or (d) with an angle (actually two graphemic lines in a junction), while (g) is a well-formed cube using a bottom angle, but not (e) with a curve or (f) with a line.

Like how phonemes can come together in phonology, graphemes combine in various *junctions*. For example, an L-junction is formed by two lines uniting at a single corner, a Y-junction forms when uniting between three graphemes, and a T-junction arises

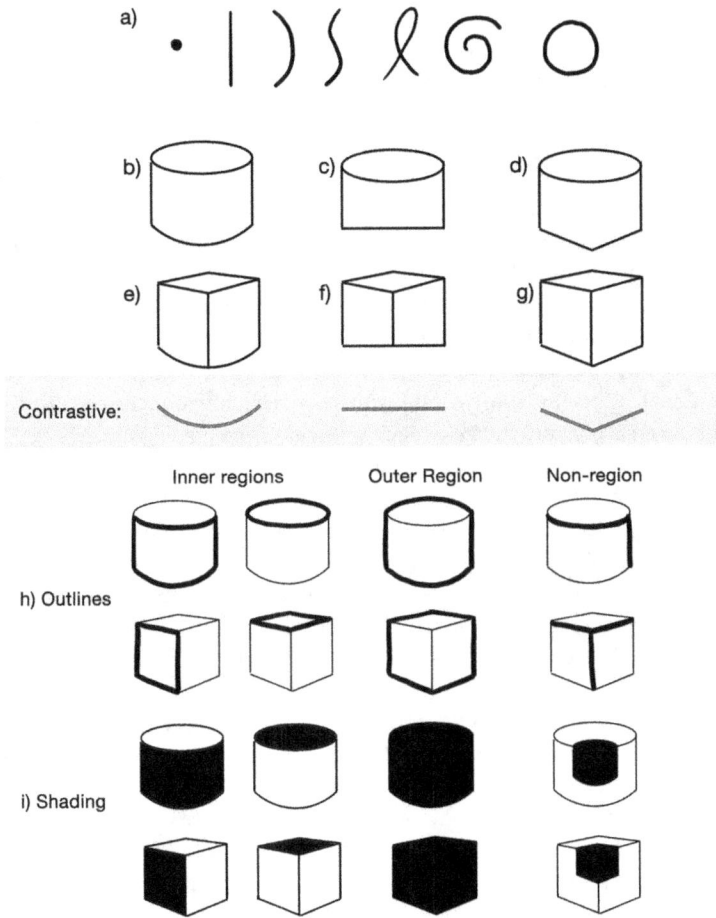

Figure 2.4 The formemes of the graphic modality: a) graphemes of different types appearing in b–g) different contrastive contexts. Regions are highlighted through h) outlines and i) shading.

from the perpendicular intersection of lines. Line junctions are crucial for recognition of shapes (Biederman 1987), and violations of such junctions can lead to ill-formed graphic expressions (Willats 1997). This occurs in the forms in Figure 2.4c–f, such as the transformation of the arrow-junction at the bottom center of the cube in 2.4g where it instead becomes a T-junction in Figures 2.4e and 2.4f. Many "visual illusions" are simply illustrations of incongruous line junctions (like the "impossible trident").

Junctions signal outer boundaries and/or meeting points between **regions**, which are the segments of a graphological structure. A region is a distinguishable compositional segment depicted or inferred in a visual representation. Regions may be a shape that corresponds to the face of an object (such as each side of a depicted square or cube) or they may reflect the outer contour that corresponds to the shape of a whole object. Because of this, regions can be embedded inside each other, with one larger region containing many subregions (and further recursive embeddings). We call the maximal definable region of a form a *figura*, which often corresponds to conceptual objects. Because regions are distinguishable segments, both subregions or a figura can be made salient by darker lines (Figure 2.4h) or shading (Figure 2.4i), but these visual highlights look more unusual when selecting non-regions (Casati and Pignocchi 2008).

Regions can also be highlighted through the visual analogue of vocal rhyming. As in Figure 2.5a, many contours of the figures are similar despite persisting differences. This similarity-but-difference in form is directly analogous to vocal rhyming, and reveals the regions. In addition, regions as a visual segment correspond to what is often comprehended through Gestalt groupings (Peterson 2001), such as the inferred shape that arises through good continuation, closure, image constancy, and other such "perceptual" phenomena in pictures.[1]

Figure 2.5b depicts a short comic with relatively simple pictures where a stick figure discovers a box and then a person pops out of the box. Figure 2.5c depicts the graphemic and region structure of the third panel of the strip, where the stick figure finds a box with a tree in the background. The maximal level here is that of the panel— what we call a *tabula*, demarcated by its frame—a region that encloses multiple figura, discussed further below. Each figura here corresponds to the conceptual content of a person, a box, and tree. The figura of the stick figure has no subregions, and is merely composed of junctions of a circle (a) and four lines (b–e), which correspond to the meaning of a person, encoded in Spatial Structure (discussed in Chapter 4), as notated in Figure 2.5d.

The figura corresponding to the concept of a box consists of multiple subregions, notated with the Greek letter "rho" (ρ). Though we here decompose the graphological structures in detail and specify regions of figura and tabula, in subsequent chapters we gloss this complexity by referring to regions generally (as we do for all formologies). The box shape itself (ρ_1) is made up of three subregions (ρ_{3-5}) each corresponding to one of the faces of the box. Each of these regions is composed of four graphemic lines, but three lines are shared between regions, which join to form the Y-junction at the center of the box shape. Thus, Y-junctions reflect not only the combinations of graphemes, but the graphotactic junctions between segments. Junctions are crucial in the interpretation of coherent graphic shapes and their correspondence to meaningful

What Is a Modality? 57

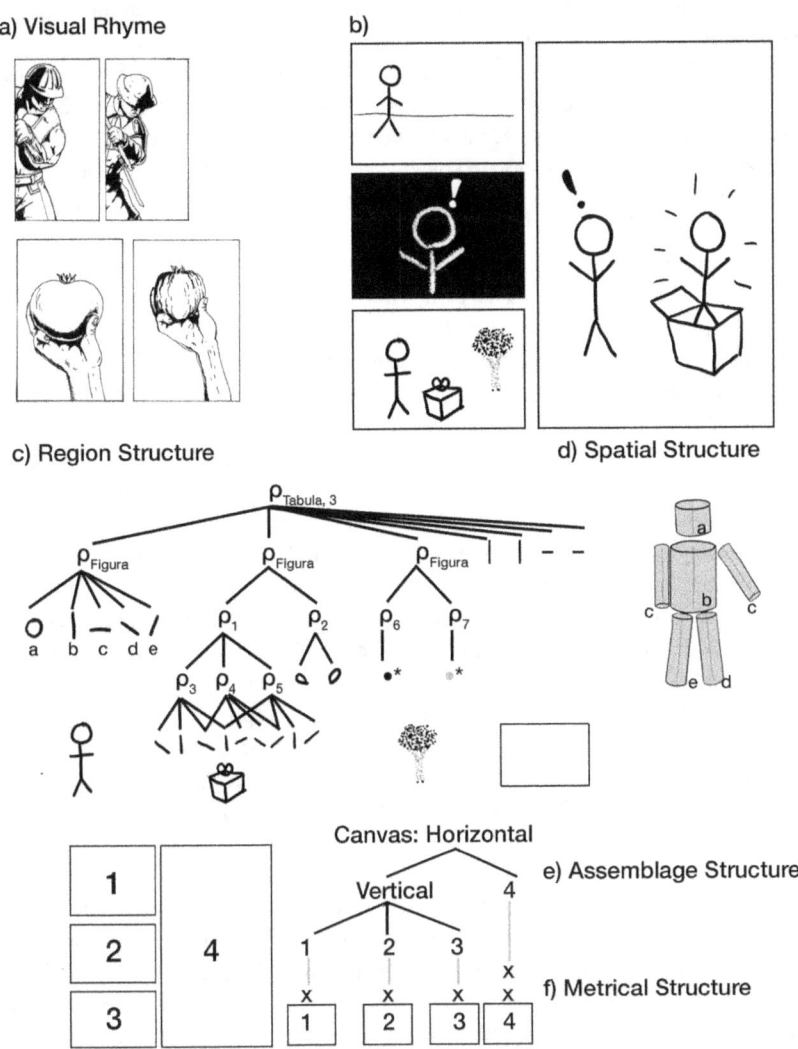

Figure 2.5 Graphological structure as illustrated through a) a visual rhyme, b) a comic strip, c) the graphemic and region structure for a panel corresponding to d) a spatial structure. An additional e) assemblage structure organizes layouts which evoke f) a metrical structure.

objects (Biederman 1987). An inappropriate junction is seen as ill-formed in creating coherent shapes (such as Figure 2.4f), while certain configurations of junctions may lead to ambiguous graphic representations (Willats 1997), such as the Necker cube being perceived as a cube facing multiple possible directions. This whole box region

($ρ_1$) also combines with an additional region ($ρ_2$) made up of two rounded shapes, corresponding to the bow on top of the box.

Finally, a figura corresponds to a tree in the background. This shape is made entirely of dots—one region made up of repeated black dots ($ρ_6$) corresponding to the upper part of the tree and one region of gray repeated dots ($ρ_7$), corresponding to its trunk. In this case, the regions are not signaled by lines marking edges of contours, but through the pointillistic mass of dots, illustrating that there are multiple ways to signal these graphical segments.

The second panel of the sequence in Figure 2.5b also has several features worth pointing out. First, this tabula is primarily black with white lines, showing that graphemes persist through inversion (Casati and Pignocchi 2008). Second, the texture of the lines of the stick figure differs from those in other tabula. These are different kinds of *marks*, but still use similar graphemes (circles, lines). Third, unlike other tabula, the figura of this stick figure does not have lines corresponding to legs, but instead ends at the edge of the frame. Here, the fact that the depicted figura indexes to only some parts of the spatial structure in Figure 2.5d leads to the inference that the tabula only shows a part of a person who still has legs, which is cropped by the borders (not that the panel shows a legless person). Finally, additional lines of an exclamation mark (!) lie outside the figura of the stick figure. This exclamation mark is not physically part of the same region as the stick figure, but they are associated in meaning, warranting a compositional relationship at a different level of structure (i.e., morphology, to be discussed in later chapters).

As discussed, figura may be embedded into larger graphic units of *tabula*, which themselves can vary in their sizes, shapes, and orientations. Within tabula, figura may relate to each other in an *internal compositional structure* (ICS), i.e., the composition "internal" to tabula. The ICS of images reflects its arrangement of regions, themselves composed of diverse graphic marks and other internal regions. In the case of depictions of perceptual environments, this internal compositional structure interfaces with the conceptual spatial representations for objects, scenes, and their parts (Võ 2021).

Because regions create an abstract segmental structure, patterned ICS templates can also be fulfilled by photography. Here, a templatic composition of regions is fulfilled by real-life percepts, not objects that are drawn or painted. We see evidence of this in the consistent arrangements, poses, and compositions that pervade many photos posted by people on social media (such as the schema for people holding up the Leaning Tower of Pisa) or that appear in tropes of filmed movies (such as the schema of a "person walking toward the camera away from a giant explosion"). These forms maintain a common graphological ICS of regions (potentially also with a morphological structure supporting it, as discussed later on), though they may not be composed of natural graphemes, but use real percepts captured by tools (photography) that compose that region structure.

Tabula can also be combined, leading to an *external compositional structure* (ECS) at the graphological level of the arrangements of tabula. This structure is often described as a "layout," whereby image-units themselves are arranged into graphic relationships depending on their alignment and/or proximity within a larger unit of a *canvas*. A single-image depiction, such as a painting, advertisement, or billboard, would have a canvas that consists of only one tabula. In the context of multi-tabula canvases, like comic pages, the graphic units may be arranged into rows or columns, may overlap with each other, may be placed inside each other, or other complex arrangements (Bateman et al. 2016, Cohn 2013b). Other types of compositional arrangements between graphic units persist in the ECS of infographics, diagrams, graphs, and various other contexts.

The external compositional structure itself may specify various physical, spatial relationships, such that layouts become organized into hierarchic segments, particularly if guided in a reading order (like the order of tabula in comic pages, instruction manuals, or infographics). Here, graphic units form segments as rows or columns, which can embed inside each other in hierarchic **assemblage structures** which inform the navigation of these units (Cohn 2020a), as in Figure 2.5e. Because assemblage structures organize this graphic information into segments that modulate how they are navigated, they can also create a pacing analogous to a prosodic intonational structure for the graphic modality. In addition, within an assemblage structure visual units may vary in their relative sizes, shapes, and orientations, which is loosely analogous to a vocal metrical grid. For example, relative size may be analogous to stress or pitch, with larger panels being more emphasized than smaller panels. In Figure 2.5f, the fourth tabula would receive more stress than the previous ones.

Finally, the graphic modality reflects a manipulation of the drawer's environment to create (semi-)lasting expressions. While this is not unique amongst modalities (i.e., manipulating sound waves does persist in an environment), it becomes most apparent for the graphic modality, which can persist indefinitely in its manifestation separate from the human body. As a result, many of the oldest records of human history persist in the graphic modality, such as cave paintings or carvings, leaving us to only make inferences about the people who made them or the contexts in which they were made (Aubert et al. 2019, Brumm et al. 2021, Tylén et al. 2020).

Because the graphic modality is put into substances in our environment, how it manifests may differ based on the properties of those substances. That is, the *materiality* of a representation may interact with how that modality structures information. For example, if drawings are produced in sand (Green 2014, Wilkins 2016), they may require more simple lines and shapes than if drawn with a pencil on paper, and thus the overall complexity and granularity of a drawing may differ because of these affordances (Cohn 2013b).

At the same time, similar graphological structures may persist across different materialities, such as between drawings and sculptures. Because these depictions rely on similar cognitive representations (i.e., graphemes and graphological structures), the same "style" may appear in both 2D drawings and 3D sculptures. These forms create different sensory experiences, though they correspond to similar cognitive representations. For example, sculpted forms may access the same graphology that underlies the graphic marks, resulting in a similar "style" between sculptures, drawings, paintings, etc. Similar graphology may thus also manifest in the bodily modality when signs may be "drawn" with fingers in air or on another body part. In these cases, a graphological structure may be conveyed in the context of bodily communication, but without the articulation of these forms leaving a persisting mark (i.e., drawing in the air leaves no mark to persist as a graphic form after its creation).

This apparent separability between sensory experiences (graphic marks vs. sculpted forms) and the persisting similarity of cognitive representations provides further evidence for the separability of these aspects within a broader notion of modality. To foreshadow discussion below, we also have cases of the reverse: where the same sensory experience persists, but linked to different cognitive representations.

2.4.1.4 Natural Non-conceptual Modalities

Our natural modalities also have the capacity to appear as non-directed expressions. It is possible for our production systems to express communicative signals which lack ties to the cognitive representations involved in more linguistic modalities. For example, the same articulators that we use to produce phonemes can also create yawning, sneezing, yelping, gasping, and other "instinctive" behaviors. These may or may not be constrained by the properties of an acquired linguistic phonology. Similarly, beyond gestures and sign languages, the bodily modality can also express "body language," facial emotions, and basic actions. Comparable use of graphic production may occur when creating non-directed and non-meaningful scribbles, such as when we scribble while attending to other meaningful signals in our environment (like listening to a lecture). These sensory signals use the same productive resources as expressive modalities, but lack the same directed (or may we say intentional?) use of formemes and formology.[1]

Just as the internal sensory and cognitive components of modalities are separable, so too are modalities disconnected from their meanings. We are able to recognize natural modalities *as modalities* regardless of whether they connect with meaning, i.e., whether they link to conceptual structures or not. For example, speech uses the natural vocal modality, but we can also create directed use of this modality in humming and whistling, which lack connections to meaning (unless they are used as structured phonological representations, as in whistle languages). In addition, even within our speech systems, we can distinguish between actual words and non-sense nonwords which may be structured using the same phonological principles of a language, even though they have no links to conceptual structure.

This separability, yet interfacing, between structures is an inherent part of the organization of the Parallel Architecture. As such, we can also have *sequentia*—expressive modalities without links to meaning—as in most instrumental music and many forms of dance. Like our vocal modality, the *musical modality* uses a sensory stimulus of sound, which is perceived through our auditory system (input through our ears). Yet, while it can be produced by the vocal tract, with primitives of articulated sound, it can also be mediated by instruments. All of these signals are durative. When produced by the vocal tract, such signals may correspond to cognitive primitives of phonemes that are organized through phonological structures (like in vocables of *la-la-la* or *sha-na-na-na-na*). However, music also uses its own cognitive representations, such as metrical, grouping, pitch, and other structures (Lerdahl and Jackendoff 1982), which may or may not interface with those of other formologies, such as phonology (when singing, humming, or whistling) or the body (such as when dancing or moving along with music).

It is certainly the case that music can interface with conceptual structures. For example, we can clearly establish emotional or associative links to meaning for leitmotifs or whole songs. A canonical example may be the Imperial March from *Star Wars*, which consistently offers a feeling of authoritarian dread, regardless of its context within the movies. Yet, music does not allow access to or unitization of propositional or compositional conceptual structures, but appears to connect with different types of meaning systems than that of speech or other expressive modalities (Koelsch 2011b). Because modalities themselves do not inherently convey meaning, some expressions of a given modality may connect with meaning, while other expressions may not: some leitmotifs in the *Star Wars* soundtrack do carry loaded meaning, but some do not, while the first notes of Beethoven's 5th symphony may carry a type of patterned meaning, but the rest of the symphony does not. This is to say that music's capacity for meaning-making is not uniform, though it is still possible. Nevertheless, we consider musical structure's natural state to be one without principled and stored interfaces to conceptual structure. As such, we classify music as a *sequentia* that uses a natural modality, but without predisposed links to meaning.

Our treatment of dance follows similar principles as those of music. Dancing uses the same bodily modality with visual and tactile sensory stimuli, which are perceived through our visual system (input through our eyes) and our haptic system (input through our skin), and produced by the body, with primitives of movement, orientation, and position, which are durative. Again, these sensory experiences may have the capacity to correspond to cognitive primitives of cheremes that are organized through cherological structures. Dancing also creates connections to the cognitive representations involved in music, such as metrical structure. Also, like music, dance can create interfaces with meaning, but it is non-uniform. Structures of partner dances (like salsa or waltz) do not explicitly convey meaning (other than possibly implicit ones involved in mating rituals), but other forms of dance might use pantomimic expressions (as in ballet) or explicitly meaningful lexicalized forms of hand positions or motion, as in forms of Indian dancing (Patel-Grosz et al. 2022). Thus, again we have a modality with various, non-uniform possibilities of interfacing with conceptual structures or not.

2.4.2 Synesthetic Modalities

Our natural modalities use principled mappings between sensory systems and cognitive representations. However, because of the plasticity of the human brain, and the creativity of human culture, we have also established mappings between natural modalities that create non-natural expressions. For example, **writing systems** involve the interfacing of the cognitive representations corresponding to speech sounds (phonemes) to those for graphics (graphemes) and their corresponding visual sensory components. While many writing systems do retain aspects of meaning within their visual representations (Coulmas 1989, Sproat 2000), all such systems use graphics to depict speech sounds, which is an *unnatural* mapping. Writing is literally *drawing sounds*. This correspondence between the cognitive representations of phonemes and graphemes creates what we call a **synesthetic modality**—i.e., the establishment of a correspondence between unrelated sensory or cognitive systems (such as the canonical correspondence between letters or numbers and colors).

We argue that writing itself is a culturally imposed synesthesia which pushes us to relate independent natural modalities (vocal and graphic) to create an unnatural, albeit useful, relationship. Indeed, studies of the brain have shown that the neural areas involved in writing have been recycled or repurposed without loss of function from existing pathways related to the "visual" system (Hervais-Adelman et al. 2019). In addition, literacy has been shown to significantly alter the structures of the brain, reflecting this non-natural status (Carreiras et al. 2009, Dehaene 2011, Wolf 2008).

Nevertheless, while writing establishes correspondences between phonological and graphological structures, writing systems may retain additional correspondences between graphological and conceptual structures. That is, written characters can provide meaningful distinctions directly, in addition to their correspondences with speech sounds. Written forms use a range of complexity for how much the graphics directly express sounds or express iconic or symbolic graphic meaning, as illustrated in Figure 2.6. The prototypical alphabetic form is exemplified by the word *dog* in Figure 2.6a, with each letter corresponding to a different speech sound. In contrast, various scripts use whole pictorial forms that maintain iconicity to their meanings, such as the Chinese character 山 for mountain (Figure 2.6b), while other characters have arbitrary depictions, such as the Chinese character 萬 for 10,000 (Figure 2.6c). Other characters have internal compositionality, with components providing cues for meaning and/or sounds. For example, the Chinese character 媽 meaning MOTHER has one meaning component (corresponding to WOMAN), and one sound component (corresponding to the pronunciation of /mā/, a rebus which lost its meaning of HORSE in this context).

In addition, alphabetic writing may also encode meanings at the levels of whole words. For example, many languages use homonyms with varied spelling, like in English: *there, their, they're*; *eye, aye, I*; or *rain, reign*, as in Figure 2.6e. While a speech-centric view might perceive these as "bad spelling," these are functional uses of the graphic form to convey varied meanings. The same meaningful qualities persist in many fossilized spellings, such as using *psych*—to signal meanings associated with the mind, despite not maintaining a homomorphic letter-to-sound correspondence, as in Figure 2.6f.

Most all writing systems involve some triangulation between graphological, phonological, and conceptual structures. These correspondences persist at different granularity of mappings, from individual letters or sub-characters to groupings of these units. Such complexity and nuance extend beyond the typical classifications of writing systems (i.e., phonographic, ideographic, logographic), which maintain a speech-centric framing that does not acknowledge the contributions of the natural graphic modality within this synesthetic mapping.

A vocal-to-graphic mapping is not the only synesthetic modality correspondence. Some sign languages also make use of fingerspelling (Fenlon, Cormier, and Brentari 2017), which gives different handshapes to letters of the alphabet (itself already synesthetic), to create a vocal/graphic-to-bodily synesthetic mapping. While these

What Is a Modality? 63

	a)	b)	c)	d)	e)	f)
GrS:	/d₁o₂g₃/₄	/山/₁	/萬/₁	/₁媽₂/₃	/eye/₁ /I/₂ /aye/₃	/ps₁y₂ch₃/₄
PS:	/d₁ɔ₂g₃/₄	/ʃan/₁	/wæn/₁	/mɑ/₂	/aɪ/₁,₂,₃	/s₁aɪ₂k₃/₄
CS:	DOG₄	MOUNTAIN₁	10,000₁	[MOTHER₃ INSTANCE-OF(WOMAN₁)] HORSE₂	EYE₁ 1SG₂ YES₃	MIND-ish₄
SpS:	🐕₄	⏶⏶⏶₁				

Figure 2.6 Different correspondences between graphological and phonological structures with meaning in written forms.

handshapes are synesthetic in origin, their incorporation into sign languages has also rendered them independent of those origins in many of their uses.

Body-to-graphic correspondences also have many forms. While the depiction of human figures is natural to visual languages (i.e., drawings), various notations use specific graphic conventions to adapt codified bodily movements, such as dance systems, into the graphic modality (Guest 1989). In addition, several graphic adaptations have been designed to create writing systems for sign languages (Grushkin 2017, Supalla, McKee, and Cripps 2014, Sutton 1995). A more hybrid form is the conventionalized drawn depictions of sign languages which often appear in academic papers or instructional texts (this book included, as in Figure 2.3), which often use the morphology of natural visual languages (i.e., drawn human figures along with motion lines, arrows, repetition of body parts to show movement, etc.), but with the grammars of sign languages motivating their sequencing across images.

Finally, it is worth noting that other synesthetic attempts at mappings between modalities have been less successful, particularly when grammatical and conceptual structures are also sought to be expressed in a target modality. For example, various invented sign systems have attempted to directly map the properties of spoken languages onto bodily gesticulations (Luetke-Stahlman and Milburn 1996). Here, in the case of English, all units from spoken English are "manually coded" in bodily signs, which is effectively a type of vocal-to-body synesthetic correspondence. These systems have largely been deemed unnatural in their properties, and do not adapt to the natural affordances of the bodily modality (Supalla 1991, Wilbur, Marschark, and Spencer 2003).

An analogous phenomenon occurs with vocal-to-graphic correspondences which also attempt to maintain the spoken grammatical structures. Various attempts at "pictographic writing" or "ideographies" have aimed for small graphic signs to be ordered in sentence-like structures with the assumptions of universal comprehension (e.g., Bliss 1965, Vandeghinste, Sevens, and Van Eynde 2015). Yet, when sentence-like structures are formed using distinguishable subjects, objects, and verbs, they are parasitic on spoken languages and fairly difficult to comprehend (Morin 2022). When graphic signs of these types (like emoji) are ordered naturally, fairly simple combinatorial structures typically emerge without grammatical categories (Cohn, Engelen, and Schilperoord 2019, Gawne and McCulloch 2019). In essence, these systems attempt to force the graphic modality to behave the way people perceive written languages to operate, rather than allowing the graphic modality to take on its own natural affordances for meaning-making (Cohn and Schilperoord 2023).

2.4.3 Tool-mediated Modalities

Additional synesthetic modalities come from the encoding of writing into other sensory experiences. For example, Braille represents letters of the alphabet into raised dots. This creates a different type of mapping than visual writing, because now the cognitive representations of phonemes are experienced synesthetically through the haptic system of touch. While it may be compelling to imagine a direct link between touch and phonemes in Braille, this is complicated by the fact that Braille is not a haptic representation of speech sounds specifically, but of the letters of the alphabet—which themselves are not homomorphic graphic mappings to phonemes. A similar situation persists in other, tool-mediated representations of writing systems, such as in Morse code (whether as beeps or flashing lights), and semaphore with flag positions. These forms use varied sensory signals to create synesthetic mappings to phonemes, mediated by productive tools and elaborating on the existing encodings of the already-synesthetic grapheme-phoneme interfacing of writing. While all of these forms could be—and in fact often are—considered "modalities," they do so as unnatural, synesthetic modalities that may or may not be tool-mediated.

"Pure" tool-mediated expressions can also persist without synesthetic interfacing between sensory and cognitive systems, like for example photography and audio recordings (but also smoke signals and other such forms). These tools simply capture sensory experiences directly, without any corresponding cognitive representations of primitives or combinatorics (with caveats to computer-*generated* representations that *look or sound like* they capture sensory experiences but actually do not). That is to say that when one takes a photograph, the sensory experiences of captured light are perceived through our visual system (input through our eyes), which have no corresponding natural productive system (other than pressing a button on a camera), and involve primitives of whatever substance emits the light that they convey (previously chemical in printed photos, now electronic in screens). Photographic visual experiences use no corresponding cognitive primitives (i.e., no graphemes of lines).

Despite not using physical marks that correspond to graphemes, photography (and video) may possibly draw from the combinatorial principles of a graphology, for example when the composition of a photograph places elements into conventionalized or established arrangements that may evoke other graphics (Arts and Schilperoord 2016, Schilperoord 2013, Schilperoord and Cohn 2023). People may take photos of figures posing like those in famous paintings, which thus refer to an established graphic composition with natural percepts, or may take photos using the same conventionalized composition without such reference, such as the millions of photos on social media of people holding up the Leaning Tower of Pisa. Both of these cases make use of established combinatoric compositions, but manifested in photos not drawings. That is to say, the combinatoric cognitive representations naturally involved in the graphic modality may be mediated through tools to manifest in visual percepts (photos) that do not involve the production system of the graphic modality (i.e., physical marks).[2]

2.4.4 Summary

With technological advancement, we enable the capturing or creation of expressive forms in ways that transcend our natural modalities. These capacities are also modalities, although they are categorically tool-mediated because of their reliance on non-natural production systems that may or may not involve correspondences with cognitive representations. Once again, this provides substance to our overall orientation that "modalities" are inherently aggregates of a mixture of sensory and cognitive components that allow us to distinguish not only what modalities are, but their broader classifications based on being natural, synesthetic, or tool-mediated, as represented in Table 2.1.

This breakdown also allows us to categorize the status of alleged modalities of taste or odor, which we view as purely sensory manifestations, but without corresponding productive systems (unless tool-mediated) and without cognitive representations apart from their sensory systems. Again, the function of formemes is not only for perception, but also to facilitate *production*. We hold that the presence or absence of producible formemes is a primary distinguishing feature of all classes of natural modalities, which can be used to create sensory signals through articulatory apparatuses via speaking, drawing, or bodily movements.

Hence, tool-mediated modalities substitute a tool for the productive apparatus, and thus also lack the typological cognitive primitives corresponding to those productive capacities. Yet, because they use a tool for production, they allow some manner of control over their production (and thus perception), and thus remain as modalities despite not being natural modalities. Purely sensory systems also lack such productive capacities and typified formology, again, unless tool-mediated (such as intentionally producing odors through a perfume … non-intentional odors can arise from a number of causes).[3]

In addition, this treatment of modalities can be extended to other species. Natural modalities are specific to species, and sensory systems that are not natural modalities in humans may rise to full modalities in other animals, such as odor being intentionally producible and perceivable by dogs or ants.

Human beings' three natural modalities of the vocal, bodily, and graphic all maintain similar overarching structures. They all use specific articulators which result in sensory signals that correspond to cognitive primitives organized by formological structures across a range of levels, from the building of single units to the hierarchic segmentation of sequential units. The question arises: do modality-general properties persist across these distinct formologies?

Table 2.1 The sensory and cognitive components of natural and other modalities. Note that we here leave out most haptic sensations, because they additionally apply to all visual and auditory phenomena. Numbers denote cognitive representations that are direct correspondences to perceptual systems (in superscript).

	Sensory signals					Cognitive representations		
	Sensory stimulus	Perceptual system	Production	Sensory primitives	Duration	Formemes	Formology	Class
Vocal	Sound	Auditory	Vocal tract	Sound waves	Durative	Phonemes	Phonology	Natural modalities
Body	Light, Touch	Visual, Tactile	Body	Light waves	Durative	Cheremes	Cherology	
Graphic	Light	Visual	Body, Tool	Light waves	(Non)-Durative	Graphemes	Graphology	
Music	Sound	Auditory	Vocal, Body, Tool	Sound waves	Durative	Notes, chords	Musical structure	Natural non-conceptual
Dance	Light	Visual	Body	Light waves	Durative	Bodily, Cheremes	Bodily/musical structure	
Writing	Sound	Auditory	Vocal tract	Sound waves	Durative	Phonemes ↕	Phonology ↕	Synesthetic modality
	Light	Visual	Body, Tool	Light waves	(Non)-Durative	Graphemes	Graphology	
Photo	Light	Visual[1]	Tool	Light waves	Non-Durative	1	1	Tool-mediated modalities
Video	Light	Visual[1]	Tool	Light waves	Durative	1	1	
Audio recording	Sound	Auditory[1]	Tool	Sound waves	Durative	1	1	

If common properties pervade modalities, they would need to operate at a sufficiently abstract level, likely within our cognitive formological structures, as they need to be invoked by distinct sensory systems. As one example, consider a potential feature of "magnitude" which might manifest as the volume of a vocal utterance, the size of a bodily movement, and the size of a picture. All such cases manipulate the relative prominence of a unit within their respective formologies. Modulation of magnitude can lead to relative differences in stress within an expression, which bears a correspondence with conceptual structure that provides focus to the element that is assigned that magnitude. This feature would thus be potentially abstract enough to span across modalities, but still able to manifest in distinct sensory systems. If such modality-general features persist, we would posit that they should also be aligned within multimodal expressions. Consider for example the additive emphasis created by a big gesture with an emphasized word *great* in *You look GREAT!* compared to a small gesture with that word, or a large gesture with no stress placed on that word. Our intuitions are both that such alignment is the most congruous, and that deliberately producing misaligned magnitudes across modalities is harder to do.

While we are not prepared to posit a full inventory of modality-general features of formologies, we can offer some benchmarks for what this would entail. First, such features should be functionally analogical within their respective formological systems. Second, such features should be subject to similar rules of combinatoriality, and third, such formological properties within each of their systems should maintain similar correspondences to conceptual structure. With the acknowledgment that modalities operate as independent and parallel structures within a Multimodal Paradigm, research can look beyond surface differences to embrace the task of asking about their distinctive and general properties of modalities, while still treating them as equal parts of a broader architecture.

2.5 Characteristic Mappings within and between Modalities

Now that we have established the components of modalities and have described the manifestation of various modalities within this framework, we now apply it to clarify relationships within and between sensory systems and/or modalities. We see mappings occurring across two sets of dimensions. The first dimension is between sensory systems and modalities. As described above, sensory systems relate to the physical signals involved in a sensation, and with the cognitive apparatuses used to decode those physical signals (i.e., sound waves are processed by the auditory system). A modality further involves a productive system and corresponding cognitive representations (formemes, formology) that facilitate both perception and production. A second dimension then involves either a *multi-mapping* (i.e., combinations of several systems) or a *cross-mapping* (i.e., where one system evokes properties of another).

We define *multisensory* experiences as those that involve two or more sensory signals at the same time. Consider co-speech gestures, where we both see a body moving and hear the sounds of a person's voice (at least). Because we are both seeing light and hearing sounds, this would be a multisensory experience. This example is

Table 2.2 Characterization of a) multisensory, b) multimodal, c) cross-sensory, and d) cross-modal mappings. Arrows denote mappings between components of modalities, and parentheses denote optionality of those mappings. Numbers for cognitive representations (primitives, combinatorial principles) correspond to structures of the sensory perceptual systems.

Modality	Sensory stimulus	Perception	Production	Sensory primitives	Duration	Formemes	Formology	Class
M1	Stimulus[1]	System[1]	Articulatory system	Percept[1]	Durative[1,2]	Unit[1,2]	Principles	a) **Multisensory**
	Stimulus[2]	System[2]		Percept[2]				
M1	Stimulus	Perceptual system	Articulatory system	Percept	Durativity ($\updownarrow$)	Unit ($\updownarrow$)	Principles ($\updownarrow$)	b) **Multimodal mapping**
M2	Stimulus	Perceptual system	Articulatory system	Percept	Durativity	Unit	Principles	
M1	Stimulus[1]	Perceptual system[1,2]	Articulatory system	Percept[1]	Durativity	1	1	c) **Cross-sensory mapping**
M2	Stimulus[2]	Perceptual system[2]	Articulatory system	Percept[2]	Durativity	2	2	
M1	Stimulus	Perceptual system	Articulatory system	Percept	Durativity	Unit ($\updownarrow$)	Principles ($\updownarrow$)	d) **Cross-modal mapping**
M2	Stimulus	Perceptual system	Articulatory system	Percept	Durativity	Unit	Principles	

also **multimodal**, because it involves the units and combinatorics of both modalities (elaborated below). However, multisensory experiences also occur within single modalities. For example, experiencing speech in a face-to-face setting also involves seeing the articulatory movements of the mouth which generates the auditory experience of the sounds. These different sensory experiences (light, sound) are all part of the single modality of vocal expression, as diagramed in Table 2.2a. Similarly, while bodily expressions may primarily be visual, they can also (or instead) be a haptic experience, if they involve touching, as in tactile sign languages (Edwards and Brentari 2020, Willoughby et al. 2018, 2020).

This categorization helps characterize what happens in the McGurk effect (McGurk and Macdonald 1976, Tiippana 2014), where the shape of different mouth positions combined with consistent auditory input gives rise to the sensation of different phonemes. For instance, if the sounds of /ba-ba/ are played auditorily along with the articulation of /ga-ga/, a perceiver may experience the phonemes of /da-da/ because of the conflict between the articulatory positions and the experienced sounds. We diagram this relationship in Table 2.3a.

Here, the articulatory system (the mouth) involves its own sensory stimulus (lightwaves, which are seen), which conflicts with the expectations of the sensory stimulus (sound), that gives rise to an unexpected cognitive primitive (phoneme). Thus, in our diagram of the McGurk effect, superscript 1 persists throughout the auditory senses, 2 persists throughout the visual senses (which is *still part of producing sound*), which gives rise to a phoneme, here denoted as the 1 and 2 creating 3 of the emergent experience. All this remains within the parameters of a single vocal modality. There is no crossing of modalities (i.e., experiencing one modality in terms of another) nor is it multimodal (i.e., different sensory systems each corresponding to their own cognitive representations). Rather, the McGurk effect exposes the multisensory properties inherent to the single vocal modality.

Thus, multisensory experiences can both be multimodal and unimodal. Multimodality specifically involves mappings between systems that use independent cognitive representations, whether or not the sensory stimulus is multiplicitous or unitary. We diagram this in our architecture in Table 2.2b, where each row characterizes a modality. Multimodal messages can involve different sensory experiences, such as seeing gestures while hearing speech. However, the crucial distinction is whether they evoke *different cognitive representations*, as specified by the distinctions in Table 2.1. We consider the combination of writing and drawing to be multimodal, but unisensory. Both writing and drawing involve the sensory system of vision, mapped to cognitive representations of graphemes and graphology, but writing further involves a correspondence to phonemes (discussed further below). This means that writing and drawing differ in their cognitive representations, despite sharing a sensory signal.

In multimodal mappings, combinations of modalities hinge on the durativity of each modality and their alignment. For example, gestures can align temporally with the durative pace of speech (Rasenberg, Özyürek, and Dingemanse 2020), such that speaking and gesturing happen at the same time, resulting in a **composite signal** (Clark 1996). Absent temporal alignment, such as pointing and a minute later saying *Look at this*, will produce two distinct unimodal messages but not a multimodal signal. This

Table 2.3 Diagrammed correspondences in a) the McGurk effect, b) sound-color synesthesia, and c) writing systems.

	Sensory stimulus	Perception	Production	Sensory Primitives	Duration	Formemes	Formology	Class
Vocal	Sound[1] Vision[2]	Auditory[1] Visual[2]	Vocal tract Mouth	Sound waves[1] Light waves[2]	Durative[1,2]	Phonemes[1+2=3]	Phonology	a) **Multisensory** (McGurk effect)
1	Sound[1]	Auditory[1,2]	–	Soundwaves[1]	Durative	1	1	b) **Cross-sensory** (sound-color synesthesia)
2	~~Light[2]~~	~~Visual[2]~~	–	~~Lightwaves[2]~~	~~(Non)~~-Durative	2	2	
Vocal	~~Sound~~	Auditory	Vocal tract	~~Sound waves~~	~~Durative~~	Phonemes ↕	Phonology ↕	c) **Cross-modal** (writing)
Graphic	Light	Visual	Body, Tool	Light waves	(Non)-Durative	Graphemes	Graphology	

absence of temporal alignment may potentially involve correspondences at the level of cognitive representations, as in beat gestures, where repetition of gestures aligns with prosody (i.e., a part of the phonological structure). Durativity is thus the aspect of the sensory signal that facilitates whether disparate modalities can become aligned in time. In the absence of durativity, such as with non-durative visual experiences of writing combined with drawings, alternate means of interfacing may be required, such as the spatial proximity between visual elements (Cohn 2013a). We elaborate on these multimodal interfaces in the next chapter.

While multi-mappings can involve multiple cognitive representations, cross-mappings connect the cognitive representations of one sensory experience to those of another. In **cross-sensory mappings**, one sensory experience is evoked with another, as diagrammed abstractly in Table 2.2c. Here, each row indicates a different sensory signal (whether a modality or not). Superscript numbers on the perceptual system map to their corresponding cognitive primitives and principles (i.e., auditory perception involves sound primitives and combinatorics). Each sensory signal has its own numbers (1 or 2), but sensory signal 1 additionally contains indices mapping to the cognitive representations of 2. That is, sensory signal 1 evokes both its own cognitive representations (1) and those of a different sensory signal (2), which does not actually manifest in experience (hence being crossed out).

Cross-sensory mappings occur in synesthesia, where atypical connections are made between systems within the brain. For example, in sound-color synesthesia (chromesthesia), experienced sounds also evoke correspondences to colors (Berman 1999). We have diagrammed this in Table 2.3b. When people with this synesthesia experience a sound (whether a modality or not), they do link it to cognitive representations for sounds (superscript 1). However, this sensory signal also evokes correspondences to cognitive representations for color (a type of light, 2), for which there is no externally experienced sensory signal (superscript 2). While color is experienced, this does not mean that the regular cognitive representation of the experience of sound is absent. Instead, the result is the triggering of two internal sensory experiences by a single external sensory stimulus.

Another cross-sensory mapping is involved in writing, as letters or characters represent sound using graphics. However, this is not only a cross-sensory mapping, but also a **cross-modal mapping**, in its connections between the cognitive representations of the graphic and vocal modalities. Because writing systems are so habituated, they may not lead to an atypical feeling of crossing of modalities, but such correspondences are reinforced over many years of rote learning, unlike our natural modalities. This has been diagrammed in Table 2.3c. As discussed above, writing maps the sensory experiences of the graphic modality (graphemes, graphology) to the cognitive representations of the vocal modality (phonemes, phonology).

This correspondence does create a cross-sensory experience (i.e., hearing sounds through light), but because these forms are both modalities—i.e., with distinct cognitive representations separate from the sensory perception alone—this creates a cross-modal mapping. We have abstractly diagrammed cross-modal mappings in Table 2.2d. Cross-sensory mappings on their own do not require modalities, and may create connections between perceptual systems where their cognitive representations relate only to the processing of the percepts alone (as in Table 2.2c).

With this organization, we can now also characterize the properties of color-grapheme synesthesia, where letters and numbers evoke specific colors (such as "blue A" or "magenta 3"). Despite being a "synesthesia," in this case, the mapped experiences all remain within the visual sensory system, except letters invoke non-relevant aspects of that visual system (i.e., colors) which may not appear in the marks, and otherwise would not be a part of the stored representations for configurations of lines. Grapheme-color correspondences do not require anything outside of what is diagrammed in Table 2.3b, other than that the graphic modality would need to specify further details about the perceptual features that are involved in the sensory experience. In this regard, grapheme-color synesthesia is not a cross-sensory phenomenon, but rather is closer to the sort of experience like the McGurk effect, which involves interactions between subparts of a single modality (here, the subparts of the visuals, color, and line, which are not typically entrenched with a relationship).[4]

2.6 Conclusion

We have argued that modalities involve an aggregation of disparate parts of sensory and cognitive components. By formalizing these components, we now have the tools to specify what modalities are, how they differ from each other, and how they interact. By decomposing behaviors into their parts, we show that the internal complexity of modalities is obscured when discussing them in terms of whole behaviors, of sensory experiences alone, or of combinations of sensory experiences and meaning. These subclassifications allow us to tease apart how modalities differ from sensory experiences alone, and clarify the various types of modalities, including natural, non-conceptual, synesthetic, and tool-mediated. Laying out these distinctions further clarifies the relationships that occur across and within sensory experiences and modalities (multi- and cross-), which are crucial for the next step of showing how modalities interact.

3

Interfacing between Modalities

Having established a foundation for understanding modalities, we now turn to asking, *how do multiple modalities interact?* All parts of the Parallel Architecture contribute to *multi*modal interactions, but aside from the connections between grammars and/or meanings, expressions can be characterized for the relationships between modalities alone. Indeed, we *experience* multimodality through the modalities themselves: their sensory signals of sounds, light, touch, etc. Yet, how do we bind together disparate sensory experiences to create a multiplicitous, but holistic experience (Holler and Levinson 2019)?

As modality interactions occur between their sensory signals, we can characterize them in terms of the component parts of such signals (Table 3.1). The components of perception (light, sound), production (articulatory systems), and the produced primitives (percepts) all would remain experienced separately for each modality. That is, regardless of whether they are produced multimodally or unimodally, our articulation of speech sounds from our mouths will always be disparate from the articulation of gestures from our bodily movements by virtue of their modality-specific production systems and the sensory signals they create.

We posit that *duration* provides a key method of characterizing how modalities actually interact. This is the only component that has the potential for being similar across modalities. Since this parameter can take two values (durative vs. non-durative), this gives us three broad possible ways by which modalities can interact. First, modalities can be involved in a ***co-durative*** interface, where both modalities have durativity, which can be coordinated across a temporal correspondence. Second, a ***mixed-durative*** interface occurs when one modality has durativity and the other one does not, requiring a mediating device for negotiating that mismatch. Finally, ***non-durative*** interfaces arise when neither modality has durativity, thus requiring additional ways of coordinating the modality contributions. As we will see, each of these categories can be subdivided, with common traits across types. Our characterization of these interactions largely focuses on the knowledge and structures used or experienced by a producer or comprehender. However, with these principles, further characterizations can be made about the multimodal interactions created and experienced by more than one interlocuter (see, for example, Holler and Levinson 2019, Rasenberg, Özyürek, and Dingemanse 2020).

Table 3.1 The component parts of modalities, with duration as the primary characteristic of modality interactions.

	Sensory stimulus	Perception	Production	Sensory Primitives	Duration	Formemes	Formology	Class
Modality 1	Stimulus	Perceptual system	Articulatory system	Percept	Durativity	Unit	Principles	
					↕	↕	↕	Multimodal mapping
Modality 2	Stimulus	Perceptual system	Articulatory system	Percept	Durativity	Unit	Principles	

Regardless of the type of interface that is used, modalities can be concatenated to function as a whole multimodal experience. When such interfaces result in a singular experience, we follow Clark (1996) in characterizing them as **composite signals**. Composite signals are aggregations of multiple modalities together into a unified unit (Holler and Levinson 2019). This creation of unitized composite signals may not be a binary matter, but instead operates across a continuum. We call the degree of integration between modalities **bundling**, a characteristic of the relationship between modalities alone (i.e., sensory signals and their cognitive correlates), regardless of additional relationships in their meanings. Strong bundling characterizes a highly unitized composite signal, while weak bundling has less integration between modalities. Strong bundling can even lead to (or emerge from) the storage of coordinated modalities in memory as multimodal lexical items. In these cases, the contributions of each modality are codified in memory as *multimodal constructions* (Dancygier and Vandelanotte 2017, Goldberg 1995, Jackendoff and Audring 2020, Schilperoord and Cohn 2023), and violation of the bundling should result in a noticeable deviation of the stored representations involved in producing the utterances instantiating this construction.

3.1 Co-durative

A first type of relationship between modalities occurs when both have a feature of durativity. **Co-durative** interfaces coordinate durativity across temporal correspondence. A canonical case would be co-speech gesture, where an auditory stream of speech and bodily motions of gestures synchronize in time. In these cases, most work has focused on the coordination of gestures with the prosody or meaning of speech (Habets et al. 2011, Jesse and Johnson 2012, McNeill 1992). Such temporal alignment can also be made between speech and graphics, where speaking aligns in time with accompanying drawings. Here, the temporal coordination mediates the alignment of representations from each modality. Temporal correspondences between modalities can be characterized by a number of features, both for the producer of those modalities and in interactive contexts (Rasenberg, Özyürek, and Dingemanse 2020). As described above, our focus will be on the modality interactions produced or experienced by a single person.

Alignments that occur between specific units within each modality will be primarily motivated by meaningful relationships, but here we are describing such interactions in terms of their forms. We use the meaning-neutral terminology of **aligned units** to describe the specific expressions within each modality that warrant a relationship. Aligned units are what contribute to the bundling of modalities, and their recognition as a composite signal. In focusing on co-durativity, we find several possibilities for how aligned units may interface, again using the canonical case of co-speech gesture as an example. We summarize these distinctions in Figure 3.1a–d, which largely progress from strong (a) to weak (d) bundled interfaces.

A first type establishes a **synchronous** alignment between the units, which are produced at the same moment and take up a roughly equal temporal span. For example, if a person utters *It was a small fish*, a synchronous pinching gesture indicating

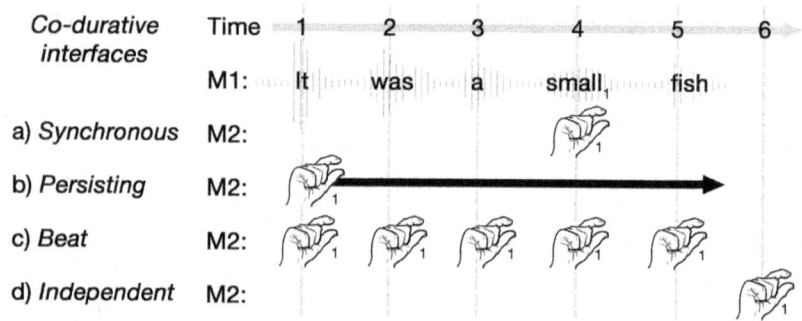

Figure 3.1 Four types of co-durative interfaces between a sentence and a gesture across time.

smallness could be produced at the same time as the word *small*. We indicate this in Figure 3.1a with co-indices marking the aligned units, which are produced at the same moment in time. However, many gestures synchronize by starting slightly before the onset of the aligning words (Habets et al. 2011, Jesse and Johnson 2012, McNeill 1992). As they are temporally aligned, synchronous interfaces allow the strongest bundling to become composite signals.

A second interaction between aligned units establishes a ***persisting*** presence of a unit in one modality up until and/or past the appearance of the aligned unit in another modality. For our example sentence of *It was a small fish*, the small pinching gesture would thus be held from the start of the sentence, continuing until at least the word *small*. Thus, the gesture is persisting in time throughout the entire time span of the speech. We indicate the relationship between aligned units again with co-indices on the gesture and the word *small* in Figure 3.1b, while we notate the persisting nature with an arrow spanning across all time points. Since they are less temporally constrained, persisting interfaces create weaker bundling than synchronous interfaces, and the resulting composite signal is thus less unitized.

A different type of persistence occurs when one of the aligned units may be iteratively repeated across the temporal span of another modality. This occurs in ***beat*** gestures where a gesture repeats with each unit of speech, creating a prosody that unitizes each vocal element. We notate this in Figure 3.1c by showing the gesture repeated across each time point with a word. In some sense, beat units create a nested synchronous relationship between each unit of a durative utterance within an overarching persisting interface. They could establish meaningful relationships between aligned units, as with the small-pinching gesture and the word *small*, but beat gestures could also use meaning-neutral handshapes (such as a fist or open hand) where the beat is used to emphasize the prosody alone. In these cases, the aligned units occur between each individual word and each beat gesture, with no co-referentiality implied.

Finally, a temporally discontinuous correspondence occurs when co-durative modalities are ***independent*** from each other. In these cases, the aligned units are actually *misaligned* in time, occurring in serial, sequential procession. In Figure 3.1d, the gesture would thus be produced after the sentence has been uttered or the other way around. Though each modality remains durative, and the modalities use their durative characteristics across time, these cases have a temporal displacement of the aligned units. That is, they do not happen at the same time. In terms of the sensory relationship between the aligned units themselves (which is where durativity occurs), there is no direct interface. Rather, the sequential production of the units mandates that alignment is established through co-referential means alone; the units are related by their meaning, not the characteristics of the modalities. This characterizes the weakest bundling, as no composite signals are created through the sensory signals, which might affect meaning integration (Habets et al. 2011).

Co-durative relationships also exist within the interactions of the vocal and musical modalities, when words are sung in coordination when particular music is played. In most cases this is a persisting relationship, since the stream of music and speech are sustained across time together. While a spoken dialogue can persist alongside music, when lyrics are sung, the rhythm and melody are intrinsic to both modalities, giving rise to further potential to synchronize. Synchronicity can thus be embedded within a persisting durativity, when particular words are aligned with particular notes, and can further create beat relationships depending on the syncopation and rhythm of the synchronized music and lyrics.

Even more complex relationships arise in film, where visuals, speech, actors' gestures, and/or music all may be coordinated in time. Given the tool-mediated nature of film and animation, co-durativity can occur between speech and graphics in videos such as those that instruct or educate. In these cases, the unfolding animated graphics can co-occur in time with speech, such as narration.

Although the aftermath of creating graphics often results in a persisting, non-durative form (as we will discuss below), graphics are produced in time, i.e., we draw using a production script. This opens up the possibility of co-durativity between the durative speech and the concurrent production of graphics. That is, where a person is drawing while speaking. This occurs in several canonical contexts including education, where a teacher explains things while drawing on a board or tablet, or sports, where a coach draws up a strategy for players to execute. Concurrent drawing and speaking also occurs in the sand narratives produced by Australian Aboriginals in Central Australia, where the drawings unfurl in real time as a speaker narrates (Green 2014, Wilkins 2016). All of these cases involve drawings that unfold in time aligned with a person speaking. Such examples also may be accompanied by gestures, particularly pointing, which may clarify the relationships between the speech and graphics, a point to which we now turn.

3.2 Mixed-durative

Another possibility for modality interactions occurs when one modality intrinsically has durativity and another does not. For example, when describing a static graphic, like a painting or a diagram, the speech is durative, while the graphics are non-durative and persisting. In these cases of **mixed-durative** interfacing, synchronicity between modalities is impossible. Therefore, co-reference must be established by the meaning alone. This is similar to our Independent co-durative interfacing described above. We diagram this relationship in Figure 3.2a, where the spoken sentence *I see nice clouds* remains independent from the persisting presence of a picture that has clouds in it.

Temporal alignment can be realized in mixed-durative interfaces, but only with the introduction of an auxiliary, mediating modality. **Indexical mediation** can link the content of the durative modality with the content of the non-durative modality, for example speaking (durative) about a picture (non-durative) which is then pointed at through a deictic gesture (mediational). Mediating devices thus bundle modalities to create a composite signal, which then inherits the same temporal correspondences as co-durative interfaces. For example, in Figure 3.2b, the painting is shown persisting, but uttering of the word *clouds* is accompanied by a pointing gesture that indicates those clouds in the picture at that moment in time. The bodily modality here provides an indexical (deictic) function to link the durative speech to the non-durative graphics via some manner of pointing. Such mediation has been shown to aid in comprehension, including in facilitating learning (Goldin-Meadow 2003a).

Indexical mediation could be achieved both with the natural bodily modality, as in our examples in Figure 3.2b–e, but also could be tool-mediated in person (such as with a pointing stick or a laser pointer) or through graphic animations (such as arrows or other graphics appearing in time within a graphic presentation).[1] These deictics thus serve a mediating function to direct attention to the appropriate places within the static modality in coordination with the speech.

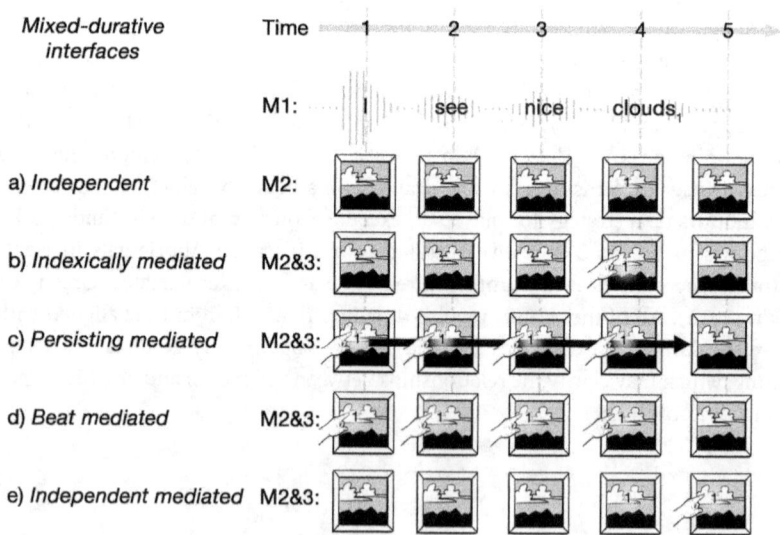

Figure 3.2 Five types of mixed-durative interfaces between a sentence and a picture, mediated by a gesture.

Mediating gestures can also ***persist*** in time, as in Figure 3.2c, until at least reaching the relevant words that co-refer to the content of the painting (*clouds*, coindex 1). Similarly, mediating gestures can use ***beats*** to emphasize the indication of a referent (Figure 3.2d). In both cases, the indexical mediation persists or repeats at least until the speech and graphics co-refer. The starting point of the indexical gesture may be variable, but should remain within the temporal stream of the durative modality. In addition, like co-durative interfaces, mediating devices can also indicate a referent after it has been mentioned in the durative modality, such as pointing to clouds after the co-referring word appears. This again would be an ***Independent*** temporal relationship, but here indexically mediated (Figure 3.2e). The crucial distinction between gestures used in indexical mediation and in co-durative expressions is that here the gestures serve a mediating function to link the co-referential contents of a durative and non-durative modality. In co-durative cases, the gesture and speech directly co-refer.

Mixed-durativity occurs in any context where graphics (whether pictorial or written) are already persisting and thus interact with durative speech and/or gestures, linked through a mediating durative device (animated graphics, gestures). In many cases, the graphic components will have originally been created (or appeared) in a durative span (such as drawing on a blackboard), but then persist afterwards in a mixed-durative context as static representations. This highlights that modality interfaces are not necessarily discrete, but can weave in and out of different interfacing types throughout the course of our dynamic expressions.

3.3 Non-durative

In cases where neither modality uses an expression that extends across a temporal dimension, it creates a ***non-durative*** interface. This relationship rules out the possibility of using temporal correspondence to facilitate an alignment between modalities. In text-image relationships (as in the pages of this book), no modality-driven temporality exists in the spatially persisting graphic representations. As a result, other methods of interfacing become required using ***spatial correspondence***. Coordination between graphic elements can rely on spatial proximity (Ginns 2006, Mayer 2009), segmentation through shared borders, and links through cues such as arrows. Such general spatial devices follow Gestalt grouping mechanisms of proximity, encapsulation, connectedness, and others (Palmer 1992, Palmer and Rock 1994).

We identify four specific types of non-durative interfacing using spatial correspondences (Cohn 2013a). ***Independent*** interfaces maintain a physical separation between the modalities such that there are no direct interfaces other than their contents (Figure 3.3a). This is similar to the content-driven independent relationships in the co- or mixed-durative interfaces. ***Adjoined*** interfaces occur when text and image become spatially grouped, whether implicit through proximity, or when encapsulated together through a border placed around them (Figure 3.3b). ***Emergent*** interfaces use indexical mediation of a linking device, such as an arrow that connects the text and image together (Figure 3.3c). As we will see, these linking devices can take on several semantic characteristics. Finally, ***Inherent*** interfaces place the text and image inside

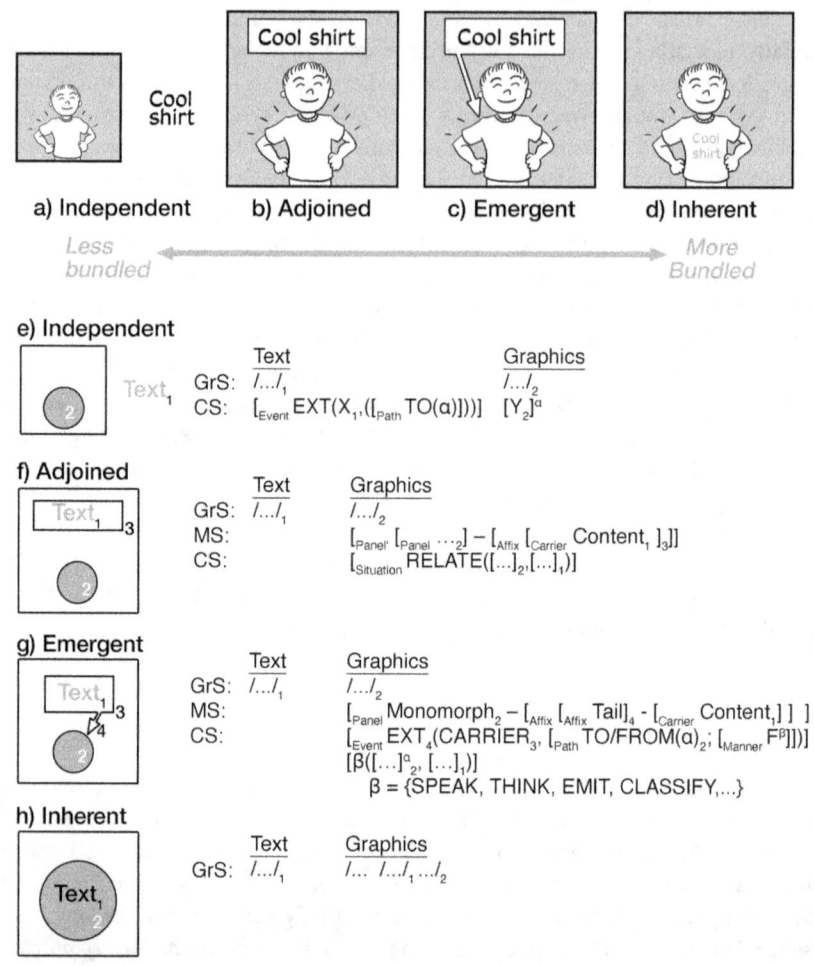

Figure 3.3 Interfaces used in non-durative relationships a–d) along a scale of bundling and e–h) their lexical entries.

each other (Figure 3.3d), e.g., a picture that shows a newspaper with a headline, where the text appears inside the "world" of the graphics. We claim these four types of non-durative interfaces display increasing bundling ability.

3.3.1 Independent

The least bundled of the non-durative interfaces comes again in Independent relationships where the modalities, specifically here text and pictures, are fully separated. A canonical example is how academic papers typically refer to figures: the body text related to a figure is physically separated at a range of distances from a figure. For example, the sentence "an Independent interface is schematized in Figure 3.3a" stands in an Independent relationship with the schematization in Figure 3.3a, separated at a physical distance from the graphic. Similar to mixed-durative cases, the text "Figure 3.3a" serves here as a mediating device that happens to be expressed in the same modality as the body text. Note however that "Figure 3.3a" is also not part of the graphics of the figure itself, and the figure caption has its own Independent relationship to the graphics, which is just more proximal.

Non-durative Independent relationships are similar to those found in co-durative and mixed-durative interfaces, where a gesture might be temporally separated from the co-referring speech. In graphic form, the spatial distance can be extreme, perhaps even separating the modalities by many pages. Thus, non-durative Independent relationships occur across many contexts, in newspapers, magazines, websites, and many others where text and images have no direct physical connection with each other, and relate only through the co-referential relationships of their content. Because of this, Independent interfaces are the least bundled of all text-image relationships, creating no real sense of a composite signal. It is thus curious—and perhaps simply a remnant of historical habits of formatting caused by early print technology—that these kinds of disconnected interfaces remain so prevalent. Indeed, despite us knowing better, we could not escape them for this very book on the topic.

We formalize these Independent relationships in Figure 3.3e. The text corresponds to a meaning of an extension (EXT) from whatever is written (formalized as "X," for example "Figure … ") which refers to some piece of graphic representation (Y) linked through a binding function (α). What this ultimately says is that the pointing function (i.e., the indexicality) is made entirely through the semantics of the text for indicating the graphics. We will further discuss such binding functions in the next chapter.

3.3.2 Adjoined

A more bundled interface comes in Adjoined relationships, which associate text and image through both a proximal relationship and/or encapsulating the text within the physical space of the image, as schematized in Figure 3.3b. This encapsulation would involve placing text on top of a picture (as if "floating above" the picture-world) and/or would be contained within the border of a picture's outer frame. For example, a narrative caption in a comic panel ("Meanwhile, in New York City … ") would have a block of text which is inside the frame of the panel, while "floating" on top of or above the picture content. Some single panel comics, like in *The New Yorker* magazine or comics like *Family Circus* or *The Far Side*, place text directly below the frame. We would still consider these to be Adjoined relationships, as they create a virtual extension of the primary frame, by being directly adjacent. Thus, these methods of spatial proximity and/or encapsulation allow the text and image to create bundled composite signals.

When text floats above a picture, often it is framed by an outer border, which we call a ***carrier***. Carriers can typically be any container of text. In the case of a caption, we call the carrier a ***satellite***, as it carries no additional semantic features other than being a holder of text (discussed below). Carriers are actually argued to exist both with a depicted container around text or even without a depicted frame. Thus, in a case where text alone remains adjoined above a picture, we consider it as [−carrier], compared to if it had a frame, it would be [+carrier].

Satellite carriers in Adjoined relationships connect the carrier to the image as a whole. We formalize this in Figure 3.3f. This relationship in fact requires the introduction of additional representations in a morphological structure (here, a tier of grammar). The image content corresponds to a unit we will call a *Panel*, which is an encapsulation of meaningful graphic information into a segmented form (Cohn 2013b). A carrier is a type of visual affix that contains the contents (i.e., the text), which must attach to a stem (Cohn 2013a). In adjoined relationships, when the satellite carriers are placed inside a panel, the carriers attach to the Panel content as a whole. We express this by saying that the imagistic content of a graphic is a Panel inside a larger Panel' to which the carrier affixes. This affixing nature is why the same content could potentially appear in different physical graphic manifestations, either floating above the image content or placed below outside the borders of a Panel.

While in Independent relationships the text provides the indexical cues for the multimodal interface ("see Figure … "), in Adjoined relationships no such indexicality persists. We merely associate the content of the text with the content of the image through their spatial relationships, facilitated by proximity and/or encapsulation. This renders Adjoined relationships fairly loose in terms of their modality connections, but may have quite strong multimodal connections through the meanings expressed by each modality. That is, the meaning of a picture and its Adjoined text may tightly couple their content, even if they remain separate in the interfacing of their modalities.

In terms of meaning, Adjoined relationships specify no overt semantics of their own. An Adjoined caption contributes little in meaning to the overall multimodal utterance, and merely acts as an invitation for a comprehender to relate the meaning of the text and images. This content in each modality then motivates the multimodal semantic relationship. There are many cases of Adjoined relationships (advertisements, single panel cartoons, news photos, etc.). To appreciate how loose the semantic relationship may be, consider placards are physically next to a painting. When such a placard reads "Untitled," it drives home the loose semantic relationships between the text and graphics in these Adjoined relationships—this gives it a title, which is otherwise semantically impoverished, and thus adds little to the overall multimodal combination.

3.3.3 Emergent

An Emergent interface is the most bundled text-image relationship maintaining the separation of each modality. Emergent relationships establish a direct interface between text and image mediated by a carrier that also has a *tail*—i.e., a linkage between pictorial contents and the contents of the carrier. For example, a satellite carrier also may have a line or arrow coming from it that points to specific content within a picture. The line or arrow here serves as the tail, to directly link the contents of the carrier to the picture. With this tail, the satellite carrier displays an Emergent interface rather than an Adjoined interface, which would have no tail.

An Emergent interface thus always evokes a tripartite structure, as illustrated in Figure 3.4. The *root* is the contents of a modality (typically pictorial) which is outside the carrier and indicated by the tail. The *carrier* is a container of content (typically text) which is somehow connected or attributed to the root. The *tail* is the linkage between the carrier (and its contents) and the root, serving as an indexical mediator of these non-durative sources of information. This tripartite structure persists even if one or multiple parts are not overtly represented. For example, a carrier could be absent with only a line of a tail connecting to a root. The carrier is still present morphologically, even if it is not depicted graphically. Similarly, a tail could be graphically omitted but implicit, while still retaining a depicted carrier. Finally, it is common within comics to show, for example, a speech balloon pointing its tail toward the edge of a panel, where the root speaker is implied but not seen (Cohn 2013a, 2019).

This tripartite structure is formalized in Figure 3.3g, where we again require a morphological structure. The root (a speaker, thinker, etc.) is what we call a *monomorph* in visual morphology, which is a free visual morpheme (or morpheme cluster) that can stand alone as an isolable form (Cohn 2018a, Schilperoord and Cohn 2023). As described above, visual affixes are bound morphemes which need to attach to other elements, like monomorphs. In our formalization of emergent relations, the tail is an affix that attaches to the carrier, and this configuration forms a larger affix bound to

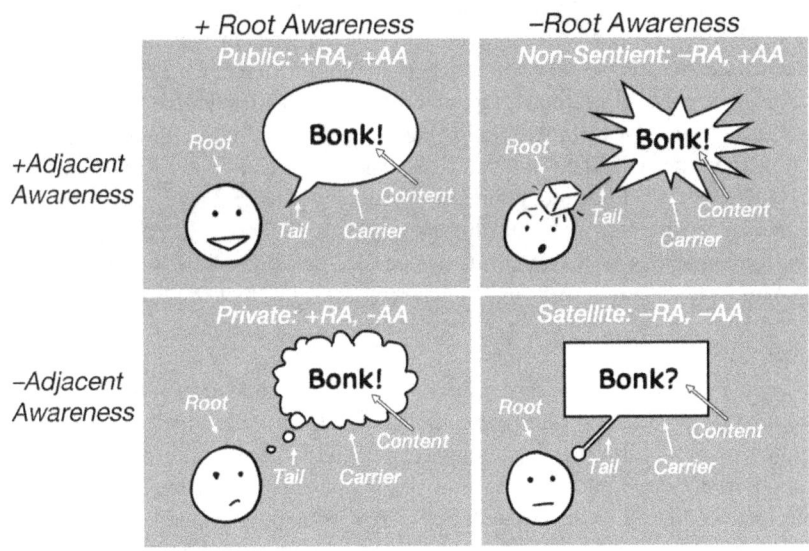

Figure 3.4 Types of carriers involved in Emergent relationships depending on their Root and Adjacent Awareness.

the root of a monomorph. The carrier (subscript 3) corresponds to a meaning of an extension (facilitated by the tail, subscript 4) to/from the root (α, subscript 2). The carrier also conveys a manner specifying the type of extension that is made, whether it is speech, a thought, a "sound effect," or a label. This manner then is bound (β) to another predicate whereby we understand that the root (a thing that is bound to α) produces the content (subscript 1) with this meaning (SPEAK, THINK, EMIT, CLASSIFY).

Because Emergent interfaces use tails corresponding to an extension in meaning, they tightly link the text and image through this visual affix. We again see a sense of pointing in this modality interface. However, unlike in Independent relationships where the indexicality was made by the semantics of the text, here it is graphically represented by the tail of the carrier, extending to/from the root (Figure 3.4).

Emergent carriers can differ from each other depending on their semantic features related to "awareness" of who in the pictorial world is cognizant of the contents of the carrier. If the root is aware of the contents of the carrier, it has the semantic feature of **Root Awareness**. A second dimension then is awareness of the contents of the carrier by any other entity within the pictorial world—"adjacent entities"—who would then have **Adjacent Awareness**. The presence or absence of these variables of Root and Adjacent Awareness gives us four types of carriers, as in Figure 3.4.

We can now place Satellite carriers within the context of our semantic features. Satellites are an "unmarked" carrier in that they have neither Root nor Adjacent Awareness [-RA, -AA]. That is to say that no one in the pictorial world is "aware" of the content of Satellite carriers. A canonical Emergent Satellite carrier is a label, where an aspect of a picture is called out by text, using a line or arrow as a tail. An atypical representation of an Emergent Satellite comes when labels are directly placed onto the items that they indicate, without a depicted carrier or tail. For example, in political cartoons, figures are often given labels that are directly on the figures themselves (sometimes to evoke a metaphoric meaning, like the Titanic having the label of "Economy" and the iceberg with a label of "Debt"). These labels are not part of the storyworld itself (i.e., the Titanic does not have the word "Economy" painted on its side, which would have no carrier at all), but they still function as labels. These would thus still be considered Satellites, but their carriers and tails become "compositionally enclosed," meaning that the functional role of carrier and tail becomes subserved by incorporating the label into the pictorial content.

The inverse of the unmarked carrier would be a **Public** carrier, which has both Root and Adjacent Awareness [+RA, +AA]—its contents are known by everyone in the picture world. The canonical example of a Public carrier is a speech balloon, which contains a verbalized utterance made by the root, hence [+RA], and can be heard by everyone [+AA]. The prototypical Public carrier is thus an oval with a pointed arrow from it, but this notion of "Public" extends to other carriers that may differ in the emotional manner of the utterance. For example, jagged-edged balloons indicating shouting are still Public carriers, as are those with flowers indicating politeness, and those that may be dripping to indicate sarcasm. All of these retain the same semantic features, even though they differ in their particular conceptual structure.

A Private carrier has Root Awareness but no Adjacent Awareness [+RA,-AA]. Here the canonical example is a thought bubble, which contains the contents of the thoughts of the root, hence [+RA], which other adjacent entities in the pictorial world cannot know [-AA]. The prototypical representation of a Private carrier looks like a fluffy cloud with circles descending as a tail toward the root. Other representations do exist though. For example, in American superhero comics, depictions of thought bubbles became less fashionable in the 1980s, which were replaced by caption-looking boxes. Yet, these boxes still showed the internal thoughts of the main character—thus also being Private carriers, just using different graphemes.[2]

The last type of Emergent carrier is a **Non-sentient**, which has Adjacent Awareness, but not Root Awareness [-RA, +AA]. The canonical case here is a "sound effect" where the sound (i.e., the contents of the carrier) emitted by the root is known to adjacent entities [+AA], but not to the root itself [-RA]. Note that the title here of "Non-sentient" is not meant to invoke a status of sentience on the root itself (i.e., a root does not have to be inanimate, and could still be animate). Like other carriers, Non-sentients can have numerous graphic representations, such as jagged lines to show volume, or variations in the font itself to convey manner (such letters that look flaming to visually convey the fiery nature of the root's state). Non-sentients can also have compositionally enclosed roots and carriers, such as when the shape of the text "points" at or otherwise graphically indicates its root.

3.3.4 Inherent

The most bundled relationship between text and images comes when the text is part of the picture-world. We call this an Inherent interface. Examples of this would be any text that belongs to the "world" of the pictures, such as text on a depicted newspaper, signage, etc. Because Inherent interfaces incorporate text inside the world of the picture, they often cannot comment on the contents of the picture itself. Their meaning is the meaning of the picture, leading to consequences for translatability, and a lack of mutability across interface types. The challenge to translatability means that if Inherent text is altered, it alters the world of the picture. For example, if a picture of a bakery shows a shop sign reading "Boulangerie" and this sign is translated to "Bakkerij," the result is altering the "reality" of the picture world.

We formalize this relationship again in Figure 3.3h. In this case, the modality interface is fairly straightforward, without the possibility for specification of morphological or meaning elements. The text here is contained inside the graphics, i.e., the structure for text with subscript 1 is placed inside, and thus is part of, the structure for graphics with subscript 2. Essentially, this is barely a type of multimodal "interface" so much as the text becomes a part of the graphics themselves.

In addition, Inherent interfaces lack mutability with the other types of interfaces. Changing this "Boulangerie" shop sign to instead be a satellite carrier with an arrow would substantially alter the picture world. By comparison, imagine text in the body of a book that discusses a distant figure in an Independent relationship. This text could easily be extracted and placed directly on top of the figure in a satellite carrier, suggesting mutability between Independent and Adjoined interfaces, thereby manipulating the bundling of the text-image relationship. However, such body text could likely not *become* part of the image, suggesting an immutable relationship between Independent (plus Adjoined and Emergent) and Inherent interfaces.

3.3.5 Graphic Planes

The presence of Inherent relationships where text is part of an image implies that in other spatial interfaces, text is *not* part of the image. What then is the relative spatial status of text and pictures in these cases, given that they share a graphic manifestation? A second clue comes from Emergent devices like a speech balloon. Though it contains the text, and this carrier is a pictorial device, the entities within a pictorial world are

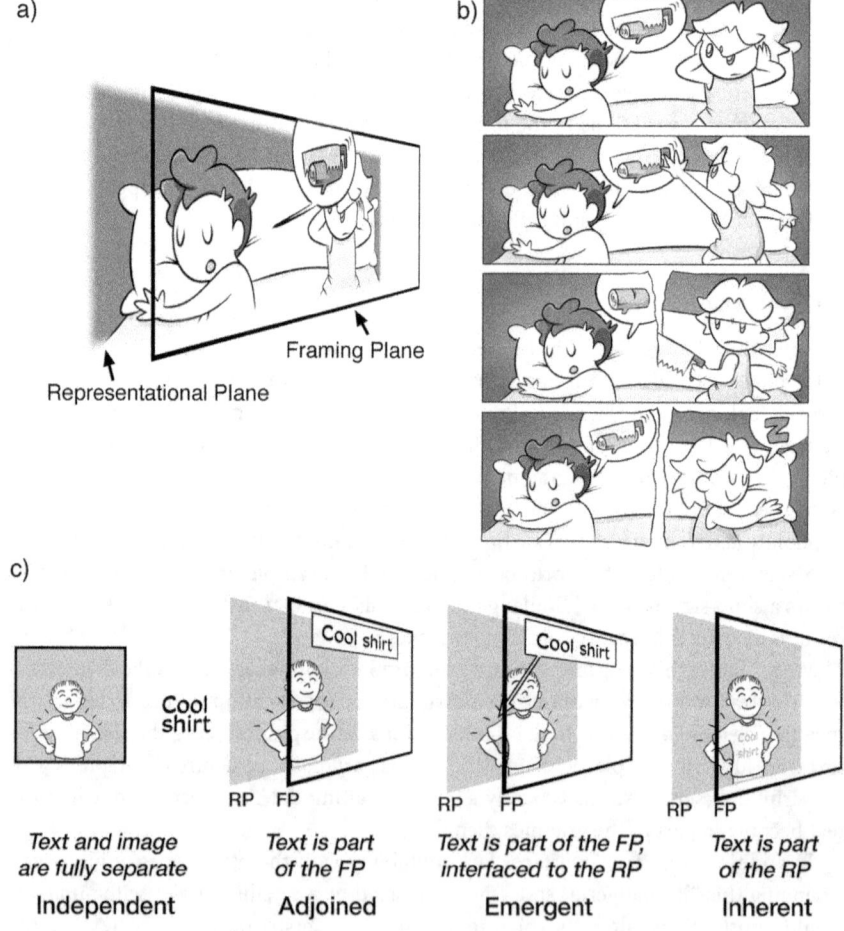

Figure 3.5 The Representational and Framing Planes in a) a panel from *JA!* by Ángela Cuéllar and Jonás Aguilar (© 2016) which b) plays with their separation, while c) shows these planes across the four types of non-durative spatial interfaces.

not cognizant that there is a floating oval with text near or above their heads, and their interactions with such a device—such as pinching or popping a speech balloon—would be deemed a "clever" meta-analysis of the graphic form, as in Figure 3.5b. So, just what is the relationship between these components?

We have argued that these observations warrant two interacting levels within graphic depictions (Cohn 2013a). A **Representational Plane** contains the depicted storyworld of a pictorial representation, while a **Framing Plane** contains the graphic devices and elements that are outside the entities in the pictorial storyworld. These elements in the Framing Plane include non-Inherent text, carriers, and other visual morphemes like motion lines, upfixes (like hearts or gears floating above characters' heads), eye-umlauts (like hearts, spirals, or dollar signs replacing characters eyes), and many other graphic conventions. In addition, the borders of a picture itself—like a comic panel—belong to the Framing Plane, hence the ability for carriers to become full panels, like when a panel is shaped like a thought bubble to depict full events and actions that are thought by a character in another panel.

Because these elements lie in the Framing Plane, they are inaccessible to the entities in the Representational Plane, unless an author plays with this division, letting such morphology become a "real" part of the pictorial world—again, like grabbing balloons, manipulating their tails, or altering the nature of upfixes. This relationship is depicted in the comic in Figure 3.5a, from *JA!* by Ángela Cuéllar and Jonás Aguilar. Here, the woman is annoyed by the snoring created by the man—graphically depicted as a saw cutting wood within a speech balloon. This device in the first panel belongs to the Framing Plane. She then grabs the saw out of his carrier (panel 2) and proceeds to cut the panel in half (panel 3) in order to sleep comfortably (panel 4/5) where the saw now returns to the Framing Plane within its balloon. Because the woman (part of the Representational Plane) interacts with both the carrier and the panel borders (typically part of the Framing Plane), these interactions collapse across the planes to pull the elements of the Framing Plane into the Representational Plane.

This division between Representational and Framing Planes allows us to further characterize the ways that text and images relate to each other. In fact, all of our non-durative spatial interfaces can be characterized by the interactions between the two planes, and along with them, the strength of their bundling, as schematized in Figure 3.5c. Independent interfaces have no spatial relationship between modalities, and no relationship between Representational and Framing Planes. In this case, the text would be fully divorced from any possible Framing Plane of a picture, because it is in a different plane. Adjoined relationships introduce the text to the Framing Plane via a satellite carrier, which is bundled through some sort of spatial relationship. However, this satellite on the Framing Plane has no direct relation to anything in the Representational Plane. They remain separate. An Emergent interface provides a link between planes using the tail, which is how the carrier (in the Framing Plane) connects to the root (in the Representational Plane). The indexical nature of the tail bridges these planes, whether or not the tail is overtly depicted, serving as a strong bundling device for the integration of those expressions. Finally, because the Inherent interface places text directly into the pictorial world, the text is part of the Representational Plane alone, with no need for mediating a Framing Plane. Thus, all of these spatial interfaces—and their bundling capacities—can be thought of in terms of the relationships between these planes.

Finally, despite these spatial interfaces emerging in a non-durative, persisting representation, we encounter them across a temporal span. We still need to engage spatial representations in a temporal order to process them, moving our eyes across a visual surface to extract the relevant information. Since there is no intrinsic temporality to the spatial form, habits and/or rules may be established for how we do this ordering, which has the potential to vary by genre or context. For example, comic readers often read the text prior to the images when engaging a panel (Laubrock, Hohenstein, and Kümmerer 2018), although this may vary depending on the content and interfacing, and the proficiency that readers have with comics (Nakazawa 2005, Zhao and Mahrt 2018). Similarly, research on advertisements suggests that people often seek the textual cues first, then look at the image (Wedel and Pieters 2017), although this may also be modulated by the complexity of the pictorial content. Thus, despite non-durative relationships occurring outside the inherent durativity of the modality, time is always present in any interaction with a modality.

3.4 Conclusion

Here we have posited several ways that modalities interact based on their shared feature of durativity: co-durative, mixed-durative, and non-durative. Each of these distinctions has subclasses varying the range to which modalities become bundled into a composite signal. Across our interfaces we observe common characteristics, as in Table 3.2. First, all interfaces can have an Independent relationship, whereby the modalities are disjunct from each other. This is essentially the null case of modality integration.

A next characteristic would be of modality-driven interfaces. That is, features of the modalities themselves directly facilitate their integration. In co-durative interfaces, this arises through the feature of durativity, which creates alignment through temporal correspondence. Because durativity is a part of the modality, no additional mediation is required. It might be odd for example, to see a speaker making a pointing gesture with one hand to draw focus to the gesture made by another hand (☞ ✋). In the case of non-durative interfaces, the Adjoined interface uses purely spatial dimensions like proximity and/or encapsulation to concatenate modalities.

We can characterize the further interfaces then as lacking this type of modality-driven relationship. Mixed-durative interfaces cannot use temporal correspondence because

Table 3.2 Characteristics across modality interfaces.

	No interface	Modality-driven interface	Mediated interface	Cross-modal incorporation
Co-durative	Independent	Synchronous, persisting, beat		
Mixed-durative	Independent		Indexical mediation	
Non-durative	Independent	Adjoined	Emergent	Inherent

one modality is non-durative, and thus either lack a direct interface and cede multimodality to content relations (Independent), or use some form of mediation, such as gestures. A similar mediated interface is found in Emergent relationships, which use morphological devices with the tripartite carrier-tail-root relation in order to bundle modalities. Finally, only non-durative relations evoke a unique type of Inherent relationship which arises because of the cross-modal nature of writing, which can then incorporate text into graphics. As we will see in later chapters, modalities can also become integrated into each other's structures using their grammars rather than their formologies.

Thus, these characteristics provide abstractions that detail how modalities interface. Co-durative interfaces are driven largely by their modalities' inherent properties. Mixed-durative interfaces must compensate for the lack of such inherent properties, and in non-durative relations, no such properties exist, and thus they need to recreate all characteristics of integration in spatial form. All such interfaces thus vary in how they *bundle* modalities together to create composite signals.

Given this range of integration, we may ask whether these gradient strengths of bundling create corresponding gradient associations in meaning. Some research has shown that Independent interfaces are harder to comprehend than those that are modality-driven. Synchronous co-speech gestures are more congruous than asynchronous ones (Graziano, Nicoladis, and Marentette 2020, Habets et al. 2011), and proximity can modulate the integration of meaning in graphics (Ginns 2006, Mayer 2009). Similarly, in mixed-durative interactions between speech and graphics, mediated gestures aid in comprehension (Goldin-Meadow 2003a). It is less clear about the fine-grained distinctions between spatial interfaces like Adjoined and Emergent relationships compared to spatial Independent relationships, but we might posit similar variance.

We thus propose two hypotheses related to our overarching notion of bundling as the integration of modalities into a composite signal. These hypotheses relate 1) to how modalities affect meaning, and 2) to our perception of multimodality. First, we posit that stronger bundling will make it easier to integrate the various conceptual contributions. Thus, the interfacing between manifested sensory signals of modalities will affect the conceptual structure. Second, we posit that stronger bundling will lead to less *awareness* that multimodality is occurring in the first place, because of the pervading holism of a composite signal.

This second hypothesis brings us to the question: What is the nature of a multimodal experience? One possibility posed by Jackendoff (1987, 2007) is the *intermediate level hypothesis*, which applied to unimodal language in positing that, in our consciousness of language, the contents of awareness come from the phonological structures. That is, we are conscious of the modality. Extending this to our discussion here, if we are aware of multimodality, such contents of consciousness are the characteristics of modalities themselves, although awareness of all signals may not be equal. We might direct more attention to one modality than another, such as when we focus on the contents of speech, but are less aware of gestures, even though we may receive their semantic content and the composite multimodal message that they create with speech. Modality interfacing is thus the most "multimodal" of the interactions that modalities have. As we will see shortly, modalities also can interact in their meaning and grammars. However, these interactions occur in ways that are more subtle and less accessible to our consciousness, or even not at all.

Part Three

Meaning

4

Conceptual Structures for Multiple Modalities

If we are to characterize the nature in which multimodal communication conveys meaning, we must first ask whether modalities affect the organization of meaning themselves. That is, are the meanings of vocal expressions encoded in the brain in a different way than that of graphic expressions? The debates around this issue typically involve two primary positions. One position holds that meaning is **amodal**, whereby the same invariant conceptual structure is activated by different types of modalities. In contrast, a **modality-specific** view holds that the form of an expression (i.e., vocal versus visual) also reflects its encoded meaning, leading to the storage of separate conceptual structures for each modality. Though these positions have long characterized debates about multimodal meaning, we will eventually arrive at a view separate from both of these positions.

The modality-specific view has primarily been championed in the theory of dual-coding (Paivio 1986), which holds that visual and textual information are encoded in the brain separately while retaining features of their sensory form, and become integrated at a later stage of processing. Arguments for modality-specificity have also arisen in theories of embodied or grounded cognition (e.g., Barsalou 2008). In contrast to this theorizing about text-picture relationships, discussion of co-speech gestures has largely emphasized a common "growth point" of conceptual origin for the production of gesticulations and speech (McNeill 1992). Gestures often convey a complementary facet of meaning to that expressed in speech, even to the point of expressing crucial information that clarifies speech or is essential for understanding the speech. Furthermore, many linguists have pointed to the necessity of some unified notion of meaning in order for people to be able to talk about what they see, smell, touch, etc. (Jackendoff 1983, 1987, Macnamara 1978, Talmy 2000a, b).

Debates surrounding the encoding of verbal and visual information have often been situated in cognitive neuroscience work investigating the character of **semantic memory**. While some findings have suggested differing brain areas corresponding to pictures and text, electrophysiological responses to different modalities have consistently yielded the same brainwave effect. The *N400* is a default neural response which arises to all meaningful information, and is modulated by the expectancy and/or congruency of a stimulus with its prior context (Kutas and Federmeier 2011, Kutas and Hillyard 1980), reflecting the access and/or integration of semantic memory (Baggio 2018, Kuperberg 2021, Kutas and Federmeier 2011, Hagoort 2017, Nieuwland et al. 2020).

While the N400 was first discovered in the context of sentence processing, it has also been observed in meaningful processing across all modalities and sensory signals. The N400 shares a similar time course no matter the modality, and no matter whether involved in unimodal, crossmodal, or multimodal interactions (Kutas and Federmeier 2011). It is also modulated by the predictability of the incoming information, whether that is words in a sentence, pictures in a visual narrative sequence, or pictures substituted for a word in a sentence (Coderre et al. 2020, Kutas and Hillyard 1984, Weissman, Cohn, and Tanner under review). This implies that words, pictures, and gestures tap into a common structure (Federmeier and Kutas 2001, Manfredi, Cohn, and Kutas 2017, Wu and Coulson 2005), further suggested by findings that the N400 effect is attenuated similarly in individuals with autism spectrum disorder for both sequential words and sequential images (Coderre et al. 2018). Thus, the similarity of the N400 response across modalities suggests similarity in their processing of meaning.

Nevertheless, these findings should not be taken to imply an amodal system without variation between modalities, since modalities have been shown to evoke some differences in their brain responses. For example, slightly different distributions of the N400 occur across the surface of the scalp for different types of information, such as between verbal (posterior) compared to visual (fronto-central) or auditory (frontal) signals. In addition, scalp distributions of the N400 also vary on the basis of concreteness within modalities, with more concrete items evincing a more widespread and/or frontal distribution than abstract items, which have a more posterior distribution (Barber et al. 2013, Cohn and Foulsham 2022, Emmorey et al. 2020, Ganis, Kutas, and Sereno 1996).[1]

Overall, these findings suggest that neither semantic memory is organized in a fully amodal way, nor is it partitioned between meaning structures unique to each modality. Rather, they suggest a **supramodal** semantic system (Calzavarini 2023, Kuhnke et al. 2023, Kutas and Federmeier 2011, Ralph et al. 2016, Xu et al. 2009). Concepts themselves are not holistic, but rather can be decomposed into **semantic features** that are partially non-overlapping across modalities, leading to both consistency and variation in the brain responses of similar meanings expressed in different modalities. We illustrate this relationship in Figure 4.1. In our example, the word *person* provides a basic level concept that only implicitly involves information like body parts, gender, sex, ethnicity, etc., while a picture may provide that information overtly and leave the basic concept to be inferred. Thus, while modalities only directly activate certain features, others remain inferred through spreading activation, and the overall semantic features add up to the totality of the evoked concept.

This modality-sensitive viewpoint is consistent with proposals that modality-specific information is encoded in different parts of the brain associated with sensory systems that access those signals, and these areas then serve as "spokes" to feed into a modality-independent hub in the anterior temporal lobe (Ralph et al. 2016). Additional work has proposed that such a hub involves hierarchic associations between modality-specific inputs (Kuhnke et al. 2023). In electrophysiology, brain responses corresponding to specific modalities thus arise early in the time-course of processing (~0–300 ms), after which the more consistent N400 responses begin. The N400 has similarly been associated with a source localization in the anterior temporal lobe (Kutas and Federmeier 2011).

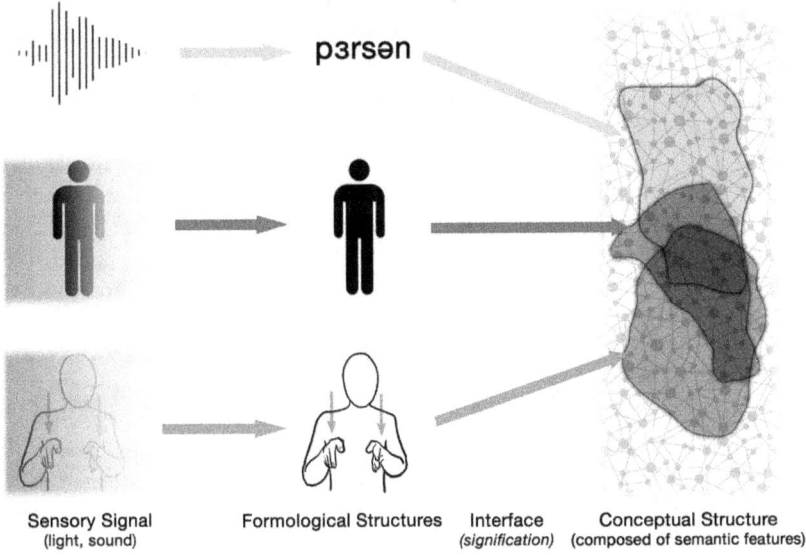

Figure 4.1 Schematization of a supramodal conceptual structure that is sensitive to affordances of modalities but is neither amodal nor modality-dependent.

Thus, the nature of meaning itself—i.e., semantic features and their combinations—appears to be of a different character than the format of modalities. The differences between modalities thus arise from how they encode and access these conceptual structures. Following Gibson (2014 [1979]), we think of these principled correspondences as modality *affordances* for the access of meaning. In the remainder of this chapter, we will make use of Jackendoff's theory of semantics to characterize the meaningful expressions across modalities and their range of signification.

4.1 Conceptual Structure

This modality-sensitive architecture of meaning aligns with Jackendoff's conception of multimodal semantics, which originally posited an abstract "hub" of Conceptual Structure, integrating varied semantic information from different sensory sources (Jackendoff 1987). This model was indeed referenced as the foundation for early conceptions of distributed and embodied cognition (Varela, Thompson, and Rosch 1991), which also stress such dispersed meaning but often without a supramodal hub (Barsalou 2008). We here use Jackendoff's theory of Conceptual Semantics (Jackendoff 1983, 1990, 2007, 2010a), the formal expression of this hub of Conceptual Structure. We believe Conceptual Semantics is well-suited for our purposes of characterizing meaning across modalities because it is conceived as an independent cognitive generative structure that characterizes the *psychological* encoding and construal of meaning. Being an independent structure, it is not derived from other aspects of expressions (such as syntax) and it is applicable to domains other than speech (such as gesture or graphics). As we will discuss below, the formulation of Conceptual Semantics has already been applied to relations with visual perception and cognition (Jackendoff 1983, 2010a, Landau and Jackendoff 1993, Landau 2017).

Conceptual Semantics makes a distinction between various primary tiers of meaning. Conceptual Structure encodes algebraic and abstract meanings. In combination with this, Spatial Structure specifies a geometric, yet abstract, spatial understanding (Biederman 1987, Jackendoff 1983, 2002, 2010a, Langacker 1987, Landau and Jackendoff 1993, Marr 1982, Talmy 2000a, b). We will focus on these primary components, but they further interact with other systems to specify auditory, olfactory, or gustatory features of concepts. We first describe the specifics of Conceptual Structure and then turn to Spatial Structure.

Conceptual Semantics posits primitives that serve as semantic categories to be fulfilled by the specific meanings of different systems. These primary primitives include Situation (Event and State), Thing (or Object), Place, and Path, which are modified by Property and Amount.[2] These conceptual categories are basic ontological primitives, and are consistent with the categories that developmental research suggests children innately know (Mandler 2004, 2010).

Common componential features extend across conceptual categories. For example, both Objects and Events use the feature of boundedness (Jackendoff 2010a, Papafragou and Ji 2023), where they can be individuated by a boundary (such as the object of a cup, or the event of a punch) or they can extend indefinitely without inherent boundaries (such as the substance of water or the process of walking). This means that concepts can be decomposed into primitive basic features that permeate across various categories. The result is that the similarities between objects and events (and other semantic classes) can arise from shared features, without needing to map them across classes (such as saying that events "are like" objects in a metaphor[3]).

Semantic categories can be combined according to three general principles. The first is that semantic categories combine in a predicate calculus of a function-argument structure, e.g. $F(X,Y)$. This structure generalizes across predicates, but specific functions persist for different categories. The primary combinatorial schemas for each semantic class are:

PLACE:
[$_{Place}$ PLACE-FUNCTION*(THING)] *={IN, ON, UNDER, OVER, etc.}

PATH:
[$_{Path}$ PATH-FUNCTION*(THING/PLACE)]
   *={TO, FROM, TOWARD, AWAY-FROM, VIA}

EVENT:
[$_{Event}$ GO(THING, PATH)]
[$_{Event}$ STAY(THING, PATH)]

STATE:
[$_{State}$ BE(THING, PLACE)]
[$_{State}$ ORIENT(THING, PATH)]
[$_{State}$ EXTEND(THING, PATH)]

The second principle is that semantic categories are elaborated using modifiers. This maintains the overarching assumption within the Parallel Architecture that all mental structures (modality, meaning, grammar) have the potential to use combinatorial hierarchies whereby core "heads" can be elaborated by peripheral "modifiers" in an "X-bar" generalized mental structure (Jackendoff 1990). Consider the example of the phrase *cat in the garden*. While a cat is a Thing that can stand alone without specification for its spatial context, the addition of a Place modifies it for richer information content. This is notated in Conceptual Semantics as:

[$_{Thing}$ CAT; [$_{Place}$ IN([$_{Thing}$ GARDEN])]]

Here, the Thing CAT, is a primary semantic category. Its location within a Place is a modifier, as indicated by the semicolon (;). Place has a function-argument structure whereby the specified function is a spatial relationship (here, IN for *in*) of the head (the Thing CAT) relative to the argument of the function (the Thing GARDEN). In this case, Places can modify most any Thing to provide context for their relative spatial orientation. Other modifiers include the properties expressed by prenominal adjectives (*small* fish), degree phrases expressing dimensional modulation (*extremely* noisy), along with manner, instrumentals, and time adverbs (run *quickly*, slice *with a sword*, arrive *at midnight*).

The third principle of combination is binding, a way to express conceptual dependency between constituents, whereby the interpretation of one constituent is bound to that of another constituent, the antecedent. The classic case of binding in verbal languages is that of the reflexive pronominal, like in the sentence *Jane likes herself*, which is expressed as:

Jane likes herself: [$_{State}$ LIKE([$_{Person}$ JANE]$^{\alpha}$,[$_{Person}$ α; FEMALE SG])]

Binding is expressed using Greek letters (typically alpha: α) which is notated as a superscript on the antecedent and a corresponding Greek letter for the bound constituent. In this case the Person JANE is both the agent and the patient of the predicate LIKE ("Jane likes Jane"), and thus this concept is expressed both by the name (*Jane*) and by the reflexive pronoun (*herself*).

As we have argued above, Conceptual Semantics can effectively express meanings across modalities, including visual information where binding is important for linking the event structures of different objects in a scene. Consider Figure 4.2, which shows a woman seeing a man run into a tree. In our treatment of its semantics, each entity has its own expressed conceptual structure, which may or may not be independent. Following Jackendoff (1990), we would notate this scene as:

Man: $[_{Event} GO_2([_{Person} MAN_1], [_{Path} TO([_{Place} AT_{+Contact}([_{Thing} TREE])_3])])]^α$
Woman: $[_{Event} WATCH_5([_{Person} WOMAN_4], [_{Event} α])]$

In this case, the conceptual structure for the man specifies that he goes to a tree and makes contact with it. This event structure is independent of the one of the woman watching, but she watches that event. This is expressed with binding such that the entire event of the runner binds the argument of watching by the woman (i.e., the woman watches "α" which is the runner's event). As we will see, binding plays an important role in multimodal semantics, as it facilitates connections between independent meanings originating in different modalities.

We should note that throughout this book, for expository reasons, we only formalize what is relevant for the points being made. Many examples across modalities have substantial complexity in their conceptual structures which would be excessive to formalize for recognizing the crucial points of our broader framework. This may result in us leaving out additional details such as the correspondences in text to conceptual structures of determiners, tense, and details in images that may not be required for integrating the meanings (e.g., the type of hair of each character in Figure 4.2).

Along with their semantic categories, these schemas are posited as inherent to the human conceptual system, but the specifics depend on the language in which they interact. Thus, different languages may distribute aspects of the same conceptual structure into different constructions. One language may encode various structures into a single word, another may require a productive combination of words. For example, languages may differ in how they correspond to events and their paths (Naidu et al. 2018, Talmy 1985). The varied ways that expressions correspond to conceptual structures also extend across different modalities. That is, the same conceptual structures may be

Figure 4.2 A scene depicting a woman watching a man running into a tree.

distributed into vocal, bodily, and graphic expressions in different ways afforded by the sensory options of that modality.

Consider the expressions in Figure 4.3 where we have a) the English sentence *The ball bounced down the hill* and b) a picture expressing a similar (the same?) event. Both expressions correspond to the Conceptual Structure shown below it, but in different ways. In English, the primary verb "bounce" includes both the motion information of GO and the manner information of BOUNCE (subscripts 2 and 5). This correspondence of motion and manner with the verb differs across spoken languages (Naidu et al. 2018, Talmy 1985). In contrast to the sentence, the picture expresses this manner of motion directly in the motion lines of the image (subscript 2). The arguments of the path function depicted by the bouncing ball (FROM, VIA, TO) are all overtly expressed (subscripts 7, 8, 9), but this is not the case for the linguistic expression of the same event, where only the goal is expressed (subscripts 3, 4).[4]

In addition, the aspectuality of the event is expressed differently. The sentence suggests that the event has already occurred through the use of the past tense morpheme *-ed* on the verb, which corresponds to the conceptualization of the event occurring in the PAST (subscript 6). In the picture, a past state is expressed by the *visual* morpheme of the motion line, which inherently implies both a current state (the location of the ball at the end of the line, subscript 8) but at least three prior states (Jackendoff

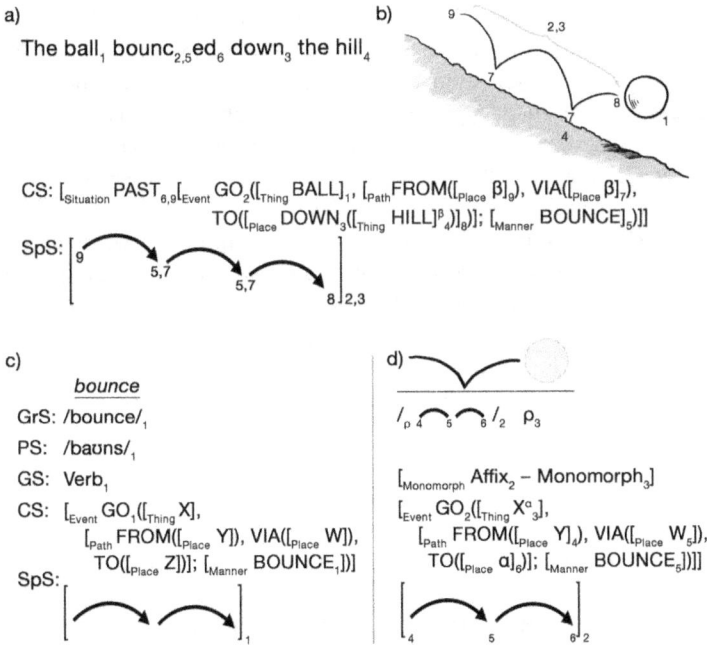

Figure 4.3 Motion events are compared across a) an English sentence and b) a graphic depiction, along with lexical entries for c) the word *bounce* and d) a motion line.

2010a): the location at the start of the line (subscript 9), and the intermediate states at each of the ends of the arcs (subscripts 7). Motion lines thus both express arguments of a path function and the past states of events (Cohn 2013b, 2018a). Note that without the line, both of these concepts are lost, and the image would solely express the present state of the shown object. Thus, both the sentence and the picture use morphemes of their modalities to express event aspectuality, but with different correspondences to Conceptual Structure, again analogous to the way various verbal languages differ in their expression of aspectuality.

In addition to Conceptual Structure, we follow Jackendoff (1983, 2002, 2010a) in positing an additional Spatial Structure which encodes a geometric meaning both for the abstracted shapes of objects (Biederman 1987, Marr 1982) and for the spatial properties of events and paths, also known as "image schemas" (Johnson 2013, Lakoff 1987b, Talmy 2000a). Spatial Structure uses independent components of meaning compared to that of Conceptual Structure, representing spatial properties like the dimensionality of an object (e.g., 0d points, 1d vectors, 2d planes, or 3d volumes), its layout or shape (e.g., circular, angular, etc.), its orientation (e.g., vertical, horizontal, etc.), and its character of movement (e.g., shape of a path). These spatial properties are often expressed implicitly in speech, but overtly correspond to bodily motions or the regions of drawings (Willats 1997).

Spatial Structure encodes dimensions of meaning which may be contrastive across concepts that otherwise may share algebraic features. For example, the difference between a swan and a goose largely comes down to the spatial conceptualization of the length of the neck (e.g., swan has a longer neck than a goose), and this dimension is not necessarily encoded as an algebraic feature such as [±long neck] (Jackendoff 2010a). A similar spatial dimensionality distinguishes the difference between cups and bowls, a graded categorization based on the relative difference between width and height of the concave object (Labov 1973). Such spatial variance can also capture the difference between manners of motion, like what it means for a person to move by skipping versus wobbling.

Again consider the examples in Figure 4.3a–b. The word "ball" would correspond to a 3d spherical shape (not depicted), which is shown directly in the shape of the graphemes in the picture. In addition, the main verb *bounce* corresponds to a Spatial Structure and indexes its manner of motion as a repeated arcing vector path across a 1d space. Yet, this spatial knowledge remains implicit. By comparison, the picture shows this path overtly, with the arcs of the motion line directly indexing the arcs in Spatial Structure. In addition, the verbal expression makes the orientation of the path overt in the word *down*, which is expressed in the graphics through a tilt in the depiction of the path. That is, where the sentence leaves these spatial dimensions implicit, the picture can make them explicit.

The contrasts between how different modalities correspond to Conceptual and/or Spatial Structure bring us to an additional feature of the Parallel Architecture: the ways that different structures interact. Structures in the Parallel Architecture are independent, and thus need **interface principles** to establish relationships. The indexation of Conceptual Structures into each modality involves such interface principles. When such interfaces become fixed and stored in memory, they constitute a **lexical item**. That is, a word is a fixed correspondence between pieces of formology, morphosyntax, and conceptual/spatial structures. Figure 4.3c specifies the lexical item for the word *bounce*. It has a Phonological Structure (PS) notated in the International Phonetic Alphabet, which corresponds to its graphological spelling (GrS). Its morphosyntax (GS) specifies it as a verb, and its Conceptual Structure (CS) specifies the event, the path, and its manner. In English, both the event (GO) and the manner (BOUNCE) are expressed by the word *bounce*, while the path information remains implicit. In addition, the lexical item specifies an implicit Spatial Structure (SpS) as a vector with intermediate midway points.

Graphic lexical items also encode conventionalized pictorial forms as fixed correspondences, here between graphology (GrS), morpho-grammar (GS), and conceptual/spatial structures (CS, SpS). In Figure 4.3d, the lexical item of a bouncing motion line has a graphological structure of curved graphemes creating a repeated arcing shape. Its morphology specifies the motion lines as an affix (Cohn 2013b, 2018a), since they cannot stand alone, and must attach to another graphic representation (i.e., the moving object). This stem is a monomorph, a free morpheme, coindexed to whatever is depicted as the bouncing object (coindex 3). The motion line corresponds to a Conceptual Structure conveying an event of a thing, traversing a path, in a certain manner. The overall line conveys the motion event (GO), while the intermediate stages represent the manner of BOUNCE. In addition, we overtly see the component parts of the path: the source (FROM) is the start of the line, the route (VIA) is the midpoint(s), and the goal (TO) is the end of the line. This final goal is also where we find the moving object (X), coindexed to the goal through a binding operator (α), because the object is always at the end of the depicted path of the motion line.

As we have demonstrated and argued throughout, all modalities can encode lexical items. Such lexical items constitute a correspondence between a regularized formology (vocal, bodily, graphic) with a combinatorial structure (morphosyntactic) and a meaning that can be both algebraic and spatial. Yet, the correspondences between a form and meaning may differ in nature between modalities because of the affordances that they offer in accessing these abstract concepts. In our next section, we show that these affordances evoke different characterizable mappings in the interface between a modality and meaning.

4.2 Signification

Having established what we mean by meaning, we can now address how this Conceptual/Spatial Structure may interface with modalities. As described above, not only are there characterizable structures within the components of the Parallel Architecture, but there are characterizable mappings between structures which constitute interface principles. We contend that these correspondences between modalities and meaning also have identifiable properties. This interface between modality and meaning is referred to as **signification** or is described in terms of **reference types**.

The traditional view on signification often endorses the Saussurean Sign (de Saussure 1972 [1916]), i.e., vocal expressions are arbitrary, and there is nothing about the vocalized sounds that motivates their meaning. Rather, because they are arbitrary, they get their meaning through conventionality. This renders arbitrariness and conventionality as linked, resulting in arbitrariness as a property of the modality itself, collapsing the signifier and signified into an indivisible unit.

A conflated form-meaning relationship is in direct contrast to the central assumption of the Parallel Architecture that form and meaning constitute distinct generative systems (Jackendoff 2002, 194). Here, arbitrariness is not a feature of the formological structures themselves, but reflects the interface between formology and conceptual structures. This parallelism is consistent with the semiotic architecture of Charles Sanders Peirce (1940), which makes a central distinction that clarifies the separate properties of the modality (*sign vehicle* or *representamen*) and the encoded conceptual structure (*referent* or *object*), along with the referent's compositional interaction with context (the *interpretant*, or integrated conceptual structure).

As discussed in Chapter 2, a modality can manifest as either idiosyncratic (tokens, Peirce: sinsigns) or regularized (types, Peirce: legisigns) sensory signals. The relationship of how sensory signals correspond to meaning is what Peirce called *the ground* (Peirce 1940). This interface can be characterized by several types of *signification*, which amount to Peirce's most well-known semiotic distinctions: **iconic**, **indexical**, and **symbolic** reference. These reference types are not "in" the structures of either the modality or the meaning, but rather emerge out of the interface between those structures. Essentially, these signification types characterize *interface rules* in the Parallel Architecture, as diagrammed in Figure 4.4.

Peircean semiotics are often described in the language sciences through the lens of a Saussurean Sign. This results because of an effort to simplify the admittedly complex

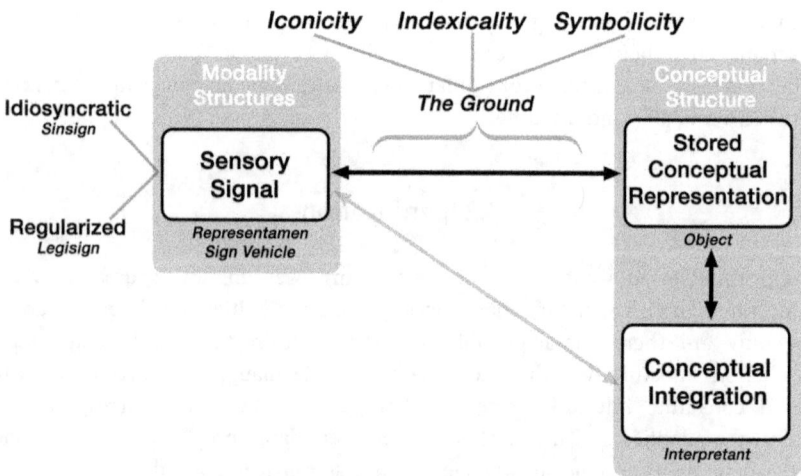

Figure 4.4 Signification arising from the components of the Parallel Architecture. Peirce's terminology is in italics.

Peircean theoretical framework, and so these works only adopt Peirce's signification types (iconic, indexical, symbolic), but without acknowledging their relationship to the independent and varied properties of a sensory signal. Because of this incompleteness, such views inappropriately maintain the framework of the Saussurean Sign, leading to misunderstandings about the characteristics of signification (Bateman 2018, Waugh 1993). For example, this lack of precision leads to the idea that signification reflects types of signals (i.e., icons, indexes, and symbols) rather than types of interfaces for how a signal relates to meaning (i.e., iconic, indexical, symbolic). It also can lead to conflation of the ideas of conventionalization and symbolicity, that iconicity is "in the signal" (e.g., "iconic phonology"), or that "linguistic signs" have only one signification type, rather than being a sensory signal that can correspond to meaning in a variety of ways at once. All of these views are inaccurate and lead to confused debates within the language sciences, yet they are clarified upfront within a more elaborated Peircean framework. The Parallel Architecture thereby allows us to better maintain the framework of Peircean signification within a cognitive model.

4.2.1 Iconicity

Iconicity is the reference type whereby properties of the modality have a *resemblance* to the properties of meaning. The canonical example is a picture of a person that resembles a person. When a drawer looks at a person and then draws them, this creates idiosyncratic iconicity—an idiosyncratic set of graphics produced from a variable percept that maps to a conceptual representation through resemblance (Figure 4.5a). In contrast, a stick figure uses regularized iconicity (Figure 4.5b); that is, the stick figure is a regularized graphic configuration (a type) that is known as a convention, but which still corresponds to its meaning through resemblance to a person, i.e., iconicity. Thus, iconicity as a method of signification can apply to both idiosyncratic and regularized signals in a modality.

We illustrate this difference by formalizing examples. Figure 4.5a shows a sketch of a person where the overall figure seems to convey no established conventions. Thus, the lines would be considered idiosyncratic. These lines correspond to a Conceptual Structure specifying that this is a PERSON in the abstract, but would also correspond to a Spatial Structure for what a person's body is shaped like. Correspondences between Graphological and Spatial Structure are marked with indices, whereby the components maintain the same configuration across structures, thereby rendering a resemblance and iconicity. This is often referred to as *projection* (Greenberg 2011, Willats 1997). Similarly, the stick figure uses the same configurational correspondences, but the graphics here are regularized into a recognizable conventionalized pattern, mapping to the same Conceptual/Spatial Structure as Figure 4.5a. As we hopefully demonstrate, iconicity here arises out of the *interface between* the structures of the modality and the meaning, rather than being characterized *within* either of those structures.

A more abstract example of graphic iconicity comes from our example of a motion line in Figure 4.3d. In this case, the iconicity is not to a concrete object, but to an abstracted notion of the path. This iconic mapping is created between the modality

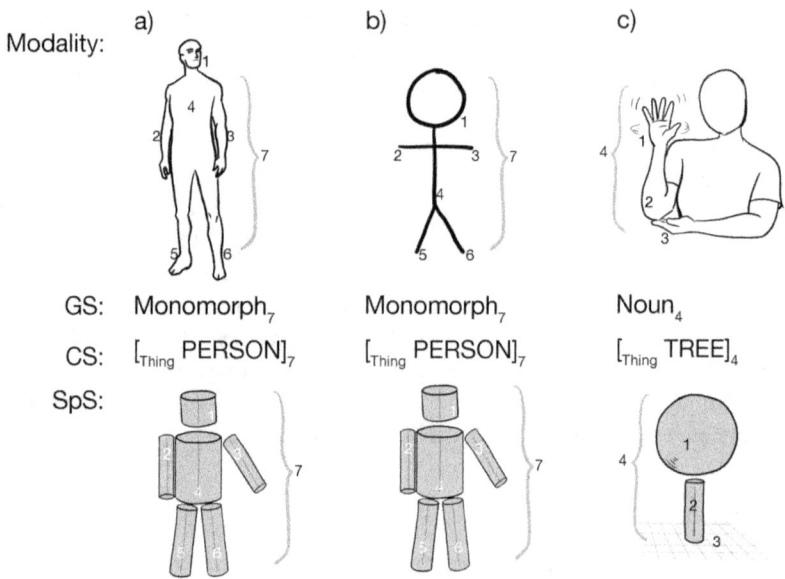

Figure 4.5 A formalization of a) idiosyncratic and b) regularized and graphics iconic of people, and c) the American Sign Language sign for a tree.

representation of the lines and the Spatial Structure of the path. That is, the lines *resemble* the spatial trajectory of the path and manner of the motion.

In the vocal modality, the canonical example of iconicity is onomatopoeia, a type of ideophone (Dingemanse 2017). Ideophones also convey their meaning through an intended resemblance of the phonemes to their meaning. For example, *woof-woof*, *wan-wan*, and *woef-woef* all are intended to express the sound that a dog makes in different languages. The conventionalization of these sounds, which indeed varies across languages, is a reflection of their regularization in the phonology. However, the intended correspondence to meaning would be that of resemblance to a stored Auditory Structure, which would parallel the types of structures found in Spatial Structure but for the auditory domain. These are examples of regularized iconicity in the vocal modality.

Nevertheless, a range of regularization to iconicity appears in vocalized communication. An idiosyncratic form of spoken iconicity is when a person imitates another's voice. For example, in a conversation if one person says "How much time do we have left?" and the other then snidely imitates their voice saying the same thing, it attempts to be iconic of the first person's voice. This vocal production is iconic because of the attempted resemblance between the voices, but is idiosyncratic because it is novel and non-patterned.

A similar thing happens in the bodily modality with pantomimic gestures, when a person seemingly embodies another person to imitate their gestures and actions. These imitated actions are idiosyncratic because they may not involve conventionalized bodily forms. In contrast, a pinching gesture can indicate smallness compared to the largeness of a wide armed gesture, but these are regularized gesticulations (Woodin et al. 2020). Similarly, sign languages use substantial regularized iconicity in their representations, of both concrete and abstract actions (Goldin-Meadow and Brentari 2017, Liddell 2003). For example, Figure 4.5c depicts the lexical entry for the American Sign Language sign corresponding to the concept of a TREE. In this case, the bodily form holds a hand upright with fingers outstretched with the elbow on the foundation of the other hand. The outstretched hand rotates and corresponds to the boughs of a tree, with the forearm corresponding to its trunk, as formalized with indices.

Iconicity uses a mapping that involves *a configuration in a sensory signal that aligns with the configuration of representations in meaning structures*. We will refer to this operationalization of iconicity as **aligned coindexation**. The sense of "resemblance" used as the primary definition for iconicity emerges out of a description of this characteristic of aligned coindexation between a modality and its meaning. In some cases of drawn representations, these mappings may adhere to principles of mathematical projection which has been used to describe how 2D drawings map to 3D understandings (Greenberg 2011, Willats 1997). However, such projection does not cover all types of aligned coindexation that occur in graphic systems (such as the stick figure or motion line where projection is straightforward). This view of projection motivating our understanding of graphic representation also tacitly assumes a perceptual basis for pictures, which is called into question by a wide range of structural, cross-cultural, and developmental evidence (Cohn 2012, Wilkins 2016, Willats 2005, Wilson 1988, 1999, 2016).

Iconicity as a signification type is thus characterized by a three-part structure: the modality, the meaning, and the aligned coindexation. Different types of iconicity vary in what fills the "slots" of structure involved in aligned coindexation. A first type is what Peirce identified as **imagetic iconicity**, which is a direct resemblance (i.e., mapping) between the sensory signal of a modality and the representations of meaning. The canonical examples here are pictures that look like what they mean. A second type is that of **diagrammatic** or **relational iconicity**, where similarity in the parts—particularly their configuration—gives rise to a resemblance across the whole.

Thus, a picture of a person involves both imagetic iconicity between each depicted body part and its referent, while the overall configuration maintains diagrammatic iconicity. A stick figure, as in Figure 4.5b, has body parts which lack imagetic iconicity (being only a circle and straight lines), but the configuration looks like a person through diagrammatic iconicity. When an image shows many recognizable body parts jumbled up, but not in their natural configuration (as in abstract art), it uses imagetic iconicity but without the diagrammatic iconicity.

While stick figures maintain relative proportions of the body parts in their diagrammatic iconicity, drawings may also show body parts out of proportion (like very large heads, noses, or ears). We often refer to these as cartoons or caricatures. Regardless of these exaggerations, the overarching diagrammatic iconicity persists. This also occurs in subway maps, where the distance and physical geography between stations are reduced or idealized as straight lines (and stations are represented by non-iconic markers like dots), but the diagrammatic iconicity of the relative positioning of stations is maintained.

A third type is **metaphoric iconicity** which maintains parallelism between both form and meaning, and also between meanings (Lakoff and Johnson 1980).[5] A picture of an hourglass may use imagetic iconicity to the spatial structure of an hourglass. However, if the hourglass was used as a sign to refer to the shape of a woman's waist (such as in the context of an advertisement), the same picture also employs metaphoric iconicity to a spatial structure of a woman (Lakoff 1987a). Thus, in metaphoric iconicity, there is first an imagetic or diagrammatic mapping to meaning, from which that meaning also maintains aligned coindexation to another concept (i.e., curvy lines → woman → hourglass).

To summarize, iconicity involves aligned coindexation in an interface between a modality and meaning that results in a sense of resemblance. We schematize these types of iconicity below, which characterize the interfaces between a formological structure (FS) and conceptual structure (CS) that maintain this aligned coindexation.

Iconicity schemas

	Imagetic	*Diagrammatic*	*Metaphoric*
FS:	$/X_1\ Y_2\ Z_3/_4$	$/X_1\ Y_2\ Z_3/$	$/X_1\ Y_2\ Z_3/_4$
CS:	$[A_1\ B_2\ C_3]_4$	$[A_1\ B_2\ C_3]$	$[A_{1,5}\ B_{2,6}\ C_{3,7}]_4$
			$[W_5\ Q_6\ R_7]$

In imagetic iconicity, the modality and meaning map directly onto each other. In our formalization, this arises with direct coindexation between modality and meaning. Note that the iconicity itself is not present in the formalization, and emerges from the correspondences marked by the coindexation. In addition, the type of meaning structure that may be accessed (spatial structure, auditory structure, etc.) may depend on the sensory and/or physical nature of the modality. In diagrammatic iconicity, the configuration of the modality maintains an aligned coindexation to the structure of the signified meaning. Thus, in our formalism, the configuration of elements in the modality reflects the configuration of elements within the meaning, but with no indices for the whole. Finally, in metaphoric iconicity, the modality has an imagetic or diagrammatic iconicity to a meaning (subscripts 1–4), but that conceptual structure also maintains an aligned coindexation with another meaning. For metaphoric iconicity our formalism thus adds an additional configuration in meaning which maps to the "base" imagetic iconicity (subscripts 5–7).

4.2.2 Indexicality

The second type of signification is that of **indexicality**, whereby the modality expresses a meaning that is indicative or pointing toward another meaning. For example, the *index* finger is so named because of its canonical use in pointing toward something to indicate meaning in that place. Indexicality manifested in the body is referred to as *deictic* gestures. Not only can we point with our index fingers, but we also may point with our thumbs, wave or point with our whole hands, jerk our heads sideways, shift our eyes in the direction of pointing, and many other gestures. Deictic gestures may also differ in their regularization across cultures (Cooperrider, Slotta, and Núñez 2018, Kita 2009, Wilkins 2003).

We formalize this indexicality for pointing gestures in Figure 4.6a. The bodily modality consists of the deictic gesture (here with the index finger outstretched), along with an implied trajectory toward an open slot wherever the pointed-to object lies. This gesture is a single unit utterance within the grammar (an emblem). Its Conceptual Structure is of an extension of a Thing from the location of the finger to the place of wherever the referred-to referent lies. The Thing here is the gesture itself, which carries no intrinsic referential meaning; that is, the hand is the Thing and maintains no other meaning than just being a pointing hand. This hand is also the source of the path, bound by β. Meanwhile, the place referent has a bound element (α) which maps to whatever fills the slot of being pointed-to. Note that no specified element receives the bound element (notated with α), because the referent in this example is out "in the world" and thus conceptual unification would occur between the meaning of that perceived referent and the open slot of the deictic gesture's conceptual structure. The modality therefore also maps to a Spatial Structure of a trajectory extending from a point outward. Again, the starting point of the trajectory coindexes with the finger, and the endpoint is the open slot of the referred/pointed-to referent.

The vocal modality also uses indexicality in various ways (Peeters, Krahmer, and Maes 2021). Pronominals and deictic expressions (*she, he, they, it, this, there,* etc.) are all indexical in that they "point" to meaning found in other places, be it elsewhere in a sentence or discourse, or within the broader context of usage (just like the index finger in Figure 4.6a points toward something in a surrounding environment). All examples

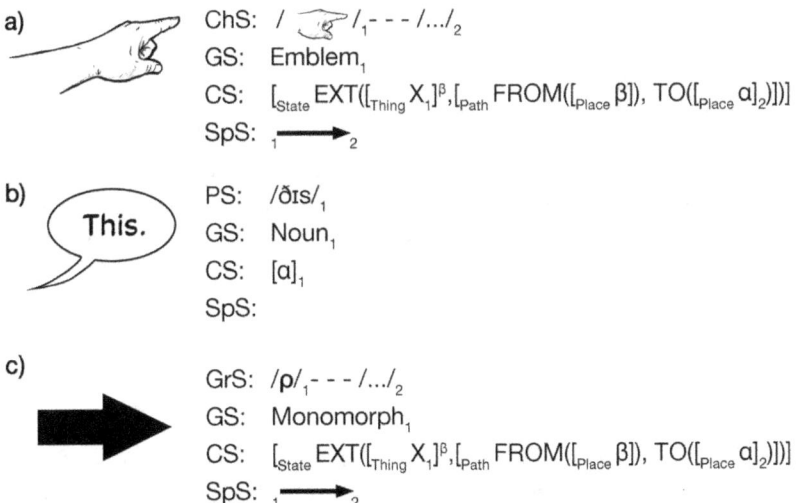

Figure 4.6 Lexical entries for indexical signs of a) deictic pointing gesture, b) the word "this," and c) an arrow.

throughout this book of "Figure X" are indexical of those images. We formalize the indexical structure of the word *this* in Figure 4.6b. The word *this* is a piece of phonology corresponding to a noun, which has a Conceptual Structure as a Thing with a bound element (α) looking for a binder. As in the deictic gesture, the meaning of the pronoun here only specifies the bound element, and the binder exists someplace in the discourse or the contextual environment. The lack of an encoded binder here is what leads to the possibility of ambiguity for what a pronoun refers to (such as when multiple candidates or not-enough seeming candidates for referents may exist, i.e., "which one did you mean?").

The canonical index in graphic form is an arrow, which *points* at an element. Its lexical entry is provided in Figure 4.6c. This lexical item is almost identical to that of the pointing index finger (Figure 4.6a) except that the modality is a graphological structure depicting a region for the arrow rather than the bodily structure of a finger. The arrow also maintains an inherent slot for what is being pointed at, and this variable can be filled by both graphics (pictures, text, etc.), and objects not part of the graphic modality, such as when a person writes an arrow on a note pointing to a real-life object or when a person puts an arrow on a photo to indicate who they are.

Indexical graphics often can be subtle or incorporated into other pictures. In a typical speech balloon that depicts what someone is saying, a *tail* emerges from the balloon as a pointer toward the speaker. This tail serves an indexical function (Cohn 2013a). Similarly, the motion line in Figure 4.3b conveys a type of indexical reference to a past event. That is, the motion line is like an arrow, pointing from the start to the end of the line, to where the object ends up. Again, for this reason, in the Conceptual Structure, the PAST state is coindexed with the start of the path (FROM).

In all modalities, we find that indexicality is *the manifestation of conceptual binding*. We formalize this as an indexicality schema:

Indexicality schema
FS: /X/$_1$ [...]$_2$
CS: [A$_1$ [α]$_2$]

The conceptual structure of the indexical sign holds an empty slot which is bound (α) by whatever the indexical sign points at. Crucially, the index itself never has an encoded binder, because it does not directly reference that which it indexes. We posit that all expressions evoking a conceptual binder have a quality of indexicality. Thus, formalization reveals the commonalities across indexical signs within different modalities, and how indexicality functions in a broader conceptual sense.

4.2.3 Symbolicity

The final type of signification is that of **symbolicity**. Peirce defines symbolicity through the absence of other types of reference. That is, symbolicity is a type of reference where the sign lacks resemblance (iconicity) and lacks indication (indexicality), and thus relies solely on the regularization of its modality as a stored representation. In other words, it uses the conventionalization of sign-meaning correspondences as its mechanism of signification. The result of relying on regularity of the signal alone, without any other type of signification, results in what is often called an arbitrary reference. This is reflected in our formalism of a symbolicity schema, where there is only a coindex between the modality and meaning, but the nature of that relationship is otherwise unspecified and lacks intrinsic or structural motivation (i.e., no aligned coindexation and no binders).

Symbolicity schema
FS: /X/$_1$
CS: [A]$_1$

Symbolic reference is thus characterizable in cases with no overt connection between the meaning and its modality. Symbolicity persists in many concrete and abstract words, like *love*, *dog*, *democracy*, *value*, and others, used either directly or metaphorically. Symbolic gestures include crossing fingers for luck, shaking one's head, etc., and symbolic graphics include the peace sign ☮ , the heart shape ♥, female or male signs ♂, and many others. Regardless of the modality, conventionalization of these signals provides an association to a meaning, giving motivation for their signification.

It is important to stress that, though symbolicity relies on regularity and conventionality, these remain traits of the modality itself. As described in Chapter 2, regularity and conventionality are traits of the sensory signal and the degree to which they are codified beyond tokens into a repeatable and abstract type. Because they are properties of the formology, regularity and conventionality occur across *all* reference types, including indexicality and iconicity. Just because a stick figure is conventional and iconic does *not* mean that it exhibits both iconic and "symbolic" traits, or that iconicity and symbolicity lie on a spectrum (e.g., Greenberg 2021, Saraceni 2003, Waugh 1993). Such views maintain relations inherent to the Saussurean Sign, but conflate conventionality (a trait of the signal) and symbolicity (a trait of the interface between signal and meaning). Rather, in line with Peircean signification and the assumptions of the Parallel Architecture, signs can be mixed if the signal allows for various interfaces to meaning (as in the iconicity and indexicality shown in the motion line), but conventionality is not the reason motivating this mixed status. Rather, a stick figure is simply a regularized iconic sign (Peirce: iconic legisign): its modality exhibits the regularity, and its mapping to meaning is iconic.

4.2.4 Summary

We have characterized the Peircean notions of signification through our formalized cognitive perspective. Iconicity as a type of resemblance involves the aligned coindexation of a modality to its referent. Indexicality involves the encoding of a conceptual binder which indicates its bound element. Finally, symbolicity uses the regularization of form solely to correspond to meaning. Though these methods of signification emerge as part of modality-meaning interfaces, they can also characterize meaning-meaning interfaces. That is, signification can potentially occur between conceptual structures, outside of their connection to a modality.

Such mappings between meanings occur in metaphors or analogies (Fauconnier and Turner 1998, Gentner 1983, Lakoff and Johnson 1980). For example, in the established metaphor relating a woman's waist to the shape of an hourglass (Lakoff 1987a), there is first aligned coindexation between a modality (graphics) and meaning (hourglass), which then has a second-order aligned coindexation between the concept of hourglass and concept of a woman's shape. Another example would be the use of the lightbulb to mean inspiration. A picture of a lightbulb first must use an iconic mapping whereby the graphics maintain aligned coindexation with the meaning of that object (lightbulb). A second-order mapping then coindexes with the concept of inspiration, which is associated through regularity and thus is a symbolic reference (despite also evoking a larger metaphoric frame that *knowing is seeing*). These second-order mappings can become so prevalent that the first-order indexation simply vanishes, leaving only the conventionalized mappings (often called "dead metaphors"). For example, the phrase *I see what you mean* also involves a first-order symbolic mapping of *see* to vision, with a second-order mapping of *see* extended to knowing (using the same metaphoric frame as the lightbulb). However, the usage of this phrase may have become so entrenched that the first-order coindexation of *see* to mean vision has fallen away.

Signification thus characterizes *interface types* which operate between modalities and/or meanings, and which we will extend to grammars in Chapter 6. In addition, the presence of meaning-meaning semiotic correspondences gives rise to Peirce's notion of cycles of signification, which is consistent with cognitive views that combinatoriality is inherent to an independent Conceptual Structure.

4.3 Modality-Reference Optimality

We have argued that human expression involves three natural modalities (vocal, bodily, and graphic), along with three primary methods of signification by which these modalities interface with meaning (iconic, indexical, symbolic). As we have discussed, all modalities can maintain both idiosyncratic and regularized signals, and all modalities can correspond to meaning through all types of signification. Thus, not only do vocal expressions use symbolic reference, but they also use iconicity and indexicality (Clark 1996, Dingemanse et al. 2015). All three types of signification are also prevalent in the bodily modality for gestures and sign languages (Goldin-Meadow 2003a, McNeill 1992), and for pictures and visual languages (Bateman 2018, Cohn 2013b, Szawerna 2017). Overall, this provides direct evidence against the structuralist assumptions of the arbitrariness of the sign (de Saussure 1972 [1916]), and of the criterion that arbitrariness alone characterizes linguistic signals (Hockett 1960).

Though all modalities maintain the ability for all types of signification, modalities differ in their *affordances* for these reference types. For example, the graphic modality has a privileged ability to create aligned coindexation with a Spatial Structure, thus being optimized for iconic signification. Likewise, the bodily modality affords communicators the ability to situate referents relative to themselves through indexicality, i.e., pointing at referents directly, or establishing a spatial location to indicate referents (Liddell 2003, McNeill 1992, Peeters, Krahmer, and Maes 2021).

Finally, despite the vocal modality's ability to create iconic and indexical reference, the creation of sound through our mouths may be optimized for symbolic signification, especially reference to concepts that lack a spatial structure (e.g., *value*, *hypothesis*, *democracy*, *categories*, etc.).

Thus, though all modalities maintain interfaces for all methods of signification, they may have preferential mappings or be optimized for certain types of reference. Optimality arises because modalities have affordances that allow access to certain features of the Conceptual/Spatial Structures which result in different types of signification. We call this the ***Semiotic Optimality Principle***:

Semiotic Optimality Principle
All modalities can maintain all types of signification through their interfaces with meaning, but a modality's sensory features afford preferential mappings creating optimized reference for that modality.

These optimized mappings are on display in our example in Figure 4.3a–b which compared a sentence and picture of a ball bouncing along a path. While both the verbal and visual modalities accessed the same primary conceptual information (BALL, GO, etc.), the visual modality was capable of creating an aligned coindexation between the motion line and the spatial structure of a path to create an iconic mapping. Meanwhile the vocal modality only conveys this information symbolically. In addition, the past tense is expressed morphologically in different ways for the modalities. It appears as an affix to the verb in the vocal modality (*-ed*), while it is implied graphically by the start of the motion line (where the object once was). Compare this to if there was no motion line graphically (or no *-ed* ending vocally): there would only be the present state with no hints of a prior state.

We would like to stress that optimized signification is not the same as exclusive signification. The optimality of the vocal modality for symbolicity is what has been overextended to the idea that arbitrariness is a primary design feature of linguistic signals (Hockett 1960), despite the proliferation of other signification in the vocal modality. Such overextended exclusivity also arises in the idea that the graphic modality merely reflects "what we see"—i.e., the optimization of the graphic modality for iconicity—despite the proliferation of indexicality and symbolicity.

The overall architecture of our communicative faculties is therefore characterized by all types of signification, not exclusive to any particular reference. Rather, because modalities afford optimized signification, they are capable of conveying information in different non-redundant ways that complement each other. This combination of affordances offers the possibility for complementary signification, and thus for creating a richer signal overall, giving motivation to why we have evolved to have a multimodal language faculty.

5

Multimodal Semantic Interactions

By definition, multimodality involves the signals from multiple modalities interacting with each other. Though there are several ways that modalities interface, no matter their integration, modalities remain separate phenomena that are perceived to be interacting. While meanings within each modality may be recognized as separate, their combination also leads to a single construed conceptual structure. Multimodal meaning-making is thus both componential and holistic at the same time. Throughout this chapter, we explore this tension between simultaneous dualism and holism to explore how multimodality creates a richer signal than unimodal expression.

Meaning across multiple modalities weighs several factors, including the meaning evoked by each modality, and any emergent meaning manifesting from their combination. Many theories have approached this by categorizing the functions of these meaningful interactions (see Bateman 2014, for review), often expanding on balanced or imbalanced semantic relationships where information expressed in one modality may support, elaborate, extend, etc., the information expressed in another modality (Bateman 2014, Kress 2009, Logi and Zappavigna 2021, Martinec and Salway 2005, Painter, Martin, and Unsworth 2012, Royce 2007). To this extent, we characterize the global "balance" of meaning between modalities as the ***semantic weight*** of a multimodal utterance. That is, an overall gist or Gestalt of a holistic multimodal message involves the component contributions of each modality. When meaning is conveyed in one modality more than another, it carries more of the weight of the overall message. Multimodal interactions with **balanced** semantic weight involve relatively equal contribution of meaning. Imbalanced relationships place the semantic weight more on one modality than another. Consider the utterances in (5.1) as if they were sent as text messages:

(5.1)

a. Would you like to eat pizza? 🍕 (imbalanced)
b. Would you like to eat pizza? 😋 (balanced)

In (5.1a) the sentence is followed by a pizza emoji, which is coreferential to the word "pizza" in the text. Deleting the pizza emoji would have little impact on the overall gist, suggesting that the writing is more informative and thus carries more semantic weight. Omission of the sentence however, leaving only the pizza, would certainly impact the meaning of the message. This implies an imbalanced relationship more weighted to the text. In contrast, the winking face emoji in (5.1b) implies an innuendo or at least some added information not conveyed by the text. Omission of either the winking emoji or the text here would alter the overall expression's gist, implying that both modalities substantially contribute, and thus have a balanced relationship.

While these broad characterizations are useful for assessing the holistic Gestalt of multimodal meaning, further nuance should be provided by formalizing these interactions. Within the Parallel Architecture, the first step would be to identify the conceptual properties within each modality, as described in the previous chapter. For a full account of multimodal meaning, we need to see how these "bottom-up" semantic contributions relate and interact with each other.

Our method targets the degree of **coreference** within and between modalities. By coreference, we here mean the phenomena of multiple distinct representations sharing a common conceptual category (things, events, etc.). Such coreference is present in the phrase *Pizza* 🍕 as might be uttered in a text message, where the word *pizza* corefers to the pizza emoji. In our formalization in Figure 5.1a, each modality expresses its own independent representation, as conveyed by the conceptual structures in $CS_{Expression}$. In this case, those representations completely overlap in meaning. Here, numbers are the distinct indices for each modality's contribution, but they share a common Conceptual Structure. Thus, these expressions are **coreferential** to a shared meaning.

Coreference means that each independent expression conveys the "same" conceptual structure, represented here with the tier of $CS_{Integrated}$. We touched on this notion of "same" in the last chapter, but we will further unpack it later in this chapter. In the case of **complete coreference**, the integrated conceptual structure is identical to that of the independent expressions. In Figure 5.1a, the word *pizza* and the pizza emoji both have similar independent Conceptual Structures (subscripts 1 and 2), which identically match the integrated structure (now coindexed with both 1 and 2). In other cases, the integrated conceptual structure contains elements coindexed from each independent

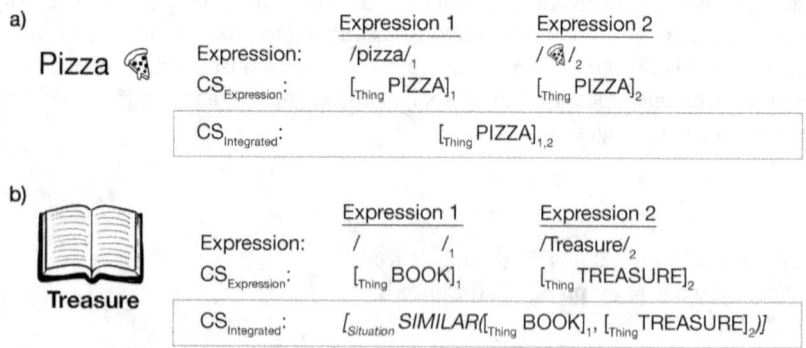

Figure 5.1 Multimodal relationships with a) complete and b) absent coreference between pictures and text.

expression but may not fully match into all expressions. A "default" version of such coreference would be formalized as below:

	Expression 1	Expression 2
Expression:	$/\ldots/_1$	$/\ldots/_2$
$CS_{Expression}$:	$[\ldots]_1$	$[\ldots]_2$
$CS_{Integrated}$:	$[\ldots]_{1,2}$	

We should note that $CS_{Integrated}$ is not a new formal contribution, but rather is the compositional semantics that arises any time multiple meaningful units are combined.[1] This also applies to individual words being combined in sentences, where the $CS_{Integrated}$ is what is usually shown in formalisms, without the breakdown between the $CS_{Expression}$ of each word and the $CS_{Integrated}$ of their combined conceptual structure. As a result, $CS_{Integrated}$ does not involve any special functions, but rather operates with the same principles as all of Conceptual Structure, whereby the component parts combine using a process of **unification**. In the case of coreference, expressions that convey the "same" concept become unified.

We here present these two tiers of Conceptual Structure in an abstracted form, but they are engaged in different directions when dealing with comprehension versus production. In comprehension, we move from top-to-bottom in our schemas: one experiences expressions (such as several modalities), which correspond to their conceptual structures ($CS_{Expression}$), which then are integrated to the ultimate understanding of the multimodal expression ($CS_{Integrated}$). In production, this process moves from bottom-to-top, starting at a common conceptual origin ($CS_{Integrated}$) which can be distributed across several conceptual expressions ($CS_{Expression}$), subsequently manifesting in different modalities. Such a shared conceptual structure—whether or not each modality taps into the exact same conceptual or spatial representations—would be consistent with notions of a "growth point" for production of multimodal meaning in co-speech gesture (McNeill 1992). The growth point is our $CS_{Integrated}$. This view is also consistent with the neurocognitive evidence of a multimodal hub for semantic memory (Calzavarini 2023, Kuhnke et al. 2023, Kutas and Federmeier 2011, Ralph et al. 2016, Xu et al. 2009).

Thus, our view does not necessarily seek to provide top-down descriptions of relations in a general way, such as text-image relationships "elaborating" or "explaining" each other. Rather, our approach renders the explicit meanings within each modality and describes how they create integrated meaning without necessarily subscribing to top-down functional categories. The emergent and interactive meanings between modalities can be described with the conceptual predicates that already exist within Conceptual Semantics that also apply to unimodal expressions. We thus stick to coreference as a basic parameter to explain the meaningful relations between modalities, and we derive categorical classes based on these coreferential relationships.

Nevertheless, we remain cognizant of how bottom-up interactions contribute to the holistic meaning. In cases of complete coreference as in our default formalism, the sources of information provide different aspects of a signal which may make them balanced or imbalanced. For example, the iconicity of a picture of a pipe along with the symbolicity of its label gives us two sources of information that can be combined in a holistic way. Similarly, a deictic gesture directs attention in a way that the deictic word *this* would not, lending them to create a sense of balance when combined. No matter how coreferential signals may be, each can contribute to the whole in distinctive ways, given their *affordances*. As argued in the last chapter, we therefore assume that coindexation between conceptual structures evoked by different modalities may not include the entirety of the exact same concept, but rather the set of features that overlaps between expressions allows us to call them "the same" concept.

While we consider the formalism above as a prototypical case of coreference, most multimodal expressions use complex coreferential interactions. We will identify the processes to integrate separate conceptual structures into a singular unified structure. This is fairly straightforward in cases of complete coreference, but a challenge arises when coreference appears *absent*, yet an integrated meaning needs to be derived from distinct contributions, again, whether unimodal or multimodal. Take, for example, an image of a book with the label *treasure*, where the word and image do not overtly share a common concept. Formally, this **absent coreference** would manifest as in Figure 5.1b, which is a simplified formalization of this relationship.

Here, each expression (i.e., unit within a modality) conveys its own conceptual information ($CS_{Expression}$), but these independent expressions do not map to a shared conceptualization. In other words, $CS_{Integrated}$ does not contain information matching across both expressions. Yet, a comprehender aims to resolve this "incongruity" of absent coreference by mediating these otherwise independent representations through additional conceptual structure. This provides a link between concepts that otherwise does not appear in the expressions themselves. Because this is not overtly expressed, this information is *inferred*. In our example in Figure 5.1b, a picture of a book (index 1) would relate to a label reading "treasure" (index 2), because of the implication that a book is a source of riches and value (or that books themselves are valuable objects), simplified here in the predicate that a book is SIMILAR to treasure. We will elaborate on this below.

Thus, in order to resolve the absence of coreference, additional conceptual structures specify the relations between the meanings of the distinct non-coreferential components. A generalized version of this formalism appears below. Each expression carries its own conceptual structure, which lacks shared features, which map to the arguments of an additional conceptual predicate F.

	Expression 1	Expression 2
Expression:	$/\ldots/_1$	$/\ldots/_2$
$CS_{Expression}$:	$[\ldots]_1$	$[\ldots]_2$
$CS_{Integrated}$:	$F([\ldots]_1, [\ldots]_2)$	

These types of inferential relations are often characterized as types of mappings by Conceptual Integration Theory and its associated theoretical frameworks (Fauconnier and Turner 1998, Lakoff and Johnson 1980), along with work on structure-mapping and analogy (Gentner 1983). They have also been described as "coherence relations" or "discourse relations" by a variety of theories (e.g., Asher and Lascarides 2003, Bateman and Wildfeuer 2014, Gernsbacher 1990, Hobbs 1985, Mann and Thompson 1987). These inferential relations are all consistent with and characterizable by existing functions within Conceptual Semantics. Our formalizations allow us to be explicit about which elements directly manifest into expressions and which *do not*, and thus need to be inferred to arrive at a sensible interpretation.

We address two primary concerns about these issues throughout this chapter. First, how does coreferentiality become assigned? The presence of multiple modalities may not on its own confer integration, and thus it's important to ask how recognition of these connections comes about. As we will see, in many cases coreference is guided by the modality interfaces discussed in Chapter 3. Second, to address how expressed conceptual structures coalesce, we need to ask: how do they create an integrated conceptual structure? Especially in cases of absent coreference, where does this additional conceptual predicate come from?

5.1 Unimodal Coreference

As coreference provides our basic mechanism of multimodal meaning-making, it is worth first exploring how it operates in a unimodal context. Indeed, coreference itself is not a feature of multimodality, and reflects basic principles of semantic composition that have been well studied across modalities. We therefore explore such coreference in the vocal and graphic modalities before proceeding to describe multimodal coreference.

5.1.1 Vocal Coreference

Coreference in sentence structure has received considerable theorizing for many decades, particularly focusing on anaphoric relations. In the sentence *Olive looked at herself in the mirror*, the word *herself* is coreferential to *Olive*, indicating that they are the same person. Following Culicover and Jackendoff (2005, 385), we treat the reflexive (*herself*) as a representation (REP(α)) which binds to the antecedent (*Olive*) in conceptual structure. This is formalized in (5.2). In spoken language, structures like *herself* are assumed to refer to the same person as the subject of the sentence. In contrast, *Olive looked at her in the mirror* renders an ambiguous interpretation as to whether *her* refers to Olive or to someone else, although the someone-else reading is more likely (given the possible lexical item of the less ambiguous *herself*). Similarly, *Olive looked at Olive in the mirror* would most likely also render a possible interpretation of there being two Olives (not to mention if the second "olive" lacked capitalization in written form, it might render a food, not another person). Similar coreference persists across different sentences, as in *Olive looked in the mirror. She saw herself*. In this case, both the words *she* and *herself* refer to OLIVE, despite the grammatical boundary of the sentence structure.

(5.2). Coreference using anaphora in a spoken and written sentence.

GrS: Olive$_1$ looks$_2$ at$_3$ herself$_4$ in$_5$ the mirror$_6$
PS: / ˈɑlɪv$_1$ lʊks$_2$ æt$_3$ hərsɛlf$_4$ ɪn$_5$ ðə ˈmɪrər$_6$ /
GS: [$_S$ NP$_1$ [$_{VP}$ V+PRES$_2$ [$_{PP}$ P$_3$ NP$_4$ [$_{PP}$ P$_5$ NP$_6$]]]]
CS$_{Integrated}$: [$_{Event}$ LOOK$_2$([$_{Thing}$ OLIVE]$_1$, [AT$_3$(REP([α]$_4$))], [$_{Place}$ IN$_5$([$_{Thing}$ MIRROR$_6$])])]

No matter how they are established, at a basic level we connect information across words and sentences in coreferential ways. That is, ultimately different words in a sentence or discourse can refer to the same information. Here, we only notate the integrated conceptual structure, but the expressed conceptual structure would independently specify each lexical item's meaning, which compositionally combines in the integrated CS. The primary inferred information within the integrated structure is the coreference of the anaphoric relationships, aided by the grammatical or discourse structure. However, an integrated semantics is not always licensed by the grammar, and additional inferences may be required, even in simple sentences. For example, the sentence *The light flashed until dawn* gives an emergent inference of repeated flashing, which is not overtly expressed (Jackendoff 2010a, Pustejovsky 1991, Talmy 2000a).

Next let's turn to cases where coreference is required to arrive at an integrated meaning, but the coreferential information is not overtly or grammatically indicated. Consider the phrase *in the garbage of Eden* which is a line from the song "Am Gold" by Nicole Atkins. This phrase makes reference to the Biblical story of the garden of Eden, and can only be understood in that context. Forms like this are called "optimal innovations" (Giora et al. 2004), whereby a recognized stock phrase is used as the base for productive variation. In this case, "in the garden of Eden" is the base, and *in the garbage of Eden* is the productive innovation. Coreference here thus does not necessarily apply between units within the expression, but between the expression and an encoded base. We formalize this in Figure 5.2.

Some parts of the utterance are maintained exactly as in the base, while others become altered. We here apply the same coindices to the utterance and the base for these repeated words (coindexed as 1,2,4,5), with "bar" notation for the altered

	Expression	Base
GrS:	/in$_1$ the$_2$ garbage$_{\bar{3}}$ of$_4$ Eden$_5$/	/in$_1$ the$_2$ garden$_3$ of$_4$ Eden$_5$/
PS:	/ɪn$_1$ ðə$_2$ ˈgɑrbɪdʒ$_{\bar{3}}$ ʌv$_4$ ˈidən$_5$/	/ɪn$_1$ ðə$_2$ ˈgɑrdən$_3$ ʌv$_4$ ˈidən$_5$/
GS:	[$_{PP}$ P$_1$ [$_{NP}$ Det$_2$ N$_{\bar{3}}$ [$_{PP}$ P$_4$ NP$_5$]]]	[$_{PP}$ P$_1$ [$_{NP}$ Det$_2$ N$_3$ [$_{PP}$ P$_4$ NP$_5$]]]
CS$_{Ex}$:	[$_{Place}$ IN$_1$([$_{Thing}$ GARBAGE$_{\bar{3}}$,^{α}; [CLASSIFY$_4$(α, EDEN$_5$)]])]$_Y$	[+VAL([$_{Place}$ IN$_1$([$_{Thing}$ GARDEN$_3$,^{α}; [CLASSIFY$_4$(α, EDEN$_5$)]$_6$])])] [+VAL([$_{Place}$ IN([$_{Thing}$ PARADISE]$_6$])])]

CS$_{Int}$:	[−VAL([$_{Place}$ IN$_1$([$_{Thing}$ GARBAGE$_{\bar{3}}$,^{α}; [CLASSIFY$_4$(α, EDEN$_5$)]$_6$])])] [$_{Place}$ IN(NOT([$_{Thing}$ PARADISE])$_{\bar{6}}$)]

Figure 5.2 Optimal innovation of the phrase *in the garbage of Eden* in reference to "in the garden of Eden."

component (3 and 3′). Thus, within the utterance, the consistency of the repeated words and syntactic structure, along with the alliteration in the phonetics between garbage and garden, helps motivate access to the original lexical item functioning as the base (in the garden of Eden). The optimal innovation is thus a productive *sister schema* of the encoded base lexical item (Jackendoff and Audring 2020).

The conceptual structure of both the utterance and the base contains the basic propositional information related to their meaning. Yet, the phrases "in the garden of Eden" and *in the garbage of Eden* also carry a particular sense of being good or bad, both individually and in relation to each other. So, to capture the full integrated meaning, we have to account for the attitude or values that are conveyed by these expressions. Both values and their valences (good, bad, neutral) are fundamental aspects of the ultimate conceptual structure corresponding to an expression. We here follow Jackendoff (2007) in treating value as a conceptual phenomenon, in that entities or actions never have intrinsic value, but that we assign such values to them through our conceptualizations.

In our formalization, we notate value assignments with outer brackets which specify the phenomenon (Thing, Situation, etc.) a certain value is assigned to (VAL), whereas the "±" specifies the valence of that value (positive or negative valence). Thus, the phrase "In the Garden of Eden" carries with it a value (VAL) with a positive valence (+), informed by our prior knowledge of the Biblical story. When put in contrast with this base, the optimal innovation of *In the Garbage of Eden* can be construed as having a similar value but now with a *negative* valence (–VAL), through the comparison of a Garbage with the positive valence of Garden (i.e., Paradise). Because of this conflict, Paradise becomes negated, which accounts for the "Paradise Lost" meaning evoked by the optimal innovation of the original base.

This base is only accessible through knowledge of the Biblical story of the Fall of the Garden of Eden. With no knowledge of this story, a comprehender would not be able to access the base form or its conceptual structure which this optimal innovation references. That is to say, the idiomatic encoded conceptual structure of the base also links to a wider encyclopedic knowledge which also must be encoded.

In the previous chapter, we argued that iconicity was a type of aligned coindexation arising out of the interfaces of structures. Optimal innovations like this one maintain this type of aligned coindexation between all structures in the optimal innovation and the base, with some elements persisting identically and some elements being altered. The aligned coindexation here in fact renders the base accessible to the optimal innovation. In other words, optimal innovations evoke a type of iconicity, which, as we will see, persists across modalities. This type of regularized vocal iconicity does not go acknowledged if the focus is merely on word-level iconicity. We schematize optimal innovations as:

Optimal innovation schema

	Expression	Base
Expression	/x_1 y'_2/	/x_1 y_2/
$CS_{Expression}$	[X_1 Y'_2]	[X_1 Y_2]
$CS_{Integrated}$	[$X_1, F(Y_2, Y'_2)$]	

This example shows that coreference can operate not only between expressed forms (like in anaphora), but also between expressed and recalled, but unexpressed, forms which are critically involved in construing an integrated meaning.

Other cases establish coreference within a sentence, but where the apparent connections may not be forthcoming. Consider a unimodal utterance evoking similar notions as our previous multimodal example, like the sentence *A book is a treasure*, as in Figure 5.3a. In this case, the expressed conceptual structure states that books are in a state of being treasure. This is congruous for its literal meaning that a book itself is a valuable thing (such as an old manuscript being discovered that is worth a lot of money). However, another interpretation is related to the contents of a book rather than its physical form (Pustejovsky 1995), which requires another domain with further information about the nature of treasure. Specifically, treasure is an object with intrinsic value of positive valence (Jackendoff 2007). The integrated meaning requires recognition that the statement is saying that books are similar to treasure, and thus that the contents of books are to be construed to have the same value as treasure (+VAL). We posit that a function of SIMILAR can integrate these domains, shifting the meaning from the expressed BE for the copula *is* to a comparative. In this case, this similarity is the inference that is made in order to make this utterance comprehensible: the knowledge gained from a book is similar to the value of treasure.

Next, consider the utterance *It got my wheels spinning* to say that something made you think with intensity or difficulty, despite no cues for coreferentiality between *wheels spinning* and thinking. We formalize this in Figure 5.3b. Here, the expression has a meaning of an unspecified agent (it) causing an event of wheels possessed by "me" (my wheels) to spin. On its own, this utterance has no invocation of conceptual structure related to thinking, and on the surface would literally mean that something spun physical wheels. In order for this to convey a meaning of thinking, it requires

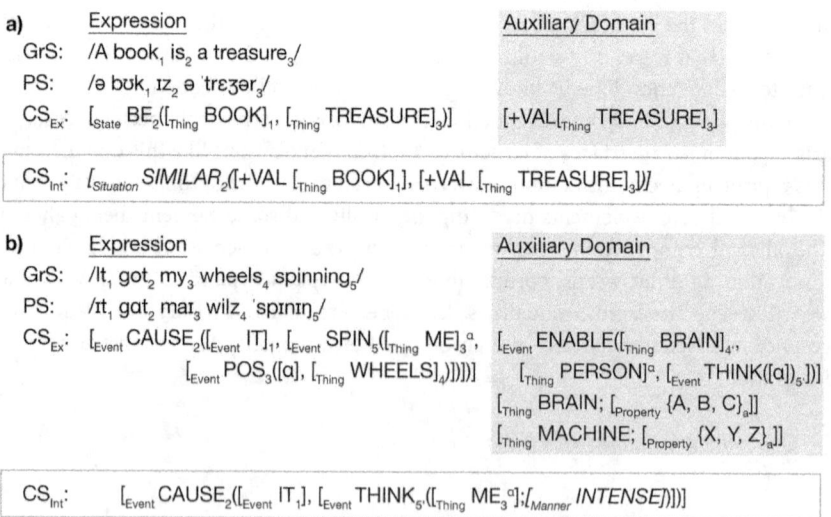

Figure 5.3 Sentences involving background knowledge from auxiliary domains.

several pieces of additional knowledge. First, we must know that brains are what enable a person to think. Metaphor theory calls such knowledge "the ground" (Lakoff and Johnson 1980) or the "generic space" in a conceptual integration network (Fauconnier and Turner 1998). Second, with this ground we can compare the workings of the brain to a machine (invoked by *wheels*), here specified as a set of certain properties (A, B, C and X, Y, Z) which coindex (subscript "a") sister schemas within our formalism. Readers who fail to understand this expression often lack this kind of background knowledge. In cases where these mappings become entrenched, such as in this idiomatic phrase, this additional knowledge becomes encoded as part of the lexical item (Giora et al. 2004).

To construe this phrase with the meaning of "thinking," we argue that a comprehender entrenches correspondences between $CS_{Expresssion}$ and this additional knowledge: between brains and wheels (subscript 4 and 4') and between brain activity (i.e., thinking) and spinning (subscript 5 and 5'). The integrated conceptual structure uses the overarching causative frame of *It got ...* as a predicate for "making me think," which pulls from the entrenched mappings between spinning wheels and thinking brains. This phrasing further adds a construed implication of the intensity of the manner of thinking, which is not present in the encoded knowledge.

When an entrenched phrasing like this (*wheels spinning*) maps to a non-literal meaning, it is referred to as an idiom. Our point here is that "metaphoric" expressions make use of an additional knowledge base to create meaning. For our account of coreference, meanings are expressed here that are not present in the uttered modality, and thus an integrated conceptual structure provides further construal for the utterance to make sense.

To summarize this section, we have provided illustrations of various ways that verbal expressions make use of coreferentiality, whether between expressions, or between utterances and unexpressed information, whether including both form and meaning (as in optimal innovations) or just meaning (as in metaphors). These same principles arise in other modalities, such as graphics, and in multimodal interactions.

5.1.2 Graphic Coreference

Let us now turn to coreference in visual representations. Consider first the sequence in Figure 5.4a. In the first panels, a man is shown juggling pins. The third panel shows a pin hit a man on the head, and the last panel shows a dizzy man. We here formalize the semantics of each panel, with corresponding indices placed directly on the images to make the notation a bit clearer. In our formalization of the meaning, we largely omit the compositional semantics of the visual morphology for simplicity. For example, in the first two panels, we focus on the actions of a man tossing the pins, but leave out the semantics of the motion lines (see Chapter 4). In panel 3, a man is hit by a pin, and again we leave out the semantics specific to the radial lines denoting an impact. The last panel shows a man in the state of dizziness, and we omit here the complexity of the compostionality of this upfix.

In order to understand this sequence *as a sequence*, certain connections across panels must be made. First, we need to recognize that all the individual depictions of male figures are coreferential to indicating the *same* man, and the different depictions of pins are also coreferential. This recognition has been described as the **continuity**

constraint (Cohn 2020a, Klomberg et al. 2023). To arrive at such coreference, each depiction of the man and pins must be recognized as being token-identical within an integrated meaning. Without this construal, each image might be interpreted as showing a different person. Indeed, this coreferential construal is not trivial, and people who are not exposed to spatially sequential visual narratives like comics or picture books do not necessarily make these connections. They may perceive such a sequence as showing different men. In addition, children only arrive at this coreferential construal between the ages of 4 and 6, with exposure to visual narratives (Cohn 2020a).

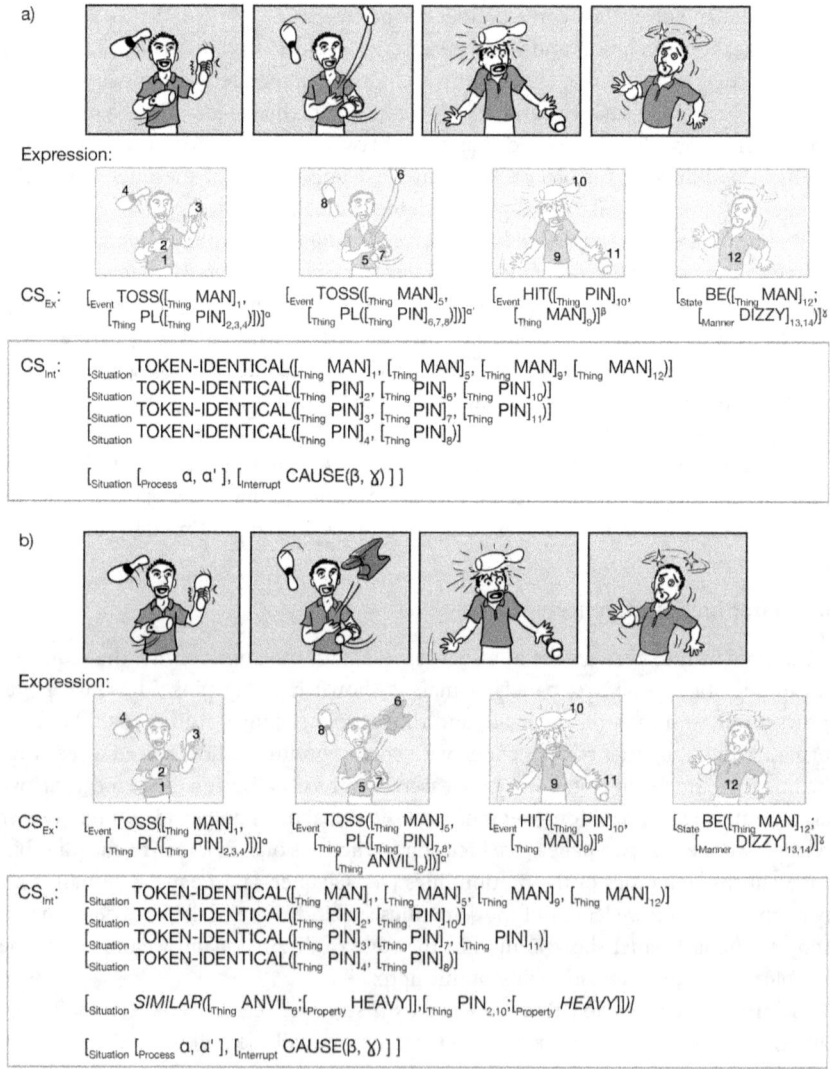

Figure 5.4 A sequence of a juggler a) tossing pins and b) tossing an anvil.

In addition to the establishment of coreference, we also need an integrated understanding of the events across panels. Such sequential meaning is facilitated by recognized differences in the depictions across panels, an **activity constraint** (Cohn 2020a, Klomberg et al. 2023). Continuity and activity taken together produce our understanding of a single man tossing three pins whose juggling actions go awry. In the first two panels, his tossing of the pins can be recognized a process of juggling, with each panel representing a snapshot of this process (as indexed with superscripts α, α'). The third panel shows an interruption of this process where one pin hits him in the head. This interruption results in his subsequent state of dizziness. That is, the events in panel 3 (superscript β) are the CAUSE of the state depicted in panel 4 (superscript γ). Altogether, this is how continuity and activity lead us to arrive at an integrated sequential understanding.

Next let's consider a modification of this sequence where the coreference across panels is less forthcoming. Figure 5.4b depicts the same juggling sequence, except in the second panel the man now throws an anvil in the air along with the pins. This anvil does not appear in any of the other panels. We now change our formalization of panel 2 to include the tossing of this anvil. How do we account for the *discontinuity* of the anvil in relationship to the pins, and how does it enter into our integrated understanding of the sequence?

To arrive at an integrated meaning, we need to associate the anvil to the pins. The message here is that the pin strikes the man very hard, and thus we could interpret this pin as being very heavy, feeling like an anvil. So, instead of a token-identical set of pins (subscripted 2, 6, and 10 in Figure 5.4), we only construe direct continuity between some of those pins (here, subscripted 2, 10) while also needing to associate them with the anvil (subscripted 6). The anvil is thus interpreted as being SIMILAR to the pins, and the pins can inherit the property of heaviness from the anvil. To re-establish continuity, we use the construal of similarity between objects.

These types of discontinuity are fairly common in comics and other media (Klomberg, Schilperoord, and Cohn 2024). Sometimes they are resolved by construing a relation of similarity, like here. In other cases, such discontinuities may be resolved by attributing the continuity to the perceptions or mental states of the characters within the sequence. For example, if we believe that the depiction of the anvil here reflects the viewpoint of the juggler, it could be construed that *he* perceives the pin as heavy as an anvil. Several such predicates are possible, including perception, imagination, dreaming, fantasizing, remembering, hypothesizing, and others. These predicates can all re-establish continuity in an otherwise discontinuous graphic representation.

We now turn to examples within a single image. Consider the example in Figure 5.5a, which is a redrawing of an automobile advertisement. Here we see a sequence of vans, apparently from different eras, lined up from left to right and getting bigger with every vehicle. The meaning of this utterance simply shows vans in a state of being, but with a spatial structure that they are in a line and that they increase in size. This spatial orientation is evocative of the image of the March of Progress, a painting that attempts to show the evolution of *homo sapiens* across several million years in a linear sequence of parading primates. Though the linearity in this image has long been discredited for implying a linear process of evolution instead of a branching process, it has become emblematic for pictorially conveying the idea of evolutionary progress. Here, the

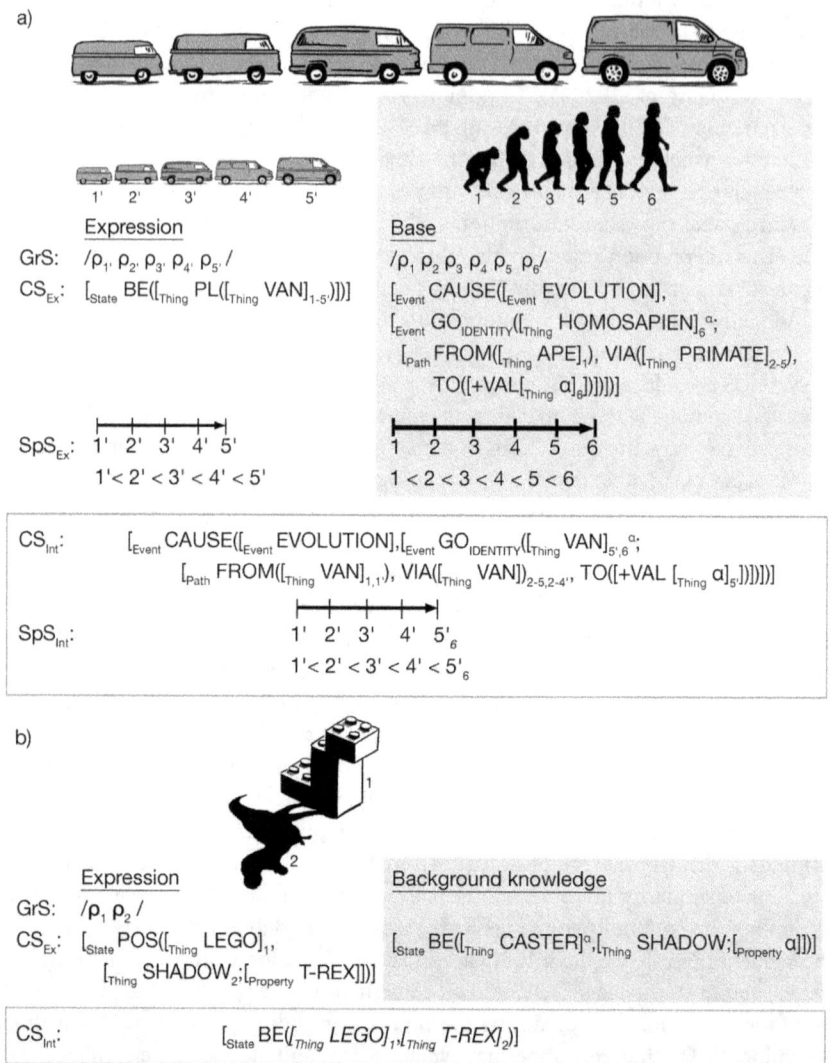

Figure 5.5 Structure of visual representations using a) a visual optimal innovation and b) integration of an auxiliary domain.

meaning of the original image now serves as the base of a *visual optimal innovation* (Arts and Schilperoord 2016, Schilperoord 2013, Schilperoord and Cohn 2023). The base conveys that evolution causes a species to progress from the stage of being apes, via other primate stages, to being *homo sapiens*. This final stage represents the ultimate state of evolutionary progress (with a value of positive valence) and thus is the topic of the image.

Because the lineup of vans makes reference to the March of Progress, it can inherit the entire conceptual structure corresponding to the base. In the integrated conceptual structure, the vans replace primates, while maintaining the overall propositional relationships of the base. The result is that the van in the rightmost position (the topic) is viewed as the endpoint of this evolutionary process, which then inherits the positive valence of this position. Without knowledge of this base reference, the image would merely remain the conceptual structure of the visual utterance: a stative lineup of vans of increasing size.

Next consider the picture in Figure 5.5b which uses a shadow in a conventionalized way to comment on its caster (Schilperoord and van Weelden 2018). Here we see a simple Lego block figure that casts a shadow that looks like a Tyrannosaurus Rex, originally from an ad campaign for Lego blocks. We notate this as a state where a thing—a Lego figure—possesses (POS) a shadow that has a property of a T-Rex. Yet, this again poses a challenge to the coreferential connection established in this picture: it is impossible for a shadow to have a shape that does not look like the caster of that shadow, which is background knowledge that we have about the nature of this relationship. This knowledge specifies that the property of a shadow (α) is bound to its caster (superscript α), and thus has the same identity (BE). In order to resolve the incongruent shadow, we apply this general rule about shadows between Lego and T-Rex, resulting in an interpretation that the Lego's true identity is a T-Rex. Of course, this is impossible, leading to a larger inference that Legos can transform mere blocks into imaginative entities and worlds in the mind of someone playing with them. We note here that this is not metaphor or analogy, because the message is not that the Legos are similar to a T-Rex but rather that the identity of the Legos actually is a T-Rex (note also that there is not an auxiliary domain brought to interpret this, only a general knowledge about shadows).

Let's turn now to an example where understanding the utterance also requires information that is not overtly expressed. Figure 5.6 is an example of an *upfix*, a visual affix that floats above a character's head to convey some aspect of their emotional or cognitive state. Conventional upfixes include elements like hearts or lightbulbs, or the gears depicted here, although this head + upfix pattern creates an abstracted schema that potentially allows for novel concatenations and is subject to a variety of constraints (Cohn 2013b, Cohn and Foulsham 2022, Cohn, Murthy, and Foulsham 2016). In this case, the gears above the head conventionally mean that the person is thinking. However, in a literal sense, gears have no overt relationship to thinking. We formalize these meanings in $CS_{Expression}$ for the head and gears separately. The head is merely a person who appears to be in some quizzical state of mind, there are multiple gears, and the motion lines indicate movement.

To make sense of this whole utterance, these meanings need to be integrated, which would result in a construal that gears above a head are spinning—a compositional meaning that still cannot account for the construal of thinking (not to mention that there are gears above the head). To reconcile this incongruity (i.e., what do gears have to do with being quizzical?) we also must draw on an auxiliary domain that has no overt manifestation in an expressed modality. As in the spoken example in Figure 5.3b (*It got my wheels spinning*), this auxiliary domain relates brains and machines. The integrated meaning, composed of both the expressed and unexpressed structures, generates an analogy (SIMILAR) between gears spinning and how a brain enables a person to think. This comes via the additional knowledge of the recognized mapping that brains are similar to machines.

Again, some visual representations require additional knowledge that is not present within the expression, and a construal does not arise out of the composition

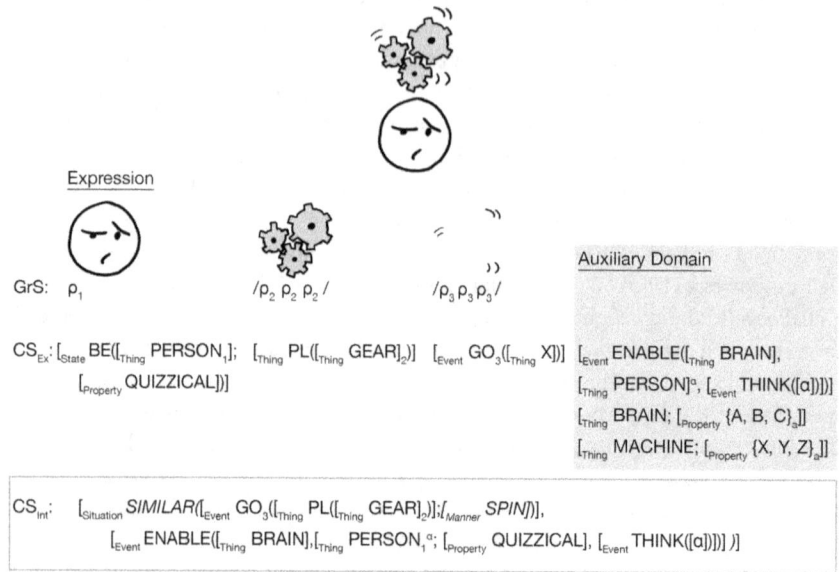

Figure 5.6 An upfix which requires a metaphor to be understood.

of expressed elements. In addition, consistent with our overall claims, we note the similarities at work within both spoken and visual expressions in terms of both their structure and their meaning.

5.2 Multimodal Coreference

In the sections so far, we have described how unimodal expressions either establish coreference or inferentially compensate for the lack of coreference. Below, we continue this analysis in terms of multimodal expressions, but we also further elaborate on the range of coreferential mappings that may occur between expressions. Though we introduce this additional nuance in terms of multimodality, the types of conceptual integrations that we discuss below in terms of coreference would also apply to cases of unimodal expressions, as discussed above.

We perceive four types of coreferential relationships, three of which establish reference and one in which coreference is ***absent*** and requires inference (as above). Our three types of coreferential relationships are ***complete***, ***included***, and ***partial*** coreference, which vary along the degree to which each expression carries distinctive meaningful information. We will describe them in increasing complexity.

5.2.1 Complete

The first type of coreference is where all primary conceptual information in one expression also appears in other expressions. We call this ***complete coreference***. In the case of multimodality, this would mean that multiple modalities express "the same" information, to the extent that coreference is afforded by a given modality. For example, it might be claimed that "complete" coreference is never possible between visual and vocal information, because pictures will always show visual information beyond that of words, such as size, texture, shape, and other dimensions. We acknowledge that such enriched information occurs in visual representations, but they mark aspects of visual meaning-making that are embedded within the affordances of the visual modality. Similarly, the affordances of speech also do not translate into coreferential properties with visuals, such as prosody or stress, which exist as ways that sound conveys information.

Thus, we here consider coreference in terms of what is possible to overlap given the feature set of a concept. That is, we are primarily concerned with the structure of situations (events, states) and the arguments that enact those situations (entities, properties), while acknowledging that each modality will always contribute its own unique ways of conveying meaning that is not translatable. We should not believe that modalities are or should be fully equivalent in their meaning-making potential because they operate with distinctive affordances.

A canonical example of complete coreference would be a picture of an object along with the label of that object. Consider the image in Figure 5.7 where we see a picture of a book along with the textual label "book." Both the text and the picture have the expressed conceptual structure of the thing BOOK. We also see here a satellite carrier (the label box and arrow), which specifies the linkage between the text and the image. As discussed in our lexical entry for carriers in Chapter 3, this satellite carrier specifies an extension of a path from carrier to the root (y), which is the function of the tail. In addition, the root (y) becomes classified with whatever meaning is in the carrier (Δ); this is the "labelling" meaning of the carrier.

The carrier facilitates labeling between the text (*Book*) and the image (picture of a book), integrated into a shared conceptual structure. If the classification content is similar between that of the text and the pictures, like here, we have a case of complete coreference. Technically, there is an additional visual element here that is *not* coreferential, namely the carrier itself. However, this visual morpheme contributes critically to establish the connection between text and picture. The satellite carrier confers classification between its content and its root, bridging the meaning of the text and the meaning of the image. Through its indexicality, it does not contribute propositional information in the same way that the picture or text offers such meaning. It simply links those meanings together to facilitate the integrated conceptual structure, but the carrier itself does not participate in the integrated meaning.

Note that the satellite carrier carries this labeling function regardless of its surface depiction, which would still persist even without a drawn box and arrow (i.e., its graphic features would be [–carrier,–tail]). Technically, the satellite carrier and its functionality would apply to both of the examples in Figure 5.1. There the classification function of a satellite carrier was left implicit, but it would also apply in those cases even when no carrier is depicted.

Another case of complete coreference is if someone asks a question like "What size was it?" and the response is "Small" with a pinching gesture indicating smallness. We formalize this in Figure 5.7b. We mark the synchronization in time within the modalities with the index "m," meaning that the word and the gesture occur simultaneously. Because both expressions correspond to scalar properties, the Thing, which is left unexpressed by both the word and the gesture, should be looked for elsewhere in the

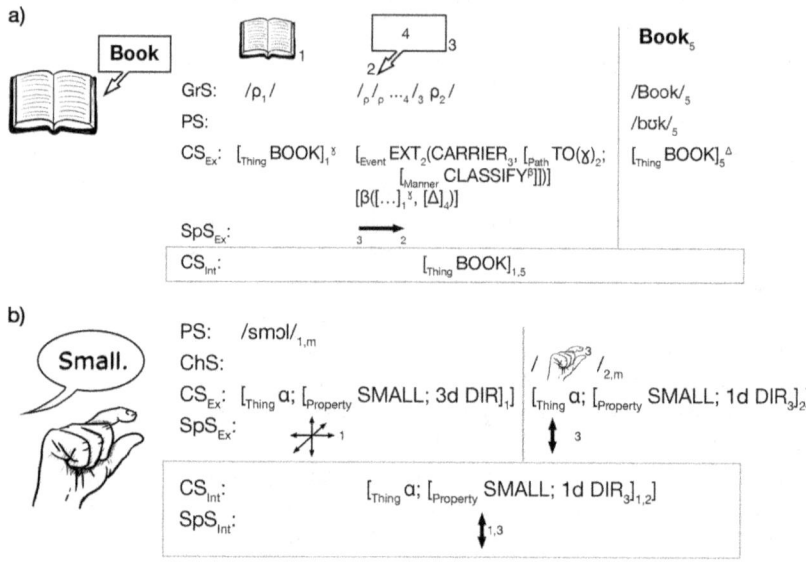

Figure 5.7 Examples of complete coreference for a) text-image and b) co-speech gesture relations.

discourse. This is notated with the binder (α), which finds its reference in the posed question (i.e., the alpha corresponds to "it" held in memory from "What size was *it*?").

Both the word *small* and the pinching gesture tap into the "same" overall conceptual structure, but do so in ways optimized for their affordances. The word *small* conveys the conceptual structure while leaving the spatial structure implicit, while the gesture makes that spatial structure explicit. This dimensionality is encoded in conceptual structure with the feature DIR (for directionality) across a 1 to 3-dimensional (1 to 3d) plane (i.e., height, length, depth). The spoken word does not specify the dimensionality of the smallness, thus implying that it occurs across three dimensions (3d DIR in $CS_{Expression}$, a three-axis configuration in $SpS_{Expression}$), reflecting a symbolic reference for expressing this property. By comparison, the gesture uses iconic reference to depict these spatial dimensions, with the separation between fingers specifying a 1-dimensional distance, and the vertical orientation of the hand implying height (1d DIR). In their multimodal integration, the gesture *constrains* the dimensionality that is left unspecified by the word, resulting in a construal of smallness specified across only one dimension. In this way, both the word and the gesture evoke a common conceptual and spatial structure, but their affordances allow for those meanings to be expressed in different ways. Thus, coreference involves access to different features of a shared concept, rather than the whole concept being expressed redundantly.

This type of pinching gesture would typically be classed as an iconic gesture, given its aligned co-indexation to spatial structure. However, it inherently maintains an alpha binding by expressing a property of an object which remains unexpressed gesturally. Thus, in addition to its iconic reference, this gesture also has indexical signification. As we argued in Chapter 4, alpha binding characterizes indexical signs. This supports our larger claim that the bodily modality is optimized for indexicality, even though signs may overtly appear iconic.

We abstract this relationship below into a generalized form for how different modalities correspond to expressed and integrated meanings. This idealization would thus interact with the encoded conceptual structures of each expression, and with the modality interfaces discussed in the last chapter (and their potential encoded structures, as in the case of carriers facilitating multimodal connections). Each expression here conveys its own independent Conceptual Structure, which is then coindexed within an integrated Conceptual Structure. We formalize this as Coreference Schema 1 (CR-S1):

CR-S1: *Complete coreference schema*

	Expression 1	Expression 2
Expression:	$/\ldots/_1$	$/\ldots/_2$
$CS_{Expression}$:	$[\ldots]_1$	$[\ldots]_2$
$CS_{Integrated}$:		$[\ldots]_{1,2}$

Though canonical cases of labeling might appear simple, complete coreference is not trivial. Consider the same exact example as in Figure 5.7a (*Book* with a picture of a book), but placed in the context of a lesson or textbook teaching the English language. In this case, complete coreference is the aim for a comprehender to establish, but to do so may also carry an overarching inference of the instructional nature of this communication. That is, there may be a pervading predicate of "in the English language, you should call this picture by the word X, or when you hear the word X you should think of the object depicted in this picture."

An additional challenge to complete coreference using labeling comes from cases where the label and the picture may refer to different levels of categorization (Rosch et al. 1976). Consider, for example, a picture of George Washington, with the label "U.S. President." In this case, the relevant features of the words overlap with a different level of categorization than the picture overtly. You must recognize that George Washington was a president of the United States (i.e., the first), and thus index that property to those invoked by the label. In this regard, there are (at the time of this writing) 45 other pictures of different people capable of co-referring with this label in the same way that a picture of Washington would.

Another complication with the Washington/U.S. President case would be that the label could be construed as indicating whatever the current holder of that title is, and Washington is no longer the President of the United States. The reader thus has to infer that this coreference was once valid temporally, but it no longer is. It is not "false" in terms of a realist semantics truth value; rather, it remains a true statement, but it is simply not the case currently. We conceive of two possible arguments for how this plays out. Either the temporality is encoded within the feature set of a given concept and is recognized as part of the coreferential mapping, or it would require an additional inferred predicate that mediates the validity of the statement. In this latter case, we would thus imagine a predicate that marks Washington as no longer being the U.S. President, despite once having been one.

5.2.2 Included

Modalities can also establish coreference across one or several expressions, but with one of the modalities including additional conceptual information absent in the other modality. We refer to this as ***included coreference***. Let us then expand on our previous book example with the label of book, but now with an image of a woman reading a book, as in Figure 5.8a. In this case, the coreference between the label of *book* and the depicted object corefers as in Figure 5.7a. However, the woman in the act of reading gives additional information in the graphic modality. Thus, the total information expressed verbally is also *included* in the information expressed visually. The concept of BOOK is integrated from both modalities, but the sense of the woman reading comes only from the graphic modality.

The generalized form of this included coreference thus appears as:

CR-S2: Included coreference schema

	Expression 1	Expression 2
Expression:	$/\ldots/_{1,3}$	$/\ldots/_2$
$CS_{Expression}$:	$[\ldots]_1, [\ldots]_3$	$[\ldots]_2$
$CS_{Integrated}$:	$[\ldots]_{1,2}, [\ldots]_3$	

To repeat, this formalization specifies that there are multiple expressions where all of one expression (2) is coreferenced ($CS_{Integrated}$) with part of another expression (1). However, additional information in one modality (3) is not present in the other. This results in a situation where some conceptual information is shared (i.e., coreferenced) while other information is distinctive to only one expression.

Co-speech gestures provide a wealth of examples of this type of coreference. Consider speaking the sentence *I caught a small fish* while at the same time making a pinching gesture which is synchronized with the word *small* (subscript "m"), as in Figure 5.8b. The spoken word *small* (subscript 4) and the pinching gesture (subscript 6) both convey the property of smallness, which corefer within the integrated conceptual structure like in Figure 5.7b. Meanwhile, the rest of the sentence "I caught a … fish" appears only in speech, providing a thing (FISH) for the gestural property to unify with. Thus, the conceptual information expressed by speech is richer than that of gestures, and the gestural concept is included in that of speech, despite the affordances of gestures inherently providing additional specification of spatial dimensionality beyond that in the speech, as in Figure 5.7b.

Nevertheless, speech may allow some affordances for expressing dimensionality. Consider the case of the word *huge* combined with an outstretched gesture (Figure 5.8c), where the gesture conveys a range of dimensionality depending on how wide the arms get from each other. However, the word *huge* can also convey dimensionality of size by extending the vowel: *huuuuuuuge* (Clark 1996, Dingemanse et al. 2015). This dimensionality is coindexed with the extended vowel itself (subscript 7) corresponding to the 1d DIR in Conceptual Structure and specifying a 1-dimensional scale in Spatial Structure, now reflecting an iconic reference between form and meaning. The

Figure 5.8 Examples of included coreference for a) text-image relationships, b) co-speech gesture, and c) co-speech gesture with further modulation of phonology.

alignment between these dimensional expressions creates additional coreference by both modalities mapping to the trajectory of the Spatial Structure.

5.2.3 Partial

Consider another version of the spoken sentence *I caught a huge fish*, but now while making a rounded gesture with both hands starting high and moving low, as in Figure 5.9a. Like the other examples, this creates coreference between the gesture and the conceptual structure of the adjective, but here the gesturing may create further

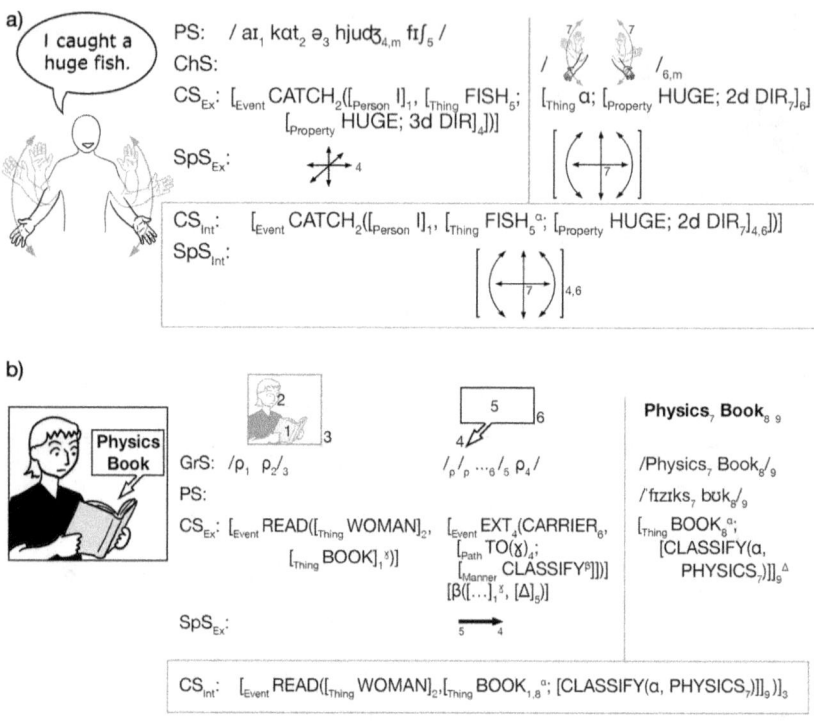

Figure 5.9 Examples of partial coreference in a) co-speech gesture and b) text-image relations.

detail depending on how wide or large the gestures become. The gesture not only takes on a single dimension (1d) of length but two dimensions (2d) of both width and height. This additional dimensionality adds features which are no longer directly coreferential with the adjective *huge*, but instead elaborate on that shared conceptual structure.

By adding dimensionality in the bodily modality, along with the additional aspects of the sentence in the vocal modality, some meaning is coreferential across modalities but also departing in both. This exemplifies ***partial coreference***, where coreference occurs across some conceptual dimensions, but each modality also maintains unique contributions. We again characterize this abstractly as below:

CR-S3: *Partial coreference schema*

	Expression 1	Expression 2
Expression:	$/\ldots/_{1,3}$	$/\ldots/_{2,4}$
$CS_{Expression}$:	$[\ldots]_1, [\ldots]_3$	$[\ldots]_2, [\ldots]_4$
$CS_{Integrated}$:	$[\ldots]_{1,2}, [\ldots]_3, [\ldots]_4$	

Elaborating on our book example in Figure 5.9b, consider the label *Physics Book*, which now specifies the type of book that is being read. This concept is only apparent in the text but not in the image. In this example, both the carrier and the text provide classification functions. The satellite carrier classifies its root (here, the drawn book) by its content (here, *Physics Book*), whatever the contents might be. The text classifies the book as a physics book, but does so regardless of its presence in a multimodal expression. Thus, in the integrated conceptual structure, these classifications are reinforced with each other.

This example now shows information that is coreferential across both modalities (book), and independently in either the graphics (woman, reading) or in the text (physics). The integrated conceptual structure coindexes BOOK to both graphics and text (subscripts 1,8), while the other components coindex with concepts in either modality.

From a communicative perspective, partial coreference may be the clearest manifestation of how multiple modalities can be optimized to create an integrated meaning. In complete coreference, information remains largely redundant across modalities, while in included coreference one modality ends up being informationally subordinate to another. Here though, each modality maintains its own independent contribution, with the shared coreferential elements serving as a lynchpin for the conceptual integration across expressions. As a result, partial coreference may be the most communicatively enriched form of multimodality where coreference still persists. As we will see below, further enrichment can be created when no such coreference is overtly apparent.

5.2.4 Absent

We now turn to multimodal interactions with no apparent coreference. As we have discussed in unimodal cases, the lack of coreference calls for additional construals beyond what is expressed. As at the start of the chapter, we formalize this as:

CR-S4: *Absent coreference schema*

	Expression 1	Expression 2
Expression:	$/ \ldots /_1$	$/ \ldots /_2$
$CS_{Expression}$:	$[\ldots]_1$	$[\ldots]_2$
$CS_{Integrated}$:	$F([\ldots]_1, [\ldots]_2)$	

To further our book-reading examples, consider Figure 5.10a now with the label *Treasure*. The message here is that books are thought of as being valuable, like treasure, but the surface meaning does not directly convey this. Rather, the satellite carrier once again classifies the book as treasure, creating a conflict because they are not literally coreferential: treasure is not a book. As in the unimodal textual example in Figure 5.3a, to integrate the meanings in this absent coreference, we must recognize that treasure is an object that has a utility value of a positive valence (Jackendoff 2007). The meaning

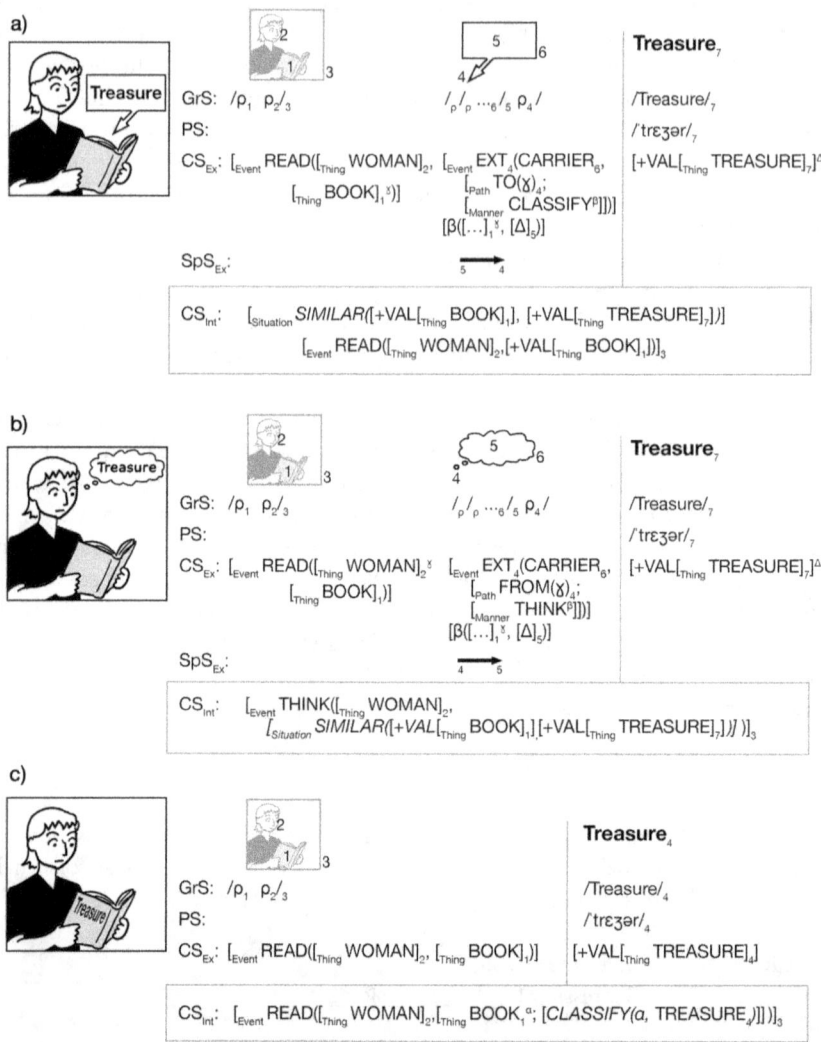

Figure 5.10 Absent coreference using a) an emergent satellite carrier, b) an emergent private carrier, and c) an inherent text-image relationship.

of treasure itself is not being applied to the book, but rather the book inherits this positive valence (+VAL) in the integrated meaning.

Next consider the same image but where the carrier has been changed from a satellite (a label) to private carrier (a thought bubble), as in Figure 5.10b. The picture and text retain the same meanings as above, but the carrier now expresses the meaning of THINK rather than CLASSIFY, which has the sense of emerging *from* the root (now the person), rather than pointing to the root (previously the book). This carrier then implies that the person is thinking about treasure, specifically that they think that the book is similar to treasure. Because there is no overt morphology that carries out this classification, like with the satellite carrier, a comprehender must infer that it is the person who is comparing the book to treasure, with again the idea of a transfer of positive valence. We find this to be the most sensible interpretation of this absent coreference. However, other possibilities do exist, such as that the person has read the word "treasure" in the book, or that they are thinking about treasure independently of their reading experience. These options would create no transfer of value from the word "treasure" to the book, but they are not impossible.

Let's close our book/treasure examples by changing the text-image interface. All of these carrier examples use an emergent relationship, but consider instead if it used an inherent relationship, where the word *Treasure* now appears on the cover of the book as part of the world of the image (Figure 5.10c). Now, this word becomes the title of the book, which again carries a function of classification. The word *Treasure* transfers no specified valence as a type of book topic (i.e., a book about treasures, a whimsical title of a novel, etc.), and thus the book inherits no valence. Nevertheless, an interpretation similar to Figure 5.10a is still possible if we interpret this text as a type of label, as one often sees in political cartoons. Though it would look as if *Treasure* is inherent to the world of the image, this interpretation would require it to be an emergent relationship with an invisible satellite carrier, thereby maintaining its classificatory function as in Figure 5.10a.

Next consider a case where a sentence is accompanied by an emotive emoji, such as *I'll call tomorrow* with a smiley face, as might be uttered into a chat conversation (Figure 5.11a). The sentence expresses that an agent "I" calls an unspecified patient "X" (presumably the recipient "you" but could be others filled in by the discourse context) at the time "tomorrow." The emoji shows a face that has a property of happiness, signaled by the curve of the mouth for smiling. The proximity of the sentence and face renders it an adjoined relationship, which as we argued in Chapter 4 invites a comprehender to simply RELATE these elements together. As this relationship does not add much, we here leave it unspecified, although we argue that it would remain a latent understanding throughout these types of multimodal utterances.

We then need to account for the relationship of the smiley face and textual utterance. Because the smiling face is happy, it is assigned a value with a positive valence (Jackendoff 2007). By combining the emoji with the sentence, we see two possible interpretations. In the first, the face is coreferential to the agent "I" to simulate that the agent is smiling while uttering this expression. This renders the interpretation (5.11ai) in which the agent and the emoji are coindexed (both subscripts 1 and 6 mapping to the Thing "I"), which then inherits both the property HAPPY and its associated positive valence. A second interpretation (5.11aii) is that the valence from the happy face applies to the whole utterance. In this case, no coreference persists between the face and the elements within the sentence, and the utterance as a whole is construed to have the positive valence (Grosz, Kaiser, and Pierini 2021).

Let's now consider the same sentence, but with an emoji expressing concern or worry (Figure 5.11b). In this case everything remains the same except that the face now has a property of CONCERN that is assigned a value of negative valence, signaled

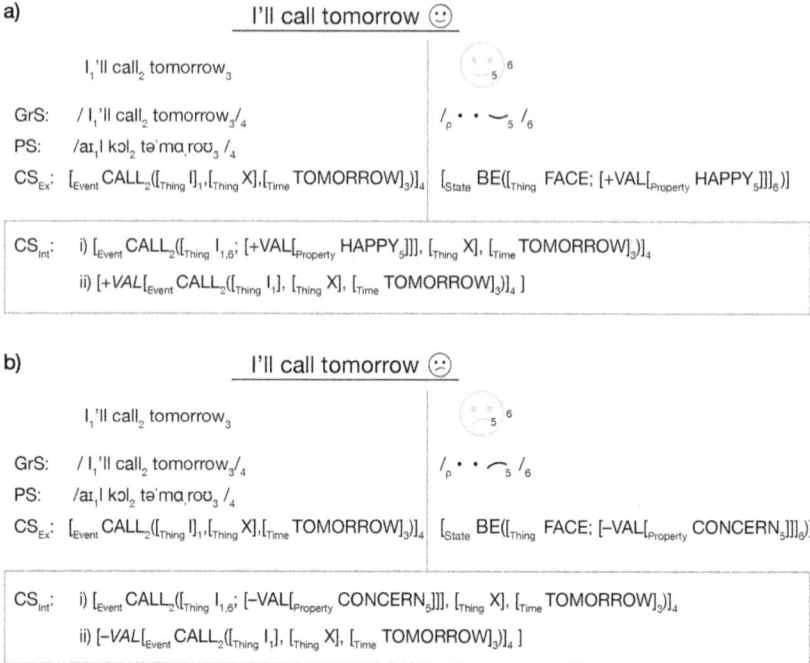

Figure 5.11 Absent coreference in text-image relationships with face emoji motivating a) positive value and b) negative value.

again by the curve for the mouth (note this contrastive role of the grapheme). This change maintains the same two possible interpretations, of (5.11bi) coindexing the face and agent to be coreferential, and (5.11bii) a construal of the negative valence of the face applying to the whole utterance. However, the coreferential option (5.11bi) may be more intuitive, as the emoji seems to suggest the state of mind of the agent (who is also presumably the sender of the message). We posit that perhaps a positive valence has a greater ability to apply to generalized statements, while the emotion of concern applies to a personal value assigned to a particular entity. We can make this broader contrast between positive and negative valence without depicting specific emotions by use of the thumbs-up/down emoji (Figure 5.12).

With a thumbs-up emoji, the literal meaning conveys a thumb being part of a hand that is oriented upwards (Figure 5.12a). This upward direction corresponds to an entrenched mapping of positive valence going upward in contrast to the negative valence going downward (Lakoff and Johnson 1980, Schubert 2005). Thus, the thumbs-up emoji has an encoded meaning of positive valence, whereby the direction UP is coindexed (subscript 7) to the upward spatial structure. When combined with the sentence, this positive valence is assigned to the whole utterance.

Nevertheless, again, the emoji could possibly be considered as coreferential to the agent. In the non-coreferential interpretation (Figure 5.12aii), the valence is applied to

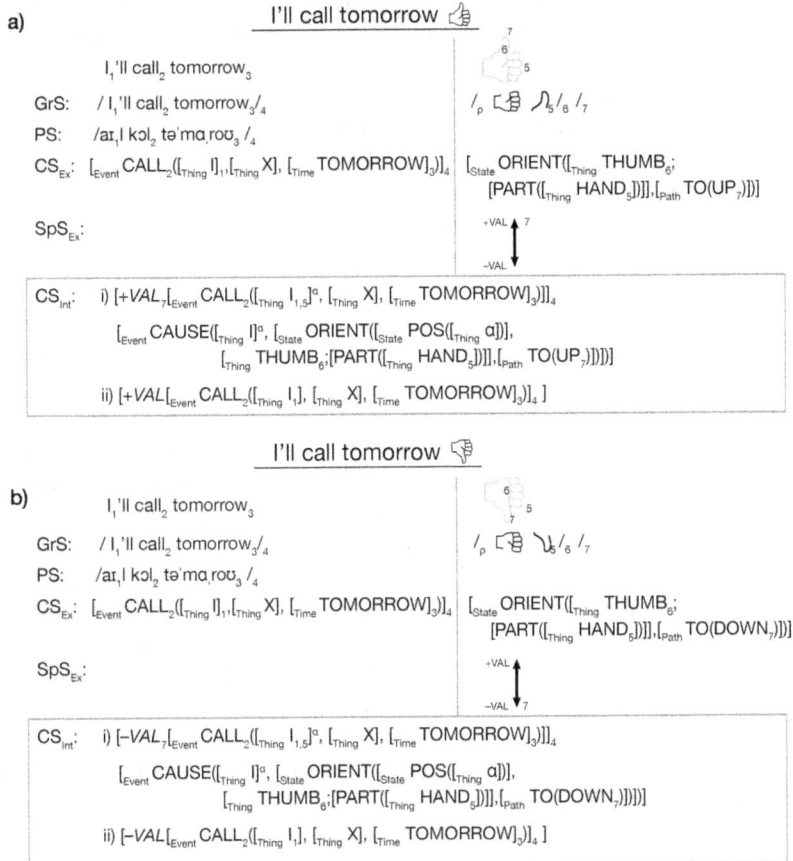

Figure 5.12 Absent coreference in text-image relationships with thumbs-up/down emoji motivating a) positive value and b) negative value.

the utterance and the emoji simply serves as a visual sign indicating positive valence that is not taken for its literal meaning as an actual body part. In the coreferential interpretation (Figure 5.12ai), the speaker is implying that the emoji reflects their own simulated gesture, i.e., that they are making this thumbs-up gesture (whether or not they physically are doing so). This results in the additional causal event that the agent "I" orients the thumb part of their hand in this upward manner.

Note again that this coreferential interpretation does not affect the overall application of valence to the whole utterance, and unlike the cases of the face emoji, this simulated action does not simply coindex an emotion to the agent, but rather implies the graphic representation of a gesture being made by the agent. We intuit here that the non-coreferential interpretation (Figure 5.12aii) is likely the preferred case, where the thumbs-up emoji simply stands as an emotive graphic expression, not as an implication of a simulated gesture. If this example was not text paired with an emoji, but was a spoken utterance with an *actual* thumbs-up gesture in the bodily modality, the coreferential, simulated interpretation would not be available, and Figure 5.12aii would be the primary interpretation.

If we reverse the direction of the thumb to be oriented downward, as in Figure 5.12b, it would map along this spatial dimension to a negative valence. The construed interpretation differs from the thumbs-up interpretation in that the valences are now negative, and in the coreferential interpretation, the thumb goes down.

Next let's consider a case where the valences of the textual utterance and the emoji conflict, which would create an interpretation of *irony* (Weissman and Tanner 2018). In Figure 5.13a, the thumbs-down emoji accompanies the sentence *The lecture was great*. The adverb *great* invites the assignment of positive valence to the lecture which conflicts with the associated negative valence of the emoji's downward orientation. In the integrated conceptual structure, the negative valence of the emoji takes precedence, giving the interpretation that the lecture was bad. The resolution of this conflicting valence across modalities leads to the sense of irony. Note that a coreferential interpretation of a simulated gesture is again possible, but we here omit it for simplicity, and it would be the same as in the prior analyses.

Let's change modalities back to co-speech gestures, again with our fish catching example in Figure 5.13b, now with the phrase *I caught a fish* accompanied by a persisting pinching gesture. We notate the persisting gesture with the index "m" spanning across the whole utterance indicated by an arrow. Because no corresponding adjective is uttered (i.e., *small* as in Figure 5.8b), it creates absent coreference between the gesture and the sentence. As before, the gesture corresponds to a property of smallness of an unspecified object (α), but which now can unify with the thing FISH in the sentence within the integrated conceptual structure.

A less straightforward example would be the sentence *I received a promotion* while making a pointing upward gesture, in Figure 5.13c. The spoken utterance conveys a transfer of possession whereby a promotion goes from an implied authority X (i.e., management, boss, organization, etc.) to the speaker ("I"). This grammatical construction of transfer originates from the physical domain, i.e., the grammar used to express transference of an actual object, e.g., *I received a present* (Jackendoff 1990). The upward gesture again maintains the same structure as other pointing gestures (as in Figure 4.6a), conveying an extension by a finger (Y) from that finger (place Z) to an unspecified location upwards (α). The orientation of this gesture maps to a spatial structure with an upward directionality of the path (coindexed 4 to 5).

With these expressed conceptual structures alone, there is no overt indication of how a change of possession maps to an upward indicated dimension. We again need to appeal to additional background knowledge. We posit a conceptual frame where an agent traverses a path from one position to another, where the old position has less value than the new position. These positions and their relative values are coindexed to a vertical spatial dimension, whereby positive values are coindexed upward and negative values are downward (Lakoff and Johnson 1980, Schubert 2005), as we also discussed with the thumbs-up/down emoji. The notion of *promotion* invokes this generalized conceptual frame, whereby the agent is an employee, and the positions are jobs within

Multimodal Semantic Interactions 139

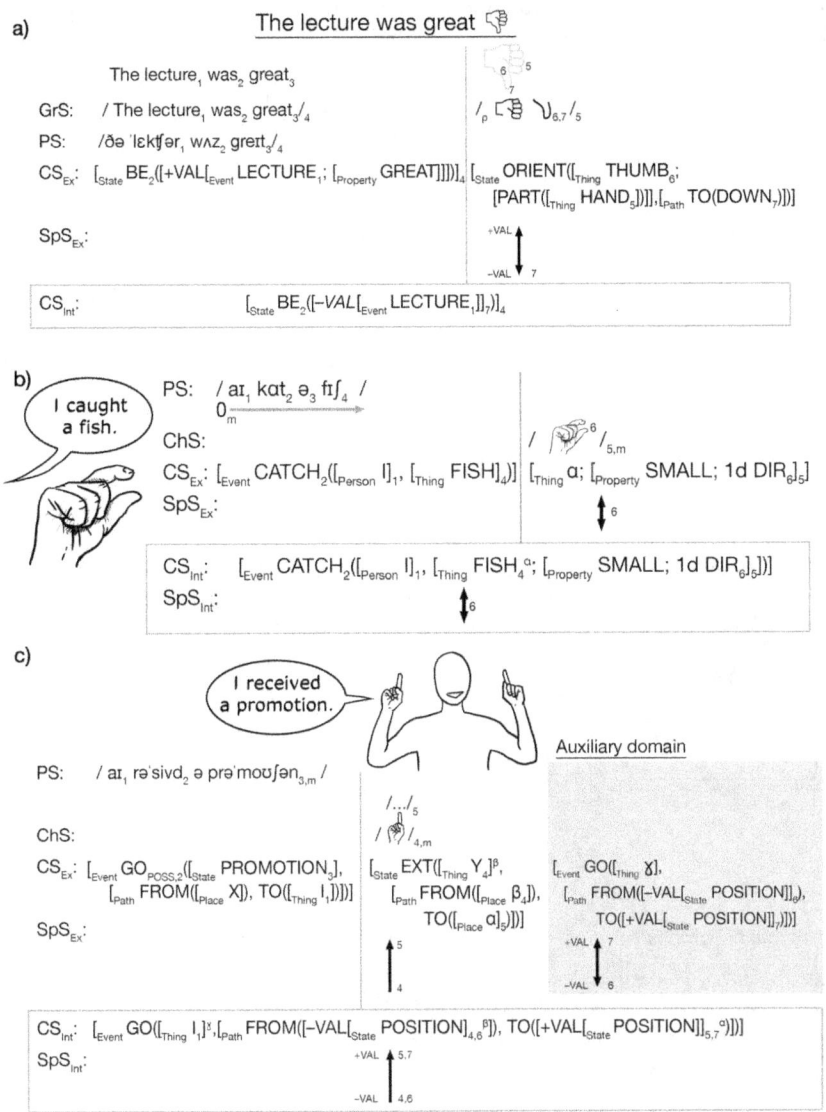

Figure 5.13 Absent coreference between a) text and an emoji, and co-speech gesture with b) a pinching gesture and c) a metaphoric gesture.

an organization. Though this value is relative, the old position is given negative value and the new position is assigned a positive value.

The integrated meaning of this multimodal utterance thus takes the entrenched meaning of *promotion* as its core, filling in the employee-agent as "I," the beneficiary of the promotion. In addition, the vertical spatial indication of the gesture is then coindexed to the path of the promotion, going from an implied "lower" value position to a gesticulated "higher" value position (coindex 5 and 7, and bound with the α from the gesture).

This example again has absent coreference expressed by each modality. Each part of the multimodal utterance taps into different parts of the conceptual structure of the background knowledge of *promotions*. The word *promotion* gives access to the algebraic path function (and would do so unimodally), while the gesture interfaces with the vertical spatial structure. Together, each modality can use their own affordances to give a richer signal. We again note that this would be classed as a metaphoric gesture, although it maintains an inherent alpha-binding that reinforces the optimality of the bodily modality as indexical.

Let us finish our analyses with an example that, to be interpreted, again requires additional construal. Consider the famous *I want you* recruitment poster from the

Figure 5.14 a) The multimodal *I want you* Uncle Sam recruitment poster and b) an optimal innovation of the poster with Darth Vader.

First World War (originally designed in 1917 by J. M. Flagg) which features Uncle Sam pointing at the viewer, as in Figure 5.14a. Below the primary sentence is the text *Nearest recruiting station*, which we will leave out of our formal analysis for reasons that will be clear below. The text *I want you for U.S. Army* conveys the thing *I* wanting *you* to join the *U.S. Army*. The picture again uses the same pointing schema as in Figure 4.6a, with extension of a finger along a path, from the location of the hand to an unspecified bounded referent (α). The integrated meaning simply brings these elements together. We interpret Uncle Sam as the symbol of the U.S. Government, which unifies the coindices from both Uncle Sam in the picture (1'), and the *I* of the text (1). Similarly, the direct object *you* is coreferential with the open slot of where Uncle Sam is pointing (α), to arrive at the integrated meaning that the U.S. Government wants you to join the U.S. Army.

Now consider a similar image of Darth Vader pointing at the comprehender in Figure 5.14b, with the text reading *I want you to join the Dark Side*. Like the verbal and visual optimal innovations discussed previously, this **multimodal optimal innovation** makes use of the original Uncle Sam poster as a base. The expressed meaning here largely follows the base poster. The text evokes the invitation to join the Dark Side, now with the verb *join* made explicit, and the picture shows the figure, here Darth Vader, again extending his index finger to point at the comprehender. The integrated meaning here unifies these structures.

While the Darth Vader representation is interpretable on its own, this multimodal utterance also inherits meaning from the base of the original poster. Specifically, by invoking the base, we add a construal of an imposing invitation, which we notate with an inferred manner of INTENSE to the wanting predicate. That is, because this is an optimal innovation, it boosts the sense of intensity of the wanting. Based on this example and many others, we can generalize the integrated conceptual structure of this "I want you ... " optimal innovation as:

$$[_{Event} \text{WANT}([_{Object\ldots}]^y, [_{Event} \text{JOIN}_7([_{Object} \text{YOU}_{3,6}]^\alpha, [\gamma]; [_{Manner} \textit{INTENSE}])])]$$

That is, the poster has open slots of an agent pointing toward you, who is intensely recruiting you to join their association. This destination of recruitment (U.S. Army, Dark Side, etc.) is the topic of the overall message. The recruiting agent is thus bound to the semantic field of this topic (denoted with γ). It would be strange for example to have Darth Vader imploring you to join the U.S. Army, and if it would occur, it would create a critical commentary about the U.S. Army in relation to what you know about Darth Vader.

This "I want you" optimal innovation thus creates an abstract, multimodal lexical item which includes the full entry of the original Uncle Sam poster as its base. An open slot in the graphological structure can be fulfilled by other graphic representations of pointing entities (Darth Vader, Captain America, a baby, etc.), while the text retains slots relating to those depicted entities (... *to join the Dark Side*, ... *to join The Avengers*, ... *to change my diaper*, etc.). Examples like these reinforce that similar properties (optimal innovations) persist unimodally within each modality (visual and verbal) and also multimodally, and need to be accounted for within the entrenched lexicons of a communicative architecture.

5.3 Conclusion

This chapter has presented an analysis of meaning across both unimodal and multimodal expressions. In doing so, we have relied on Conceptual Semantics, which has not required additional machinery to account for multiple sources of information and how they integrate into a coherent whole. The same basic coreferential operations persist within and across modalities, whether they remain in a unimodal or multimodal expression. Nevertheless, our analyses highlight how different modalities carry affordances for how meaning is manifested, and how such expressed meanings contribute to a holistic integrated meaning.

We have distinguished four types of coreference based on the differing contributions of each expression. In cases of absent coreference, various interpretative strategies resolve the lack of direct meaningful connections between expressions. These strategies sometimes include adding some or all of the conceptual structure that already exists within the distinct expressions (such as inheriting the valence and values). In other cases, additional stored knowledge needs to be activated in order to arrive at a sensible or relevant integrated meaning (as in knowledge of how shadows work, or making connections between domains like minds and machines). Finally, sometimes additional construal needs to be introduced with predications like analogy (SIMILAR) or contrast (NOT-SIMILAR) in order to integrate non-coreferential meaning.

This range of strategies suggests that multimodal inferencing is not uniform, and requires accounting for the specific contributions of each expression and possibly the explicit additional knowledge brought to bear on an integration. This implies that multimodal inferencing cannot simply be thought of as induced entirely through context and relational construals (e.g., Bateman, Wildfeuer, and Hiippala 2017) or accounted for by simply positing functional relations (Forceville 2020, Kress 2009, Logi and Zappavigna 2021, Martinec and Salway 2005, Painter, Martin, and Unsworth 2012, Royce 2007). Rather, addressing multimodality requires specifying the explicit semantic contributions encoded by separate expressions and characterizing the particular ways that they integrate. Certainly, context plays a role in the interpretation of any utterances, whether unimodal or multimodal. However, that context needs to interact with semantics encoded within the expressions themselves.

Regardless of the theory used for this purpose (we have used Conceptual Semantics) a formal treatment of these issues is required, whereby both the semantics of the separate contributions and their integrated meaning are made explicit. Leaving out these details not only misses important aspects of unimodal and multimodal meaning-making, but it would also ignore opportunities to characterize the constraints and strategic options employed to arrive at these integrations. Formalization forces us to confront these issues with precision, without leaving the details to be inferred, assumed, or hand-waved.

In addition, by illustrating the properties and principles of conceptual structure in multimodal utterances, we have demonstrated how such meaning-making interacts with the interfaces between the modalities themselves, as discussed in Chapter 4. In spatial interfaces between writing and pictures, the nature of the interface matters whether the text is part of the image (Inherent), is connected through a visual device

(Emergent), or is left loosely associated (Adjoined). These interfaces between the modalities themselves constrain the range of strategies that may be employed in multimodal conceptual integration. Again, such constraints and relationships should be accounted for by any theory of multimodal meaning-making.

Though the Parallel Architecture maintains the independence of its components, interactions within one component of the architecture (like between modalities) have consequences for the ways that structures in another component integrate (like between meanings). We will see this further as we next turn to our final substructure of grammar in the next chapters. Such interactions highlight the interplay within the Parallel Architecture between its component parts and its inherent holism, which exactly represents the type of part-whole relationships that we find in multimodality itself.

Part Four

Grammar

6

The Complexity Hierarchy

For modalities to be able to access meaning, they must be organized in some way. This organizational system is a type of **grammar**. Various works have categorized a range of complexity for types of grammars. This most famous comes in the classic Chomskyan hierarchy (Chomsky 1956), which posits mathematically idealized grammatical structures of increasing complexity. These logical idealizations can be useful for distinguishing different complex systems in a theoretical sense, but they do not necessarily provide an ecologically valid characterization of how communicative systems in the world actually function, particularly with regard to the mapping of modalities with meaning.

Jackendoff and Wittenberg (2014) propose an alternative taxonomy with a more ecologically valid intent. Their **Complexity Hierarchy** characterizes the mappings between form (a modality) and meaning, as facilitated by the grammatical system (Wittenberg and Jackendoff 2023), better accounting for the variety of sequencing that appears across the range of communicative systems. The diversity in this range of grammars implies no difference in value or status to each level in the hierarchy, aside from the constraints on communication that they afford.

Jackendoff and Wittenberg (2014) originally posited their Complexity Hierarchy in terms of the structures of spoken and signed languages, to describe the maximal level of combinatoric complexity for a given system. We argue that this hierarchy can be applied to sequencing across all modalities—and possibly beyond modalities—and thus we have modified the terminology to apply to this broader context. In addition, these constructs can characterize combinatorial complexity in a bottom-up manner within a given system. As we will see in future chapters, this nuance is necessary for the proper analysis of different modalities and their interactions.

For these reasons, our modified approach to the Complexity Hierarchy emphasizes it as a structure-independent capacity not bound to "grammar" specifically. In this sense, the Complexity Hierarchy can be viewed as a modality-independent capacity, and combinatoriality in different modalities may vary in the representations that they use. Although a spoken word and a graphic picture obviously differ in how they convey meaning, as discussed in prior chapters, both represent a single isolable *utterance*, and thus we argue both are characterizable by the types of combinatoriality in the hierarchy.

In many cases, the differences between modalities are less about the modalities *per se* than the types of combinatoriality that they afford. For example, Conceptual Structure can map to different levels of combinatoriality based on the affordances of the expressions. Individual pictures afford more internal conceptual complexity than a typical single spoken word. Ultimately though, both modalities employ the same combinatorial principles within the structures of their respective systems. The Complexity Hierarchy thus distinguishes the abstract means of combinatoriality, which manifest as the representational schemas encoded in memory for a given modality's system.

6.1 Complexity Hierarchy

Table 6.1 shows the Jackendoff and Wittenberg (2014) Complexity Hierarchy, modified to have modality-general terminology. While Jackendoff and Wittenberg specify the units as Words and the constituents as Utterances or Phrases, we render the hierarchy as comprising basic principles of segmentation, sequencing, and combinatoriality applicable beyond the context of "grammar" specifically. We also introduce modifications in terms of classification and scope that will be described below.

In Table 6.1, schemas consist of several basic components. The smallest component is a **Unit**, which is some piece of an **Array**. An Array is a concatenation of units combined according to some schematic principle. When Units and/or Arrays are embedded within a superordinate structure, we refer to them as **Phrases**. We use hyphens (-) to indicate concatenation between components, a Kleene star (*) to indicate repetition of components, and a slash (/) to indicate optionality between listed components. While we provide the whole hierarchy here, we describe each level in detail throughout this chapter.

Some additional features of the Complexity Hierarchy are highlighted in Table 6.1. We categorize the complexity of schemas. **Simple combinatoriality** merely specifies that units exist or become concatenated. In the case of meaningful units, simple combinatoriality means that the conceptual structures of the units (and any additional inferences they sponsor) carry all of their organizational properties. That

Table 6.1 The Complexity Hierarchy.

Combinatorial Complexity	Combinatorial Type	Schemas
Simple	One-unit	$[_{Array}$ Unit]
	Two-unit	$[_{Array}$ Unit - Unit]
	Linear	$[_{Array}$ Unit - Unit*]
Complex	Phrase structure	$[_{Array}$ Unit/Phrase*] $[_{Phrase}$ Unit - Unit] (two-unit phrase) $[_{Phrase}$ Unit*] (linear phrase)
	Categorical	$[_{Array}$ X - Y ... n]
	Recursive	$[_{Array}$ Unit/Phrase*] $[_{Phrase}$ Unit/Phrase*]

is, the schemas contribute little to the organizational structure of an array beyond the information provided from the units themselves. They package information a single unit, two-units, or linear array (the "Combinatorial Types" in Table 6.1), and their corresponding schemas are provided in the third column of Table 6.1.

In contrast, **complex combinatoriality** contributes structure to the organization of the expression, by assigning categorical roles to differentiate units and by segmenting arrays into constituents, possibly with recursive embedding of phrases. Because working memory capacity is limited, representations of distinguishable types (categories) and segmentation (simple phrase structures) are posited to facilitate the processing of more complex expressions. These combinatorial types and their schemas are provided in the bottom half of Table 6.1.

Simple combinatoriality contributes little to the manifestation of expressions, so their function is simply to concatenate the elements involved, either in a limited (one-unit, two-unit) or unlimited (linear) array. This only requires a cognitive principle of *linearization*. In addition to these linearization mechanisms, complex combinatoriality yields embedding (simple phrase, recursive) involving *hierarchical* processing, facilitated by the cognitive operation of Unification, a principle of assembling schematic structures (Jackendoff 2002). The distinctions between simple and complex combinatoriality within the Complexity Hierarchy characterize the processing functions of linearization and hierarchy. These principles are fundamental in many models of language and cognition (Boeckx, Martinez-Alvarez, and Leivada 2014, Coopmans et al. 2021, Dehaene et al. 2015, Fitch 2014, Kemmerer 2012, Matchin and Hickok 2019, Zaccarella and Friederici 2017).

Indeed, other models posit similar mechanisms operating in the neurocognition of human sequencing. Dehaene et al. (2015) for example propose five types of sequence knowledge: 1) transitions and timing, 2) chunking, 3) ordinal knowledge, 4) algebraic patterns, and 5) nested tree structures. In our terms, both transitions/timing and ordinal knowledge involve linear sequencing, only based on the relational properties of the units (i.e., ordered vs. unordered). Dehaene et al.'s chunking corresponds with phrase structures, allowing a single level of embedding or segmentation. Algebraic patterns distinguish strings into salient types beyond tokens, which corresponds well to a notion of categorization of those strings. Finally, nested tree structures involve multiple levels of embedding, characteristic of hierarchy and recursion. Dehaene et al.'s taxonomy therefore aligns well with the Complexity Hierarchy, modeling the basic principles of combinatoriality in human cognition. Such principles are domain-general and applicable across all structures within our model (modalities, grammars, meanings), and also to cognitive systems involving sequencing and hierarchy (perception, event structure, etc.).

This abstraction enables us to describe both the structure of arrays and the structures that may persist within individual units. This results in not only having complex utterances consisting of simple units, but also simple utterances potentially consisting of complex units, depending on the levels at which the segmentation applies.

Here we now clarify distinctions between omnia systems and semia systems outlined in the first chapter, which were distinguished by the presence or absence of grammar. We can now better characterize these types in terms of their combinatorial complexity. Omnia (and sequentia) are characterized by complex combinatoriality and semia are characterized by simple combinatoriality, as motivated by this Complexity Hierarchy. These details will become clearer as we elaborate on the traits of each of these combinatorial types and corresponding schemas.

6.1.1 One-Unit Schemas

The simplest combinatoriality appears as a ***one-unit schema***, which organizes meaning into a single unit of a particular modality, thus lacking any combinatorial capacity. We formalize this as Complexity Hierarchy Schema 1 (CH-S1):

CH-S1: *One-unit schema*
[$_{Array}$ Unit]

One-unit schemas apply to all our natural expressive modalities as semia, but also extend to other behaviors. For example, if they stand alone, one-unit schemas manifest in a single note or the single ring of a gong or a clock. They could also be a single mark made on a tree, rock, etc., or a single light flash (as in traffic signs). Such utterances remain as one-unit expressions.

6.1.1.1 Vocal One-Unit Schemas

Examples of single units in vocal expressions include single monomorphemic words. While all words may be characterized as single units, they most often take part in more complex grammatical structures. One-unit schemas are canonically used in words encoded to only be one unit long. These words cannot function as parts-of-speech in more complex grammatical structures (although we will discuss this point later on). For example, words like *abracadabra*, *gadzooks*, *ouch!*, or *ummmmm* ... do not interface with syntactic categories (like nouns or verbs) that function in sentence structures (Jackendoff 2002, Jackendoff and Wittenberg 2014).

In addition, ideophones, like *pow* or *kablam*, form an extensive class in many languages, which generally maintain morphosyntactic independence—i.e., one-unit types—from their sentence contexts (Dingemanse 2017). A formalized example of the onomatopoeia *pow* is in Figure 6.1ai, where the modality corresponds to an array of a single unit, which expresses the conceptual structure of a sound-emission for an impact. This schematization can also be generalized for almost all ideophones (Figure 6.1aii).

One-unit schemas can also characterize the one-word stage of speech development, where a single word can take on multiple meanings (Wittenberg and Jackendoff 2023). For example, as formalized in Figure 6.1b, when a child utters the word *cookie* it may mean the child wants a cookie (Figure 6.1bi), whereby only the conceptual structure for *cookie* is expressed (co-indexed across structures with "1"), and the predicate (WANT) and agent (I) remain unexpressed. This correspondence between an expressed word of

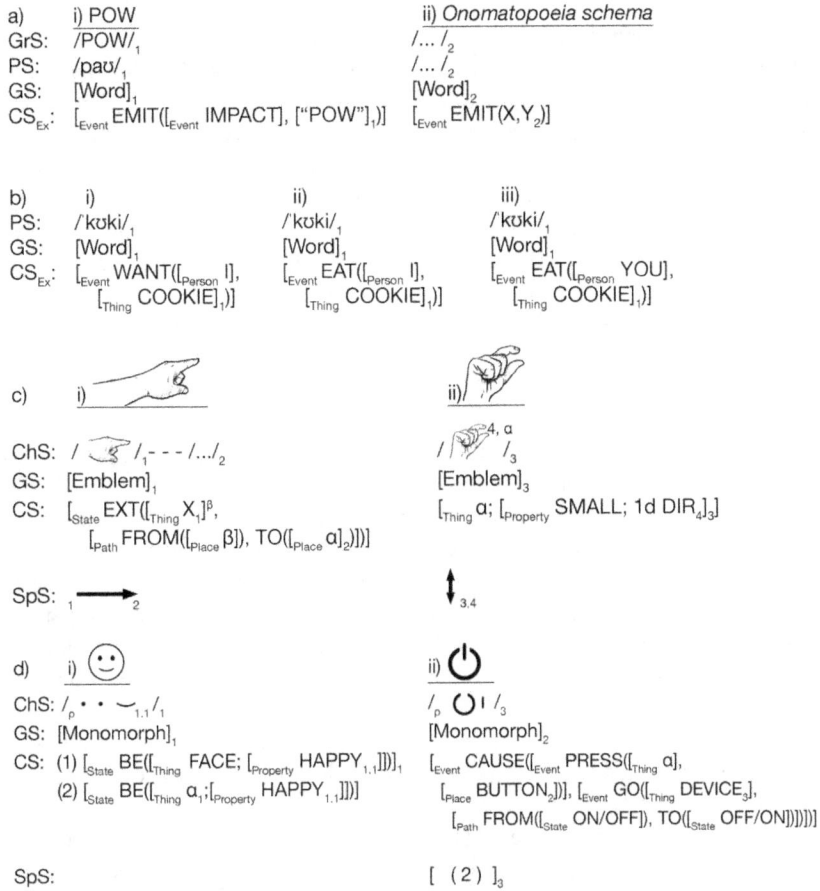

Figure 6.1 One-unit schemas in expressions in a) onomatopoeia, b) two-word speech, c) gestures, and d) visual signs.

cookie and an unexpressed predicate and agent maintains in other possible utterances of the word, such as if the child is eating a cookie (Figure 6.1bii), sees someone else eating a cookie (Figure 6.1biii), and many other possible interpretations that would be known to the child, but would require pragmatic inference for the child's interlocutors.

Note that in our formalization, we notate *cookie* here simply as a word. This maintains the spirit of these utterances being only one-unit arrays, which have not yet taken on the distributional properties displayed by grammatical categories, like nouns. While *cookie* may be a noun within a mature English speaker's mental lexicon, a child at the one-word stage of development has not necessarily demonstrated acquisition of such distributional intuitions. Figuring out such grammatical categories through their distributions is part of the challenge of acquiring language.

6.1.1.2 Bodily One-Unit Schemas

In the bodily modality, most gesticulations use one-unit schemas which cannot be put into a coherent sequence (Gawne and Cooperrider 2022, Goldin-Meadow 2003a, McNeill 1992). Gestural emblems would also be characterized by one-unit schemas which are form-meaning interfaces in the bodily modality, such as thumbs-up or down, waving as a greeting, and many gestural explicatives. We have already formalized some of these gestures in prior chapters. We repeat these formalizations for a pointing gesture (Figure 6.1ci) and a pinching gesture (Figure 6.1cii). Gesticulations are bodily movements whereby the form is not regularized in the mental lexicon, but most often appear as single units. In co-speech gestures, these forms typically appear at a rate of once per spoken clause.

6.1.1.3 Graphic One-Unit Schemas

One-unit schemas are used in the graphic modality in individual pictures. These may be simple graphic expressions like emoji, icons, or other pictographs (Cohn, Engelen, and Schilperoord 2019). For example, a simple smiley-face emoji is formalized in Figure 6.1di. Here, the graphic structure of the face corresponds to a single-unit monomorph, which has an iconic representation (1) as a face that is in the state of being happy. An extended, contextual conceptual structure (2) may instead place the agent of being happy as a pragmatically defined element, be it the communicator, the overall sentiment of an utterance, etc. We formalize this as an alpha (α) which is in a state of being happy.

As another example, consider the picture typically used as a power button on devices. Our knowledge of this button is formalized in Figure 6.1dii. This is also structurally a single-unit monomorph, which carries the expression that a user (α) who presses it causes the device to go from off to on (or vice versa). This button also carries a Spatial Structure of the knowledge that it (subscript 2) is placed somewhere on a device (subscript 3).

Single-unit expressions can also manifest as complex compositions of whole scenes, as we find in paintings, advertisements, editorial cartoons, and others. Though these complex compositions may persist as single-unit utterances, this does not imply that they do not have internal complexity. Indeed, within their status as a one-unit utterance, they may be composed of complex combinatoriality, as we will discuss below. Such cases can persist because of the specific representational systems that may distinguish complexity at different levels, for example morphological structures may vary in their complexity while simultaneously acting as a unit for the varying complexity of grammatical structures.

6.1.2 Two-Unit Schema

An incrementally more complex combinatoriality occurs in a ***two-unit schema***, when an expression is restricted to having only two componential parts. We formalize this as:

CH-S2: *Two-unit schema*
[$_{Array}$ Unit - Unit]

Arrays using two-unit schemas can vary in the dependency of their component parts. Units can be either *free*, meaning that they can stand alone, or **bound**, meaning that they must combine with a free unit. For example, bound units are characterized by affixation in morphological structure, which occurs in all modalities. As will be demonstrated, these characteristics of free and bound properties of units persist throughout almost all levels of the Complexity Hierarchy. Across modalities, two-unit schemas also often involve a wide range of implicit construals between juxtaposed units, as will be demonstrated.

6.1.2.1 Vocal Two-Unit Schemas

Jackendoff and Wittenberg (2014) argue that two-unit utterances in speech characterize the nature of children's two-word stage of language learning where only two slots seem available for a range of argument structures. For example, the utterance *Mommy cookie* may mean *Mommy eats a cookie*, *Do you want a cookie Mommy?*, *Give me a cookie Mommy*, and others. We formalize these in Figure 6.2. Essentially, in all cases the expressed elements (subscripted 1 and 2) are the arguments for Mommy and Cookie, while the binding predicate between them remains unexpressed.

These forms also exist in constrained utterances like greetings (*Hello X, Goodbye X*) or epithets (*Fuck X*), and manifest within individual units formed of two component parts, like forms of address (*Ms. X, Governor X, Professor X*) and pivot schemas (*Lake X* vs. *X Lake, Mount X* vs. *X Mountain*). Such constraints also characterize simple compounds, which involve a wide range of meaningful relations between units. Jackendoff (2009a, 2010a) counts up to 14 basic conceptual relations in compounding, including classification (*Molotov cocktail*), similarity (*baby doll*), composition (*strawberry pie*), possession (*writer's cramp*), causation (*sunburn*), and several others.

We may also consider affixation as using a two-unit schema that concatenates a unit to another, only with different characteristics given to the properties of those types, i.e., the stem-unit could also potentially exist on its own, while the affix-unit cannot. Here, the elements of the two-unit array involve one that is free and another that is bound. This contrasts with the two-unit arrays already discussed, which would consist of two free units.

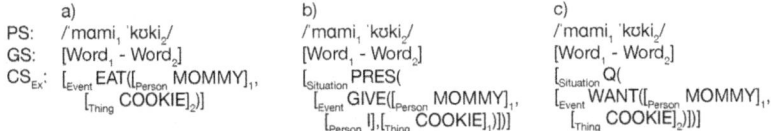

Figure 6.2 A two-unit child utterance *Mommy cookie* meaning a) *Mommy eats a cookie*, b) *Give me a cookie Mommy*, c) *Do you want a cookie Mommy?*

6.1.2.2 Bodily Two-Unit Schemas

In the bodily modality, two-unit sequences have been studied especially in regard to sign languages (particularly emerging sign languages) and homesign. Two-unit arrays structure the production of signs or gestures that consist of smaller, but also meaningful signs. If the meaning of those larger structures is compositional from the units, it results in a bodily phrase, but if it cannot, it results in a bodily compound. Both of these circumstances are frequent in sign language and gesturing. Two-unit compounding has been shown to be a highly regularized and productive mechanism in combining (two) signs (Meir, Aronoff, et al. 2010). Signed compounds display properties similar to those schemas in other modalities, such as head-modifier or coordinated units. The compound status of two-unit signs is also apparent in sign compounds, like the combination of signs for *bed* and *soft* in American Sign Language to create the sign of *pillow*.

Two-unit schemas also underlie the phrases or first-stage sentences produced by homesigners (Goldin-Meadow 2003b). These two-unit utterances not only concatenate smaller signs into larger ones, but they also benefit from using the first or second position of two-unit schemas to convey basic semantic relations. These schematic slots are filled systematically with preferences for certain semantic heuristics, including: entities are preferred to occur before actions or recipients, actions to occur before recipients, and actors to appear before actions. This patterning persists in homesigns from various cultures, no matter the spoken language in the child's environment. These deaf children cannot access such spoken patterns, and they are not receiving these cues for their homesigns from the influence of their caregivers. In fact, similar sequencing appears for the gestures produced by speaking individuals when they are restricted to only communicate using their hands and without speaking (Gershoff-Stowe and Goldin-Meadow 2002, Goldin-Meadow et al. 2008). Under our interpretation, when limited to only two slots, these productions would characterize a two-unit array with a variety of possibilities for their correspondences to Conceptual Structure.

6.1.2.3 Graphic Two-Unit Schemas

In the graphic modality, utterances comprising two-units are used across several constructions consisting of two pictures. These patterned forms may express yes/no contrasts (as in signs showing which foods one can and cannot have in a classroom), or they may show pairs of images denoting before-after causal relations between depicted states or comparisons between depicted items (Plug et al. in prep., Schilperoord and Cohn 2023).

Consider the examples in Figure 6.3a, which all use a common before-after pattern where the first panel shows an object or situation in one state, and then the second panel shows the same object or situation in a different state. The inference here is that the object has changed from one state to the next, motivated by some causative force which is the topic of the sequence. For example, if a shirt goes from dirty to clean, the topical causative force is likely detergent that an advertisement is selling. We formalize this in Figure 6.3a. The graphic structure here specifies two juxtaposed regions (ρ_1 and ρ_2)

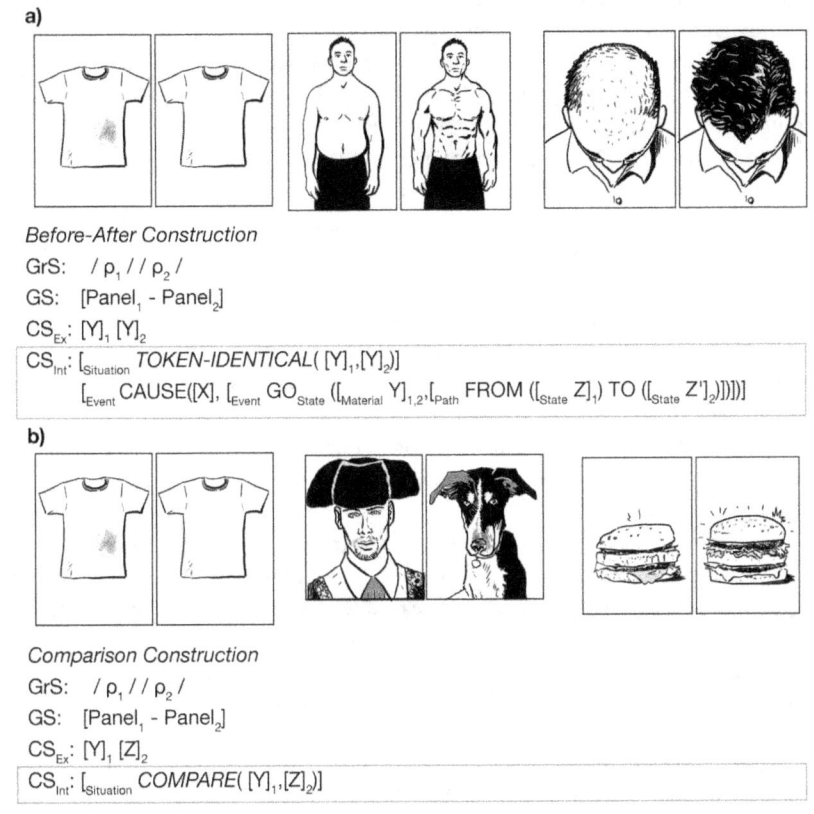

Figure 6.3 Two-unit visual arrays using a) a Before-After Construction and b) a Comparison Construction.

which correspond to the two-unit array of two panels. Panels here are an encapsulated unit that may contain a range of morphologically complex internal parts, as will be discussed further on. These panels correspond to a Conceptual Structure whereby a state, property, or feature of a material (Y) goes from a before state (Z) to an after state (Z'). This change in states is caused by some entity "X," which can be a range of semantic categories (Thing, Event, etc.). We call this the ***Before-After Construction*** or BA-Construction (Schilperoord and Cohn 2023), which has several constraints which are demonstrable in violations of the canonical structure, such as when the objects in each panel are no longer coreferential (for example, showing a skinny person in the first panel and a muscular person in the second panel to imply that the person has gained muscle, only to actually show two entirely different people).

Another two-unit construction occurs when showing different objects in each of the panels, as in the examples in Figure 6.3b followed by their formalization. Here, the regions correspond to panels that express different materials (Y and Z), with the construal that the viewer can compare these materials or properties in order to make sense of their juxtaposition. For example, the juxtaposition of a dirty shirt and a clean shirt might not show the change over time, but may simply be comparing two different shirts, in which case the shirts depicted in each panel would not be coreferential (i.e., with no inference of being token-identical). Another example may invite analogies through the comparison. The juxtaposition of an eagle and an airplane in a travel advertisement may invite you to map properties from the eagle to the plane, i.e., that the plane moves as fast as an eagle, and thus is a good way to travel. Other construals may evoke similarities between how something looks, like the man and dog in Figure 6.3b, or the features of components, like quality of different hamburgers in Figure 6.3b. We call this the **Comparison Construction** (Schilperoord and Cohn 2023).

The Before-After and Comparison Constructions use different types of unexpressed construals for negotiating the relationship between two visual images. A different construal would also persist in the yes/no contrasts where one image shows what is allowed (water in a classroom, acceptable items to throw in a toilet, etc.) and one image shows what is not allowed (food in a classroom, unacceptable items to throw in a toilet, etc.). These combinations are loosely comparable to verbal compounds, with a wide range of relational construals.

Two-unit arrays also arise when people communicate in "sentences" with emoji, that use only two units and omit what could be (perhaps generously) characterized as grammatical subjects or objects. Figure 6.4a shows the formalization of a two-unit emoji sequence produced within the experiment of Cohn, Engelen, and Schilperoord (2019) where participants had a conversation with each other using only emoji. Here, a participant conveyed "booking a flight" with 📚 ✈. The verb *book* here was conveyed with a pile of books as a rebus (that is, using the typical phonology associated with the object "book" but discarding its iconic meaning), while the plane emoji indicates the event of a *flight*, specified through flight being a classification of a plane-flight. This creates an unexpressed phonological association that carries with it the verbal idiom *book a flight* and its syntax and semantics. Because of this, we have conflicting sets of conceptual structures. The graphic conceptual structure only conveys an object of a book (subscript 1) and of a plane (subscript 2), while the associated vocal conceptual structure conveys two events (to book and to fly). The integrated CS inherits the vocal meaning, but uses the rebus meaning of "book" as in "reserve" (without the expressed object meaning) and the "flight" meaning of the emoji draws on the metonymy of the object of "plane" expressed through the alpha binding. These two emoji are graphically monomorphs in a two-unit array, which, because of the rebus, also have correspondences to a syntactic structure.

Pictures as single units may also use two-units with visual affixation. For example, many signs float above characters' heads (gears to mean thinking, hearts to mean love, lightbulb to mean inspiration, etc.) as a visual affix related to the emotional or cognitive state of the person (Cohn 2013b, Cohn and Foulsham 2022, Cohn, Murthy, and Foulsham 2016). Other visual morphemes in comics and cartoons involve lines to show motion, sweat drops to show anxiety, and a range of other signs. Such bound morphemes have also been applied outside the natural graphic modality to tool-mediated use of photographs or video, such as in placing hearts above the head or in

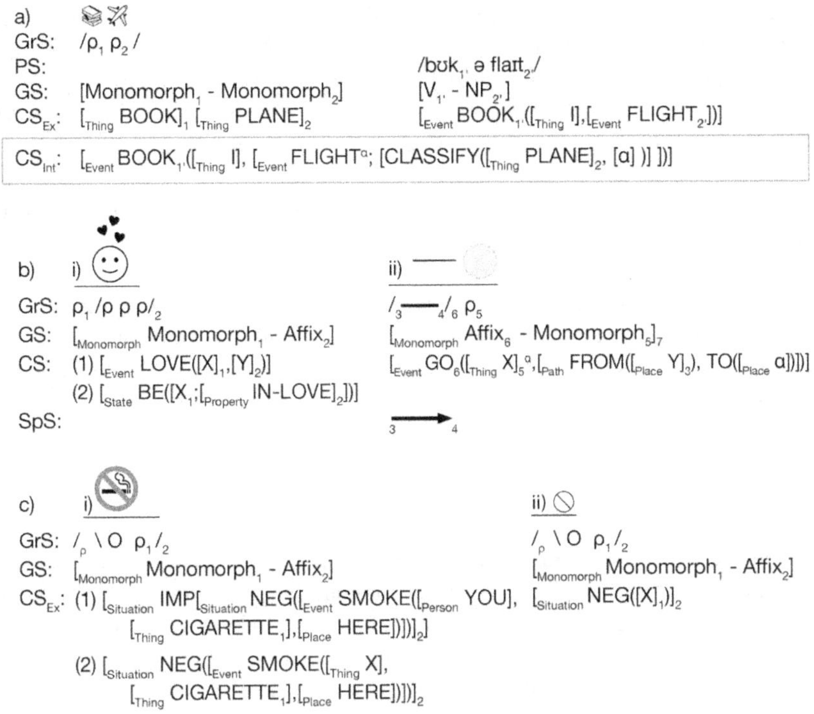

a) 📚✈️
GrS: /ρ₁ ρ₂/
PS:
GS: [Monomorph₁ - Monomorph₂]   [V₁, - NP₂,]   /bʊk₁, ə flaɪt₂/
CS_Ex: [_Thing BOOK]₁ [_Thing PLANE]₂   [_Event BOOK₁,([_Thing I],[_Event FLIGHT₂])]

CS_Int: [_Event BOOK₁,([_Thing I], [_Event FLIGHTᵃ; [CLASSIFY([_Thing PLANE]₂, [a])])])]

b) i) 😊💕   ii) ———▶
GrS: ρ₁ /ρ ρ ρ/₂   /₃———₄/₆ ρ₅
GS: [_Monomorph Monomorph₁ - Affix₂]   [_Monomorph Affix₆ - Monomorph₅]₇
CS: (1) [_Event LOVE([X]₁,[Y]₂)]   [_Event GO₆([_Thing X]₅ᵃ,[_Path FROM([_Place Y]₃), TO([_Place a])])]
     (2) [_State BE([X₁;[_Property IN-LOVE]₂])]
SpS: ₃———▶₄

c) i) 🚭   ii) 🚫
GrS: /_p \O ρ₁/₂   /_p \O ρ₁/₂
GS: [_Monomorph Monomorph₁ - Affix₂]   [_Monomorph Monomorph₁ - Affix₂]
CS_Ex: (1) [_Situation IMP[_Situation NEG([_Event SMOKE([_Person YOU],   [_Situation NEG([X]₁)]₂
             [_Thing CIGARETTE₁],[_Place HERE])])]₂]
        (2) [_Situation NEG([_Event SMOKE([_Thing X],
             [_Thing CIGARETTE₁],[_Place HERE])])]₂

Figure 6.4 Two-unit schemas in the graphic modality including a) an emoji rebus, b) visual affixes of heart upfixes and a motion line, c) a negation affix.

the eyes of real people using mobile apps with "filters." Such filters apply principles of visual morphology to realistic percepts mediated through technological tools.

We formalize two visual affixes in Figure 6.4b. First, consider an affix of a heart floating above a character's head, in Figure 6.4bi. Here, the heart is an affix bound to the stem of the head, a monomorph that could stand alone as a free morpheme. This representation typically has two possible meanings, indicating either that the person loves someone (an event), or that the person is in love (a state). A second visual affix of a straight motion line is formalized in Figure 6.4bii. In this case, the motion line indicates a path of a moving object. The start of the line marks the source (FROM) of the path, while the end of the line depicts the goal (TO). The moving object is located at the end of the line, and thus is bound with the goal (a). This path is also reflected in a Spatial Structure of a one-dimensional directional vector.

In addition, many street signs morphologically use two-units where an outer, encapsulating representation (yellow triangle, blue circle, red outline, etc.) gives a predicate to whatever is depicted inside it or superimposed on it (e.g., a bicycle inside a blue circle, inside a red outline, etc.). A similar construction persists in the widespread use of the visual negation sign (Figure 6.4cii), which has an open slot within the circle for whatever is negated (Giora et al. 2009, Oversteegen and Schilperoord 2014). We formalize this in Figure 6.4ci for the no-smoking sign, and in Figure 6.4cii for the generalized construction. Here, the negation sign is an affix which surrounds a monomorph (which may have its own internal complexity). This corresponds to a predicate that negates what the monomorph depicts, which can be an event ("no smoking") or an object ("no dogs"). In the case of the no-smoking sign, the monomorph depicts a cigarette, which belongs to a larger predicate of an imperative (IMP) for telling the unexpressed *you* not to *smoke* that object in some designated area (Figure 6.4ci-1). Alternatively, this sign could be expressing that smoking will not take place by anyone (X) in this location (Figure 6.4ci-2), thereby giving assurance to non-smokers. Note that in this latter interpretation, the imperative *you* is no longer inferred and it instead becomes a declarative. Once again, this two-unit array depicts certain elements, but leaves a substantial amount to be inferred.

6.1.3 Linear Schema

The least limited simple combinatoriality uses a **linear schema**, which imposes no constraints on the number of units that become concatenated into an utterance. These semia allow for longer strings of expressions, without combinatorial complexity. We clarify here that "linear" is not used to mean a particular presentation (i.e., "in a line"), but rather a simple concatenation of units, no matter their manifested presentation given the constraints of a particular modality (i.e., in a sequence, a grid, simultaneous presentation, etc.). We formalize this as:

CH-S3: *Linear schema*
$[_{Array} \text{Unit - Unit*}]$

In linear schemas, the representations of the units determine their relationships to each other, which can result in different ordering within an array. An **unordered linear schema** imposes no structure on the order of the expression, resulting in a relatively free order that could be rearranged without consequence. This corresponds to transitions and timing from Dehaene et al. (2015), and to the mathematical notion of "set" that has also been invoked for human sequencing (Uddén et al. 2020). In contrast, an **ordered linear schema** does impose restrictions on the arrangement of the units within the expression, corresponding to Dehaene et al.'s (2015) ordinal knowledge, and to the mathematical notion of a "sequence" (Uddén et al. 2020). We formalize these possibilities below, with curly brackets indicating the unrestricted order, and subscripts emphasizing the ordinal sequencing:

CH-S3: *Linear schema subtypes*
    a) Unordered ("set") - $\{_{Array} \text{Unit - Unit*}\}$
    b) Ordered ("sequence") - $[_{Array} \text{Unit}_1 \text{ - Unit}_2 \ldots \text{Unit}_n]$

6.1.3.1 Unordered Linear Schemas

Unordered linear schemas typically correspond to semantic fields which are basic lists associated by a binding conceptual category. Classic work in psycholinguistics has found that processing of items is facilitated when participants are provided the superordinate category prior to the list (Bransford and Johnson 1972, St. George, Mannes, and Hoffinan 1994). However, if the superordinate category is not specified overtly, this binding concept must be inferred. Consider both the textual and graphic lists in Figure 6.5a. Here, the items (beer, pretzels, pizza, football) are unordered units within an array, and could be rearranged with little consequence on its well-formedness. Each of these items corresponds to an expressed thing or event that can be integrated into a larger category of something like RECREATION. However, this category is not overtly expressed, and thus receives no coindexation into the modality, thereby leaving the binding association between elements to be inferred.

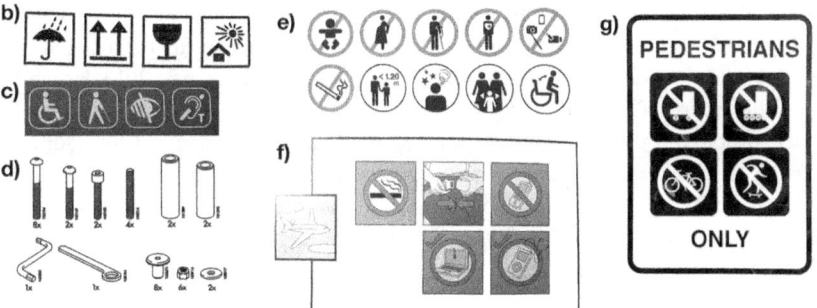

h) *Unordered linear arrays (lists)*
FS: / $X_1, Y_2, Z_3 ... n_4$ /
GS: {$_{Array}$ Unit$_1$ - Unit$_2$ - Unit$_3$ ... Unit$_4$ }
CS$_{Ex}$: [X]$_1$, [Y]$_2$, [Z]$_3$ ... [n]$_4$
CS$_{Int}$: [$_{Category}$ F([X]$_1$, [Y]$_2$, [Z]$_3$ ... [n]$_4$)]

Figure 6.5 Unordered linear arrays including a) a formalization of a visual list of emoji, and linear arrays from b) the side of a box, c) an airport sign, d) a furniture assembly manual, e) a rollercoaster ride, f) an airplane safety manual, and g) a park sign; h) shows a general schema for unordered linear arrays.

Unordered linear schemas are used verbally in various lists, such as those showing the ingredients in a recipe, the tools for a project, or the items on an errand or shopping list. They also occur in the speech of some aphasics that results in a "semantic soup" of words (Jackendoff and Wittenberg 2014, 2017). Graphic unordered schemas abound in signage and instruction manuals (Cohn 2020a), where lists indicate what to do or not to do in various places (airplanes, parks, etc.) or what elements may be involved in a project (such as all the tools and parts needed for putting together a piece of furniture). We depict some of these examples in Figure 6.5b–g. Unordered linear schemas also appear when people use numerous related emoji in an unstructured way, as in Figure 6.5a, or when a person sends several emoji related to birthday parties (Cohn, Engelen, and Schilperoord 2019, Gawne and McCulloch 2019), as in: 🎂 🎁 🎈 🎉 🎊 🎁.

A general formalization of these patterns appears in Figure 6.5h. The binding category of these semantic fields often remains unexpressed, and thus appears only in the integrated conceptual structure. However, sometimes this category may be provided overtly as either a textual label or an image on its own. For example, Figure 6.5f comes from an airplane safety manual that features a list of pictures of what to do or not to do (buckle seatbelt, no smoking, etc.) next to a picture of a plane flying. This "plane flying" picture provides the overarching topic of the semantic field applying to the other pictures (i.e., these are all commands for when the plane is in flight).

6.1.3.2 Ordered Linear Schemas

Where unordered linear schemas put no semantic constraints on the arrangement of the units, ordered linear schemas do restrict their arrangement: rearranging these units alters their meaning. These constraints may involve basic semantic heuristics for the ordering of conceptual information, or they may reflect the basic ordering of event structures.

In speech, ordered linear schemas may invoke rules like agents precede patients, entities precede actions, topic first, or focus last (Cohn and Paczynski 2013, Jackendoff and Wittenberg 2014). These semantic principles allow for the guidance of word order without any contributions of the combinatorial system imposing any additional representations (i.e., the linear schema). Such linear schemas also appear in the reduced forms created when people type into search engines (Smirnova 2021), for example turning a question like "What do I do if my dog eats catnip?" into a bare form of "dog eat catnip."

Ordered linear sequencing is also argued to persist in a variety of places within bodily communication. For example, when speaking individuals are asked to communicate using only their bodies, they produce gestural orders maintaining an agent-patient-act structure, regardless of the word order of their native language (Goldin-Meadow et al. 2008). This agent-patient-act structure could arise from the interaction between heuristics of "agents precede patients" and "entities precede actions" (Cohn and Paczynski 2013). Variation from this basic ordering has also been shown to be affected by the properties of the elements (such as event reversibility or a human first heuristic), indicating that these orders arise from the pressures of the conceptual structures (Hall, Mayberry, and Ferreira 2013, Hall, Ferreira, and Mayberry 2014, Meir et al. 2017). Similarly, agent-patient-act and agent-act-patient ordering of units also most commonly arise within the homesign systems created by deaf individuals who do not receive exposure to external languages (Goldin-Meadow 2003b), and they often appear within emerging and rural sign languages that develop within small communities (de Vos and Pfau 2015).

In the graphic modality, ordered linear schemas also appear in instructions, such as providing the step-by-step procedures for doing various actions, like assembling furniture or toys, or when cooking. They may also be used in infographics, often guided by arrows between each of the ordered elements. Ordered sequences may also be produced in emoji when conveying a simple temporal sequence, such as 🌱🌿🌳. Consider the examples in Figure 6.6 along with their formalization. Here we see sequences of emoji with objects that correspond to different holidays. Figure 6.6a shows these emoji in the order that those holidays would appear throughout a year, while Figure 6.6b rearranges this chronological order. Figure 6.6a thus uses an ordered linear schema in the grammatical structure (with square brackets), while Figure 6.6b uses an unordered linear schema (curly brackets).

With regard to their Conceptual Structure, these emoji each directly express objects or people. However, they all metonymically connect to holidays of the year, which we here notate as belonging to the integrated conceptual structure similar to our analysis of unordered sequences above. We will not provide the formalization here for establishing such metonymy, but we note the connections between these objects and their corresponding events through their indices. Holidays receive a bar-notation (ex. 1') corresponding to their associated objects (ex. 1).

A second metonymy associates the holidays to the months they occur, notated with double-bars (ex. 1"), recognized as belonging to a stored chronology. We store similar orderings for our schematic ordinal knowledge of meals of the day, days of the week, letters of the alphabet, etc., often referred to as "scripts" (Schank and Abelson 1977). We bring this background knowledge to our understanding of this ordered sequence of emoji. While this knowledge may be recognized for the unordered version of these elements as well, it is not activated in their interpretation (outside of,

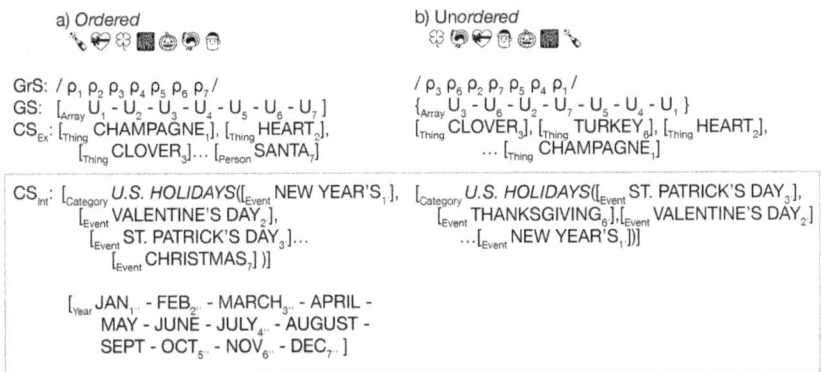

Figure 6.6 a) Ordered and b) unordered arrays for the same visual units of U.S. Holidays.

162   *A Multimodal Language Faculty*

potentially, the recognition that they are indeed out of their chronological order). This second, unordered version could potentially be rearranged into any order other than the chronological one and maintain a similar construal. In cases like this, we could imagine a generalized structure similar to Figure 6.5h, just with the added script of stored ordinal knowledge. Thus, the ordered versus unordered quality of these schemas is motivated by the semantics of the elements that are sequenced, not imposed by the schema itself.

An additional example of an ordered linear schema comes from step-by-step instruction manuals. These appear in science diagrams, assembly instructions (furniture, Legos, etc.), recipes, and others. Consider Figure 6.7, which shows typical instructions for putting on an oxygen mask from an airplane safety manual. This sequence shows a series of events (meant to be imitated by the passenger) where a woman reaches for a mask (panel 1), puts it over her head (panel 2), tightens the

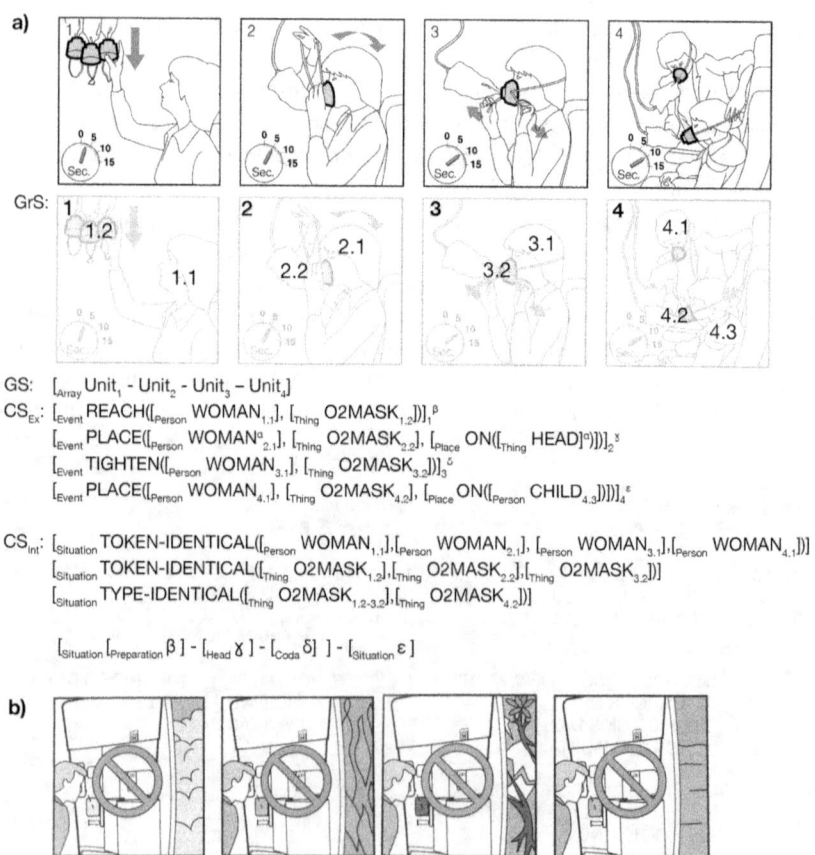

Figure 6.7 Linear arrays that are a) ordered and b) unordered from airplane safety manuals.

mask to her face (panel 3), and then helps place a mask on a child (panel 4). In our formalization in Figure 6.7a, we simplify the notation to the primary events, and leave out additional information such as that provided by the arrows. We also skip over extensively formalizing partitive knowledge (such as that the head belongs to the woman in panel 2, which we shorthand through the alpha-binding).[1]

The meaning of each of these panels is specified in $CS_{Expression}$. The integration of these events into a larger event structure guides our understanding of them as occurring in this particular order. Unlike the semantic fields bound within unordered linear sequencing above, the panels here do not offer you a set of options to be carried out in any particular order, but instead the integrated event structure guides this order.

Though these panels convey complex event structures, the linear schema involves only relationships between each pair of adjacent panels, and the event structure drives the ordering. The first three panels create a constituent for their events (woman putting on a mask), but this event is not the preparation for the subsequent event with the child. Rather, the presentation of these independent events belongs to an ordered linear schema, while the constituency belongs solely to the event structure. We express this in Figure 6.7a by the linear schema in the grammatical structures having no internal constituents.

In addition, panels do not seem to play roles outside their meaning. As we will see further on, images can play functional roles in a narrative structure, such as to set-up, climax, or resolve a sequence. However, this instruction manual sequence conveys no such functional properties for the panels. They merely convey the properties of events (preparation, head, coda) without additional guidance from a narrative categorization. Evidence for the lack of functional roles comes from the relative possibilities for units to be deleted. Narrative categories have relative preferences for their deletion from a sequence, with some being more acceptably deleted than others (Cohn 2014b). However, this instruction manual maintains no such relative preferences for different panels.

In addition, ordered linear schemas often involve coreference of elements across panels. We know that the woman and the mask are the same in each panel. This differs from the ordered sequence of holiday emoji in Figure 6.6a, which had no such repetition. By repeating similar-looking characters across panels, a comprehender may be motivated to assess their relative similarities and differences, establish them as referring to the same entities (i.e., the continuity constraint), and thus order them in connection with event structures motivated by the perceived changes across panels (i.e., the activity constraint). The presence of coreference thus contributes to the understanding of a visual sequence being ordered.

Nevertheless, this semantic dimension of coreference is orthogonal to ordered versus unordered sequencing. As we saw in Figure 6.6, it is possible to have an ordered linear sequence with no coreference across images. In addition, coreference can also occur without being ordered. Consider the array in Figure 6.7b, which is from another airplane safety manual. Here a person looks out the window at a variety of disastrous possibilities (smoke, fire, forest debris, or water). In each image, the exact same lines are used for the person, which could motivate a coreferential interpretation. Yet, this does not necessarily motivate the sense of ordering. We do not interpret this array as a single person having a very bad day: first seeing smoke, then fire, then debris, and then water, in this particular order. Rather, this is a list of possible circumstances that a passenger might encounter in a plane disaster, with the recommendation not to open the door if they experience anything of this list. Any order of these panels would motivate the same unordered meaning.

6.1.4 Simple Phrase Schemas

In contrast to simple combinatoriality, complex combinatoriality contributes representational structure to the constituent parts. ***Simple phrase schemas*** segment a sequence into constituent parts with one level of embedding, formalized as:

CH-S4: *Simple phrase schemas*
a. [$_{Array}$ Unit/Phrase*]
b1. [$_{Phrase}$ Unit - Unit] (two-unit phrase)
b2. [$_{Phrase}$ Unit*] (linear phrase)

First, the schema of the expression (Array) specifies that it either contains Units or Phrases to an unrestricted amount, as indicated by the Kleene star (*). A "Phrase" in this context specifies a segment embedded within the larger scheme, which can manifest as one of two types, in line with the prior types described already: a two-unit phrase or a linear phrase. This formalism effectively specifies that a simple phrase schema embeds linear types inside of other linear types resulting in a single level of embedding.

Because linear schemas provide no structure of their own to an expression, they may become difficult to process or remember at larger lengths. Embedding provided by a simple phrase schema may offer a way to represent chunking that facilitates storage and memorization. Thus, the claim is that simple phrase schemas—and phrase structures more generally—use memory capacity more effectively, giving rise to the possibility of more complex behaviors.

Simple phrase schemas arise in several systems. If a system only uses simple phrase schemas and no categorical roles for units (discussed in the next section), they may fall in a middle-ground between omnia and semia. Some fully developed languages are fairly restrictive in their combinatorial embedding, only reaching the level of a simple phrase schema in their grammars (Jackendoff and Wittenberg 2014). Like the use of linear schemas, in these systems, simple embedding may interact with semantic heuristics, or potentially more complex grammatical structures that just happen to be restricted in their embedding structure.

In the graphic form, various instruction manuals use simple phrase schemas to convey a particular order of sub-actions. For example, Figure 6.8 shows how to pull out a sofa-bed or return it to being a couch. Each process of pulling-it-out or pushing-it-back involves a linear order of the events, similar to the sequence of events in the examples for ordered linear schemas above. However, each of these sequences forms a cluster, which are arranged relative to each other in an unordered linear array, since the whole events of pushing or pulling the sofa can happen in either order. At this higher

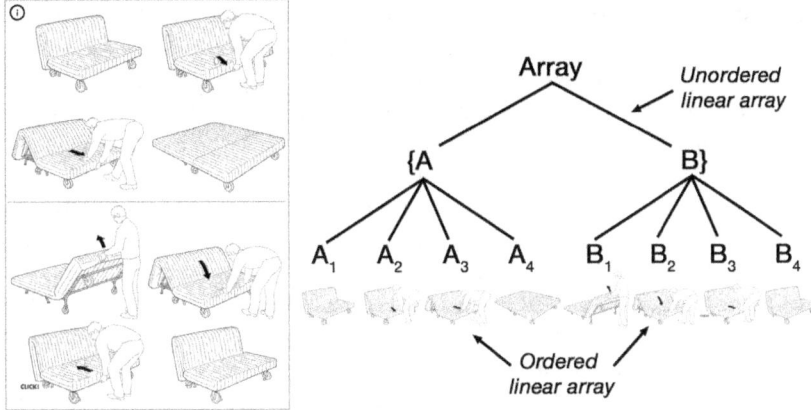

Figure 6.8 An instructional manual that uses a simple phrase schema, where linear ordered constituents are embedded within an unordered linear sequence.

level, there is not necessarily a binding semantic relationship (e.g., the first sequence could be said to cause or set up the second, but the same would be true in reverse). This creates a single level of embedding where ordered linear sequences are organized within a larger unordered linear array.

Simple phrase schemas can also characterize the basic embedding found in other systems. For example, phonological structure involves simple phrase schemas in the embedding structure of syllables (Selkirk 1984). Each syllable consists of an onset and a rhyme, with the rhyme consisting of a nucleus and coda. Syllables are then ordered linearly within spoken utterances, but with no additional embedding structure (though they may exist in parallel with other higher-order structures involved in prosody or intonation).

6.1.5 Categorical Schemas

In *categorical schemas*, called "part-of-speech grammars" by Jackendoff and Wittenberg (2014), units play functional roles with varying salience and distributions in an array. Though we list simple phrase schemas and categorical schemas sequentially, they maintain the same level of complexity. Because categorical schemas reflect system-internal regularities, they represent the shift into omnia systems. We formalize categorical schemas abstractly as:

CH-S5: *Categorical schemas:*
$[_{Array} X - Y \ldots n]$

In this abstracted formalism, multiple units are distinguished in their categorization, with X and Y representing units of different categories, and the potential for additional numbers of such categories (n). Categories of units result from an abstraction across patterned tokens which come to belong to different types, thereby resulting in the tokens inheriting the salience of the types. For example, the categorical role of a noun applies to many different conceptual categories (e.g., things: the *dog*, events: the *dance*, properties: the *redness*, etc.). In addition, nouns have many distributional patterns inside the schemas of the syntax of various languages, which are maintained internally to the structures of those systems (e.g., nouns are modified by adjectives, and fulfill roles as Subjects and Objects of sentences in relation to verbs). Through this abstraction, various specific words with a range of meanings can play the same grammatical roles (nouns, verbs) within various grammatical patterns.

While our broad categorical schema thus characterizes category assignment, their ordering becomes specified in the various constructions found in representational systems. The category of noun is specified in various syntactic constructions, both generalizable across spoken and signed languages but also specific to diverse languages. This tension between the language-specificity versus language-generality of grammatical categories has given rise to debates over the universality of various grammatical categories (Evans and Levinson 2009, Haspelmath 2018). Examples from English might be that a clause consists of a noun, verb, and noun, in that order, [$_{\text{Clause}}$ N—V—N], while a noun phrase consists of a determiner, adjective, and noun, in that order, [$_{\text{NP}}$ Det—Adj—N].

Because categorical schemas generalize across individual tokens, their combination can yield the same structures with different words. For example, as in Figure 6.9a, the sentences *The woman ate a hamburger in the park* and *A thief stole the purse from the granny* both have a common syntactic structure, using the same grammatical categories in the same order. Though these categories may be similar on the surface, in more complex arrays, how they combine may require higher-order relations (such as that the prepositions *in the park* and *from the granny* connect differently to their preceding clauses). This variability in constituency is not covered by categorical schemas alone, and requires machinery at a higher level, as discussed below.

This entrenched structure also allows for combining words with categorical roles into a felicitous schematic order, but which may lack a cohesive meaning. The sentence *Some water dreamed a bagel on the moon* has the same structure as the other example sentences, but makes substantially less sense. This observation was popularized by Chomsky's (1957) famous sentence *Colorless green ideas sleep furiously*, but this idea precedes his work (Goldsmith and Laks 2019). Psycholinguistic research on syntactic-only sentences like these has confirmed that syntactic structure provides a processing benefit beyond scrambled orders of words (Marslen-Wilson and Tyler 1980) but remains independent of semantic processing (Van Petten and Kutas 1991).

Categorical roles also persist at other levels of representation. Below the syntactic unit, morphological structure involves potential categories of "word" and "affix" among others, as defined again by the abstracted relations across patterns of tokens. In addition, structure can also correspond to a level of meaning higher than that typically found in sentences, with narrative roles assigned to clauses of speech or signs, parts of text, or pictures (or film shots) in a visual narrative sequence, among other contexts (Cohn 2013c, Labov and Waletzky 1967). Such categories are often characterized by

Figure 6.9 Structural categories in a) three sentences, including one with well-formed syntax but incongruous semantics, and b) three visual narratives, including one with well-formed narrative grammar but incongruous semantics.

the classical notions of narrative, such as Aristotle's three-act structure of Beginning-Middle-End, or by Gustav Freytag's (1894) triangular five-act structure. In our own work, we have posited a structure of [$_{Arc}$ Establisher-Initial-Peak-Release] which constitutes a canonical schematic structure within a larger narrative grammar (Cohn 2013c). Indeed, no matter the specific models of narrative categorization, functional roles for units across theories remain consistent (Brewer 1985, Cohn 2013c, Cutting 2016).

These narrative roles can be identified by distributional patterns in their arrays, as determined by tests like deletions, rearrangements, substitutions, and other such diagnostics typical of syntactic research (Cohn 2020b, 2015b, a, 2014b). However, narrative categories may maintain prototypical correspondences to aspects of event structure, such that the initiation (Initial), climax (Peak), and resolution (Release) may ideally interface with the preparation, head, and coda of an event (Cohn 2013c). This would be parallel to the ways that syntactic categories have prototypical correspondences to aspects of conceptual structure (thing-noun, event-verb, etc.), though structural categories themselves are not semantic categories.

Recent work has demonstrated that these narrative categories are separable from the meaningful elements that they arrange, and are not reducible to states of characters' goals or to the specific events that they contain (Cohn 2020b). Consider the three sequences in Figure 6.9b. All of these sequences maintain a similar structure of a location (Orienter), set-up (Establisher), initiation (Initial), extension (Prolongation), climax (Peak), and resolution (Release). However, the specific semantics of these elements vary across the sequences, and combinations of pictures playing similar roles can also be arranged coherently without making sense. Like syntactic structures, the narrative grammar manifesting in these narrative-only sequences has been found in psycholinguistic research to provide a processing advantage over scrambled sequences of images, while also remaining independent of semantic processing (Cohn et al. 2012). Thus, the processing of syntactic and narrative structures involves similar organization and processing, despite operating at different levels of representation, as would be expected from our view of the abstracted principles of a Complexity Hierarchy.

As reflected in the visual examples, narrative structures characterize the sequencing of pictures beyond the complexity of linear or simple phrase schemas. This discourse-level categorical structure may be optimal for images, as they can contain fairly complex information within their units. Visual representations appear to be less optimal for representing the types of syntactic categories (nouns and verbs) found in vocal or bodily modalities. Various approaches to "translating" speech into pictures have attempted to create visual sequences with noun-pictures and verb-pictures (e.g., Bliss 1965, Vandeghinste, Sevens, and Van Eynde 2015), although such sequences largely remain unnatural and incomprehensible without making the synesthetic connections to the spoken languages (Cohn and Schilperoord 2023, Morin 2022). Such notions have been extended to "rebus writing" with emoji (Danesi 2016), although studies of actual emoji sequencing indicate a preference for linear schemas, and they remain fairly unstructured or limited when attempting to take on syntactic categories like nouns, verbs, or even subjects or objects (Cohn, Engelen, and Schilperoord 2019, Gawne and McCulloch 2019).

These attempts to push the graphic modality to operate with syntactic structures typical of the spoken and signed modalities are unnatural, and they maintain a mistaken view of how the graphic modality works by shoehorning it to look like writing (which itself is co-opting the natural graphic modality to operate in an unnatural way) (Cohn and Schilperoord 2023). We posit that the information-dense capacity for the graphic modality leads it to more optimally afford categorical roles corresponding to more complex conceptual structures. That is, pictures can contain more information corresponding to entire scenes or events, instead of individuating basic ontological categories (things, properties, locations), and thus more prototypically correspond to narrative categories rather than syntactic categories. This renders the application of syntactic categories (nouns, verbs) to pictures to seem fairly suboptimal by going against their natural affordances. It would be similar to the use of Manually Coded English in the bodily modality, where the syntactic structure of spoken English is forced on a signed vocabulary, ignoring the affordances of how syntax naturally manifests in the bodily modality (Supalla 1991).

The advantage of categorical schemas lies in their salience for sequencing information beyond individual tokens. From a cognitive processing perspective, categories would be advantageous for memory by reducing the number of elements needed to parse. Instead of needing unique processing for the meaning of each token, an abstracted class provides structure to the information that becomes independently categorized. In line with this, most primary theories of structure—be it morphology, syntax, or narrative—typically arrive at a small inventory of base categories falling within the range of the optimal memory load (i.e., somewhere in the range of 5 to 7 core categories).

Within these structures, certain categories may establish dependencies in their relationships, again like between free and bound units. For example, affixes fall into a category that is dependent on the presence of a morphological stem, which then constitutes a head (word) and modifier (affix) relationship. Similar structure persists in syntax, for example, between nouns (head) and determiners (modifier), among others. In narrative structure, the climactic, information-rich Peak component of a sequence (head) is supported by the preceding "rising" information or the subsequent "falling" information (modifiers) (Cohn 2013c).

These head components have been argued to determine the character of a larger constituent structure, i.e., a head-modifier schema, also known as an *X-bar schema* (Chomsky 1970, Culicover and Jackendoff 2005, Jackendoff 1977). This schema provides an additional level of abstraction to the types that arise from the categories of individual units. Thus, typification across individual tokens of units (words, pictures, etc.) allows for categories of units (nouns, verbs, Peaks, etc.), and similar abstraction can be made across the consistencies in the schematic ordering of the relations between these categories ([Noun-Verb-Noun], [Establisher-Initial-Peak-Release]). We formalize this as:

CH-S5.1: *Head-modifier schemas:*
$[_{\text{Array/Phrase-X}} (Y^*) - X - (Z^*)]$

In this schema, a central head category (X) determines the nature of the constituent. The other categories (Y, Z) either precede or follow this core and are typically optional, indicated with parentheses. We mark these modifiers with a Kleene star (*) to indicate that multiple modifiers are possible within a flat structure, following Culicover and Jackendoff (2005). The functions of these modifier categories (Y, Z, etc.) thus differ in relation to the head and to the nature of the schema, e.g., modifiers at the sentence level may function differently from those at the word or narrative level. Head-modifier schemas may operate at the Phrase level within simple phrase schemas, but they also may facilitate more complex embedding found in our next schematic type.

6.1.6 Recursive Schema

The most complex combinatorial schema allows for the units or constituents of one type to embed in constituents of that same type, i.e., **recursion**. Recursive expressions are prototypical of omnia systems. We formalize the schema that allows this as:

CH-S6: *Recursive schemas:*
a. $[_{\text{Array}} \text{Unit/Phrase}^*]$
b. $[_{\text{Phrase}} \text{Unit/Phrase}^*]$

Here, a phrasal schema (b) can be embedded either within a higher-level array (a), as in simple phrase schemas, or also in a phrase of itself (b). By embedding phrases within phrases, we arrive at the possibility of recursion. In our notation, "Unit/Phrase" indicates a concatenation of either units or phrases, while a Kleene star indicates that either units or phrases can extend to unlimited length.

Recursive schemas allow for embedding beyond the single level of simple phrase schemas, again manifesting within the entrenched constructions of a particular system, yielding complex structures like the continual embedding of phrases inside of other subsequent phrases. Consider an English sentence like *Jared said that John thought that Ted was an excellent teacher*. Here, the sentence *Ted was an excellent teacher* embeds inside the syntactic frame of [*John thought* X] which itself is embedded in the frame of [*Jared said* X]. This results in a right-branching embedding structure that could potentially keep extending with additional repetitions of this similar frame of [Y *said/thought/wished/etc.* X]:

[$_S$ *Jared said that* [$_S$ *John thought that* [$_S$ *Ted was an excellent teacher*]]]

Another possible organization would be to embed a constituent inside of another constituent, in a center-embedding. This arises in a sentence like *My friend who went to Spain for the summer recently bought a surfboard*. This single sentence can be divided into an outer, matrix sentence *My friend bought a surfboard*, within which the sentence (*My friend*) *went to Spain for the summer* is embedded. The ability to separate these two clauses and have them each stand alone shows that they are each grammatically fully formed sentences. In addition, the matrix clause would need to connect across the distance of the embedding (*My friend ... bought a surfboard*) no matter how large the center-embedded clause would grow (... *who went to Spain for the summer before traveling around Europe until his partner called with an emergency to bring him home* ...). In principle, recursive structures impose no limits to the depth of embedding or the length of the embedded structures. Excessive embedding may confront limits of processing like memory capacity, but in principle are not features of the system itself.

A byproduct of complex structures is the possibility of ambiguity between how constituents may embed, particularly in correspondence to their conceptual structure. Consider a typical ambiguous example sentence like *Maria watched the girl with binoculars*. Here, it is unclear whether the binoculars are used by Maria to watch the girl or that Maria sees a girl who has binoculars. These different meanings evoked in conceptual structure depend on whether the prepositional phrase [$_{PP}$ with binoculars] connects to the verb phrase [$_{VP}$ watched ...], rendering the first instrumental interpretation, or connects to the preceding noun phrase [$_{NP}$ the girl ...], rendering the second possessive interpretation. These multiple possibilities arise because prepositional phrases maintain promiscuous placement in the schematic constructions of English syntax. That is, ambiguities arise due to how recursive structures manifest in constructions of specific languages, rather than to a universal principle of recursive schemas in general.

Recursive schemas also can appear within the individual units of a system. For example, within English morphology, the word *unbelievable* unites the stem word of *believe* with the suffix of *-able* to form the word *believable*, which then provides the stem for the prefix *un-*, to form:

[$_{\text{Word}}$ [$_{\text{Affix}}$ un - [$_{\text{Word}}$ [$_{\text{Word}}$ believ-] [$_{\text{Affix}}$ - able]]]]

Recursion also appears in complex compounds (Jackendoff 2010a), such as the noun compound:

[$_N$ [$_N$ mocha] [$_N$ [$_N$ [$_N$ chocolate]-[$_N$ chip]] [$_N$ [$_N$ cookie]-[$_N$ dough]]] [$_N$ [$_N$ ice] [$_N$ cream]]]

Here, the words *chocolate-chip*, *cookie-dough*, and *ice cream* are all compound nouns, and they combine recursively such that there is cookie dough that is made with chocolate chips, that is inside mocha-flavored ice cream. Such complex compounding proliferates across many languages with little restrictions to its recursion outside of its corresponding conceptual structure.

It is worth emphasizing that even if a system uses recursive schemas, each level within the Complexity Hierarchy is inclusive of the lower levels (Jackendoff and Wittenberg 2014). Thus, if a system reaches the complexity of using recursive schemas, other types of schematic sequencing may appear as well. In our English examples, we have already mentioned how various one-unit and two-unit phenomena occur, though English also has the possibilities of more complex recursive schemas. Though our examples of linear schemas have primarily focused on lists and instances of reduced complexity (such as search terms or newspaper headlines), linear schemas also may appear embedded within more complex structures. Consider the case of conjunctions, where a grammatical category is repeated in a flat structure, such as several noun phrases making up a larger noun phrase (*The butcher, the baker, and the candlestick maker*) or several adjectives making up an adjective phrase (*red, white, and blue*). These phrases can have unlimited length, but the conjunction remains at a flat, linear structure, though it may appear within a larger recursive sentence structure.

All of these insights about the combinatorial properties of recursion and other sequencing types have been extensively discussed in the linguistics literature. We discuss them here in order to situate them within this broader architecture. The necessity for this will become clearer as we progress to discussing multimodal interactions between the combinatorial properties of different modalities. On this point, while recursive structures most famously appear in the syntax of many languages, both for speech and sign, such complexity also appears within other modalities.

Consider the sequence in Figure 6.10a, which is a visual analogue of the right-branching [Y said X] pattern discussed above. Like in the right-branching English sentence, this sequence shows a chain of people conveying what other people have said or done (i.e., 1 says that 2 says that 3 says that 4 watches TV). This chain of speech arises because the panels of the visual sequence are also speech balloons, each emerging from a character within its preceding panel.

This pattern can be characterized by a lexicalized construction similar to the [Y said X] pattern in English, but manifesting in the graphic modality, which appears in Figure 6.10b. This narrative construction modifies the canonical narrative schema

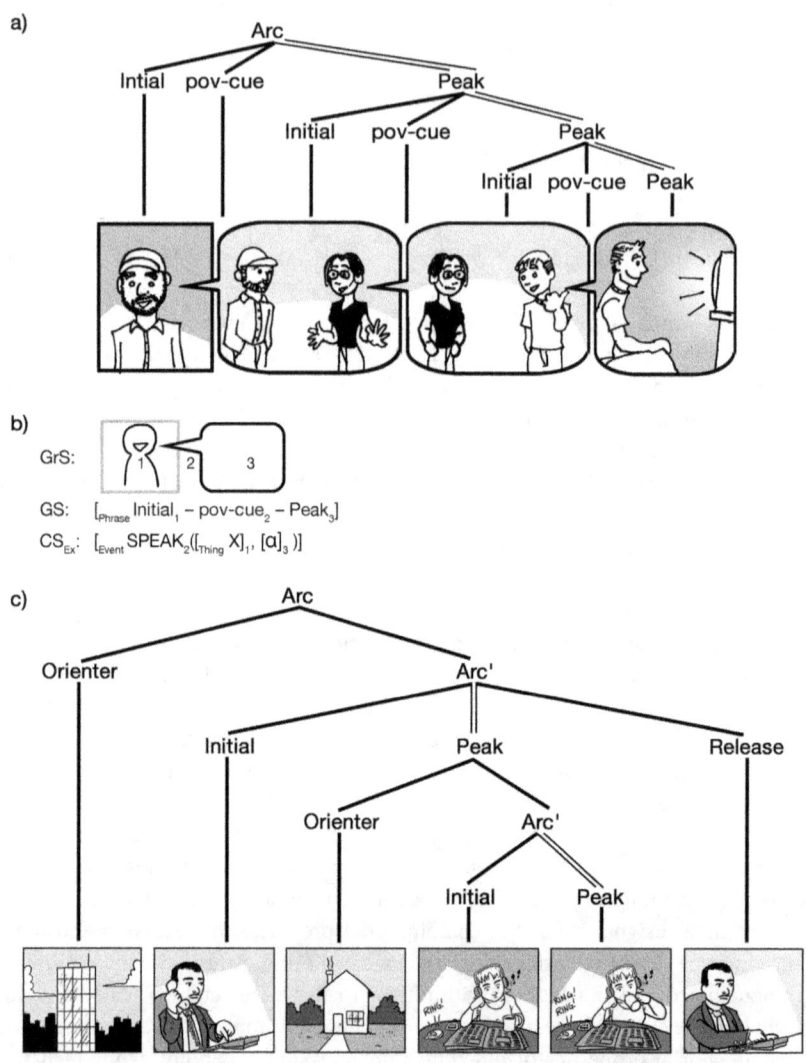

Figure 6.10 Embedding in the narrative grammar of visual languages, including a) a recursive right-branching structure, and b) recursive center-embedding.

discussed earlier. In this case, each source-panel for a balloon-panel functions as a narrative Initial, with the subsequent production being a Peak. An intervening "pov-cue" marks the morphological cue of the speech balloon (which we formalized in Chapter 3, and will not re-formalize here), but could also be a thought bubble or a range of different cues depending on the intended meaning (i.e., speech, thought, memory, imagination, etc.). The contents of this Peak-balloon panel correspond in conceptual structure to whatever is uttered, here marked as alpha.

Though the tails of the balloon-panels appear to be linearly ordered, each successive "speech" constitutes a further level of embedding within the prior speech act. The balloons here do not show this embedding, but an alternative graphic representation could visualize it with each balloon panel encircling the next (panel 4 inside of panel 3 inside of panel 2), rather than the linear sequence shown here; both are felicitous productions. Like in the spoken English sentences described above, the embedding begins at the end, with panel 4 being spoken by the righthand character in panel 3. This pair is in turn spoken by the righthand character in panel 2, and these three panels are all spoken by the character in panel 1. The result is, like the verbal utterance, a right-branching structure using recursion.

An additional right-branching structure can be seen in Figure 6.10c, which also uses center-embedding. This sequence has two Orienters (panels 1 and 3), a category which functions in a narrative structure to provide a superordinate setting for a subsequent, embedded narrative schema. In this case, those settings are an office building (panel 1) and a house (panel 3). We infer the man to be within the office building and the woman to be within the house, even though no physical cues within the panels show us that they belong in those locations. We infer this information solely through the juxtaposition of the Orienters to these subsequent panels. Structurally, Orienters provide a superordinate structure for an embedded narrative arc, functionally analogous to the way that complementizers (*that*, *which*) embed a clause in a sentence. Orienters inherently provide recursion, with an Arc within an Arc, and this occurs several times within Figure 6.10c.

Consider also the final panel in Figure 6.10c. This panel shows the man, which we infer to belong within the office building, despite the change of location to the house starting with panel 3. This final panel thus uses a distance-dependency to connect with the second panel (both showing the man), and the sequence with house and woman is thus center-embedded within the upper-level narrative schema, playing a role as a Peak. This center-embedded status can be confirmed by extracting the inner clause (panels 3–5), to stand alone as a well-formed sequence, while the matrix sequence (panels 1, 2, and 6) can also exist independently. Thus, visual narrative sequences also exhibit center-embeddings, just like in sentence structure.

The complexities of these interacting embeddings again give rise to the possibilities of structural ambiguities. Consider the sequence in Figure 6.11, which shows a man lying in bed, then a view of a clock, a window, and the clock at a later time, before finally showing the man on the phone. Ambiguity arises in this sequence because there are multiple options for how these panels combine together (Cohn 2013c, 2015b). A first option, diagrammed in Figure 6.11a, is that the panels of the man (1 and 5) connect with each other across a distance, with the progression of time shown by the clocks (panels 2 and 4) providing a center-embedded clause. This would structurally be similar to the example in Figure 6.10c, but without the Orienters, and with a different category played by the embedded clause (there, a Peak, here a Prolongation, a category depicting a medial extension). This structural configuration would correspond to an interpretation that the clock panels occur at different points in time than the panels of the man.

At least one other interpretation of this sequence is also possible, as in Figure 6.11b, where we understand the first and last pairs of panels each to occur at the same

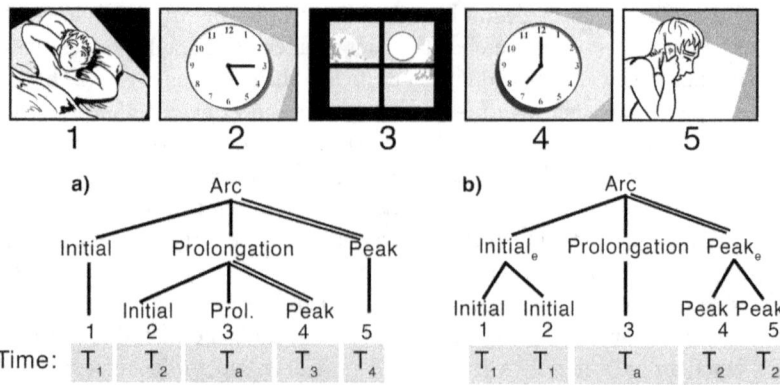

Figure 6.11 A structurally ambiguous visual narrative sequence, with two interpretations depending on whether panels are viewed as a) separate narrative states, resulting in a center-embedding, or b) grouped into common environments at the same narrative state.

moments. That is, we infer that the man (panel 1) and the clock (panel 2) occupy the same spatial environment at the same time. The same inference would persist between panels 4 and 5. This spatial inference is not required for the first interpretation. According to this second interpretation, the first and last pairs of panels would be grouped together into common constituents. Like in syntax, a conjunction schema combines similar categories (Initials or Releases) into a phrase of that same category. In this case, the resulting conjunction phrase corresponds in Conceptual Structure to the inference of a shared spatial environment for the constituent parts. We do not show this correspondence overtly, but this interface with Conceptual Structure is notated by the subscript "e."

Note that in the sequence in Figure 6.11, this structural ambiguity can be ameliorated by rearranging the final two panels. If panel 5 occurred prior to panel 4, this would rule out the first interpretation, since no center-embedding would be possible between the clock panels, and no distance-dependency would persist between the man panels.

Thus, like syntactic structure, the combinatorial principles of narrative structure give rise to recursive embedding, center-embedded clauses, and structural ambiguities. Though it may be an optimal method of conveying complex sequential information in the graphic modality, this narrative structure operates across modalities and media. For example, the same narrative structure guides filmic sequences (Cutting 2016), although the first stage of specifying the visual narrative structures of film often begins in drawn form, with storyboards, which provide the groundwork for subsequent filming and editing where that narrative structure may be altered or elaborated on. This narrative grammar also characterizes the organization of verbal discourses (for example, the same structures would persist in verbal translations of each of the visual sequences above). Like in the graphic modality, such a verbal narrative grammar would characterize the structures that guide the pacing and flow of verbal discourse, which then corresponds to meaningful relationships in Conceptual Structure. Research on such structural properties of discourse have persisted for decades (Clark 1996, Labov and Waletzky 1967, Lakoff 1964, Mandler and Johnson 1977, Rumelhart 1975), though recently most focus has been placed on the meaningful coherence relationships (Asher and Lascarides 2003, Hobbs 1985, Mann and Thompson 1987, Zwaan and Radvansky 1998), which would arise in the Conceptual Structures.

Recursive structures also appear in other aspects of the graphic modality. We have already described how visual affixation can combine elements like hearts and motion lines to graphic stems, and further complexity arises when embedding these visual forms into larger scenes. We will discuss this more down below. In addition, as was described in Chapter 2 about modalities, the basic components of the graphic modality consist of embedded regions that make up drawings (Willats 1997, 2005), and in the layouts of graphic arrays, like comic pages, which embed rows and columns inside each other (Cohn 2013b).

Recursion has also been described in many other facets of cognition. For example, the conceptual understanding of visual perception has been argued to use recursive embedding of basic spatial structures (Biederman 1987, Marr 1982). Event cognition has long been known to involve complex embeddings, which would reflect the event knowledge in our Conceptual Structures (Jackendoff 2007, Zacks and Tversky 2001). Music has also been argued to use multiple tiers of recursive structures, including hierarchies for time-span reductions and metrical structures (Lerdahl and Jackendoff 1982). Similar structuring has been argued for dance (Patel-Grosz et al. 2022), and other domains.

6.2 Combinatorial and Conceptual Correspondence

Throughout, we have shown that all levels of combinatoriality, including recursive structures, persist across modalities and cognitive domains. This well aligns with our arguments that all of these schemas belong to a general Complexity Hierarchy which manifests in specific representations for various systems. A fundamental question that remains is of course how the Complexity Hierarchy corresponds to Conceptual Structure.

One expectation may be that prototypical correspondences exist between certain types of representational systems and particular levels of meaning. In morphology, units, whether bound or free, correspond to ontological semantics, such as a Thing, a Property, or a Situation. In addition, syntactic structures would correspond to a function-argument structure, such that the predicate itself becomes a unit, as would its arguments (i.e., *PUNCH(X,Y)* becomes *X punches Y*). Finally, elements at a narrative or discourse level would prototypically correspond to an entire event structure where multiple function-argument structures would be connected. We schematize these prototypical correspondences as:

Prototypical correspondences between combinatorial and conceptual structures:

	Morphology	Syntax	Narrative
GS:	$[_{Unit} \ldots]_1$	$[_{Array} \text{Unit}_1 - \text{Unit}_2 - \text{Unit}_3]$	$[_{Array} \text{Unit}_1 - \text{Unit}_2]$
CS:	$[_{Category} \ldots]_1$	$[_{Situation} F_1(X_2, Y_3)]$	$[_{Sit.} F([_{Sit.} F(X,Y)]_1, [_{Sit.} F(X,Y)])]_2$

Though these prototypical correspondences are straightforward, the links between combinatorial systems and meaning may be more multifaceted. Combinatorial complexity can interface promiscuously with different levels of conceptual complexity, which we discuss below in several examples.

The challenge to a deterministic mapping between morphology and ontological categories comes from "nominalization" in spoken languages (Jackendoff 1977).[2] Nominalization is a unit corresponding to a predicate or event structure. For example, the nouns *marriage, destruction,* and *payment* are all sister schemas to the verbs *marry, destroy,* and *pay*. In Conceptual Structure, these words all refer to conceptual events with a predicate-argument structure, though they manifest in different parts of speech with varying structural assignments. The nouns are isolable as units in their grammatical distributions (i.e., *marriage* has no built-in dependencies), while the verbs maintain open schematic slots facilitating an array (i.e., *NP marry NP*).

Typological research has also shown that traditional divisions between morphology and syntax often break down. Classifications of morphological complexity have long shown distinctions between lexical items that can stand alone compared to those that contain internal complexity (Sapir 1921). For example, polysynthetic morphology uses stored units (morphemes) that are smaller than the level of an isolable unit (word), but can combine to create such a unit at a "sentence" level of information (Haspelmath 2018). This notion of polysynthetic words arising at a "sentence level" of meaning occurs because of the stereotypical view of how sentences should correspond to Conceptual Structure: *words convey ontological semantics* and *sentences convey predicates*. Indeed, intuitions of the inadequacy of maintaining such correspondences in the face of the world's languages often arise in questioning the notion of a "word" as a construct or about the adequacy of separating constructs of morphology and syntax (Haspelmath 2017).[3] Under a different view, such isolable polysynthetic units merely map to a conceptual structure of a complexity beyond those of the correspondences shown in typologically different systems. Under our interpretation, polysynthetic words are not "one-word sentences" but rather are single multimorphemic units that maintain a correspondence to a predicate-argument conceptual structure. We schematize this possibility as:

	Analytic word	Polysynthetic word
GS:	$[_{Unit} \ldots]_1$	$[_{Unit} \text{Unit}_1 - \text{Unit}_2 - \text{Unit}_3]$
CS:	$[_{Category} \ldots]_1$	$[_{Situation} F_1(X_2, Y_3)]$

Thus, dissociating such expectations of structure-meaning correspondences allows for better capturing each system's unique capacities to map varying levels of combinatorial complexity to varying levels of conceptual complexity.

Outside of the vocal modality, signs within the bodily modality often concatenate predications within a single unit. For example, two fingers held downward resembling legs might be wiggled to indicate walking along a linear path, as in Figure 6.12. This gesture combines both the agent of the action (fingers for legs), who directly does the action (walk), while also showing the manner of the action (wiggling "legs"), and the path of the motion (the linear trajectory of the arm movement). This substantial amount of conceptual structure all corresponds to one overall gesticulation.

Because of this complexity, such examples have raised questions about how many "morphemes" or "words" may be represented in the bodily modality, and thus whether it reflects prosody, morphology, and/or syntax (Sandler 2010, Aronoff, Meir, and Sandler 2005). Such questions betray an expectation for the ways that units versus arrays correspond to ontological categories versus predicates. In our terms, this expression uses a schema that combines units that appear simultaneously through the affordances of the bodily modality, but which interface to a complex predicate which involves numerous aspects of an event (actor(s), orientation, direction, motion, manner). Nevertheless, multiple interpretations are possible within our framework depending on the unitization of the correspondences to formological and conceptual structures, as in Figure 6.12, whether as (i) a single holistic unit (like an idiom), as (ii) a compositional multimorphemic unit, or (iii) syntactic array.

In addition, the graphic modality uses complexity at many levels of representation. Consider Figure 6.13, which is a panel from the comic *That Deaf Guy* by Matt and Kay Daigle. It shows a central character signing rapidly, with his son and wife on either side. Each character is a **monomorph** (abbreviated "Mm"), an isolable graphic entity, but these forms each expand into more complex components. Complex drawings are composed of combinations of **micromorphs** (abbreviated "mm"), which are constituent morphological forms that make up a monomorph, but which cannot stand alone. In

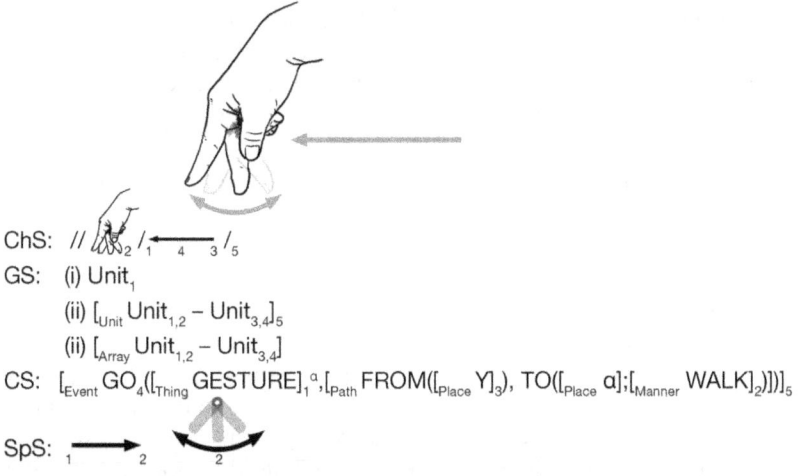

Figure 6.12 Formalization of a motion gesture.

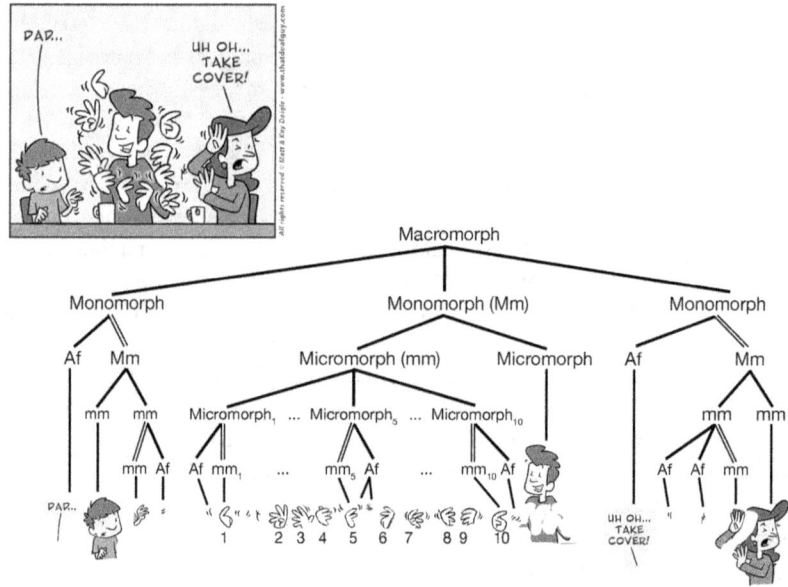

Figure 6.13 Hierarchic structure of a panel from a comic. *That Deaf Guy* © Matt and Kay Daigle (www.thatdeafguy.com).

this case, micromorph clusters for each character's bodies combine with micromorphs for hands/arms that use visual affixes of motion lines. The central figure additionally repeats micromorphs of hands to show further motion (i.e., reduplication), where each hand has a motion line. Each of these forms a micromorph-affix constituent combining to form a larger micromorph. As there are so many of these, we only formalize the first (1), middle (5), and last (10) of these micromorph constituents. The peripheral characters also have affixes for speech balloons. Each of these figures is a monomorph which corresponds to a spatial object (people), which attaches to affixes to convey abstract information (motion, speech), to create complex morphological constituents. Altogether, these monomorphs create a scene-level morphological concatenation (a ***macromorph***) that would correspond to the semantics of visual scenes (Võ 2021).

In the Complexity Hierarchy, this graphic unit uses a recursive schema that corresponds to a complex scene semantics (Võ 2021) and to a complex event structure (Jackendoff 2007). This contrasts with image-units that more concisely correspond to ontological semantics, such as a heart-shape (Figure 1.4b) or smiley face (Figure 6.1di), which use a one-unit schema corresponding to an ontological event (LOVE) or emotion (HAPPY) respectively. The internal combinatorial complexity of visual units like in Figure 6.13 has motivated the comparison to polysynthetic verbal morphology (Cohn 2013b), whereas simple units like a heart-shape or smiley face have been compared to analytic morphology. That is, like in spoken or signed languages, visual languages maintain morphological complexity that spans the whole Complexity Hierarchy.

This difference in morphological complexity of visual units also can be observed in sequences. As we have shown above, linear schemas manifesting in the graphic modality can use simple units (like the emoji in Figures 6.5 and 6.6) but also complex units (like the panels in Figure 6.7). The simple units largely correspond to ontological categories, while those with internal complexity, some with recursion, may correspond to predicate structures. Thus, linear schemas provide sequencing for units that may vary in their complexity.

Throughout, we have posited a promiscuous relationship in the correspondence between combinatorial structures of units and arrays and their conceptual structures. Nevertheless, within representational systems, some work has proposed trade-offs in complexity between units and arrays. Studies of linguistic typology have indicated that as the units of a language increase in their morphological complexity, the sentence-level combinatorics decrease in complexity, and vice-versa (Bentz et al. 2022, Ehret 2018, Koplenig et al. 2017). Within our system, this view allocates the range of conceptual structures to different levels of segmentation (units versus arrays), while at the same time to different levels of combinatorial complexity (from one-unit to recursive schemas). Similar trade-offs between the complexity of units and sequences have been demonstrated in the structure of comics around the world (Cohn 2024), where the information density of panels trades off with the complexity of patterns in the visual narrative grammar. As such trade-offs arise across modalities, they imply a domain-general negotiation of how meaning corresponds with levels of combinatoriality and segmentation.[4]

While all modalities appear to use a range of correspondences between combinatorial complexity and meaning, these correspondences may vary based on modalities' affordances. For example, the graphic modality may better afford complex units that more readily express conceptual event structures because of the natural affordances for complex information combined into visual representations. It is more natural to convey a "person running" in a single visual unit (Figure 6.14a) rather than parceling out units of a single person followed by a separate unit showing running legs (Figure 6.14b).

Figure 6.14 Graphic depictions of a "person running" as a) a single unit, b) broken up into parts.

Indeed, experiments have shown that such decompositions of images into a linear sequence are harder to comprehend than natural holistic images (Weissman et al. in prep.), because they force the predicate structure of the vocal language onto the visuals in an unnatural presentation (Cohn and Schilperoord 2023). By comparison, expressing the same event in the vocal modality requires each component of the event structure to be separately expressed (whether in different units or in a single polysynthetic unit). Thus, the sensory properties of modalities may constrain or allow for different combinatorial complexity in their units, which correspond to different levels of conceptual complexity.

6.3 Semiotics of Grammar

In Chapter 2 on modalities, we introduced the notions of C. S. Peirce's semiotics to distinguish different types of representations. Idiosyncratic signals (Peirce: sinsigns) vary as unique tokens in each of their manifestations, while regularized signals (legisigns) reflect types that are encoded in memory and manifest as unique *replicas* (tokens of types). Regularized signals often result from a process of typification that abstracts across the commonalities found in individual instances. As we have alluded to in our discussion of the Complexity Hierarchy, similar typification happens in concatenations of representations, which results in combinatorial schemas characterized by categories and phrase structures (i.e., words abstract into grammatical categories, which belong to constructions, and constructions abstract into a head-modifier schema).

This regularity means that combinatorial schemas hold the same characteristics of conventionalized regularization (legisigns) as the types found in formologies. The difference between these representations is that the regularized structures found in formologies have a correspondence to articulation in actual vocal, bodily, or graphic signals, while the regularized schemas in combinatorial structure remain solely as mental representations that operate abstractly across manifested signals. The various sequences produced using these combinatorial schemas represent replicas of these types (i.e., each unique sentence using a transitive syntactic construction is a Peircean replica of the legisign of the general combinatorial schema).

In that combinatorial schemas reflect regularized patterns, they allow for similar types of signification to arise out of their interface with conceptual structures. In Chapter 2, we explained how, consistent with Peirce, signification types of iconicity, indexicality, and symbolicity reflect interfaces between signals and meaning. Similar interfaces thus arise between combinatorial schemas and conceptual structures.

Take for example a sentence structure that uses a combinatorial schema of conjoined elliptical clauses. At the combinatorial level, this can be characterized as a regularized schema encoded in memory in some form similar to: [NP—[$_{VP}$ VP—VP—VP]]. On its own, this is simply a regularized schema. However, it allows for interfaces with Conceptual Structure of varying signification. In the manifested sentence of *She went to the store, bought ingredients, and baked a cake*, each verb phrase corresponds symbolically to three separate events; however, the ordering of those verb phrases maintains an iconic reference to the temporal (and possibly causal) ordering of the conceptualized events. This correspondence between syntactic and conceptual ordering has been called the *iconicity assumption* (Zwaan and Radvansky 1998). Nevertheless, this same syntactic schema can be invoked without such iconicity. For example, the sentence *She played football, baked cakes, and lifted weights* invokes the same regularized syntactic schema, but with no correspondence to meaning mandating a temporal ordering of the events. This would thus characterize a symbolic interface between the combinatorial and conceptual structures. Thus, the same regularized combinatorial schema can maintain different types of semiotic correspondences to meaning.

It is worth giving a few more examples of different types of signification. Symbolic reference between combinatorial schemas and conceptual structures has been identified in many grammatical constructions (Culicover and Jackendoff 2005, Fillmore 1988, Goldberg 1995, Verhagen 2005) where the sequencing of units maintains no motivated correspondence to meaning. However, iconic and indexical reference may be possible. For example, iconic reference maintained by combinatorial schemas includes the iconicity assumption in serialized verbs, but we also find iconicity in direct quotes. The syntactic frame of *They said "X"* inherently implies iconicity of the direct quote "X" from its source. Various other syntactic constructions also evoke iconicity (e.g., Marx and Wittenberg 2022, Schlenker et al. 2022).

In visual narrative sequences, readers typically maintain an iconicity assumption that each subsequent image may represent a successive temporal progression (Klomberg et al. 2023). However, many graphic sequencing constructions involve no such temporal ordering. In Figure 6.10a, the content within each successive panel would have taken place in a prior state (each being uttered by a prior person), implying a temporal order that is reversed from the order of panels in the strip. However, the entire sequence occurs at the time of the utterance in panel 1, while each balloon maintains the same type of iconicity as direct quotes. Also, in Figure 6.10b, there is no implied temporality between the Orienters and the subsequent events that occur in those locations. In Figure 6.11, the center-embedded interpretation (a) of the clocks does imply a progressing temporal sequence, but the other interpretation (b) does not, as the man and clocks combine in spatial environments with no implied temporality. These examples show that the graphic modality maintains varied possibilities for signification in its sequencing.

Combinatorial schemas may also create indexical reference. As we argued in Chapter 4, indexicality structurally involves the use of conceptual binding, whereby a representation "points" to content in another place. Such binding arises in syntactic structure in constructions involving ellipsis, such as the sentence *John gave Mary a book and Jim a cake*, where the second clause (*Jim a cake*) omits the verb, which is then indexically implied as the same as the first clause (*gave*), no matter who does the giving (John or Jim). Relative clauses use similar indexicality, as do constructions which allow for the omission of subjects or objects in a sentence. All of these cases

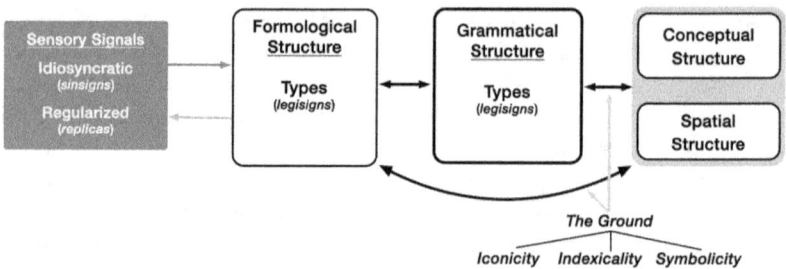

Figure 6.15 Semiotic properties of the Parallel Architecture.

of syntactic schemas use encoded omissions with the intent for inference-via-indexicality to fill in the blanks. Sequencing in visual narratives can also invoke indexicality, such as schematic sequencing whereby units show zoomed-in views of content present in another panel, thereby maintaining a part-whole indexicality (Cohn et al. forthcoming).

Within the Parallel Architecture as a whole, Formological Structures and Grammatical Structures both give access to and present Conceptual Structures. With this "presentation" function, it makes sense that they display similar characteristics as idiosyncratic or regularized representations, which then maintain similar semiotic interfaces to conceptual structures. This is illustrated in Figure 6.15. Again, these characterizations are a natural consequence of the properties of the Parallel Architecture, i.e., how information is encoded at each structure and how they interface.

Finally, it's worth reflecting on this notion of semiotic regularity further. When linguists and cognitive scientists talk about the "symbols" in mental representations, they often refer to the conventionalized and patterned nature of these representations, while maintaining a conflation between "arbitrariness" and conventionality that holds in the notion of a Saussurean Sign. "Mental representation as symbol" typically just invokes the notions of patterned conventionality (i.e., Peircean legisigns), but not necessarily a symbolic reference. Such conflation often leads to confusion about whether conventionality or signification is being discussed, and dissociation between them is crucial for clarifying the arguments about both language and cognition.

6.4 Conclusion

Altogether, combinatorial schemas operate across both units and arrays, which correspond promiscuously to levels of conceptual structure, leading to various types of signification for different sequencing. We could refer to these levels of combinatorics mapping to conceptual structure as microsyntax (for expression of semantic ontological categories), mesosyntax (for expression of predicate-argument relations), and macrosyntax (for expression of relations between predicate-argument relations).

While these conventionally (and speech-centrically) may be known as morphology, syntax, and narrative/discourse, we have shown that these combinatorial structures often cut across the boundaries of established terms for how they access Conceptual Structure with their particular representations. Although this may seem to be purely terminological, we highlight this because a multimodal approach requires that we recognize the complexities and consistencies within and across modalities. Our established terminology does not always reflect this and constrains as much as it can illuminate. We leave it to the broader field what terms are ultimately preferred, but our approach shows how similar principles of combinatoriality apply across both units and arrays, and both within and across modalities.

7

Interactions between Combinatorial Schemas

We have now established a Complexity Hierarchy with methods of combinatoriality that appear in ecologically diverse ways, both within and across modalities. As multimodal interactions may involve expressions at various levels of combinatorial complexity, we now need to describe how these schemas might interact. Here we posit two dimensions for combinatorial interactions.

The first dimension is **symmetry**. We have argued that combinatorial schemas broadly fall into classes of simple and complex types. Simple combinatorial schemas provide little structure of their own, and merely facilitate a mapping between a modality and meaning without additional representations. Complex combinatorial schemas further contribute representations of categorical roles and/or phrase structure. Given these possibilities, combinatorial interactions are either *symmetrical* between schemas of the same type (i.e., simple with simple, or complex with complex) or *asymmetrical* between schemas of different types (i.e., simple with complex).

The second dimension is **allocation**, which concerns the relative independence of a combinatorial schema to another schema. In *independent* relations, the combinatorial schemas remain fully formed with no direct connection to each other. In *substitutive* relations, the units or combinatorics of one schema function within, and are determined by, another schema.

In this chapter, we elaborate on the formalisms of these interactions, but we will describe their manifestations in unimodal and multimodal interactions in Chapters 9 and 10.

7.1 Symmetry

Symmetry involves the relative complexity (simple or complex) of interacting schemas, as detailed in Table 7.1. Crossing simple and complex combinatorial schemas gives rise to both symmetrical relations, maintaining the same complexity of schemas, and asymmetrical relations, using schemas of different complexity. As we will demonstrate, the variety of ways that omnia (complex) and semia (simple) interact falls out as a natural consequence of these symmetries.

Table 7.1 Possibilities for multimodal interactions between combinatorial schemas of two expressions.

		Simple			Complex		
		One-unit	Two-unit	Linear	Simple phrase	Categorical	Recursive
Simple	One-unit						
	Two-unit		Simple Symmetrical			Asymmetrical	
	Linear						
Complex	Simple phrase						
	Categorical		Asymmetrical			Complex Symmetrical	
	Recursive						

7.1.1 Symmetrical Simple

When multiple combinatorial schemas are simple, we describe them as *Symmetrical Simple* interactions. We here collapse all simple types (i.e., one-unit, two-unit, and linear grammars) into a single formalism using optionality (notated with parentheses, and a Kleene star * for potential repetition) whereby two schemas are interacting in Combinatorial Interaction 1 (CI-1):

CI-1: *Symmetrical Simple*
Schema$_1$: [$_{Array}$ Unit - (Unit*)]
Schema$_2$: [$_{Array}$ Unit - (Unit*)]

Each of these schemas describes a simple utterance with at least one unit, possibly elaborated into two or a linear sequence. This interaction occurs when a single gesture comes with a single word (like making a deictic pointing gesture along with uttering "that"), or a single textual word along with a picture, such as a meme with an image and one word, or a single word along with an emoji ("Nice!♥").

7.1.2 Symmetrical Complex

Symmetrical relationships can also persist between complex schemas. We again collapse all three complex schemas (categorical, simple-phrase, and recursive) into a single formalism. As before, simple-phrase and recursive schemas require two interacting structures, which allows the embedding of the phrasal-level schema into the array-level schema. Thus, we here divide these parts by a comma in CI-2:

CI-2: *Symmetrical Complex*
Schema$_1$: [$_{\text{Array}}$ Unit$_x$/Phrase$_x$*], [$_{\text{Phrase}}$ Unit$_x$/Phrase$_x$*]
Schema$_2$: [$_{\text{Array}}$ Unit$_x$/Phrase$_x$*], [$_{\text{Phrase}}$ Unit$_x$/Phrase$_x$*]

Both schemas specify that a unit or phrase, potentially of a particular category (subscript X), forms an array or a phrase. An example that involves two complex combinatorial schemas would be a comic strip, with a complex visual narrative sequence interacting with sentences in text (such as in emergent carriers like balloons or captions). Another example might be the expression of a bimodal bilingual who both speaks and signs at the same time (Emmorey et al. 2008). In video, subtitles appearing while a person talks would also use a Symmetrical Complex interaction, with degrees of redundancy of the meaning between text and speech for whether it is the same language (depending on the quality of subtitling) or different languages (depending on the quality of translation).

7.1.3 Asymmetrical

Interactions between one simple schema and one complex schema are described as asymmetrical. Using the same formalisms as above, asymmetrical interactions are characterized as in CI-3:

CI-3: *Asymmetrical*
Schema$_1$: [$_{\text{Array}}$ Unit - (Unit*)]
Schema$_2$: [$_{\text{Array}}$ Unit$_x$/Phrase$_x$*], [$_{\text{Phrase}}$ Unit$_x$/Phrase$_x$*]

A typical example of an asymmetrical interaction is a gesticulation that runs concurrently with speech, often using a one-unit schema in the body along with a complex sentence structure (Clark 1996, McNeill 1992). Similarly, a single emoji placed at the end of a typed sentence entertains the same relationship (Cohn, Engelen, and Schilperoord 2019, Gawne and McCulloch 2019). A visual sequence with onomatopoeia, such as a fight scene with sound effects (like a sequence of a comic where one person punches another with the text "Pow!"), would have a complex narrative grammar along with the one-unit word. All of these examples are asymmetrical in the interactions between their combinatorial schemas.

7.2 Allocation

While symmetry involves the relative complexity of combinatorial schemas, allocation relates to how those schemas are distributed relative to each other. This distribution gives us two types: *Independent* and *Substitutive*. Independent allocation allows each schema to exist on its own without any direct interaction, while Substitutive allocation places one combinatorial schema as a unit within another schema. These notions align with Clark's (1996) "concurrent" and "component" co-speech gestures, here now elaborated across all modalities and operationalized to combinatorial interactions specifically. In the Parallel Architecture, allocation can be formalized by how different schemas are coindexed.

7.2.1 Independent

We begin with Independent allocations, where the units of both schemas are autonomously distinguishable for whatever categorical roles may be played (if any) within and across expressions. The critical insight here is that the combinatorial allocation is mediated by the interactions between the modalities. That is, the temporal or spatial correspondence between modalities themselves allows for the interfacing of schemas, but on their own, the schemas remain independent. Allocation between combinatorial schemas here is imposed by the circumstances of the modality interfaces. Consider an interaction between text and an emoji like: *I love pizza* 🍕, formalized in Figure 7.1a.

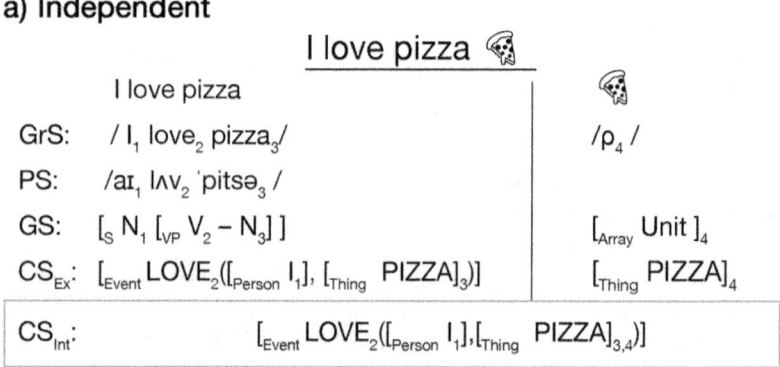

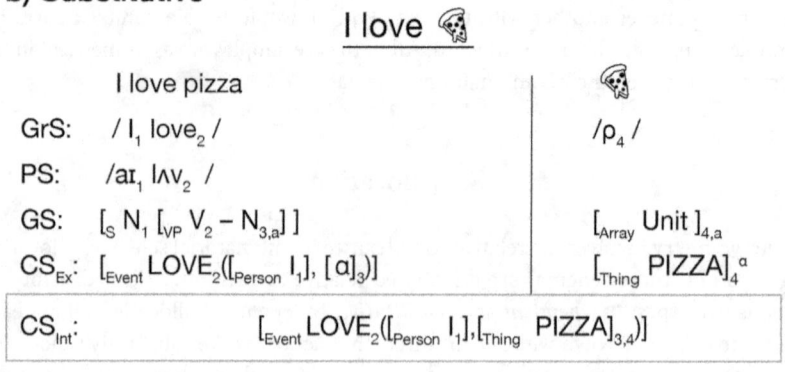

Figure 7.1 Multimodal interactions of a) Independent and b) Substitutive allocations.

Here, the pizza emoji is spatially integrated with the sentence by following it, creating an interface between the adjacent word *pizza* and the emoji. By maintaining both the word *pizza* and the pizza emoji, it warrants a coreferential relationship which is resolved in the integrated conceptual structure (i.e., PIZZA receives subscripts 3 and 4 from both modalities). The combinatorial schemas themselves (one-unit emoji and a textual sentence) remain independent. A similar interaction appears between the spoken sentence *I caught a small fish* with an accompanying pinching gesture to reinforce the small magnitude (Woodin et al. 2020), as in Figure 5.8b in Chapter 5.

Because these combinatorial schemas remain separate, so do their individual semantics. This independence is what invites coreference between the meaningful elements (complete, included, partial, absent). In the gesture example, this interaction creates an imbalanced relationship because the speech carries more semantic weight than the gesture. This displays an *included* coreferential relationship where one word semantically overlaps with the gesture, but the rest of the verbal utterance is not reflected in the bodily modality. In independent allocation, the combinatorial schemas work to package the meaning of each modality separately, creating the need for multimodal meaning to emerge outside the context of combinatorial constraints. That is, multimodal meaning in this case arises at the level of conceptual structure alone, given the combinatorial independence of each expression.

In independent allocations, the modalities interface to create sensory alignment and/or integration in temporal or spatial correspondence. The combinatorial schemas of these modalities work to package the message of each expression independent from each other. This independence puts greater demands on the conceptual structure to integrate the meanings of those separate messages, requiring the establishment of coreference between the semantics of each modality and the inferences necessary to resolve such coreference. All the schemas for symmetry as formalized in the last section (CI-1 to 3) implicitly maintain independent allocation.

7.2.2 Substitutive

While independent allocation keeps each schema separate, substitutive allocation incorporates the schemas together into one sequence. Substitution is here defined as when the combinatorial schema used by one expression is inserted as a unit within another schema. We refer to the inserted expression as the **substitution** and to the receiving schema as the **matrix schema**. Thus, the categorical role of the substitution may be determined by the top-down sequencing of the matrix schema. For example, in the sentence *I love* 🍕, the pizza-emoji is substituted for a noun in the matrix schema, here as the Direct Object noun of a sentence. Compare this to the *I* ❤ *NY* construction that we described at the start of Chapter 1. While the heart is entrenched in the lexicon with the categorical role of verb, the pizza emoji is not encoded in the lexicon with the role of a noun. This poses a problem for structural unification, whereby the pizza emoji does not readily match the specification of a noun slot in a syntactic construction. For example, the pizza emoji may be odd when expressing case (plural: 🍕-s, possessive: 🍕's) like regular nouns.

For *I love* 🍕, we assume that the emoji's placement into a canonical noun position following the transitive verb *love* allows it to fulfill both the semantic and grammatical argument structures, as depicted in Figure 7.1b. Here, the modalities have no explicit interface, because the expressions of each modality become units within a single sequence, rather than co-occurring expressions. In the combinatorial structure, the pizza emoji appears as an unmarked unit, while the text invokes a canonical transitive sentence construction. Substitution is thus characterized formally by an index to the whole substituted utterance (here, subscript "a"), which coindexes to a single unit within the matrix schema (here, the direct object noun). In Conceptual Structure, the verb *love* licenses a transitive event with an argument structure specifying both an agent (here *I*) and a patient. As the patient is not expressed by text, this argument is fulfilled with a binding operator (α) which links to the conceptual structure of the pizza emoji, fulfilling the semantic argument of the event structure. Overall then, the substitution results in one modality fulfilling a grammatical role within, and determined by, the grammar of another modality, thereby coalescing their meaning.

The formal challenge of substitution is to explain how representations of one type of expression (e.g., "unit") unify with those of another (e.g., "noun")? Our proposal is that unification occurs solely within Conceptual Structure, such that a conceptual category corresponding to Expression 1 (like the Thing of PIZZA of a pizza emoji) is licensed to be unified with a conceptual category corresponding to Expression 2 (like the Thing slot made available by the transitive event LOVE). Thanks to the prototypical correspondences of that unified conceptual structure, the substituted unit can thus play a role within the matrix schema (i.e., the unified Thing prototypically corresponds to a noun, which can satisfy the grammatical constraints of the transitive verb *love*). We articulate this as a generalized correspondence schema:

Substitution Schema

	Expression 1: Matrix schema	Expression 2: Substitution
GS:	[$_{\text{Array}}$ Unit - Unit$_a$ - Unit]	[$_{\text{Array}}$ Unit]$_a$
CS:	[... [$_X$ α] ...]	[$_X$ X]^a

To reiterate, the binding operator (α) reflects the unification of meaning of the substituted unit into the matrix expression's conceptual structure. This creates the possibility of the substituted unit's combinatorial structure (whatever it may be) being inserted into a grammatical unit within the matrix schema (coindex "a").

Under this view, unification does not occur directly within the combinatorial schemas, but is in a sense conceptually "coerced" within the grammar. The meaning of the substituted unit can satisfy the allowable meanings of the combinatorial schematic slot, and thereby lead to acceptability of being a combinatorial substitution. In some cases, this may lead to less satisfactory meaning unification. For example, if a substituted unit does not satisfy the constraints of the conceptual structure offered by the matrix schema, a less well-formed combinatorial substitution may result. Consider substitutions like *I love* ♥ or *I* 🍕 *eating lunch* where, despite the shared semantic fields of the substituted elements with the matrix schema, the substitutions appear less felicitous. Indeed, substitutions of emoji that align with their grammatical context are readily integrated into the combinatorial structure, but substituted emoji with less appropriate meanings creates downstream processing costs (Cohn et al. 2018, Scheffler et al. 2022).

Given that combinatorial allocation and symmetry remain orthogonal, substitutions can vary across all types of symmetry. Substitutive allocation in the context of Symmetrical Simple interactions can be formalized as a modification of schema CI-1, here adding a ".1" to indicate substitutive allocation:

CI-1.1: *Symmetrical Simple Substitution*
Schema$_1$: [$_{Array}$ Unit - (Unit*)]$_a$
Schema$_2$: [$_{Array}$ [Unit] - [Unit]$_a$ - [Unit]*]

In this case, each schematic structure is an array whereby the units have no prespecified categorical roles, and may be one-unit, two-units, or a linear schema of an unlimited length (as suggested by the Kleene star *). For a sequence to allow for substitution, the matrix schema in a Symmetrical Simple substitutive allocation needs to use a linear schema (here Schema$_2$), while the substitution can vary across levels of simple complexity (Schema$_1$). For example, imagine a list where one of the items is fulfilled by an image rather than a word: *beer, chips, 🍕, football*. We formalize this as in Figure 7.2.

Again, the pizza emoji is integrated in the modality by virtue of its sequencing with the text, and it remains a single utterance with a conceptual structure consistent with the substitution in Figure 7.1b. This consistency retains the integrity of the lexical entry of the pizza emoji as a unit. The textual list uses a linear schema whereby units lacking a grammatical category are ordered sequentially, and the whole utterance of the pizza emoji is coindexed to a single unit within that linear schema (subscript "a"). The conceptual structure here just specifies a broader semantic field related to recreation, where the semantics of the pizza emoji joins the list of other instances, facilitated by the linear array. Thus, in Symmetrical Simple substitutive allocation, units from one expression can be inserted into a matrix schema of another, but no further categorical role is fulfilled because the linear schema itself does not specify categorical roles, such as the pizza emoji playing the role of a noun in Figure 7.1b.

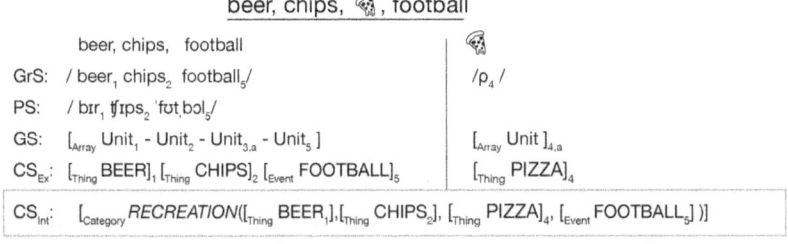

Figure 7.2 Substitution in a linear array.

Grammatical roles do become specified in Asymmetrical substitutive allocation. Here, the complex schema of one expression uses categorical roles, which the substitution using a simple schema can inherit. This occurs in our example sentence *I love* 🍕 in Figure 7.1b, where the pizza emoji acts as a noun in the textual sentence. Generalized, asymmetrical substitutive allocations can be formalized as in CI-3.1:

CI-3.1: *Asymmetrical Substitution*
Schema$_1$: [$_{Array}$ Unit - (Unit*)]$_a$
Schema$_2$: [$_{Array/Phrase}$ [Unit$_x$/Phrase$_x$] - [Unit$_y$/Phrase$_y$]$_a$ - [Unit$_z$/Phrase$_z$]*]

Again, substitutions coindex the whole array of the substitution to a unit inside the matrix array. While our formalized example in Figure 7.1b shows an image inserted into a textual sentence, multimodal substitutions of "component" (Clark 1996) or "language-like" (Kendon 1988, McNeill 1992) gestures into the syntax of speech are also well attested (Clark 1996, Fricke 2013, Kendon 1988, Ladewig 2020, McNeill 1992). This occurs when speaking *I caught a <small pinching gesture> fish*, where the pinching hand gesture fulfills the role of an adjective in the sentence corresponding to the notion of small magnitude (Woodin et al. 2020). We diagram this scenario in Figure 7.3b which again contrasts with its Independent allocation (Figure 7.3a), in terms of co-indexation of schemas and alpha binding of conceptual structures. A reverse modality relationship occurs in bimodal bilinguals, who have proficiency in both a spoken language and sign language and have been observed to codeswitch where spoken words substitute into the sign language grammar (Emmorey et al. 2008).

Units of text can also be inserted into a visual sequence that uses a complex schema, such as in Figure 7.4a. Here, we first see one boxer reach back his arm while approaching another boxer, followed by the word *Pow*, and a depiction of the first boxer standing over the second. We infer here that a punch occurred which must have knocked out the second boxer. However, we do not see this action: the climactic event of the visual narrative is replaced by an onomatopoeia, which sponsors inference of an event through the sound that it emits (Goldberg and Jackendoff 2004, Jackendoff 2010a). This again is Asymmetrical substitution, here of a single word into the narrative grammar of the graphics.

Relationships between complex schemas can also use substitutive allocation. In these cases, the substitution uses a complex schema of its own such that its internal parts have their own categorical roles, but the whole utterance acts as a unit in the matrix schema of the other expression. Formalized, this appears as CI-2.1:

CI-2.1: *Symmetrical Complex Substitution*
Schema$_1$: [$_{Array/Phrase}$ [Unit$_x$/Phrase$_x$] - [Unit$_y$/Phrase$_y$] - [Unit$_z$/Phrase$_z$]*]$_a$
Schema$_2$: [$_{Array/Phrase}$ [Unit$_x$/Phrase$_x$] - [Unit$_y$/Phrase$_y$]$_a$ - [Unit$_z$/Phrase$_z$]*]

Again, the whole substitution coindexes with a unit in the matrix schema. An example of Symmetrical Complex substitutive allocation occurs when a whole sentence replaces the Peak in a visual narrative sequence, as in Figure 7.4b. This is structurally similar to the Asymmetrical example in Figure 7.4a, only here the text

Interactions between Combinatorial Schemas 193

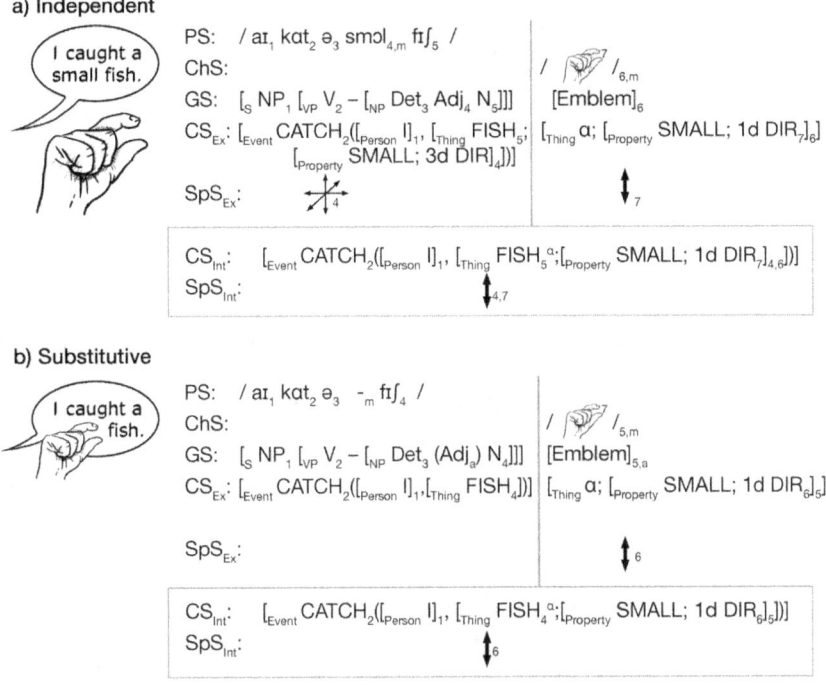

Figure 7.3 Co-speech gesture interactions using a) Independent and b) Substitutive allocations.

Figure 7.4 Visual narrative sequence with a) Asymmetrical and b) Symmetrical Complex substitutive allocation.

is a whole sentence rather than a single unit (Cohn 2019, Huff et al. 2020). The reverse situation arises when an image sequence appears between words or clauses within a sentence. We will return to formalizing these examples in Chapter 10.

It is worth emphasizing that these relationships characterize interactions between combinatorial structures, not between modalities per se. Indeed, similar combinatorial allocation occurs in unimodal contexts. For example, many spoken languages use ideophones (e.g., onomatopoeia) as a class of one-unit words which show morphosyntactic independence in their allocation, either at the end of sentences (independent) or playing grammatical roles within sentences (substitutive) (Dingemanse 2017). Similar asymmetrical allocation occurs in the bodily modality by gestures inserted into the grammar of sign languages (Emmorey 2001, Marschark 1994). Substitutive allocation also characterizes the interactions within codeswitching, where units of varying sizes from one language are inserted into the matrix schemas of another language (Kootstra 2015, Muysken 2020). All of these are unimodal cases of substitutive allocation.

7.3 Conclusion

Though symmetry relates to the relative complexity of contributing schemas, allocation in many ways drives the overall multimodal (or unimodal) interactions. When combinatorial structures remain separated in independent allocations, it entails that the modalities themselves remain separate. In these cases, modalities interface on their own (through temporal or spatial correspondence) and require coreference across signals. By integrating schemas in substitutive allocation, the multimodal messages themselves become integrated. Thus, while the overt sensory experience of multimodality occurs through their modalities, and their understanding results through the integrated conceptual structure, we remain unaware of the covert interactions of the combinatorial schemas that largely characterize how multimodal messages arise.

Part Five

Multimodality

8

Unimodal Expressions in a Multimodal Model

At the start of this book, we introduced a multimodal Parallel Architecture that includes the formologies of humans' three natural modalities—vocal, bodily, and graphic—using a combinatorial system (grammar) to express and construct meaning. In the previous chapters, we have elaborated on the basic structures of each of these three primary components, along with the interactions that occur within each of these structures. The full model is now depicted in Figure 8.1, including the sensory inputs and motor outputs for each formology, the range of combinatorial schemas used in grammars, and both the Conceptual and Spatial Structures that comprise the meaning.

We have argued that expressive behaviors like speech, gesturing, signing, or drawing emerge out of interactions between these structural components. This warrants the question: If the overall system is bigger than one modality, what do individual modality expressions look like within it? In this chapter, we detail how unimodal expressions arise as emergent states from this holistic model. This will foreshadow our subsequent discussion on how these unimodal systems manifest in multimodal expressions.

To sum up our arguments from the previous chapters, let's review the primary principles regarding each of these structures within the Parallel Architecture. First, modalities provide the accessible expressions by which humans communicate. The natural modalities include the vocal, bodily, and graphic modalities, which persist in parallel to each other, but humans' communicative potential can be expanded using tools. The natural modalities use a combination of both sensory signals (the properties of light, sound, touch, etc.) and cognitive representations (the mental correlates which organize those signals). These signals in a modality can appear as either idiosyncratic (non-patterned, novel) or regularized (patterned, systematic, lexicalized), which leads to the generalization of signals in a modality from tokens to types. Modalities also interface with each other temporally using their feature of durativity, or spatially, using spatial features and/or graphic morphology.

In order to communicate meaning, interlocuters must access conceptual structures. Modalities serve as the "handles" to access the meaning in a supramodal semantic memory. Meaning is encoded both as an algebraic conceptual structure and as a geometric spatial structure. Though semantic memory is modality-independent, modalities provide affordances for how these features can be accessed. These relationships between modality and meaning also arise in systematic interfaces, characterizable as types of signification like iconicity, indexicality, and symbolicity.

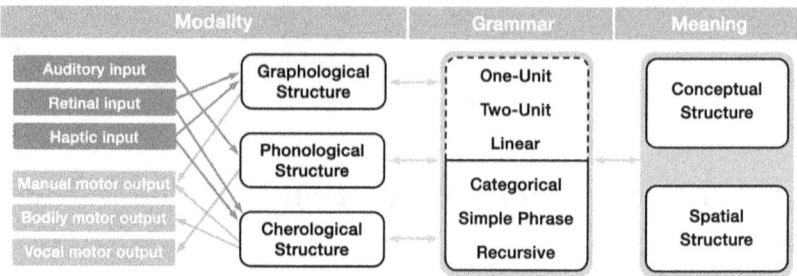

Figure 8.1 The multimodal Parallel Architecture.

Meanings further combine through coreferential relationships, whether within or across modalities.

The relationship between modalities and meanings is mediated by combinatorial properties which package the communicative information. This system has conventionally been described as a grammar, but involves combinatorial schemas of varying complexity which arise both for units (morphology) and relations between units (syntax, narrative). These combinatorial schemas exist in a Complexity Hierarchy that begins with simple schemas, like one-unit, two-unit, and linear arrays, which do not contribute their own representational structure to the expression of meaning. Complex schemas add representational structure like segmentation in simple phrase schemas, abstraction across tokens into types with categorical roles of units ("parts-of-speech"), and recursion. These complex properties provide additional aid to the salience and segmentation of expressions, supporting memory in their processing. Combinatorial interactions arise across two dimensions: symmetry, for whether the interacting schemas are simple or complex, and allocation, for whether schemas are independent or substituted into each other.

Given these component structures of the Parallel Architecture, we can now describe how they interact. Expressions arise as *emergent states* out of interactions between these structures, which we have categorized as omnia, semia, sequentia, and modalia. We focus here on omnia and semia, which can now be better understood in terms of our distinction between simple and complex combinatorial schemas rather than the wholesale presence or absence of a grammar. Omnia are a combination of a modality that gives access to meaning using a *complex* combinatorial schema. Meanwhile, semia combine a modality that gives access to meaning using a *simple* combinatorial schema.

With the idea that combinatorial structure motivates these classifications, we can also extend these notions beyond whole systems. Omnia and semia provide useful categorization for structural types that cut across individual modalities. Because they are emergent states, these categories apply both to whole systems and to utterances within actual usage. For example, English as a whole could be characterized as an omnia system, but the use of English may involve semia, such as encoded single units (ideophones, interjections, or proper names) and spontaneous single unit utterances (e.g., *Thanks. Why? Banana.*). That is, the notions of omnia and semia describe both structural properties of whole systems and the dynamic usage of those systems.

We now turn to these emergent states in unimodal expressions, starting with semia as the simpler structures before progressing to omnia.

8.1 Semia

The simplest emergent state is that of a single unit. In the vocal modality, single units may be encoded as isolates, or may arise in usage if utterances merely consist of a single unit. Isolates are units encoded without specifying combinatorial possibilities with other units, such as interjections, performatives, and exclamations. Words like *abracadabra, gadzooks, ouch!,* or *ummmmm ...* are not encoded with syntactic categories, which is why placing them into sentence structures is not licensed (Jackendoff 2002, Jackendoff and Wittenberg 2014). Similarly, ideophones, like *pow* or *kablam*, also maintain morphosyntactic independence from their sentence contexts (Dingemanse 2017). In addition, single-unit utterances may use forms that do have combinatorial possibilities within sentences, but arise in context as single-unit semia. These would include questions (*Why? What?*), reduced responses (A: *Would you like wine?* B: *Red.*), imperatives (*Stop! Sit!*), or exclamations (*Shit! Fuck!*). All of these semia would arise in the Parallel Architecture as an interface between the vocal modality, a one-unit array, and Conceptual Structure, as diagrammed in Figure 8.2a.

Simple arrays also arise in the vocal modality. Two-unit semia appear in two-word expressions made by children, and in various constrained utterances like greetings (*Yo X, Goodbye X*), epithets (*Oh hell! Holy shit!*), forms of address (*President X, Doctor X*), and pivot schemas (*Lake X* vs. *X Lake*). Simple compounds also allow diverse meaningful relations between units. These expressions manifest in the Parallel Architecture similarly to the single-unit semia, only that they use a two-unit array (Figure 8.2e). This same tripartite structure within the Parallel Architecture persists with linear arrays (Figure 8.2i), either unordered or ordered. Again, unordered semia manifest as lists, while ordered semia manifest in various reduced forms, like when people type into search engines (Smirnova 2021).

These vocal expressions can also manifest in the graphic modality via writing. As discussed in Chapter 2, spoken languages which maintain a writing system involve an additional interface to Graphological Structure beyond just to Phonological Structures. As argued, this creates a synesthetic modality whereby connections are made across natural modalities. Because of this, all of the single-unit vocal semia (or any expressions in the vocal modality) can also persist with this additional interface to the graphic modality, as diagrammed in Figure 8.2b, 8.2f, and 8.2j.

In the bodily modality, one-unit semia proliferate that cannot be put into a coherent sequence (Goldin-Meadow 2003a, McNeill 1992). Gesture research has identified a distinction between the encoding of different bodily movements in memory (Kendon 1988). Gesticulations are semia that are not entrenched in a mental lexicon, such as the various novel bodily expressions made in a conversation. These bodily expressions are semia that remain as idiosyncratic manifestations in the bodily modality. To

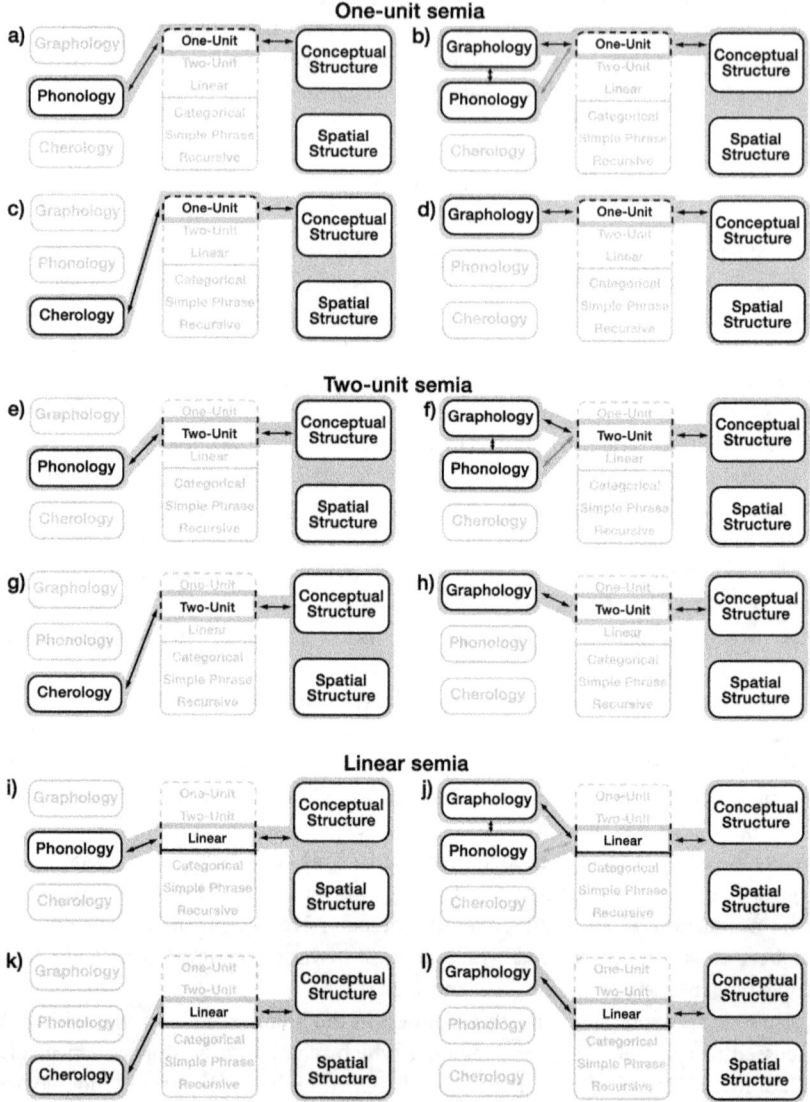

Figure 8.2 Emergent semia in each modality manifesting as a–d) One-unit, e–h) two-unit, and i–l) linear semia in each modality.

reiterate from Chapter 2, conventionality (or lack thereof) is encoded in the modality itself, regardless of its interface with meaning, and this notion of idiosyncratic form thus aligns with the Peircean notion of a sinsign. Gestural emblems meanwhile are entrenched in the mental lexicon with an encoded, regularized form, which include thumbs up or down, waving, nodding or shaking the head, or a range of obscene hand gestures which vary depending on culture (Gawne and Cooperrider 2022).

Neither gesticulations nor gestural emblems belong to a wider system, such as a sign language. However, though sign languages are omnia with a lexicon of signs with combinatorial possibilities, these can be expressed in context as single units, similar to our semia examples from speech above. Again, all of these interactions persist using an interface between the bodily modality, a one-unit array, and Conceptual Structure, as diagrammed in Figure 8.2c.

The bodily modality also allows for sequential semia without yet displaying complex combinatoriality. For example, systematic sequencing of signs has been demonstrated by homesigners who develop the properties of their own bodily sign systems (Goldin-Meadow 2003b). These sequences often display consistent ordering of the signs, but appear largely motivated by their semantic structure, not by additional combinatorial representations (e.g., categorical roles, hierarchic embedding). In addition, when hearing people are asked to communicate without speech and only using their bodily motions, they often manifest consistent sequencing structure (Goldin-Meadow et al. 2008, Hall, Ferreira, and Mayberry 2014). Again however, this structure is motivated by the meaning of these signs, rather than additional combinatorial representations, and in fact, consistent structures arise no matter the native spoken languages of the participants (Goldin-Meadow et al. 2008, Meir et al. 2017). In all of these cases, sequencing occurs using linear combinatoriality where the meaning drives the structure of the utterances, and as such renders them as bodily semia (Figure 8.2k).

Like the vocal and bodily modalities, the graphic modality also expresses semia in a range of ways. The distinction between idiosyncratic and regularized semia that we find in the bodily modality also persists in the graphic modality. However, perhaps a more salient distinction in graphics concerns the amount of information that each unit expresses. Some graphic semia remain constrained in their conceptual content. Contemporary visual culture is filled with icons, pictograms, and other basic single-unit expressions, including the various icons that persist throughout signage (bathroom signs, street signs, etc.), in technology (on buttons, volume buttons, Wi-fi icons, etc.), and the logos for various brands and companies. Simple graphic semia have also become a mainstay of digital communication with emoji, and constitute a fairly fixed visual lexicon for expressing a range of constrained meanings. Though many of these graphic semia use internal combinatorial properties like affixation (ex. the negation symbol is an affix for whatever is negated), these graphic semia largely convey basic conceptual content like simple events, objects, manners, emotions, properties, and others.

Simple graphic semia are contrasted by more complex graphic representations that still persist as single units. Graphic representations can naturally depict more complexity because of the affordances allowed by an analog representation with iconic mapping to a conceptual structure including complex scenes (Võ 2021). This renders the possibility of single-unit representations to convey a range of complexity, which is on display in contexts including paintings, sketches, political cartoons, comic covers, advertisements, and other media. Highly complex one-unit graphic semia also include search puzzles in books like *Where's Waldo?* Across all these examples, scenes convey objects and their events situated within a larger spatial context. No matter their complexity, all of these examples arise as graphic semia in the Parallel Architecture as an interface between the graphic modality, a one-unit array, and conceptual structure (Figure 8.2d).

Graphic semia also occur using two-unit arrays. As discussed in Chapter 6, the Before-After Construction (Schilperoord and Cohn 2023) in the graphic form depicts a first unit of a "before" state followed by a second unit of an "after" state, which motivates a comprehender to recognize the change between states arising through some causal force (such as exercise to become healthy). These Before-After Constructions occur in a range of places, including advertisements, political cartoons, memes, and other contexts. Two-unit arrays also can involve other construals, such as drawing contrasts between the depicted elements (such as showing two competing products next to each other), yes/no commands (yes: drinking water in a room, no: eating food in a room), or analogies (one picture showing a guitar, and another showing an atomic bomb blast, comparing their shapes to convey the energetic nature of the advertised guitar). All of these graphic semia involve an interface between the graphic modality, a two-unit array, and Conceptual Structure (Figure 8.2h).

Graphic semia can also use linear arrays. As discussed in Chapter 6, unordered linear graphic semia depict lists of elements, as appearing in signage, instruction manuals, scientific diagrams, and many other contexts. Signage might indicate unordered linear graphic semia which tell you what to bring or not to bring on an airplane or what things are allowed in a park. Instructional manuals may give you both ordered or unordered linear graphic semia. Consider assembly instructions for furniture: the list of included parts and tools would be an unordered array, while the step-by-step instructions for assembly are an ordered linear array. Like the linear semia that occur in other modalities, these graphic semia use sequences motivated by the conceptual structure of what is being expressed, rather than more complex combinatorial representations. In these cases, the conceptual structure itself may vary in its complexity—ex. a list versus the ordered series of events in a step-by-step assembly—however the combinatorics facilitating these sequences does not reflect that same complexity. These graphic semia use the same types of interfaces in the Parallel Architecture as other graphic semia, except using linear arrays (Figure 8.2l).

In addition, linear graphic semia range in the complexity of their units, particularly for unordered sequences (Figure 8.2l). They can use simple units like pictograms or emoji, but can also show more complex scenes (as in safety-manuals or instructions). Nevertheless, the complexity of visual sequences may be constrained by the affordances of the graphic modality. Simple images like emoji do not seem to be able to create more complex combinatorial structures, and largely use repetition and linear arrays (Cohn, Engelen, and Schilperoord 2019, Gawne and McCulloch 2019). We have posited that more complex combinatorial sequencing in the graphic modality requires more complexity in the units, governed by narrative rather than syntactic structures.

8.2 Omnia

Where semia only maintain simple combinatoriality, omnia involve more complex combinatorics that introduce categorical roles, phrase structures, and potentially recursion. Unlike semia which can either be encoded or arise simply through usage, the complex representations involved in omnia reflect the structure of an encoded system.

Spoken language is a vocal omnia, which uses an interaction within the Parallel Architecture between the vocal modality (Phonological Structures), complex combinatorial schemas, and Conceptual Structure (Figure 8.3a). For speech, these are what have traditionally been described as sentences, phrases, clauses, etc., which all use complex combinatorial schemas to guide their syntax beyond the content of their conceptual structures. Though omnia best characterize the *emergent states* possible by full languages, this is not to suggest that full languages consist exclusively of omnia. As we have discussed, full languages can also encode or express semia.

This interaction between the phonology of the vocal modality, complex combinatorics, and conceptual structures was characterized by Jackendoff's (2002) original Parallel Architecture. The relative relationships between these three structures are also what most linguistic models previously have attempted to characterize (Goldsmith and Laks 2019, Harris 1993, 2021). We maintain our own preferences for characterizing the nature of these component structures, such as constructions and schemas that retain the possibilities of internal hierarchy (e.g., Culicover and Jackendoff 2005, Jackendoff and Audring 2020). However, the notion of omnia itself is neutral to specific theories about the structures of a modality, grammar, or meaning, and we leave open the possibility of debate, while requiring the basic principles and mechanisms of our multimodal architecture.

Writing systems introduce a mapping of graphology to the structures involved in speech. These expressions use all of the same interactions as spoken languages (Figure 8.3a), only introducing an additional interface with the graphic modality (Figure 8.3b). In the context of omnia, these would include written sentences, phrases, and clauses.

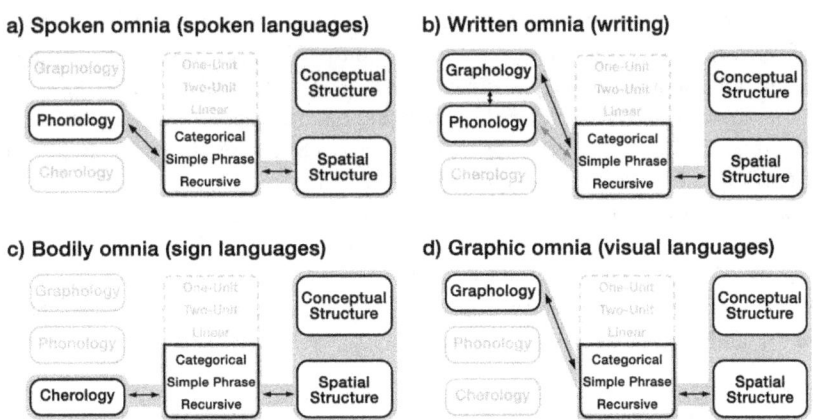

Figure 8.3 Omnia in various modalities, including a) spoken languages, b) written languages, c) sign languages, and d) visual languages.

Bodily omnia are sign languages. These systems involve an emergent state with an interaction between the bodily modality (Cherological Structures), complex combinatorial schemas, and Conceptual Structure (Figure 8.3c). Sign languages thus differ structurally from semia by using fully encoded lexicons and complex combinatorial schemas that extend beyond just meaningful relationships. Again, it is worth emphasizing that while the prototypical bodily omnia are sign languages, the terms should not be equated. In recent years, several "emerging" sign languages have spontaneously arisen in communities with high incidences of deafness (de Vos and Pfau 2015, Meir, Sandler, et al. 2010), and these systems are often characterized as transitioning in their structures from more idiosyncratic expressions to a more regularized and conventionalized lexicon, and a shift from a conceptually driven sequencing to a full-fledged grammar. These systems should rightfully be called "sign languages" but in our scheme they would be characterized as developing from being semia to omnia.

Finally, in the graphic modality we also see omnia produced in visual languages. These systems involve an expression in the graphic modality (Graphological Structures) that uses complex combinatorial schemas to express conceptual structures (Figure 8.3d). Like other modalities, it's again worth remembering that the notion of "visual language" is not equated with "graphic omnia," and visual languages use semia as well. Full omnia systems arise in the context of drawn visual narratives, such as those found in comics, which use systematic lexicons encoding items ranging from small morphemes (like the ways of drawing hands or eyes) to systematic templates of whole scenes (such as regularized comic panels), and even regularized patterns of narrative sequencing (Cohn 2013b, 2024). Like omnia in other modalities, graphic omnia manifest in different visual languages around the world, which are characterized by cross-culturally diverse visual lexicons and combinatorics (Cohn 2024). The structures in manga from Japan are distinct from those in comics from the United States or Europe, and all of these are significantly different from the structures of the visual languages used in Central Australian Aboriginal sand narratives, Mayan pottery, Aztecan codices, Japanese scrolls, and all other systematic graphic systems throughout history.

Structures from visual omnia can also be conveyed outside the graphic modality through the use of tools like photography and video. The visual content of films also uses an interaction between complex combinatorial narrative schemas and meaning, but conveyed using natural percepts rather than graphically produced pictures (Cohn 2020a). These complex visual sequences in film indeed are often preceded by drawn visual sequences in the form of storyboards, which lay out the primary combinatorics of the visual narrative structures which eventually become manifest as moving natural percepts. Thus, the visual content of films is also a type of omnia (which usually appears within a broader multimodal context), but mediated by tools rather than a natural modality of expression.

8.3 Conclusion

Given the behaviors discussed in this chapter, we can see that humans use a wide range of expressions across various levels of complexity. There should be no argument that humans indeed have all of these capacities. Incorporating all of our modalities into a single architecture with combinatoriality based on common principles can thus account for these diverse unimodal expressions in a generalized manner.

It is worth reiterating that our model primarily focuses on emergent states, though such states may be encoded in the structures as well. We think of languages as omnia, but languages also include semia, and what are labeled as "languages" often involves more sociocultural factors than structural ones (as argued in Chapter 1). By focusing on emergent states, we can also trace the development or shift from semia systems to omnia systems, a process that is characterized by increasing regularity and conventionalization across all structures (i.e., grammaticalization). In such cases, this shift is gradual and somewhat amorphous for when to demarcate the line between an omnia system and a semia system. This is often why it is difficult to know when a system "becomes a language," particularly given the investment in sociocultural factors that might be involved with that labeling. This possible fuzzy boundary is why it is important to think of these notions not solely as characterizing whole systems (and not "language" per se), but as emergent states within a broader architecture, whether characterizing lexical items, dynamically produced utterances, or whole encoded systems.

In this light, prior theories of the architecture of language have largely focused on only one particular *portion* of this overall architecture, what we would call vocal omnia. An amodal assumption more or less reinforces this limited scope by definition, by either relegating non-vocal behaviors to the periphery, or by maintaining the vocal modality as the prototypical linguistic form while generalizing it as an "amodal" capacity. This amodal view dictates that only a single modality needs to be examined in detail, because the rest are assumed to come for free. By situating all modalities in parallel into a unified architecture, we can more adequately address the full range of human expressive behaviors, simultaneously acknowledging their unique properties and affordances and their shared cognitive principles.

9

Independent Multimodal Interactions

In prior chapters, we have argued that multimodality does not arise from interactions between indivisible behaviors like "speech + gesture" or "text + image," but those behaviors are byproducts of interactions between their substructures, which are shared in a common architecture. This means that variation in multimodal messages can arise from independent interactions within each of the architectural structures, i.e., between modalities, between grammars, or between meanings. With at least 13 types of modality interactions (4 co-durative, 5 mixed-durative, 4 non-durative), 4 types of semantic coreference, 3 types of combinatorial symmetry, and 2 types of allocation, it results in at least 312 different types of possible bimodal interactions. In addition, these are not static properties with singular interactions, but rather multiple interactions may arise within dynamic emergent states that may weave in and out throughout multimodal expressions. All of this renders too many multimodal possibilities to categorize as specific types, which possibly explains why multimodality appears as such a complex issue when viewed without decomposing those expressions.

We have already shown how these various interactions manifest within the context of each component of the Parallel Architecture. To further highlight these interactions, this chapter and the next provide examples with a range of complexity. Our framing of these interactions can usefully illustrate how different multimodal messages maintain similar structures. For example, the analogy that emoji-text interactions are like digital co-speech gesture (Gawne and McCulloch 2019, McCulloch and Gawne 2018) reflects an acknowledgment of similar architectural relationships between semia and omnia. Our approach allows for the recognition of such architectural alignments, despite surface modality differences, and without the need for analogies. As such, our framing highlights the broader systematicity in multimodal messaging that might otherwise seem more idiosyncratic.

In this chapter, we focus on multimodal interactions with independent combinatorial allocations. As argued in Chapter 7, in independent allocations the combinatorial structure of each modality operates separately, with conceptual interactions primarily facilitated by modality interactions. In Chapter 10, we will discuss substitutive allocation, where the conceptual interactions are primarily facilitated by combinatorial interactions, and modalities remain separate. That said, we now discuss various examples, which will increase in their complexity based on their combinatorial symmetry.

9.1 Symmetrical Simple Relations

We start with cases where all modalities use simple combinatorial schemas, a **Symmetrical Simple** interaction. These types of interactions abound in contexts like identification documents (such as photos and names on passports, driver's licenses, etc.), street signs with pictures and single-words, menus and shopping catalogues with pictures of items plus their names, memes, advertisements, single-panel cartoons, and single-word utterances with gestures, among others. These emergent states are diagrammed in the Parallel Architecture in Figure 9.1a for interactions between simple speech and gestures, and Figure 9.1b for interactions between simple images and text.

Consider first a simple example like you might find in advertisements or online shopping in Figure 9.2a, where a picture of an object for sale (here a pen) is shown with a description of the object (here the word *Pen*). The picture as a whole (subscript 4) contains a visual region for the monomorph of the pictured pen (subscript 1) and the written word *Pen* (subscript 2). These visual elements are interfaced using an adjoined relationship, with a carrier (caption) containing the word *pen*. This carrier is left undepicted but persists morphologically as an affix for the stem of the monomorph (the picture of a pen). As we described in Chapter 3, adjoined carriers facilitate a conceptual structure that relates the graphic and textual content, which is then resolved in $CS_{Integrated}$ as complete coreference, as discussed in Chapter 5.

This basic relationship of an object and its label is maintained across many media, whether in shopping listings, advertisements, identification documents, and many others. Given this prevalence, we posit an abstracted multimodal lexical item as schematized in Figure 9.2b. Here, a depicted object X is labeled by a word Y, with the remaining correspondences consistent with the pen example in Figure 9.2a. The default interpretation here is some form of coreference (i.e., the label describes the object depicted), but with varying degrees of overlap (e.g., the label may provide more or less categorical specificity, such as *dip pen* or *office item*). The entrenched nature of this multimodal lexical item allows comprehenders to expect a coreferential relationship, which can then be played with creatively in examples like Figure 9.2c.

In Figure 9.2c, we now see the same picture of a pen but alongside the word *Weapon*. Everything here is the same as with the label of *pen*, except that the co-referentiality warranted by the multimodal relationship is challenged because of the lack of overt coreference between what is shown and what is described. This sponsors a comprehender to resolve the incongruity of the absent coreference (Fauconnier and

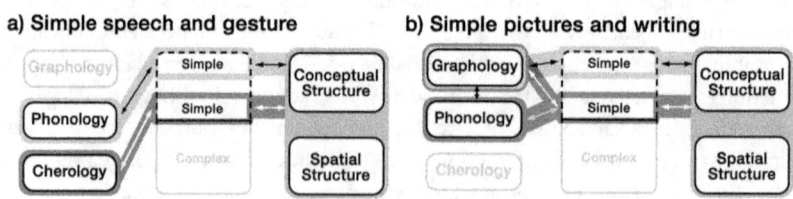

Figure 9.1 Symmetrical Simple interactions in the Parallel Architecture for a) simple speech and gesture and b) simple pictures and writing.

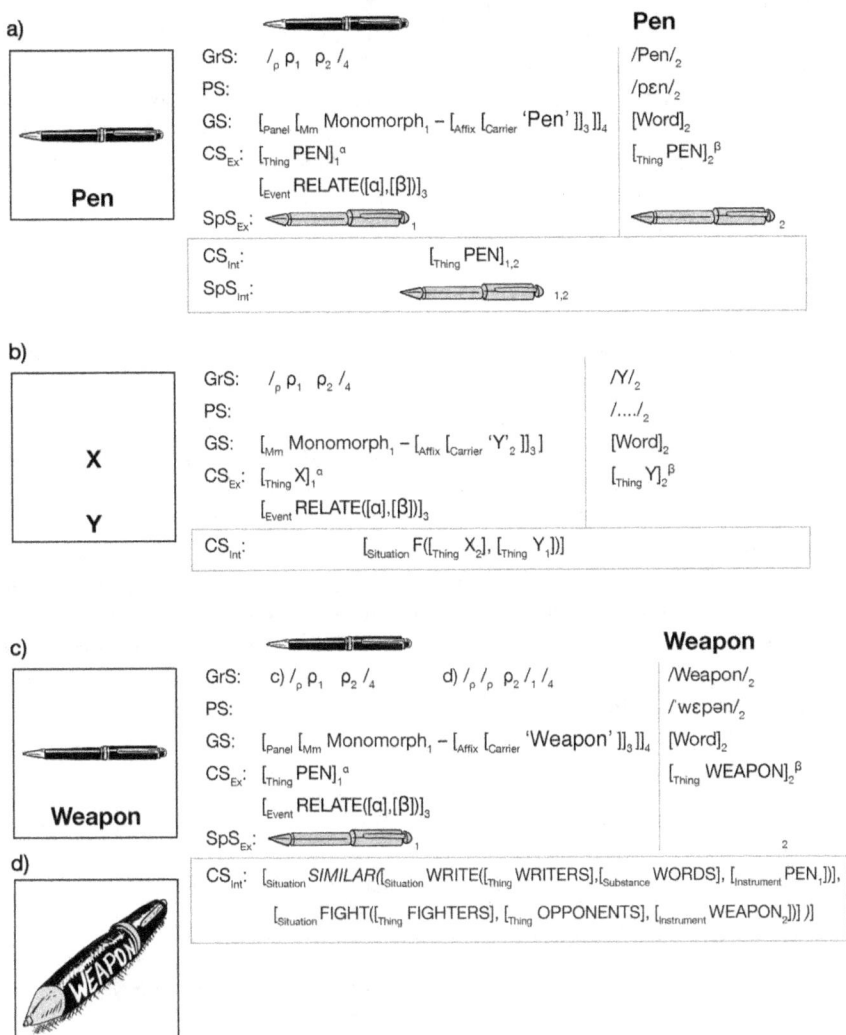

Figure 9.2 Symmetrical Simple interactions between text and image for a) complete coreference, b) a general schema of this labeling relationship, and its use in absent coreference c) with modalities kept separate or d) with text on the image.

Turner 1998, van den Hoven and Schilperoord 2017), which in this case evokes an analogy based on the use of each of these items (Gentner 1983). Specifically, a weapon is an instrument used to fight against opponents and a pen is an instrument used to write words. This comparison renders an analogy where a pen is similar to a weapon through the words they facilitate. Both Figures 9.2a and 9.2c evoke the same lexical item as in 9.2b, but differ in how the two evoked objects should be related at the level of $CS_{Integrated}$. Because we recognize the need for additional construal within the context of these depictions, it reinforces the entrenched nature of the basic labeling schema.

Finally, an alternative depiction of the relationship in Figure 9.2c appears in Figure 9.2d. Here, the only thing that changes is the manner in which the elements are depicted—i.e., placing the label directly on the object, which results in an altered graphological structure. However, the same labeling function persists along with its structure (unless the text is interpreted literally, with the word written inherently on the pen). This on-object labeling is also entrenched for different types of media, like political cartoons, which may carry the expectation of an analogical relation rather than a complete coreferential description. Similar functions occur with other depictions, like a label placed overlapping with an image in many conventionalized image-macro memes (Dancygier and Vandelanotte 2017). Within any of these depictions, if a comprehender fails to establish a relationship, the same basic labeling schema would lead them to expect that the two messages would be completely distinct or just be an error. All of this implies that the formological manifestation of these relationships as spatially adjacent or overlapping persists as sister schemas within the multimodal lexicon.

Another Symmetrical Simple interaction comes when someone speaks a single word and makes a gesture. To invoke an example from earlier, consider a person pointing at an object, such as clouds, with a deictic gesture along with speaking the demonstrative *This*, as in Figure 9.3a. The gesture is an emblem with a conceptual structure of an extension (EXT) from the gesture itself to whatever it points at (indicated by the variable α). The noun *this* similarly maintains indexical reference to an unknown thing, again indicated by α, since the gesture and word both co-refer with the unexpressed thing in the integrated conceptual structure. Note that in this case, the referred-to thing remains unexpressed in conceptual structure of the multimodal utterances, but the

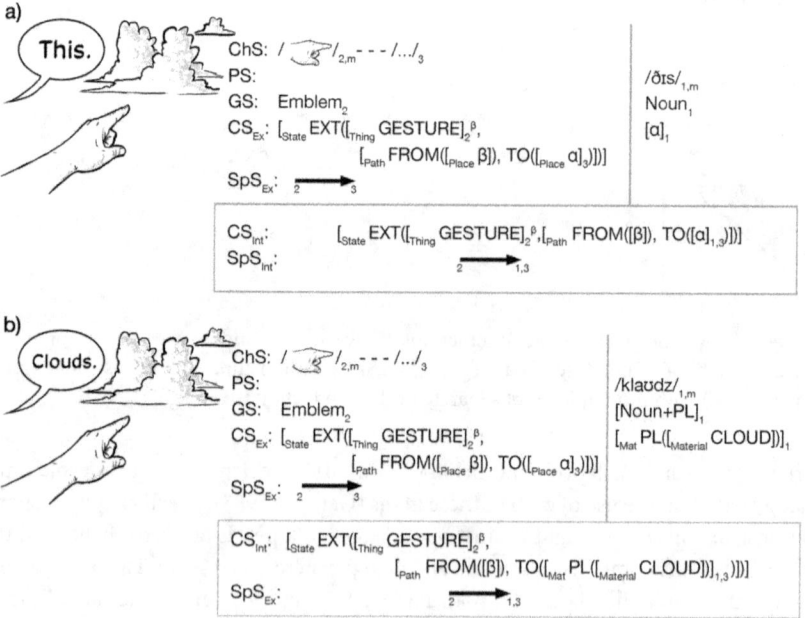

Figure 9.3 Simple Symmetrical interactions of a deictic pointing gesture toward clouds while speaking a) the word *This* and b) the word *Clouds*.

Independent Multimodal Interactions 211

binding variable (α) is associated with something in the environment along the vector of the deictic gesture, such as clouds in this example.

Next consider a case with the same deictic gesture, but where the spoken utterance refers to what is being pointed at, *Clouds* in Figure 9.3b. Unlike the demonstrative *This*, the word *Clouds* carries an overt conceptual structure (i.e., CLOUDS), which can be associated with elements in the environment which are being pointed at. The integrated conceptual structure then unifies the referent CLOUDS with the open slot in the TO function of the gesture.

Symmetrical Simple interactions can also involve slightly more complex expressions. Consider the short sequence in Figure 9.4a which shows a vibrant looking man with the label *No kids*, and then a haggard looking man with the label *Kids*. Each of these words evokes a similar labeling function as in Figure 9.2; however, now an additional relationship needs to be construed because of the sequential images. In the integrated conceptual structure, we need to recognize the coreference between the depictions of the man: they are the same man but with different properties (vibrant versus haggard). Because of this referential continuity, the difference in properties can be interpreted as a type of change, and the cause of which is provided in the text: *Kids*. The integrated conceptual structure thus describes that kids cause the man to go from vibrant to haggard.

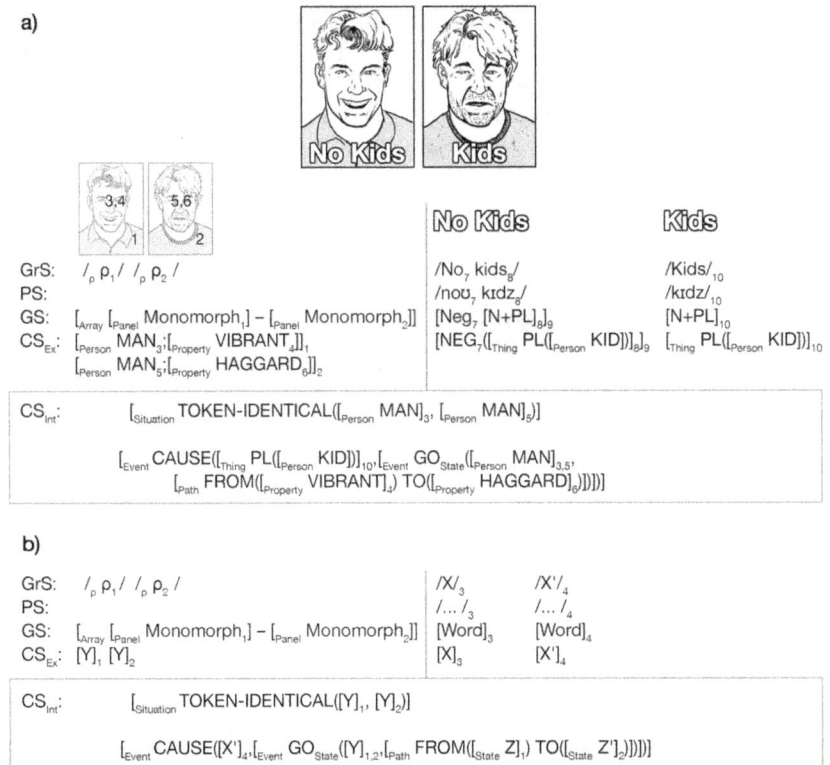

Figure 9.4 The multimodal Before-After Construction in a) an example and b) an abstract schema.

In this case, the interpretation of causation is entirely inferred, but the text and images provide the different arguments for this construed predicate of caused-change.

As discussed in Chapter 6, the Before-After Construction evoked in this sequence is encoded as a multimodal lexical item which manifests in advertisements, cartoons, memes, and many other contexts. Extending the unimodal formalism provided in Chapter 6, the abstract multimodal lexical item is shown in Figure 9.4b. In multimodal Before-After Constructions, the text often provides the causative force. If the text simply says *Before* and *After*, it corresponds to the arguments of the Path (i.e., FROM and TO). As argued before, the Before-After Construction is part of an inheritance hierarchy of two-unit multimodal constructions that express a wide range of conceptual relations, including causation, contrast, analogy, range, and others (Schilperoord and Cohn 2023). Because two-unit sequences often contain no overt marking indicating the causative force, these other conceptual relations may be possible, such as construing this sequence as contrastive between the same man in two different circumstances.

Let's consider two additional examples that both use simple combinatorial structures with linear arrays. Figure 9.5 depicts a burger along with its ingredients. The visual depiction is a region corresponding to a monomorph with the conceptual structure of a BURGER. Because it is a burger many of its ingredients on display compose (COMP) the whole dish. The text lists several of these same ingredients in a linear array, which become coreferenced in the integrated conceptual structure to the depictions of those ingredients. This relationship again maintains what was discussed in the labeling schema in Figure 9.2b (again, omitting carrier information).

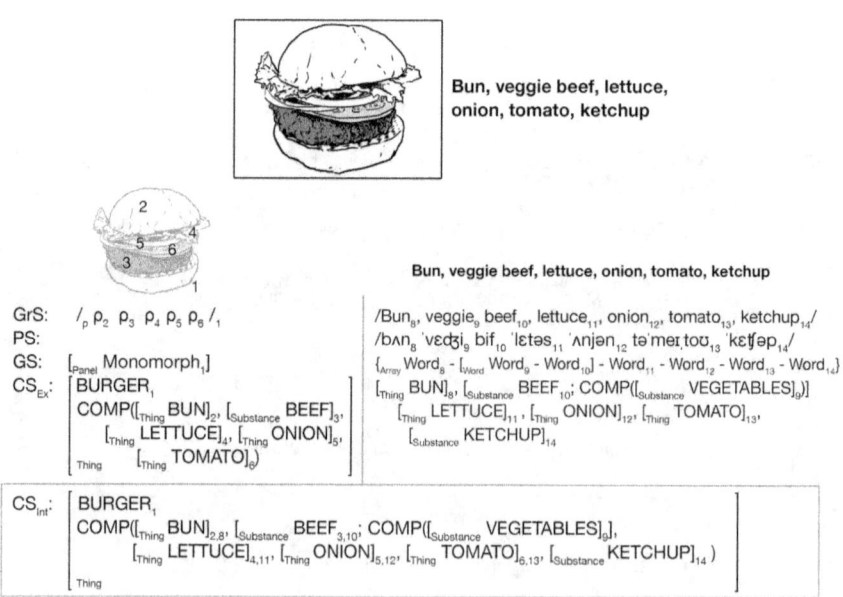

Figure 9.5 Symmetrical Simple interaction using a single picture and a linear written array.

Nevertheless, some ingredients listed in the text cannot be seen in the picture such as ketchup and the composition of the beef (vegetables). This information is only inferred as ingredients of the burger in the integrated conceptual structure. One can imagine other such examples where ingredients are less visible on the whole, such as soup or stew, or extending such constructions to many other objects (e.g., a picture of a computer and text with its properties).

Finally, consider the sequence in Figure 9.6a of a street sign from Nara, Japan which warns about the dangers of the deer that roam freely throughout the city. Each panel maintains a symmetrically simple labeling interaction, and we again omit the additional details related to carriers. Overall, panels are sequenced in an unordered linear array, each showing deer carrying out actions to a female patient, along with text in Japanese, English, Chinese, and Korean corresponding to those actions. Our formalization corresponds only to English, but additional parallel formalizations could be made in all of the languages. Each word only invokes the conceptual frame of that predicate, with an unspecified agent and patient. The pictures correspond to the same events, but with the agent (deer) and patient (woman or girl) specified. In addition to this expressed conceptual structure, we also recognize the pragmatic function of the sign as a whole issuing caution, formalized as the government warning "you" about unspecified events (X). This warning predicate is not overtly in the expressed content (or floating in the "pragmatic ether"), but is knowledge that we bring to bear each time we encounter such signage.

The integrated conceptual structure thus first takes the warning stance as its broadest predication. The sign as a whole conveys a warning from the government to you that deer do these various actions. Because the warning holds YOU as its superordinate patient, recognition of the sign as a warning leads to the inference that each of the subsequent events also can inherent YOU as the patient (notated with the binding function α), and the depicted females are proxies for YOU. Thus, the text and images specify the warned-of events, the image alone provides the agent (deer), and the situational knowledge provides the patient (you). Overall, this leads to an interpretation that you should be warned that deer may do various things to you. Note that if the pragmatic stance of the sign is ignored or not understood, the conceptual integration merely maintains the labeling functions we discussed earlier, whereby the empty slots of the textual frames become filled by the contents of the images (i.e., deer and women/girls). This would be purely descriptive, and have no imperative interpretation.

This type of signage is not unique, and again we posit lexicalized knowledge of all signs with an abstracted similar schema, whether found on signs, in safety manuals, or other contexts. We formalize such a lexical item in Figure 9.6b, where the linear array again shows a depiction of several events (or things) with words corresponding to each of those situations. This lexical schema persists whether the words are present or not (i.e., it also pertains to a sign with an unordered linear array of images). Additional unexpressed knowledge about the sign informs us that such contexts carry an imperative function from some authority (warning, informing, obliging, etc.), and this purpose then informs our subsequent interpretation about all of the expressed events (or things) as pertaining to us.

214   A Multimodal Language Faculty

a)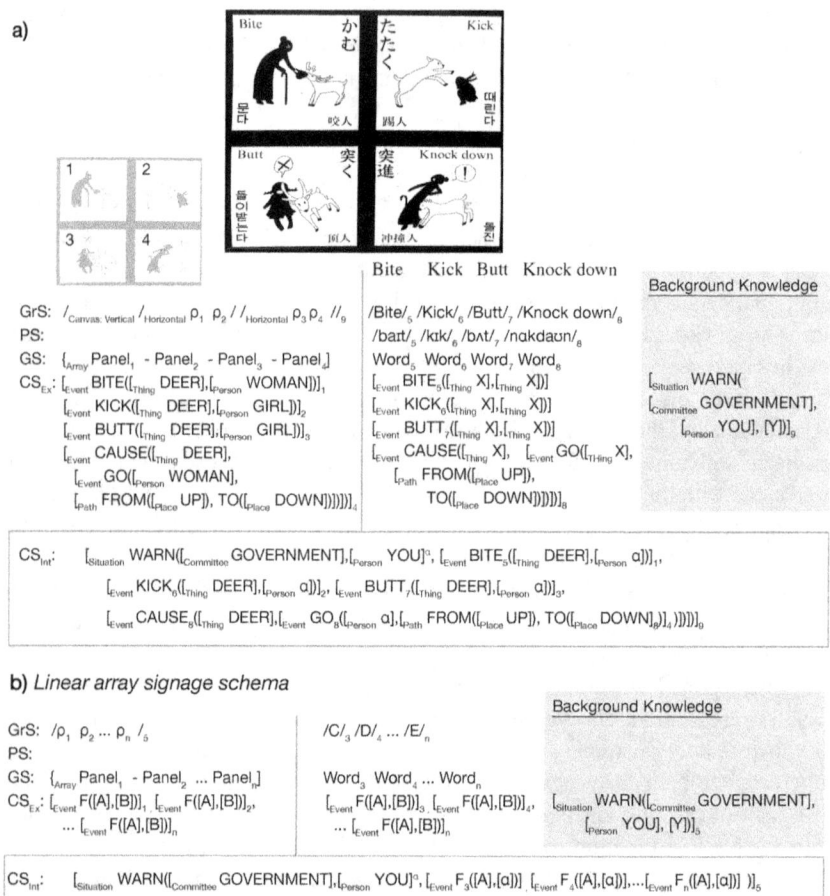

Figure 9.6 Symmetrical Simple interaction a) in a street sign from Nara Japan using linear arrays of image and words and b) in an abstract schema for street signs.

9.2 Asymmetrical Relations

More complex interactions occur when one modality uses a complex combinatorial schema and another modality uses simple combinatoriality, an ***asymmetrical*** interaction. These prevalently appear with spoken sentences alongside gestures, with written sentences that appear alongside single images (be it simple like emoji, or complex like full scenes), or with sequential images appearing with single textual words. These various multimodal expressions are diagrammed for their emergent interactions in the Parallel Architecture in Figure 9.7a–d.

We have formalized many examples of asymmetrical co-speech gestures throughout earlier chapters. Here, let's revisit our recurring example of *I caught a small fish*

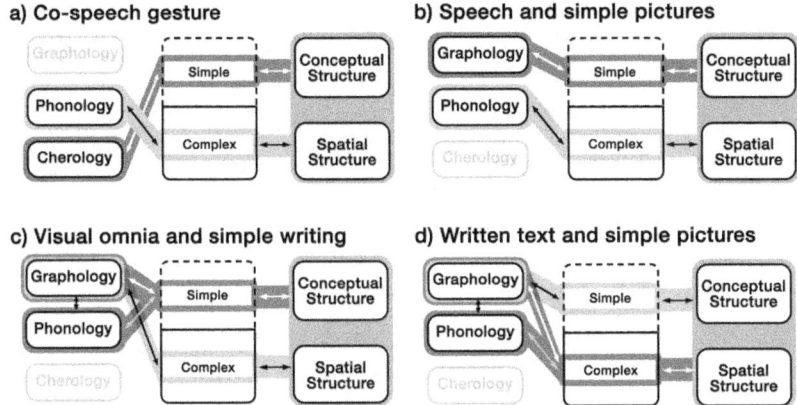

Figure 9.7 Asymmetrical interactions in the Parallel Architecture between a) spoken sentences and gestures, b) spoken sentences and simple pictures, c) visual sequences and simple writing, and d) written sentences and simple pictures.

accompanied by a pinching gesture indicating smallness, as in Figure 9.8. We have already analyzed the semantics of this multimodal expression in Chapter 5, but here we provide the full formalization. As is apparent in the grammatical structure, we have an interaction between a complex array (a sentence) and a simple array (a one-unit gestural emblem). We provide two options for the co-durative temporal correspondence of either a) a synchronous alignment between *small* and the coreferential pinching gesture (subscript m) or b) a persistence of the gesture across the span of the whole sentence (subscript n). Though we show these two modality interactions, the integrated conceptual structure remains the same, with the gesture and adjective *small* being coreferential, leading to the expression as a whole to demonstrate an included coreference.

Other cases of persisting alignment in the modalities may leave room for ambiguity. Consider if we added a modifier to our sentence to render it as *I almost caught a fish* produced with the same persisting gesture. Because the gesture persists temporally across all of the words, it can have more than one coreferential option. In this case, the pinching gesture may also refer to the word *almost*, to give a metaphoric sense of how close the speaker was to actually catching a fish. Because of the temporal persistence of the gesture, its co-referent remains ambiguous (*almost* or *small*) in a way that synchronous alignment would clarify. That is, despite the modality and meaning interactions operating independently, the modality alignment may have consequences on their conceptual integration.

By comparison, imagine if this same sentence was written as text, with an emoji of the pinching gesture placed at the end of the sentence. In this case, the same ambiguity of coreference would persist, but now with a non-durative spatially adjoined correspondence in the modality. Because emoji are often placed at the ends of sentences,

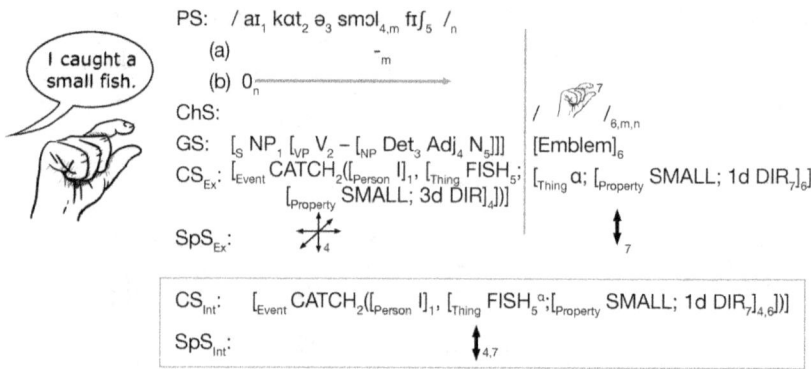

Figure 9.8 An asymmetrical co-speech gesture interaction a) synchronized to a coreferential word and b) persisting across the duration of a sentence.

this ambiguity often occurs (Grosz, Kaiser, and Pierini 2021). Again, the coreferential scope could be disambiguated by inserting the emoji directly next to the co-referring word in a spatial analogue of temporal synchronicity. Yet, people seem to infrequently place emoji next to their referring words compared to at the end of sentences (Cohn, Engelen, and Schilperoord 2019, Cramer, de Juan, and Tetreault 2016), implying a preference for maintaining the structural integrity of the modalities within the forced linear presentation of written text and emoji. This further reinforces the independent allocations of the text and emoji within these asymmetrical relationships, as opposed to the spatial incorporation of emoji into text in substitutive allocation, as we will discuss in the next chapter.

Asymmetrical interactions between written languages and images are also highly prevalent, as they occur whenever sentences combine with a single image. We find them in figures and figure captions (including many of the figures in this book), in scientific articles, newspapers, magazines, websites, and other contexts. Many advertisements also combine sentences with single images, as do single-panel cartoons (political, jokes, etc.), and many memes. Multimodal expressions between text and emoji also often involve asymmetrical interactions, with sentences followed by single emoji or unordered linear arrays of emoji. Further asymmetrical interactions occur when sentences combine with linear arrays, such as a sentence providing a conceptual frame for a list of images (ex. "These things are prohibited in this park" with various graphic depictions of prohibited objects and actions). We have already formalized many of these types of asymmetrical interactions throughout the earlier chapters.

A different type of asymmetrical interaction occurs when written text maintains complex sentences which are combined with a sequence of images that do not necessarily connect with each other. Here, the images themselves form a linear array, but each image is largely parasitic to its accompanying text. The bundled nature of each text-image association leads to a "sequencing illusion" where the graphics appear to have more sequentiality than their actual content warrants. For example, Figure 9.9a has a conversation between two people where the text carries more semantic weight for the meaning of the sequence, with the images providing context. The coreference of text and image within each panel may give the sensation of variance between panels, yet, in fact, each panel merely repeats the same image.

A more complex example is found often in non-fiction comics with interactions between text and pictures, and also in dynamic contexts like documentaries between video and narration. In these cases, the text largely carries the semantic weight and the images often illustrate or elaborate on the textual content. The excerpt in Figure 9.9b

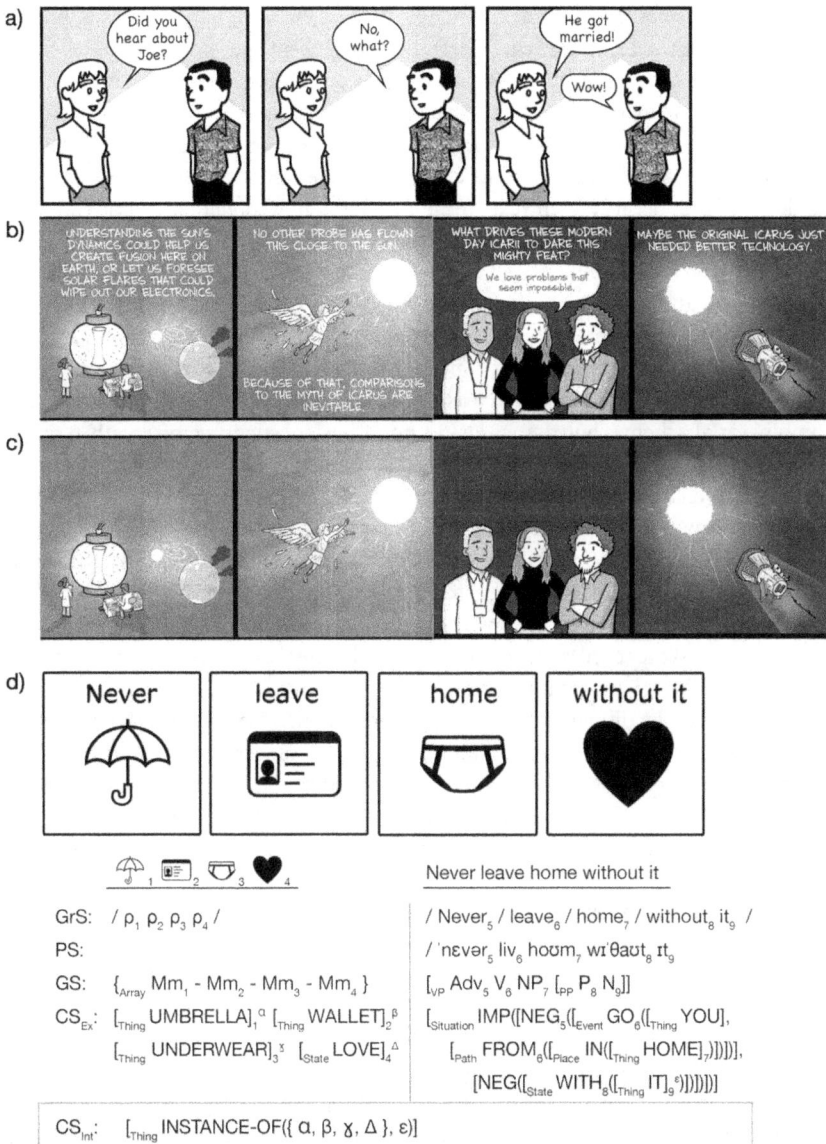

Figure 9.9 Asymmetrical interactions between complex text and simple image sequences, including a) where no changes occur across panels, b) in illustrative panels, c) compared to images alone, and d) in segmentation of a sentence across a linear array. (b and c) © Jorge Cham from *Physics Magazine* 14, 178, December 14, 2021 (https://physics.aps.org/articles/v14/178).

describes solar missions of probes, and each image is coreferential with key information within each panel (for example, the images in the first panel co-refer to "create fusion" and to "solar flares ... wipe out our electronics"). Nevertheless, the pictorial content of each panel does not connect to the other panels in an integrative way, which becomes more apparent when omitting the text (Figure 9.9c), rendering a more incoherent sequence of images. Because of the lack of connections across images, this interaction overall remains asymmetrical.

Finally, consider the sequence in Figure 9.9d where each panel shows a different item (umbrella, wallet, underwear, heart) and a single sentence is distributed across the panels to read *Never leave home without it*. Again, an illusion of sequentiality is created through the text-image interactions. In actuality, the images here create a linear array of objects. Because of this flexibility, any object could appear alongside any word within each panel, making the within-panel relationships between text and image effectively random. This is because each text-image pairing is not coreferential, but rather the coreference arises between all of the depicted items with the final word of the sentence *it*. The integrated conceptual structure expresses that all the items belong to an *ad hoc* category provided by the text, i.e., these are all things you should not leave the house without. This renders the overall sequence as asymmetrical in its combinatoriality, with the conceptual interactions operating globally rather than locally per panel.

Asymmetrical interactions also arise when a sequence of images uses a complex combinatorial schema, but the words do not. These occur in comics with narrative sequences that use only single words in the panels, such as ideophones, or single words expressed as characters' speech or thoughts. Such multimodal interactions have been shown in corpus work to have been increasing in frequency over time in American comics over the past 80 years (Cohn 2024). Similar asymmetry persists in movie trailers where narrative sequencing is integrated or interspersed with promotional text ("mesmerizing," "tour de force," "a wild ride").

Consider first the short sequence in Figure 9.10a, where two boxers are shown fighting and the second panel shows the ideophone *Pow!* next to the act of one boxer punching the other. Let's begin by dissecting the visual sequence alone. The first panel shows a boxer reaching back to punch (a narrative Initial), the second panel shows the punch (a Peak), and the final panel shows the defeat of the punched boxer (a Release). The integrated conceptual structure for these three panels could be described purely with causative functions; however, this can become unwieldy in the notation. Instead, we invoke a slightly more descriptive notation of events through their subparts of a Preparation (the "about to" part of an event), Head (the event itself), and Coda (the aftermath or refraction period of an event). This tripartite structure for discrete events is an alternate notation for the causative relations between sub-events (Jackendoff 2007), supported by empirical research (Cohn, Paczynski, and Kutas 2017). For example, "reaching back" instantiates a general GO function, which is encoded within the knowledge about the event of punching, and this stored information allows for the prediction of upcoming events (Aglioti et al. 2008, Cohn, Paczynski, and Kutas 2017). We here frame our notation in terms of the actions of the agent of this event, though a full treatment of the event structure of this sequence would involve tracks of events for all characters involved.

Turning to the textual component, as discussed previously, the sound effect alone is an emission of a particular event (here an impact of a punch), but which has its

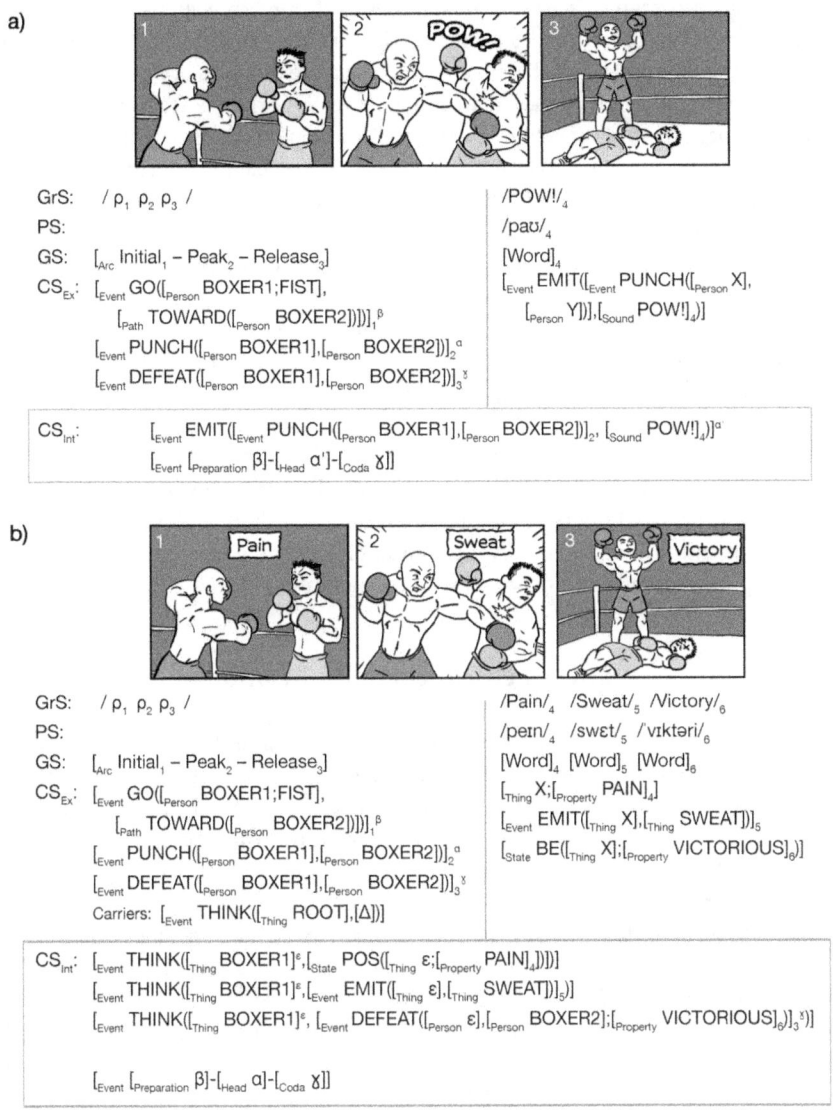

Figure 9.10 A short boxing sequence with a) an ideophone (Pow!) and b) single words depicting thoughts.

arguments left unspecified (Jackendoff 2010a). These arguments are filled in the integrated conceptual structure, with the boxers acting as the agent and patient as specified in panel 2, which then emits this sound. The integrated conceptual structure for this panel is incorporated into the broader event frame, with a slightly more elaborated head event (indicated as ɑ′, since the unimodal representation expressed as ɑ would also suffice on its own without the integration of the ideophone).

For a different example, consider Figure 9.10b, with captions with single words accompanying each of the boxing panels. These words could be interpreted as a noir-style thought process of one of the boxers, amongst other interpretations. For simplicity, we again leave out the semantics for the carriers, as described in Chapter 3. We here formalize the interpretation where the words reflect the thoughts of Boxer1 (although this is ambiguous). Here we have diagrammed a version where PAIN is a property of one of the boxers; however, additional possibilities would include a desire for a boxer to cause pain or an anticipation to receive pain, or that pain is a metonymy for the preceding hard work of being in this athletic situation. It is also ambiguous whether these words refer to the boxer(s) as they are presented at this state. We have chosen to formalize this only for the final panel, where *Victory* can be coreferential with the defeat of one boxer by the other. A similar coreference could occur for all words describing content within each panel, or this could be left independent.

Whatever interpretation is chosen, it would affect the integrated conceptual structure, not necessarily the expressed conceptual structure. Though each word expresses a different property or state, in all cases the agent is left unmentioned. This information is filled within the integrated conceptual structure by Boxer1 playing the role of this agent, while also interpreting these words as thoughts of that same boxer (filling the conceptual frame of the carrier as conveying thinking). This coreferential construal is entirely inferred however, as the ambiguity of the bare single words leaves several options for integrating the text with the pictures.

9.3 Symmetrical Complex Relations

The most complicated interaction occurs between modalities that both use complex combinatorial systems, resulting in **Symmetrical Complex** interactions. These occur in places like visual narratives that use both a syntactic structure and narrative grammar, in films where the narrative grammar may be dynamic and in motion, and in production by bimodal bilinguals who both speak and sign their language concurrently. Emergent states for such interactions in the Parallel Architecture appear in Figure 9.11.

Let's first consider an additional modification to our boxing example in Figure 9.12a. We have added a full sentence to the second panel, with the descriptive *The fist connected with his jaw*. Here, *fist* and *jaw* are coreferential with the depicted events, and *connect* is synonymous in this case with the punching event in that panel. The integrated conceptual structure thus reflects this basic coreference. In addition, the simple array of *New York, 1963* added to the first panel does not use a complex combinatorial structure, but does provide additional meaning not present in the visuals. In this case, the integrated conceptual structure results in the text modifying the whole event of the sequence, not just the first panel, with a time and place. That is, the caption holds scope semantically over the full expression.

Altogether, this example uses a Symmetrical Complex interaction of the sentence and the visual sequence, but the caption at the start also uses an asymmetrical relationship. In addition, the captions render differing types of semantic relationships to the visuals, which do not depend on their complexity. The full sentence in panel 2 uses a complex syntactic structure, but maintains fairly simple coreference with its spatially bundled image. Meanwhile, the caption in panel 1 uses only a simple array, but

Independent Multimodal Interactions 221

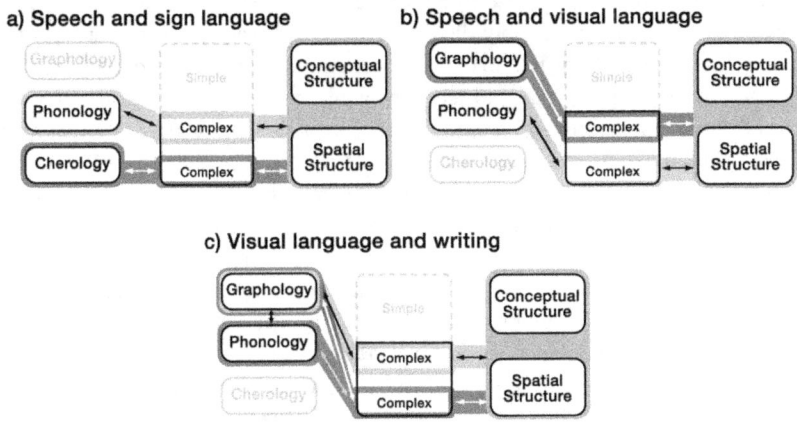

Figure 9.11 Symmetrical Complex interactions in the Parallel Architecture between a) spoken and signed languages, b) spoken and visual languages, and c) visual languages and writing.

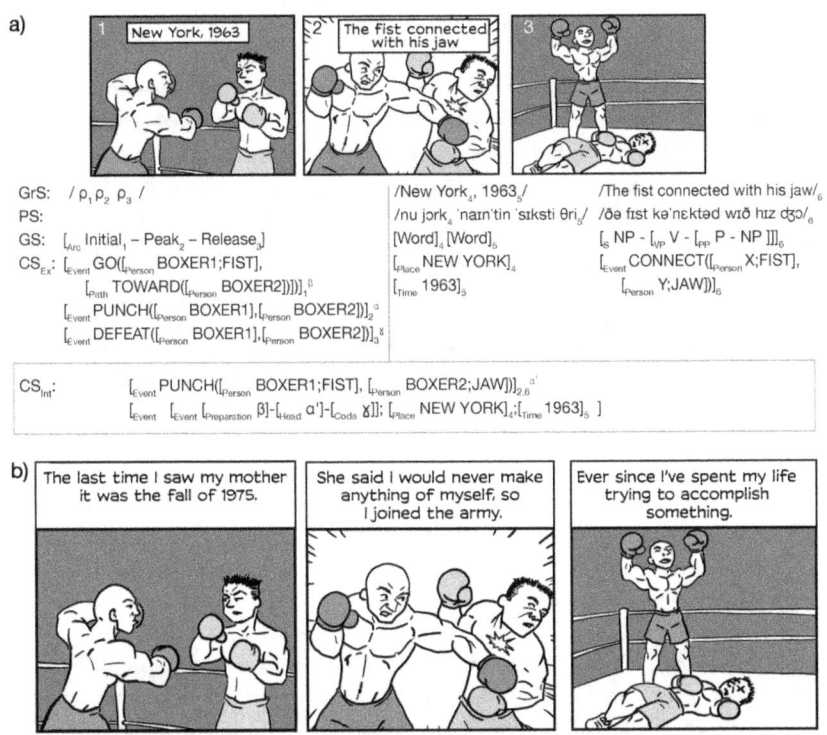

Figure 9.12 Symmetrical Complex relations between a visual sequence and text.

provides meaning that is otherwise absent in the pictures with scope across the whole sequence, not just to its spatially bundled image. This relatively simple example reveals the complicated interactions that may persist across both structure and meaning.

Next consider Figure 9.12b, which uses a more elaborated textual narration across all three panels. In this case, the producer of the text relative to the images remains ambiguous. The speaker ("I" in the text) may corefer to either of the boxers that are depicted, or neither of them (a sports commentator, a person in the audience, etc.). This ambiguity also renders the final panel as ambiguous, with the strived-for-accomplishment in the text being coreferential with the depicted victory of the boxing match, but with the sentiment differing depending on who speaks the text: if it is the victorious boxer, it shows them actually accomplishing something, but if it is the loser, it reinforces the prediction of the mother. If there is no coreference between the narrator and the picture, the boxing image merely illustrates the broader idea of accomplishment. Effectively, this example illustrates how non-apparent absent coreference leaves open many possible interpretations to integrate the multimodal interaction where both modalities provide substantial structure and meaning.

9.3.1 Translations

A special case of independent multimodal interactions occurs with simultaneous production of the same expressions, whether in the same or different modalities. These cases can maintain any of the types of combinatorial relationships that are discussed above, depending on what is expressed. Consider the case of a video where subtitles persist in the same language as is spoken in the video. The text and spoken language are supposed to correspond to the exact same conceptual structures, with (hopefully) the exact same words and grammar being used by both modalities. In some cases, this replication of expression does not always occur, with unintentional variants when the subtitles unfortunately do not match the spoken expression, thereby creating multimodal oddities.

Subtitles may also provide a multimodal signal where the message in the spoken modality may not be accessible (Schilperoord, de Groot, and van Son 2005). For example, translated subtitles provide text for a viewer who does not speak the language spoken in the video. In these cases, complete coreference can only be maintained to the degree that different vocal languages are able to translate between each other. In addition, concurrent subtitles may provide the only access to the spoken languages in the video when the sound is inaccessible, whether for people with hearing impairments or if sound is muted or in a noisy environment. In such cases, the relationship between the translation and the translated utterances is not experienced as a multimodal interaction, despite being produced in multiple modalities. This occurs in any simultaneous translations, including those that occur in face-to-face communication, such as when people are both speaking and signing, or simultaneous translation of multiple spoken languages.

Throughout, different expressions are meant to converge on the same conceptual structure. This arises because they use either different representations across modalities (e.g., speech and text) or different systems within the same modality (e.g., different spoken languages). These varying options are all accounted for as interacting emergent states within the Parallel Architecture.

9.4 Conclusion

As should be evident, multimodality involves complicated interactions throughout all structures of the communicative architecture. Though we use basic examples and often have simplified our formalizations, a substantial amount of complexity remains. In addition, multiple modalities and levels of complexity can combine all within one expression. Consider the comic strip in Figure 9.13a. We already showed the extensive morphological complexity of just the first panel from this strip in Figure 6.13 in Chapter 6. It combines natural pictorial graphics with the synesthetic expressions of speech (writing) and sign language in graphic form. Despite being only three panels long, it includes a complex visual sequence of images, text using both simple and complex combinatoriality which also is substituted into the visual sequence, and a graphic depiction of sign language.

Figure 9.13b depicts these interactions diagrammatically for the entire strip, where we can see multiple independent emergent states all interacting, resulting in both Symmetrical Complex and Asymmetrical interactions, along with both Independent and Substitutive allocations. Though they are diagrammed here all at once, in actuality such interactions weave in and out of various states as part of a singular communicative experience.

All this complexity may give the appearance that there is no consistency, and that all multimodal expressions are unstructured and idiosyncratic. Yet, this is not the case. Even in Figure 9.13a, multiple conventionalized multimodal constructions persist, both for the interfacing between text and image (with the emergent carriers depicting characters' speech), the substitutional construction for text playing a role as a narrative Peak (Cohn 2019), and the general spatial template that signals this as a comic strip (i.e., the title and authorship is provided in text on top of panels). Such multimodal patterns are further substantiated by constructions within each modality, such as the fixed expressions *take cover*, *no more X for you*, and the optimal innovation *broke the "sign" barrier* playing off the base *break the sound barrier*. In addition, highly conventionalized graphic patterns persist in the repetitive visual vocabulary for these particular authors' way of drawing people (maintaining many similar graphemes for the same characters across the first and last panels), and the use of entrenched patterns for depicting motion, with both motion lines and repetition of moving objects (the hands in panel 1). Finally, lexical items from American Sign Language are also depicted in the final panel from all three characters. The son is signing something close to *made a record*, the father is signing *me* and a *question mark* corresponding to his speech of *I did?* or "really?," while the mother is signing *enough*. If a comprehender is fluent in both English and American Sign Language, additional semantic composition arises between the text and these signs.

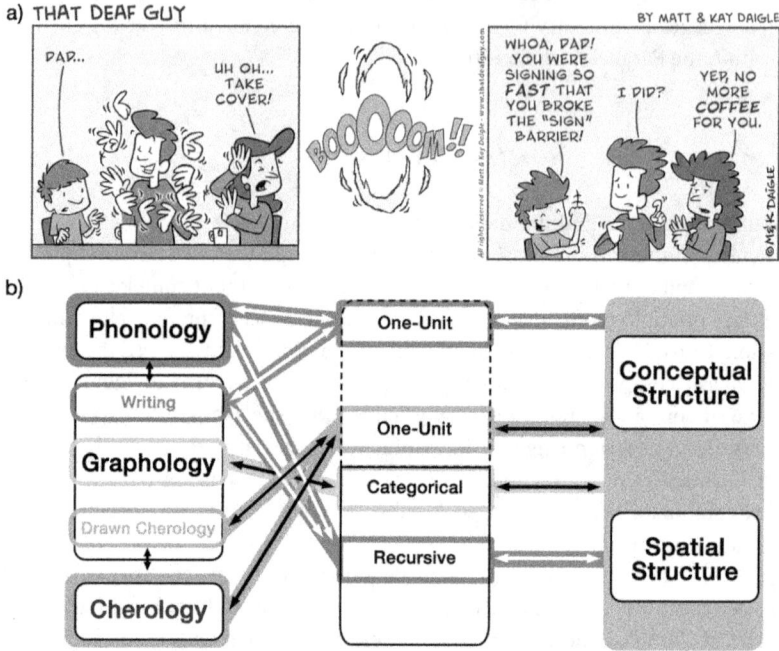

Figure 9.13 A multimodal a) *That Deaf Guy* comic strip and b) the interactions diagrammed in the Parallel Architecture. *That Deaf Guy* © Matt and Kay Daigle (www.thatdeafguy.com).

Thus, as in all linguistic expressions, multimodality balances productive and novel combinations with those that are entrenched in memory as lexical items. This balance between the novel and the lexicalized is maintained both within the systems that manifest in separate modalities, and in multimodal combinations where these systems interact. We have highlighted throughout this chapter and, in this book, multiple instances of multimodal lexical items which encode correspondences between multiple modalities into abstract and productive schemas. Lexicalized multimodality demands a multimodal architecture, and any realistic theory of the structure and cognition of language and communication must account for the full range of complexity of *all* these phenomena.

10

Substitutive Multimodal Interactions

We have finally arrived where we can address the patterns discussed at the outset of this book, namely the phrase *I ♥ NY*. In this canonical sentence, we see the heart shape fulfilling the role of a verb in the verbal syntax. We also highlighted that this stock phrase has been extended into other patterns, such as when the heart functions as a verb meaning LOVE, overall with a [Subject-♥$_{Verb}$-Object] construction. Other extensions use a variety of images as verbs, typically with the images having a semantic relationship to the object (ex. I 🍺 Octoberfest), to form a [Subject-Verb$_{Image}$-Object] construction. Just what is going on here?

All of these patterns use **substitutive** allocation, where one expression is inserted into the combinatorial structure of another expression. *I ♥ NY* is a canonical example where we observe substitution occurring across modalities, with the graphic modality here inserted into the vocal-graphic expression of *I [verb] NY*. This same substitutive allocation is observed when we use gestures to replace words while speaking, what has been called language-like gestures (McNeill 1992) or component gestures (Clark 1996). As we will see, substitution persists both across modalities and within modalities, and this allocation in fact provides critical evidence that the language faculty is a broader multimodal system.

Under an amodal assumption, substitutions are predicted to be incongruous—or deemed as peripheral phenomena—as they involve multiple outputs in a singular syntax, and they would involve shifting from the core modality of speech/writing to a secondary modality of graphics or gestures. In a Multimodal Paradigm, substitutions instead provide evidence for the connectedness of our multiple modalities belonging to a holistic architecture. Such substitution should not be possible, or should be highly incongruous, if our modalities did not exist in an integrated way.

Experimental research supports the idea that substituted elements from one modality readily integrate into the combinatorial structure and meaning of another modality. Yet, we do see costs of switching between modalities in substitutions. Reading times for grammatically congruous substituted emoji were slower compared to words in sentences, but viewing times for grammatically incongruous or homophonous rebus emoji were even slower (Cohn et al. 2018, Scheffler et al. 2022). In addition, viewing times for sentences substituted for images in visual sequences (Symmetrical Complex substitution, as in Figure 7.4b) were also found to be slower than their substituted pictures (Huff et al. 2020). However, onomatopoeia in visual narratives were actually viewed faster than the pictures they substituted (Klomberg and Cohn 2022). Thus, while some work suggests that switching modalities may incur costs, this may either be due to the front-end change in the modality itself (graphics to text, or vice versa), or simply be a matter of relative complexity in the representations.

Nevertheless, the felicity of substitution is suggested by their grammatical and semantic processing. Pictures inserted into sentences are comprehended with accuracy comparable to all-verbal sentences (Cohn et al. 2018, Potter et al. 1986). Substituted emoji within sentences that better maintain the expectations of the written grammar incur no sustained costs (ex. *John loves eating* 🍕 ...), while "ungrammatical" pictures (ex. *John* 🍕 *eating pizza* ...) create spillover costs that persist after the substitution (Cohn et al. 2018). Substituted emoji are also viewed faster than independent allocations of emoji placed at the end of sentences (Cohn et al. 2018). Substituted gestures and animations into vocal sentences also render a range of felicitous implicatures of different types (Tieu, Schlenker, and Chemla 2019).

Finally, neural responses indexing semantic processing (the N400, as measured by event-related potentials) are modulated by congruity or predictability of a substitution with the content of its matrix sequence. This occurs for images substituted into text (Federmeier and Kutas 2001, Ganis, Kutas, and Sereno 1996, Nigam, Hoffman, and Simons 1992, Weissman, Cohn, and Tanner under review) or for text substituted into a visual narrative sequence (Manfredi, Cohn, and Kutas 2017). In addition, such semantic processing is facilitated by iconic gestures with an onset that precedes a corresponding spoken word, functioning momentarily like a substitution (Hintz et al. 2023). Together, these findings imply that, while modalities themselves may incur front-end costs, substituted elements readily integrate with their matrix modality across both their semantics and combinatorial systems.

In this chapter, we will further interrogate substitutive allocation. We continue our formalization of these phenomena, and show that substitution arises both within and across modalities. We will arrive at an overall interpretation that substitution is not merely some peripheral, exceptional phenomena, but in fact reveals the permeating interconnectedness of components within the multimodal architecture. This connectedness can already be seen in our abstracted formalization of substitution which we first introduced in Chapter 7:

Substitution Schema

	Expression 1: Matrix schema	Expression 2: Substitution
GS:	$[_{Array}$ Unit - Unit$_a$ - Unit$]$	$[_{Array}$ Unit$]_a$
CS:	$[... [_X α] ...]$	$[_X X]^a$

Here we formalize the substitutive allocation of two expressions, where Expression 1 serves as the **matrix schema** for Expression 2 which is a **substitution**. The grammar of Expression 1 uses multiple units within an array, while the structure of Expression 2 remains as a single unit (although substitutions may not be restricted to being single units). Expression 2, subscripted with "a" on the outside of the unit, manifests in the grammar of Expression 1, with "a" coindexed to the inside of the array. This outside-to-inside coindexation is the primary formal characteristic of substitution. Substitution has further consequences on the Conceptual Structure, where the meaning of Expression 2 is additionally bound to the meaning of Expression 1, which is marked by the binding operator (α). The end result is that the unit of Expression 2 plays a role within the combinatorial structure of the matrix schema of Expression 1, and that the meaning of Expression 2 is thereby integrated into that of Expression 1. We now turn to showing how this overarching schema manifests in various interactions both across and within modalities.

10.1 Multimodal Substitutions

Let's finally formalize the structure of the *I* ♥ *NY* expression, and the additional constructions it entails. It appears in Figure 10.1a. The matrix expression of *I __ NY* appears in the vocal/textual modality while the heart shape appears in the graphic modality. The matrix expression uses verbal syntax, with a canonical SVO sentence structure, while the substitution is a graphic monomorph that coindexes with the verb in the matrix syntax (coindex "a"). One could perhaps argue that instead of being a monomorph, the heart itself is already encoded as a verb. We will discuss this issue below.

The conceptual structure corresponding to the matrix schema specifies an event with "I" and "NY" as its arguments; however, the verb itself is not specified in the modality. This predicate function remains empty for the verbal expression through a prototypical correspondence between verbs and predicates, but is bounded by the conceptual structure evoked by the substitution, here the heart-shape. The heart-shape encodes a conceptual structure of the predicate LOVE with two open arguments, which in other contexts may be filled by unexpressed arguments. For example, if a person sends a supportive or affectionate message with only a heart-shape to another person, the unexpressed arguments are contextually inferred as ME and YOU.[1] In this context, the heart's predicate of LOVE becomes bound to the unspecified function of the verbal expression through the binding operator (α). These conceptual structures then come together in the $CS_{Integrated}$ to place I and NY as the arguments of LOVE.

This overall construction becomes extended in contexts where the heart widely plays a role as a verb, with varying subjects and objects, as in a variety of places discussed in the first chapter, such as *They* ♥ *weddings* or *We* ♥ *our children*. As argued previously, this creates a construction with the heart as a verb with unspecified subject and object slots. We formalize this **Productive Heart Construction** in Figure 10.1b. This construction uses the same components as the canonical phrase *I* ♥ *NY*, only here the subject and object are open slots with no specified modality or conceptual structure, other than the general interfaces specifying that the subject corresponds to a conceptual agent/experiencer. Because these components are left unspecified, the construction becomes productive, scaffolded around only the expressed heart substitution.

As described above, under this analysis, the Productive Heart Construction technically does not encode the heart as a verb. Rather, it uses the canonical SVO construction but where the verb is filled by the concept of LOVE, which coindexes to the conceptual structure of the heart-shape. Note that we have articulated an alternative

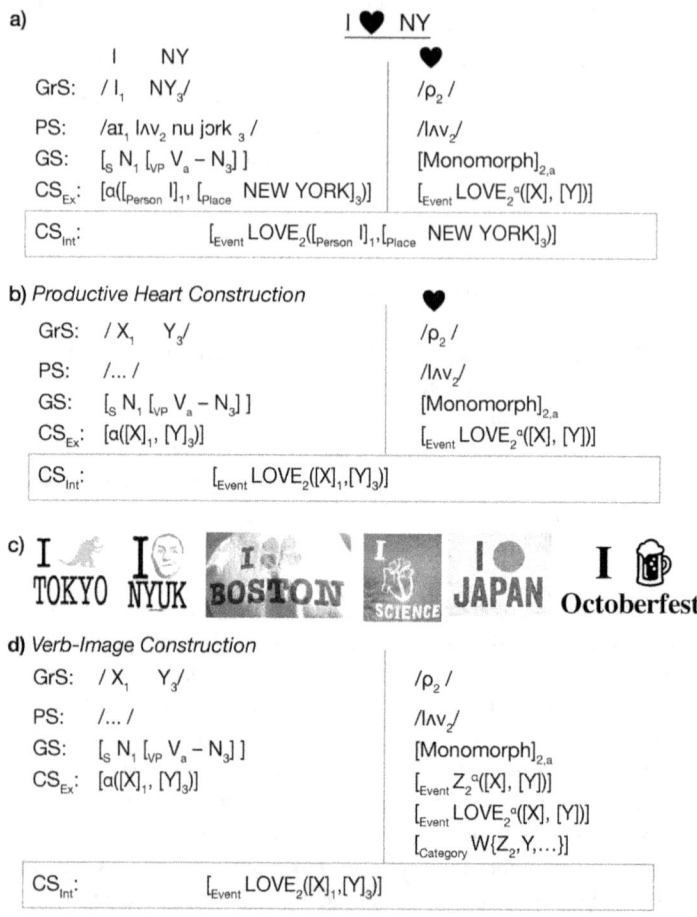

Figure 10.1 Substitutions of images for verbs a) in the classic *I ♥ NY*, b) in the Productive Heart Construction, c) in several substitutions, and d) in the Verb-Image Construction.

interpretation in prior works (Cohn and Schilperoord 2022) where the heart itself is encoded as a verb with the frame of the canonical SVO structure. This analysis works perfectly fine for accounting for the same structure. What is at issue then between these analyses is whether graphic units have the ability to directly encode grammatical units from another modality. To some degree this is a question of affordances: can the graphic modality afford syntactic structure (i.e., nouns, verbs, etc.) or does it only allow more graphically afforded combinatorial structure (i.e., visual morphology and narrative structure)? No matter the specific analysis of where the verb information is encoded, the heart-shape as a verb in these contexts is most definitely entrenched in long-term memory.

If we maintain the interpretation of the heart as a monomorph which substitutes into the verbal syntax as verb, it raises the question of how this unification occurs. Unification operates by linking structures that are specified with similar encoded categories, such as a lexical item encoded as a verb filling the verb slot in a syntactic construction. Ill-formed constructions thus arise when categories mismatch, like a noun in a verb slot. So, how does a monomorph then fill the slot of a verb, when those categories mismatch even in the nature of their structures?

Our answer is that to some degree unification does not fully occur within combinatorial schemas, because indeed these elements do mismatch. This gives rise to a marked situation in grammar where the substitution is recognized as atypical, but where we "coerce" the substitution into the matrix schema through its conceptual structure. In other words, the meaning of the substituted unit can satisfy the allowable conceptual structures corresponding to the combinatorial slot, leading to a coercion of the combinatorial substitution. In some cases, this may give rise to less satisfactory meaning unification as well. In contexts of the heart-shape, this coercion may be less demanding and more acceptable because of the entrenched nature of the whole multimodal construction which includes a conventionalized mapping of the monomorph to the verb. We will elaborate on the constraints on substitutive unification further in this chapter, and as we will see, cross-type unification is often central for issues of substitution.

This construction has become even more productive in expressions where the verb slot is extended beyond the heart-shape to other graphic images which are not directly encoded. Several examples are provided in Figure 10.1c, along with those in Figure 1.1 of Chapter 1. We formalize this **Verb-Image Construction** in Figure 10.1d.

This construction sometimes maintains an association between the verb-image and the meaning of LOVE (coindexed through subscript 4 between LOVE and whatever additional predicate "Z" may be expressed), but sometimes it does not. For example, in the case of *I 🍺 Octoberfest*, the beer as an object does link to the predicate of LOVE, while simultaneously indicating something like "drink beer at." In the case of an image of Godzilla filling the slot of *I __ Tokyo*, there is somewhat of an inference of the predicate LOVE, but at the same time some association that Godzilla destroys Tokyo via our background knowledge about the relationship between Godzilla and Tokyo.

A similar metonymy persists in *I ☘ Boston*, where the clover-leaf invites an association to Boston's Irish-American population and basketball team that uses the clover-leaf as a logo, while invoking the LOVE predicate inherited from the broader constructional frame. To arrive at a coherent interpretation of the sentence, and most all Verb-Image Constructions, we usually require a categorical or metonymic association between the substituted image and the grammatical object of the sentence (and only rarely the subject). We attempt to capture this with a predicate of a category that includes the superordinate associative field (W) which contains both the meaning of the image (Z) and that of the object (Y). This helps explain why for example Godzilla as substitution would be less coherent in *I ___ Boston* than *I ___ Tokyo*, or in *I ☘ Tokyo*. This is not to say that an interpretation could not be construed, just that it would not immediately belong to an available semantic frame via our background knowledge of those cities.

Thus, semantically, the Verb-Image Construction involves different combinations of the conceptual structures that could be involved. In the canonical case, the image invokes a predicate associated to the object while also maintaining an invocation of LOVE. There are also cases where only one predicate is invoked. For example, in Figure 1.1 from Chapter 1, an image of the face of Curly from the Three Stooges is placed in the sequence *I <Curly> Nyuk*. The image of Curly does not correspond to an event but to an object, and *Nyuk* is a sound he made. In this example, the expression still evokes the LOVE predicate inherited from the construction along with the semantic frame to arrive at an interpretation of "I love the Three Stooges," but without a compositional predicate sponsored by Curly. Consider also the expression *I ☠ Bush* (seen on a shirt at a 2005 anti-war protest) which expresses something like *I hate Bush*. In this case, the LOVE predicate is inhibited and the skull-and-crossbones motivates the antonym event structure of HATE, with little semantic association between verb and object other than the predication. Thus, while the prototypical Verb-Image Construction might involve the three conceptual components specified in Figure 10.1d, various instantiations only evoke some of them.

We arrive at an inheritance hierarchy of constructions which developed from the concrete *I ♥ NY* and was further abstracted by turning subjects and objects into variable slots, and then further by making the verb a variable mandatorily filled by an image. This is thus a family of multimodal constructions. Despite this verb-driven substitution, additional work has shown that images substituted into verbal sentences often play roles as nouns or adjectives within online conversations (Cohn, Engelen, and Schilperoord 2019). Below, we discuss why we think this preference for nouns and adjectives occurs, yet the prevalence of substitution to not be verbs in conversations further reinforces the status of the Verb-Image Construction *as a construction*, often associated with particular contexts (like T-shirts).

Let's now turn to multimodal interactions with co-speech gestures, starting with our oft-invoked example of catching a small fish. Imagine the sentence *I caught a ... fish* where a pinching gesture is produced while finishing the word *a* and starting the word *fish*. We formalize this example in Figure 10.2a. As in Chapter 3, we here notate the interface of the gesture to speech beneath the phonological structure that marks the expression of the gesture (-) with a correspondence across modalities (subscript m). As with the image substitutions above, this pinching gesture corresponds to an unexpressed adjective (subscript a) for which the vocal expression has no correspondence in Conceptual Structure. As discussed in Chapter 5, the pinching gesture itself is a unit which corresponds to the property of smallness (Woodin et al. 2020) that modifies a gesturally unexpressed object (α).

The integrated conceptual structure then unifies this property to the thing of FISH, to arrive at an overall interpretation that the fish was small. There is of course an interpretation with no unexpressed adjective in the verbal syntax, and thus no substitution. Within our Parallel Architecture, such an interpretation works just the same as in Figure 10.2a only no adjective would be specified and it would be interpreted as an independent, Asymmetric allocation leading to the addition of a predicate applied to the concept of FISH. We formalized the semantics of this in Figure 5.13b in Chapter 5. This interpretation would become more explicit without

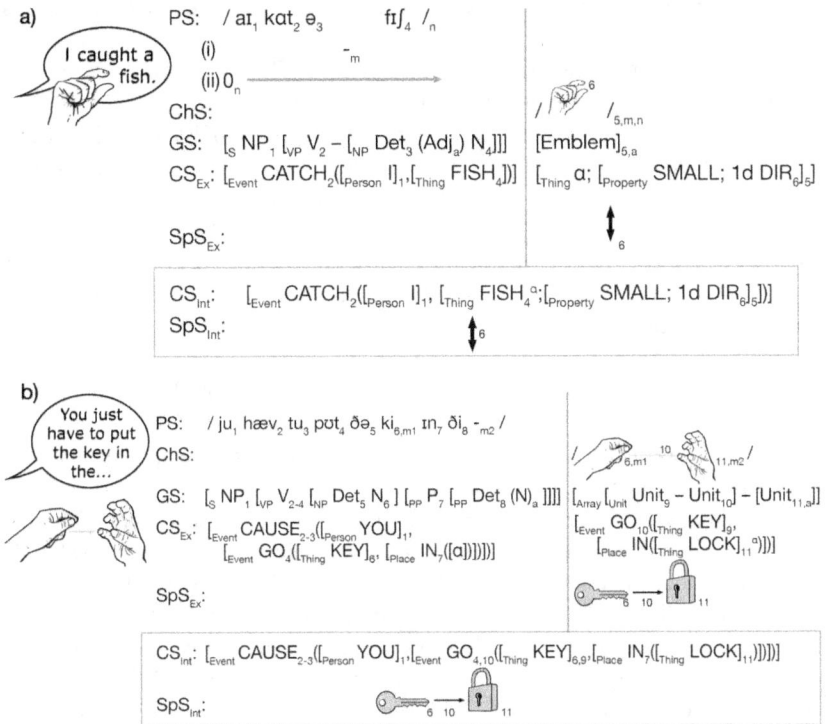

Figure 10.2 Substitutive allocation in co-speech gestures.

the timing of the substitutive gesture, such as if the pinching gesture was produced at the start of the sentence and persisted across its whole duration, as in Figure 10.2aii. In this independent Asymmetric allocation, there would be no temporal implication of an unexpressed adjective, and the association of smallness to the fish would be even more pragmatically assigned than in the substitution.

This difference between modality interfacing—as either synchronous-substitutive gestures or persisting-independent gestures—thus has consequences for the meaning of the multimodal interaction. Persisting gestures make no use of the durative affordances of both modalities to temporally index units together. Here it is left to the receiver to conceptually integrate the gesture and utterance. This same relationship would hold in text-image interactions with independent allocation of an image in relationship to text, whether as an emoji placed at the end of a sentence or a caption accompanying a picture. Aspects of the modality interactions thus have consequences for construing the integrated conceptual structure.

Consider also an example reminiscent of a gesture in a tip-of-the-tongue situation (Pyers et al. 2021), where someone utters the sentence *You have to put the key in the ...* with a gesture of one hand as if holding a key appearing at the same time as the spoken word *key* which moves repeatedly toward an open hand as if holding a lock that occurs after the determiner *the*, but where the word "lock" is never uttered. We formalize this in Figure 10.2b.

This example combines a synchronous independent allocation with a substitution. The gesture resembling a key is synchronous with the word *key* (subscript m1). In this case, the gesture provides an iconic reference to the form of holding a key, while the word provides symbolic reference to the same overall cluster of concepts. This key gesture in one hand is joined by a second hand (subscript m2) which appears as if holding a lock, which together form an iconic depiction of the scenic action. This second lock-gesture creates a grammatical substitution with an unexpressed noun (subscript a) which is cued by the preceding determiner *the* (Delong, Urbach, and Kutas 2005, Huettig, Audring, and Jackendoff 2022, Schilperoord and Verhagen 2006, van Berkum et al. 2005). If the sentence ended with *You have to put the key ...*, it could also be considered as a substitution for the whole prepositional phrase, though the grammatical cues would be less compelling. This lock-gesture provides an iconic reference to a concept of a lock, which is then integrated with the Thing slot left open in the speech (*in the ...*) to arrive at the overall interpretation that the key goes in the lock.

We should note here one detail about our choice for the combinatorial structure of the gestures, given debates about the scale of morphemic segmentation in the bodily modality (Aronoff, Meir, and Sandler 2005). Here we take the option that the key-gesture and its movement maintain an isomorphism between their modality, grammar, and meaning, i.e., the handshape and its movement correspond to two morphemic units that concatenate in a larger unit, which also corresponds to the object KEY (handshape) and the predicate GO (movement). There is another non-isomorphic interpretation where the handshape and its movement are different articulators that correspond to separate aspects of meaning, but which both index to a single monomorphemic unit (i.e., both subscripts 9 and 10 would correspond to the same unit). While our approach does not resolve this issue of segmental scale, it does provide the possibilities for both isomorphic and non-isomorphic segmentation which we leave as an open question.

The reverse relationship with modalities also exists. Bimodal bilinguals with proficiency in both a spoken language and sign language have been observed to "codeswitch" between modalities (Emmorey et al. 2008). This substitution of spoken words into the sign language grammar is the inverse of the modality situation in co-speech gestures. However, co-speech gestures involve the interaction of a semia (gestures) with an omnia system (speech), while in this case of bimodal bilingualism, the units come from fully developed omnia systems in both modalities (spoken and signed *languages*). We will address the issue of codeswitching more generally below.

Let's now turn to another substitutive allocation, this time with a vocal/textual expression manifesting within a visual sequence. Consider Figure 10.3a which has a visual sequence where the onomatopoeia of *POW!* substitutes for the Peak, i.e., the climax, in the visual narrative sequence. The matrix schema of the visual sequence depicts the Initial and Release states of the narrative, which correspond semantically to the agent boxer reaching back to punch and to his subsequent celebration at his opponent's defeat. The graphic structure here leaves the punching event unseen, but it is implied through the corresponding onomatopoeia which represents the causative function of a sound emitted by a punch or impact (Jackendoff 2010a).

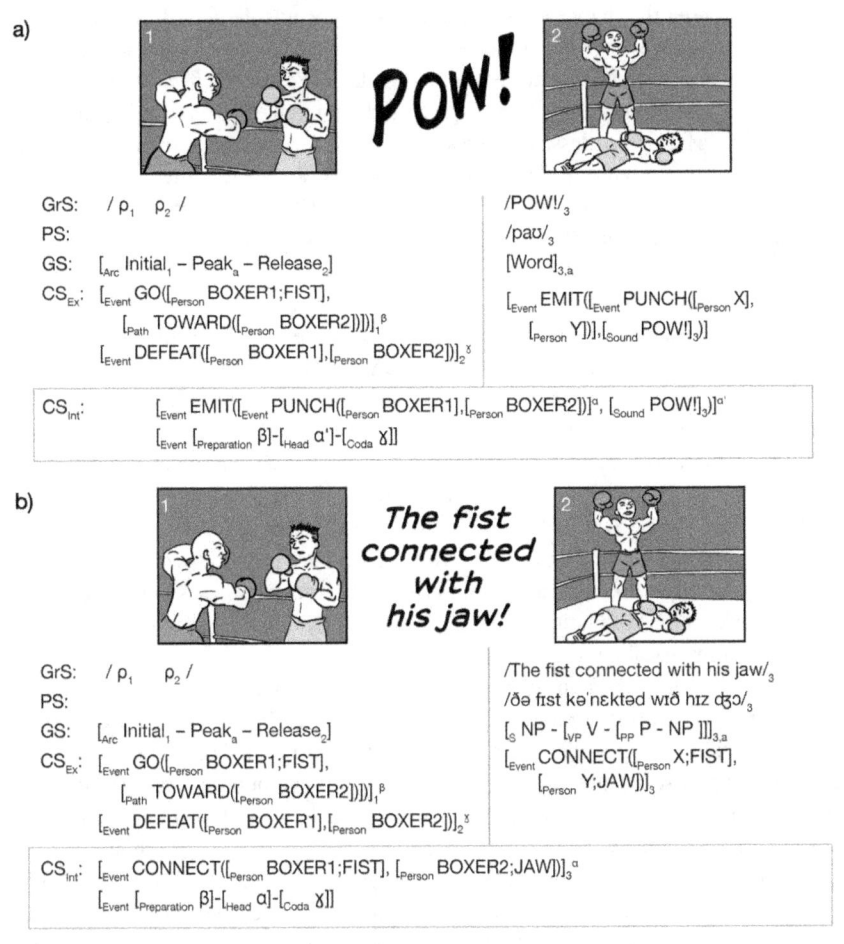

Figure 10.3 Substitutive allocation in a visual narrative sequence with a) Asymmetric (single word) and b) Symmetrical Complex (sentence) symmetry.

The sound effect provides an element that fills the role of a climactic narrative Peak in the narrative grammar, again marked by coindex "a." Because this textual cue fills the narrative role of an otherwise visually motivated structure (Initial-Peak-Release), it is another example of substitution. Such substitutions are both a frequent-type Asymmetrical substitutive allocation and an entrenched constructional pattern for sponsoring inferences in visual narratives (Cohn 2019, Klomberg and Cohn 2022). The onomatopoeia cues the unexpressed event, helping facilitate the inference, combining with the knowledge from the other panels of the boxers as agent (puncher) and patient (punchee). This punching event then is integrated in conceptual structure, as the head (α), together with the visually expressed preparation (β) and coda (γ) resulting in a full event structure.

We can also imagine a more explicit Asymmetric substitution where instead of the sound effect *Pow!*, the word *Punch!* appears between the two panels. This expression would only render the change in our notation to not include the sound-emission event, with the punching event overtly expressed. Corpus analysis has suggested that this type of descriptive label (stylistically shown as if it were a sound effect) does appear in various comics, although at a lower proportion than onomatopoeia (Pratha, Avunjian, and Cohn 2016). Nevertheless, neural responses indicate these descriptions do not vary from onomatopoeia in terms of their semantic processing, but that they are recognized as being low probability, given their rarity (Manfredi, Cohn, and Kutas 2017).

More complicated substitutive allocation is also possible, such as in a Symmetrical Complex interaction where both expressions use a complex grammar. This would again be an interaction between two omnia systems: the visual language of the graphics and the written language of the text. In Figure 10.3b, we see a full sentence within the matrix visual sequence instead of just a single word. The sentence *The fist connected with his jaw!* is more semantically explicit about the unseen event structures, only that it leaves the possessors of the fist and jaw to be inferred (X and Y respectively). We understand that "connected with" signals a stylistic way of expressing the punching event which would ultimately be integrated as the head in the broader event structure.

Because of the explicitness of the text, the conceptual integration is more forthcoming than the onomatopoeia in Figure 10.3a. The full sentence constitutes an utterance that can stand on its own, but here again fulfills the Peak role in the visually evoked matrix clause. The result is a substitution using a Symmetrical Complex interaction rather than an Asymmetrical interaction like the previous examples.

Overall, in substitutive allocations, the modalities are not interfaced in a temporal or spatial correspondence, but rather feature a sensory "switching," such that one modality concludes, a different modality begins and ends, and the original continues. As a result, no interfacing arises at the modality level, because no composite signals result from separate expressions integrating into a holistic unit. In other terms, in independent allocations, the modality interfaces provide cues (synchronicity of speech and gesture, spatial proximity or connection for text and images, etc.) which give rise to unification operations within the conceptual structures. In substitutive allocation, on the other hand, combinatorial schemas work to integrate multimodal messages by inserting an expression of one modality as a unit into the matrix schema of another modality. The result is that the combinatorial structures facilitate the access to and unification of meaning from both modalities. This precludes co-referentiality between the semantics of the modalities, thus giving rise to the need for a binding operator (α) to link the meanings. The grammar facilitates this meaning, whether or not it invites conceptual integration.

In this section, we have demonstrated that substitution occurs across most all modalities, and can involve different symmetrical interactions (Asymmetric, Symmetrical Complex). There is flexibility in the various categorical roles played by substitutions (adjectives, verbs, nouns, Peaks, etc.), where the conceptual structure evoked by the substitution is governed by the combinatorial structure of the matrix modality. In addition, substitutions can both be encoded as constructions within the Parallel Architecture but attuned to the lexicon of the matrix modality, or they can be novel, and fully compositional. Altogether this demonstrates the scope of substitution as an important indicator of the multimodal nature of expression, a point we will return to below.

10.2 Unimodal Substitutions

Though we have emphasized substitutive allocation as central for our arguments about multimodality, allocation is a property of the relationships between combinatorial structures, not necessarily just between modalities. It follows that this allocation arises in unimodal contexts as well. Unimodal examples of substitution include, and generalize across, a wide range of phenomena that have thus far been well studied and attested in the literature, but have largely been treated as distinctive. By recognizing that these phenomena involve consistent and abstract structural relationships, they allow us to highlight the generalizing scope of our architecture and the distinctions it entails.

Consider examples where semia within a modality are integrated with the omnia of that same modality. In the vocal modality, ideophones are a lexical class of typically one-unit words (semia) that are prevalent in many of the world's languages (Dingemanse 2017). These expressions show morphosyntactic independence—often placed at the end of sentences—yet they can also be inserted into sentences to take on grammatical roles (Dingemanse 2017). In the bodily modality, similar asymmetrical allocation occurs with gestures that accompany grammatical sign language (Emmorey 2001, Marschark 1994).

Consider the English sentence, *He pow-ed him in the face*, similar to other sound-emission verbs like *The car rumbled around the corner* or *The ball whizzed by his head* (Goldberg and Jackendoff 2004, Jackendoff 2010a). While verbs like *rumble* and *whizz* are encoded in the English lexicon as verbs, *pow* is not, which makes it more demonstrative as a type of ideophone with morphosyntactic independence (i.e., semia). This shows that similar conceptual expressions (i.e., sound-emission) can manifest in both entrenched and novel forms, yet only the novel forms qualify as substitutive allocation because they have no encoding as verbs in the lexicon. However, semantically, the essence here is that the verb expresses something about the action via the sound that it emits. We formalize this in Figure 10.4.

We again separate out the components of the matrix schema and the substitution, despite them manifesting in the same modality. On its own, the onomatopoeia *pow* is a unit with no encoding as a verb or other part-of-speech, and could thereby also substitute for other categories, like nouns (e.g., *He gave him a pow*). This productivity is

	He pow-ed him in the face	
GrS:	/He$_1$ -ed$_2$ him$_3$ in the face$_4$/	/paʊ/$_5$
PS:	/hi$_1$ d$_2$ hɪm$_3$ ɪn ðə feɪs$_4$/	/pow/$_5$
GS:	[$_S$ NP$_1$ [$_{VP}$ V$_a$+PST$_2$ – NP$_3$ - [$_{PP}$ P Det N]$_4$]]	[Unit]$_{5,a}$
CS$_{Ex}$:	[α([$_{Person}$ HE]$_1$,[$_{Person}$ HIM]$_3$^{β},	[$_{Event}$ EMIT([$_{Event}$ PUNCH([$_{Person}$ X],[$_{Person}$ Y])],[$_{Sound}$ POW]$_5$)]
	[$_{Place}$ IN([$_{Thing}$ FACE;[$_{Thing}$ PART([β])]]$_4$)])]	

CS$_{Int}$: [$_{Event}$ EMIT([$_{Event}$ PUNCH^α([$_{Person}$ HE]$_1$,[$_{Person}$ HIM]$_3$^{β},[$_{Place}$ IN([$_{Thing}$ FACE;[$_{Thing}$ PART([β])]]$_4$)])],[$_{Sound}$ POW]$_5$)]

Figure 10.4 Substitutive allocation within a language with an ideophone.

unusual for sound-emission words encoded as verbs in the lexicon (e.g., ?*The car went for a rumble around the corner*). The word *pow* uses the same conceptual structure as we saw in its multimodal context, which is as a sound emission for a punching event. The matrix schema uses a canonical sentence structure, with the morphology of a past tense marker that helps facilitate the substitution being recognized as a verb (e.g., in *He pow him in the face* the substitution remains less recognizable). The substitution once again is marked with subscript "a" for the onomatopoeia to coindex with the verb. The conceptual structure of the matrix schema here resembles what we saw above for the Verb-Image Construction, where we have a predicate structure that is filled in by the substitution. The integrated conceptual structure thus once again allows for the predicate of punching associated with the sound emission to be filled with the arguments (*he, him*) provided by the matrix schema.

In this example, grammatical unification contends with a unit that has no licensed lexically specified category. That is, the ideophone here is encoded as a unit, while the grammatical unification would be "looking for" something to fill the role of a verb. The result is a combinatorial "coercion" where the categories mismatch (Jackendoff 2010a, Pustejovsky 1991), and indeed though it is construable, the sentence should feel marked as atypical. We might hypothesize that substitutive allocation is a type of *unification mismatch* that remains semantically resolvable because of the matrix grammar—regardless of the modality being used—and may be easier when the substitution has no competing categorical role (i.e., the unspecified "unit" of the substitution is not a competing syntactic category with the matrix "verb").

Unimodal substitution also arises in interactions between different representational systems, such as in codeswitching between two languages—i.e., where the units, of varying sizes, of one language are inserted into the matrix schema of another language (Kootstra 2015, Muysken 2020). In these cases, substitution occurs not between an omnia and a semia, but rather between units in omnia systems. Like multimodal substitutions, "insertional" codeswitching is motivated by cognates for substituted words or clauses between languages, and in many cases the morphosyntax of the utterance comes from the matrix schema (Myers-Scotton 1997, 2002). As a result, codeswitches are more often content words (like nouns) than function words. Multimodal substitutions of emoji into sentences are consistent with this, as people more often replace pictures for certain grammatical categories (nouns, adjectives) in sentences over others (verbs, adverbs) (Cohn, Engelen, and Schilperoord 2019).

Sometimes replacement of units occurs as "legal" substitution where the categorical roles match and without the grammatical coercion. We just have a noun in one language substituted by a noun in another language. For example, in the sentence *My tomodachi comes from Nihon*, the words *tomodachi* (friend) and *Nihon* (Japan) are nouns in Japanese and appear as nouns in the English matrix schema. This would be more recognized as atypical of the modality than the grammar. More complicated structure occurs when there is mismatch between the roles of the encoded substitution with its matrix grammar in their respective languages (Backus 2015).

Similarly, unimodal substitution between graphic forms is evoked by different registers or contexts in their representations. This occurs with switching "styles," i.e., changing between the visual vocabularies of different visual languages. Consider the sequence in Figure 10.5a from *One Night* by Tym Godek, which shows a man lying in bed who then turns out the light to sleep. In the third panel, the action of turning off the light is no longer part of the bedroom scene in panels 1, 2, and 4, but rather shows a darkened lightbulb directly. This lightbulb is shown diagrammatically, out of context of the lamp which is being turned off in the actual scene. Semantically, the lightbulb maintains a part-whole relationship to the lamp, and thereby to the action of turning it off (Cohn 2019). However, structurally it appears as the climactic Peak of the narrative, only using an object to represent what would usually be shown as an action. This semantic mismatch (object instead of event) along with the change in register (diagrammatic instead of scenic) creates the substitutive allocation.

A similar phenomenon occurs in Figure 10.5b, from *Night Fisher* by R. Kikuo Johnson. Here we see a man changing a tire before giving up. We never see the man and the tire in the same panel at the same time. Rather, the man reaches downward past the lower border of each panel, where we assume the tire is located. The tire itself is shown in alternating panels with the man, but in a diagrammatic register signaled by being isolated and with arrows (and numbers) characteristic of the visual lexicon of instruction manuals. The tires are once again a type of substitutive allocation because

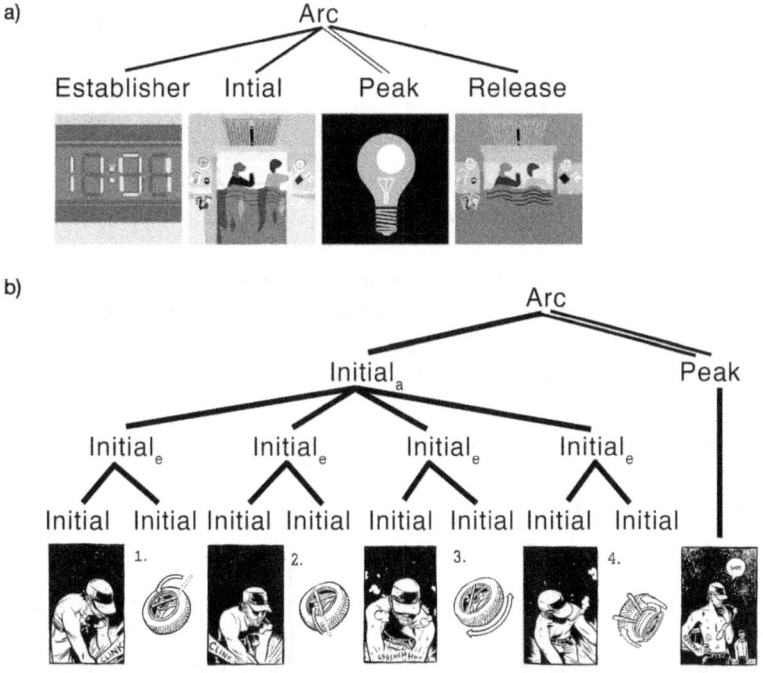

Figure 10.5 Switching in visual register in a) *One Night* by Tym Godek and b) *Night Fisher* by R. Kikuo Johnson. *One Night* © 2006 Tym Godek. *Night Fisher* © 2005 R. Kikuo Johnson.

of their difference in register, as bare objects diagrammatically presented rather than objects integrated as elements into a scene (i.e., showing the man's hands on the tire). The panels of the man (panels 1, 3, 5, and 7) do not actually show the tire-fixing actions taking place, but these elements (man and tire) are associated through the narrative grammar. Each pairing of man and tire combines in a conjunction that evokes inference that they belong to a common environment (subscript e), and further as an iterated action (subscript a) within the narrative Initial, which altogether sets up the subsequent climactic Peak of the man giving up on his activities.

In both of these visual examples, the substitutions are semia inserted into an omnia sequence. The lightbulb in Figure 10.5a is merely an isolated object, with no cues or indications of connections with a broader sequence, unlike the panels that surround it which represent omnia with categorical roles. The tires in Figure 10.5b form a linear array—also a type of semia—which would be evident from creating a sequence from only the tire panels (note also their numbering). This contrasts from the omnia of the matrix schema of the scene of the man, which has categorical roles and constituent structures. These are again examples of Asymmetric substitutive allocation.

Altogether, these examples use substitutive allocation in a unimodal context. If it helps to think of this in terms of the established notion of codeswitching, we might think of substitution between languages as "unimodal codeswitching," whereby the units come from representational systems within the same modality, rather than a "multimodal codeswitching" of substitution from different modalities. This aligns with the idea that a broader lexicon distinguishes lexical items with features for different languages (Jackendoff and Audring 2020), which here extends to a lexicon across and between modalities. Thus, again allocation characterizes the interactions between grammars, no matter the modality or representational origins of those combinatorics.

10.3 Constraints on Substitution

As we have demonstrated, substitutive allocation involves the insertion of units from one representational system into the combinatorial structure of another. However, are there limitations on what can substitute across systems? Without any such constraints, there would be unlimited degrees of freedom for substitution between systems that may have widely varying structures. Given the empirical evidence discussed above, such unconstrained possibilities for interacting do not seem to be the case. We posit constraints coming from each of our tiers of the Parallel Architecture.

A first constraint is on the coordination of the modalities involved in the substitution. Because substitution involves the insertion of a unit (or array) into the array of another expression, it appears within the sequential production of the matrix array. This requires both coordination between the expressions and within a pacing adaptable for the flow of information from the matrix array. This coordination relies on equivalent durativity features: speech and gesture go together well because they are both durative, as might speech with pictures that are rapidly drawn. The durativity required to create a complex image would take too long within the flow of speech for it to substitute, but very simple images may suffice (Green 2014, Wilkins 2016). Pictures and text also mix well, because both are non-durative. In all of these cases, the expressions require the right conditions in order to switch back and forth between units of different origins.

A second restriction on substitutive allocation may come from the conceptual relationships of the elements involved. The primary constraint would be that the substitution should maintain *comparable conceptual content* to the slot made available by the matrix schema. That is, if the available grammatical slot is a verb, it should correspond to a substitution that can carry a predicate (as would a narrative Peak). Substitution involving a noun may be more semantically flexible, but prototypically a thing or an action. This is seen most simply where the substitution directly conveys the type of information that could be filled by the matrix expression, such as using a pizza emoji in a noun slot instead of the word *pizza*, or a heart-shape in a verb slot instead of the word *love*. Substitution with ideophones, whether within speech or multimodally with a visual sequence, operates through the inference of the sound emission, but does not necessarily conflict in its semantic associations. Indeed, mismatches between a substitution's semantics and its available slot can create processing costs (Cohn et al. 2018).

The quantity of information involved in a substitution may also matter. If a substitution conveys more information than needed, additional challenges arise for construal. We posit that single arguments can be fulfilled by words or simple images, but whole argument structures (predicate + arguments) likely cannot. For example, in Figure 10.6 substituting an image of a single person running as either a verb (10.6a) or noun (10.6b) seems better than substituting two people in the act of punching as a transitive verb. In this case, the arguments of the action appear twice, as both subject and object pronouns in the matrix schema and pictorially depicted for the event. The substitution of a fist in (10.6d) is better because it no longer has the competing arguments. This same relationship holds for the mutual event of kissing, with the more abstracted depiction in (10.6e) being better than the transitive depiction in (10.6f), while a sentence structure with no implication of agent or patient appears to allow for both (10.6g,h).

The byproduct of this constraint for the visual modality is that productive substitutions are easier for fairly concrete nouns which involve less argument structure.

a) I 🏃 to the store
b) I went for a 🏃
c) He 👥 him
d) He 👊 him
e) He 😘 him
f) He 💋 him
g) They 😘 for an hour
h) They 💋 for an hour

Figure 10.6 Substitutions of graphics into sentences with varying degrees of acceptability.

Experiments analyzing substitution of emoji into written text suggest that nouns and adjectives are the most substituted grammatical classes in conversational messaging (Cohn, Engelen, and Schilperoord 2019), despite the Verb-Image Construction. We hypothesize that it would be harder to substitute more abstract concepts or those with fuzzy boundaries, such as the word "graduation" which may involve a range of duration and activities within it. Here, substitution by an image may require metonymy, such as for showing an indexically related object, like in Cohn, Engelen, and Schilperoord (2019), where a participant conveyed the concept of graduation through the emoji of a graduation cap.

Finally, we can posit combinatorial constraints on substitutions. Substitutions involve the placement of a unit within an available slot of a matrix schema, and so this unit and its slot need to align in their structure. Morphological forms can be distinguished that can stand alone (words, monomorphs) and those that are bound (affixes). There are also configurations where morphological units combine to express a larger statement, whether as words adding up to a sentence, morphemes adding up to a polysynthetic word, or visual morphemes adding up to a visually depicted scene. Because these different forms have a range of complexity, there may be limits on how they can substitute for each other across modalities.

We here posit that *forms* that can stand alone (i.e., free morphemes)—and comparable available positioning within a matrix array—would better be capable of substitutive allocation, but not more complex morphological forms. Spoken languages with complex morphological systems (like Turkish) may be harder for images to substitute into, because they do not allow equivalence in structure across modalities, and you would lose grammatical relations embedded as inflectional morphology within the isolable word form. In English, substitution readily applies for uninflected verbs or nouns (*I* ♥ *NY*), but becomes more marked when it is inflected (*I* ♥ *ed NY*) or uses inflection without affixation (*I did* ♥ *NY*), although not impossible. Languages with more complex inflection may be less prone to allow such substitution (again, also with limits on being isolable forms).

Substitutive granularity is also why it is harder to insert a complex picture for a single word in a sentence. The conceptual structure is asymmetric, as is the combinatorial structure. However, it may be possible to substitute a single word for a complex scene within a visual sequence, as in the substitutions of the words *POW!* or *Punch!* instead of showing a person punching another person (Figure 10.3a). Thus, simpler units may be substitutable for more complex units, so long as they maintain the structural adherence to being isolable, and the ability to convey the conceptual structure in a reduced form (for example, *Pow!* or *Punch!* expresses the predicate and leaves the arguments inferred). Effectively, we predict it is easier to substitute less information than a slot allows than to provide more.

10.4 Conclusion

Substitutions provide critical evidence for the interconnectedness of modalities, carrying implications for the characteristics of the wider faculty of language. As substitution appears to apply unimodally within a language (ideophones, signers gesturing), unimodally across languages (codeswitching), and in multimodal interactions (speech/gesture, sign/speech, text/image, image/text), it implies that substitution does not merely occur between modalities, but between *combinatorial structures*, no matter their representational origin.

Modalities have long been considered as distinctive representational faculties, meaning that substitution would mark exceptional interactions between otherwise independent systems. However, substitutive allocation appears in natural communication, is produced effortlessly without being marked as exceptional, and is fully productive both for novel and constructional forms. All of this provides evidence that substitution is not an exceptional phenomenon occurring between independent systems. Instead, one can substitute across expressive systems **because** these systems share their cognitive architecture. If an expression is not integrated into a shared architecture, it should not naturally be able to substitute across modalities.

Substitution naturally demonstrates the properties of *complementary distribution*, which are foundational diagnostic tests in linguistics for establishing abstracted paradigmatic and syntagmatic relationships. Taking such tests to their logical conclusion, as we would in any unimodal context, substitutive allocation provides straightforward evidence for a multimodal linguistic faculty.

Part Six

A Multimodal Language Faculty

11

Consequences of a Multimodal Language Faculty

Throughout the prior chapters, we have proposed a multimodal faculty accounting for language and other types of communication. We have argued that different behaviors of varying complexity (omnia, semia, sequentia, modalia) arise as emergent interactive states within a holistic Parallel Architecture that balances contributions of modalities, grammars, and meanings. We repeat our diagram of this model in Figure 11.1.

This reformulation of the linguistic system from an amodal system into an inherently distributed, multimodal system has several consequences and raises several fundamental questions: Why would humans' communicative capacity be multimodal (as opposed to amodal) in the first place? How do expressive systems arising from different modalities interact within this shared system? What are the consequences of a multimodal model on notions of diversity, universals, and innateness? We will address each of these questions throughout this chapter.

11.1 Why a Multimodal Architecture?

Why would humans' capacity for communication be inherently multimodal? We have identified at least two functions for multimodality in a basic sense, which are **multiplicity** and **utility**.

11.1.1 Multiplicity

Multimodality provides a communicative system with built-in **multiplicity** because it inherently has several modalities which persist in parallel. Multiple channels for expressing meaning provide *redundancy* that serves as a functional benefit in two ways. First, a multimodal signal during communication provides access to meaning through more than one channel. Second, multiple modalities offer different options for expressing meaning given the accessibility of modalities, whether biological or in particular situational contexts.

Under one interpretation, having multiple modalities that can express meaning might be considered as inefficient or unnecessary. In this view, unimodal expression is the default and sufficient for all communicative needs. In a unimodal viewpoint, a similar signal appearing in two modalities would be superfluous. However, as we

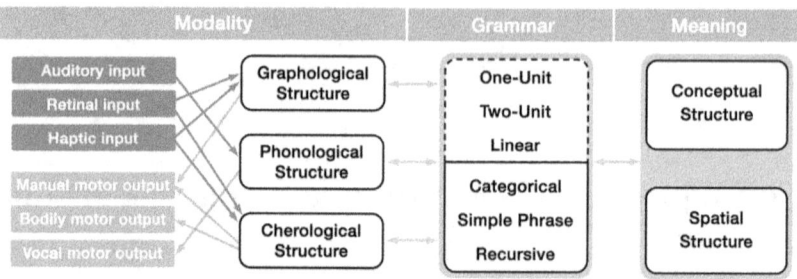

Figure 11.1 The multimodal Parallel Architecture.

have discussed, most communication is not unimodal to begin with, and the pervasive multimodality has simply gone unacknowledged.

Redundancy in communication is fundamental to the human capacity to evoke meaning. A signal that uses multiple channels allows for the reinforcement of the most important aspects of that signal (through co-reference), while also providing the potential compensation for inattention to particular parts of that signal. Take our repeated example utterance of *I caught a small fish* while making a pinching gesture. By conveying the notion of size through both the adjective *small* and the gesture, it provides salience to this particular concept. At the same time, if a person was either not seeing the gesture or not hearing the speech clearly, the redundancy of multiple modalities at once provides different possible access points to that salient meaning. In addition, the gestures provide information about that concept that may be absent in the speech stream (size, orientation, etc.), although we will return to this point in the next section.

Multiplicity also provides an advantage for having multiple options for communication given limited access to modalities or situational contexts. For example, both deaf and hearing individuals can acquire and use bodily omnia of sign languages. However, lack of access to the input of the vocal modality through deafness is often a driver of the development of bodily semia into omnia (i.e., from gestures or homesign to the emergence of full sign languages). Indeed, deaf communities make up the primary users of sign languages. Because the bodily modality persists in *parallel* to the vocal modality, the broader communicative architecture maintains another pathway to an omnia system when access to the vocal modality is limited. Similarly, when both auditory and visual sensory systems are inaccessible, the tactile qualities of the bodily modality can provide a pathway to a communicative system, as in tactile sign languages (Edwards and Brentari 2020, Willoughby et al. 2018, 2020).

Situational contexts also provide constraints or different demands on how modalities are used and which are most efficient. For example, in some cultures such as the Arrernte in Central Australia, times of bereavement involve a period of silence, and thus a sign language and possibly a visual language can be used to maintain communication without speech (Green 2014, Wilkins 2016). Similar constraints persist in other communities where speaking is prohibited, such as monks who take a vow of silence (Umiker-Sebeok and Sebeok 1987).

Different modalities can also provide relative advantages for communication given certain situational constraints. In some contexts, a person might not want their speech to be heard or might not be able to be heard. For example, while hunting, speech may inadvertently alert others (predators, prey, competitors) to a person's presence, and thus signing or drawing provide silent options for communication. These visual modalities are also beneficial when attempting to communicate in a loud context, when having a full mouth, when being underwater, or when communicating across a large physical distance. At the same time, speaking might be optimal when a person cannot see their interlocuter, such as in the dark, on the telephone, or when communicating with full hands. These different relative strengths for situational contexts are based on the affordances offered by the sensory signals carried by each modality. All of these situations benefit from the multiplicity of different modalities being available in parallel to convey a message in different ways when the need arises.

To summarize, multiple modalities within a holistic architecture provide flexibility through communicative redundancy and optionality. However, multiplicity should not be interpreted as support for language being amodal and "flowing into" different modalities indiscriminately. Multiplicity and its advantages rest on the distinctive and parallel nature of modalities, rather than modalities themselves not mattering. We return to this issue in depth in Chapter 13.

11.1.2 Utility

An additional advantage of a multimodal faculty is its **utility** for communicative richness. Having multiple modalities persisting in parallel allows different channels to express meaning in complementary ways, with more sources of information providing a richer signal (Clark 1996, Ferrara and Hodge 2018). This parallelism allows for the access of meaning through different channels in a range of relationships, whether redundant in their content (complete co-reference) or complementary (absent co-reference). Meaning is thus distributed across modalities, while at the same time comprising a singular holistic expression.

Because modalities use distinctive sensory properties, each of them gives access to conceptual structures relying on their affordances. The vocal modality allows for iconicity in ideophones, direct quotes, serial verb constructions, and many other contexts, indexicality in pronominals and deictics, and symbolicity in many, many words. The bodily modality also allows for iconicity in many gestures or signs, indexicality in deictic gestures or signs using space in a referential way, and symbolicity in many emblems and signs. Finally, the graphic modality also conveys iconic pictures, indexical arrows and other pointers, and symbolicity in many graphics including hearts or visual affixes like that for negation. Throughout, we see a proliferation of signification not because they are encoded in the forms themselves, but because a sensory signal can interface with meaning in a variety of ways.

Though all modalities allow for *all* types of signification (iconicity, indexicality, symbolicity), each modality possesses its own affordances to optimize their referential capacities. In Chapter 4, we dubbed this the **Semiotic Optimality Principle**, which we repeat here:

Semiotic Optimality Principle
All modalities can maintain all types of signification through their interfaces with meaning, but a modality's sensory features afford preferential mappings creating optimized reference for that modality.

For example, the graphic modality is optimized for iconicity, as many visual representations are based on their resemblance to percepts in our primary visual sensory system. As such, pictures are prototypically iconic, despite their capacity for other signification. While the bodily modality also uses iconicity and symbolicity, it excels at indexicality, by locating the body in space relative to other meanings. For example, gestures abound with deictic reference, whether as full pointers or embedded into their conceptual structure (as in the pinching gesture for smallness being a property with an open slot for the object it applies to). Sign languages are also filled with indexicality, such as establishing a physical signing space for a referential entity and then pointing to that space as a pronominal (Liddell 2003). Finally, despite being able to convey iconic or indexical signals, the vocal modality excels at symbolicity by disconnecting the features of sound to their meaning.

It is only because of the optimization of the vocal modality that "arbitrariness" is perceived as a design feature of speech (Hockett 1960). Arbitrariness is a description that applies to the form—i.e., to the sounds that are uttered—with regard to how it relates to meaning. This application of arbitrariness to the form itself leads to conflation and confusion with the orthogonal property of conventionality. As we have emphasized throughout, conventionality is a property of a sensory signal, but symbolicity is how the form interfaces with meaning. Indeed, all sensory signals are arbitrary: on their own they simply are sound, light, movements, haptics, etc., and these sensory experiences have their own combinatorial principles independent of what they signify (i.e., phonological, cherological, and graphological structures).

Though each modality has the ability to use all types of signification, their semiotic optimization allows them to take advantage of their relative strengths. Therefore, combining different channels results in different types of signification, which in turn leads to a richer composite signal. Thus, one can optimize the access to meaning by distributing information into different modalities to express an overall holistic message (Clark 1996, Ferrara and Hodge 2018).

11.1.3 A Note about Processing ...

Though the multiplicity and utility of multimodality confer human expression with the ability to distribute information into various channels, it is worth acknowledging that more is not always better. We argue above for the advantages that multimodality offers; however, costs also persist in terms of processing and integrating multiple signals at once. More demanding multimodal relationships should require more resources (attention, working memory capacity, fluency, etc.), particularly with greater complexity of both the combinatorial and conceptual structures.

With regard to our Parallel Architecture, we would posit that Symmetrical Complex combinatorial interactions may be harder to process than Asymmetrical interactions. This would explain why combinations of semia with omnia appear more frequent throughout communication, such as in most co-speech gestures, single images with text, or sentence-emoji interactions. More complex interactions between omnia require fluency in all of those systems, such as encoding constructions into a multimodal lexicon for negotiating that complex structural relationship.

In addition, these traits of multiplicity and utility provide a balance for each other in processing. The higher demand of processing multiple signals may be compensated or ameliorated by each of those signals using different types of signification, thereby reducing competition with each other in accessing conceptual structures. For example, if speech conveys a more symbolic reference while gestures simultaneously provide a more iconic reference to the spatial dimensions of a concept, these signals complement each other rather than competing for our limited resources of attention, memory, etc. This possibility of negotiating between competing multiplicity and complementary utility is possible because of the parallel yet holistic nature of our multimodal architecture. More is not always better, but also more is not always more costly.

11.2 Reimagining Diversity, Universals, Relativity, and Innateness

Given that the multimodal Parallel Architecture maintains all modalities in parallel, what does that imply for the relationships between these modalities? Under a unimodal or amodal conception of our communicative faculty, speech is given a primary position and the other modalities are perceived as peripheral. In the Parallel Architecture, modalities persist independently and equally alongside each other, which entails changes in the way that we think about their relationships.

Here, we highlight three primary dimensions by which modalities relate to each other, as entailed by the Parallel Architecture. The *parallelism of modalities* within our architecture suggests a re-understanding of the fundamental dimensions of **diversity**, **universals**, **innateness**, and **relativity**.

11.2.1 Diversity

A fundamental principle of linguistics of the last century has been the distinction between language as an abstract phenomenon ("big L" Language) and the specific manifestations of that structure ("little l" languages). The typical treatment of this distinction is amodal, without specification for systems of different modalities, as diagrammed in Figure 11.2a.

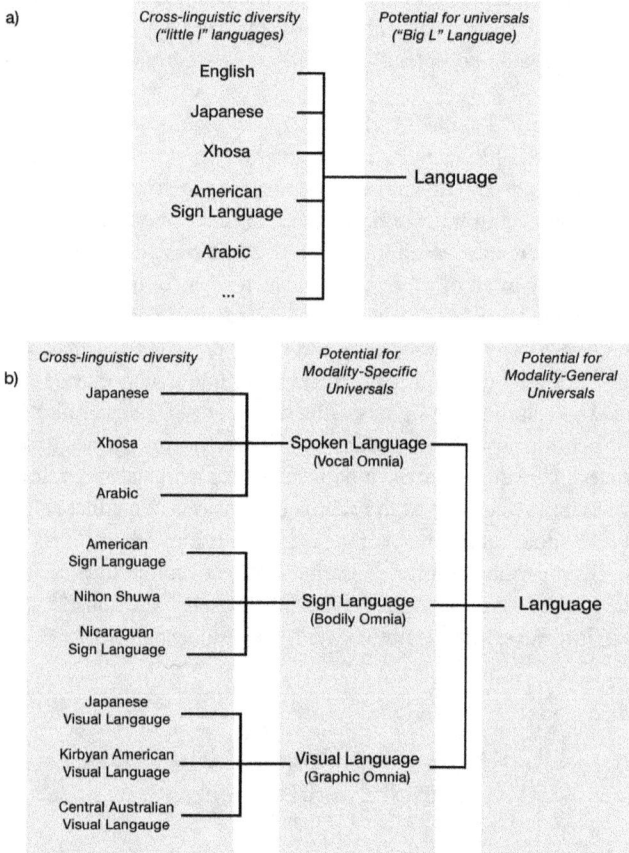

Figure 11.2 Relationships between an abstract Language and cross-linguistic diversity in a) an amodal and b) a multimodal paradigm.

Given a multimodal orientation, this notion should be extended to each modality. While superordinate notion of "big L" Language remains—essentially referring to the multimodal faculty itself—each modality also has an abstracted system, as diagrammed in Figure 11.2b. Here spoken omnia/language, signed omnia/language, and visual omnia/language all refer to a level of abstraction for the general principles of systems that emerge in those modalities. These abstractions do not appear in usage, but rather we use diverse variation of systems (i.e., "little l" languages ... or "little o" omnia) within each modality. That is, within the abstract category of vocal omnia, we see variation across systems like Xhosa, Cantonese, Walpiri, and Dutch. Likewise, in the abstract category of bodily omnia, we see variation across American Sign Language, Nihon Shuwa, and Nicaraguan Sign Language, and in the abstract category of graphic omnia we have Kirbyan American Visual Language, Japanese Visual Language, and many others (Cohn 2024).

The notion of linguistic diversity extends through all distributional possibilities within the multimodal communicative faculty. We not only have diverse and codified omnia, but we also have regularized and diverse systems of semia, sequentia, and even modalia. Codified semia appear in the differences between how people gesture across cultures, which points to systematic patterns in their bodily expressions, just not at the full level of omnia. Graphic semia also have diverse systems in different graphic "styles of drawing" and artistic traditions, which may or may not lack a complex combinatorial system as in graphic omnia.

Sequentia also clearly have codified systems. Bodily sequentia vary across dance styles, sports, miming, and other conventionalized actions. Different musical traditions are auditory semia with regularized patterns that differentiate them, and within which they may have "varieties" comparable to different diverse omnia. For example, within the category of rock music, there may be varieties of folk, punk, grunge, metal, prog, etc., and rock itself may be subordinate to a broader category which also contains pop, reggae, blues, and others.

Even modalia have diverse systematic manifestations, such as between categorical types of abstract artwork (graphic modalia) which vary as emphasizing more or less splatter, geometry, color, or curvature, among other dimensions. Vocal modalia also vary as a subcategory within spoken languages, where non-meaningful vocalizations may have diverse but recognizable manifestations. For example, the same basic musical scale is represented in different phonemic manifestations in Western music (*do-re-mi-fa-so-la-ti-do*) and Indian music (*sa-re-ga-ma-pa-dha-ni-sa*). These are different systematic vocal modalia.

In a cognitive sense, these diverse systems are reflected in **lexicons**. To repeat, a lexicon here reflects the representations encoded in long-term memory composed of pieces of structure of one or several of the components of the Parallel Architecture. There is no separate place for a lexicon, but rather the lexicon permeates throughout the whole architecture. To this extent, because the multimodal architecture inherently includes parallel modalities, every modality has the possibility of lexicalization, with gradient levels of complexity for the contributions of the modality, grammar, and meaning (i.e., as omnia, semia, sequentia, and modalia).

While we have thus far emphasized the cross-linguistic diversity that manifests within each modality, the multimodal nature of this architecture also allows for diverse multimodal constructions to be encoded within lexicons. It is not just the case that unimodal gesticulations vary across cultures, but so do combinations of speech and gesture. We also see codified combinations of text and pictures which vary across cultures and contexts, such as the differences arising in the text-image relationships stereotypical of advertisements compared to comic strips.

All of this is to say that the multimodal Parallel Architecture warrants a consideration of diverse communicative systems characterized by unimodal and multimodal lexicons both within and across all of our modalities. The main emphasis here is that diverse systems arise in all modalities, and no modality is fully universally transparent in itself. Just as there is no singular spoken language, there is no singular universal sign language nor a universal visual language. All modalities manifest in diverse varieties corresponding to specific populations, cultures, and contexts, and all of these systems require proficiency gained through exposure and practice.

11.2.2 Universals

The multimodal Parallel Architecture also alters the view of linguistic universals, which are complementary to what is considered to be diverse. We could consider the architecture itself to be a type of universal, insofar as we posit this overarching holistic architecture to persist within human cognition. The universality of this architecture is its potentiality to be further developed based on exposure to diverse systems. We will elaborate on this point below when we talk about innateness.

More specific aspects of universals persist within the architecture. The notion of linguistic universals comes from observations that, despite the proliferation of diverse structures across (spoken) languages of the world, various structures or structural alignments cut across or underlie this diversity (Chomsky 1986, Croft 2003, Greenberg 1966). These consistent features are often thought of as *universals*, and at a more abstracted level they may provide a *cognitive toolkit* on which our manifested languages are built (Jackendoff 2002). This is to say that universals reflect a basic core cognitive capacity for our linguistic knowledge, which can be elaborated on in diverse systems. This is to some degree reflected in the idea of a "big L" Language which abstracts across the diverse manifestations of "little l" languages, as depicted in Figure 11.2.

As described in the last section, an inherently multimodal model introduces another dimension of diversity beyond cross-linguistic diversity, with diversity of systems within modalities, as in Figure 11.2b. It is reasonable to propose that universals persist within modalities, with consistent typological trends and/or underlying potentialities persisting as **modality-specific universals** for the vocal, bodily, and graphic modalities. For example, universals may cut across spoken languages but not signed or visual languages, or vice versa. In these cases, modality-specific universals are hypothesized to rely on the affordances of the modality itself. Again, for example, the universals specific to spoken languages would be expected to involve aspects of sound (such as the universal qualities of vowel-consonant relationships in syllabic structure), or how sound constrains combinatorial and/or conceptual structures. Similar constraints motivated by affordances can be posited for modality-specific universals in the bodily or graphic modalities. For example, all sign languages may make use of movement and/or space relative to a body in ways distinctive to that modality.

In the same way that the original conception of universals pointed to the consistencies that cut across diverse languages within the (mostly) spoken modality, universals may persist across modalities' diverse systems. This is to say that truly universal qualities of our communicative faculty in the sense of a cognitive toolkit should persist across all modalities. We will refer to these as **modality-general universals**, which are diagrammed in their relationships to diversity in Figure 11.2b, and within the Parallel Architecture in Figure 11.3.

Modality-general universals need to be abstract enough that the sensory aspects of modalities themselves do not necessarily affect their properties, arising as architectural similarities persisting across modalities. For example, the abstract schemas of the Complexity Hierarchy have been posited to have varying manifestations in expressive systems. The schemas involved for sentence structures, narrative structures, and prolongational structure in music all differ greatly in the specific representations

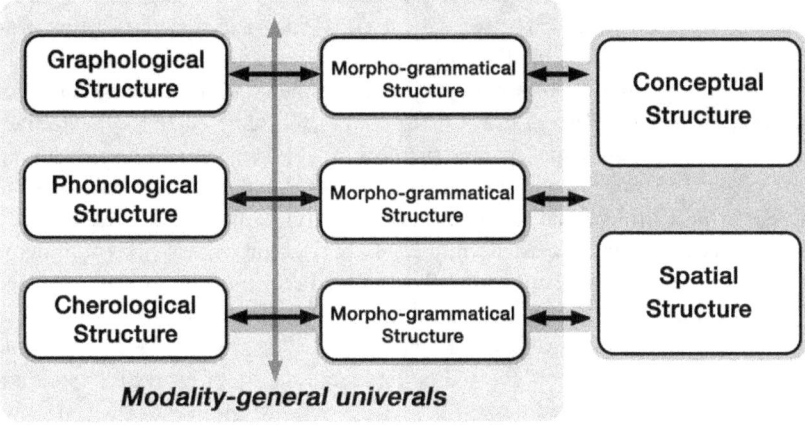

Figure 11.3 Modality-general universals manifesting in the Parallel Architecture.

they use, yet they all potentially invoke recursive combinatorial schemas at the most abstract, architectural level. This places the cognitive capacity for combinatoriality as a type of modality-general universal.

In line with this, we posit several universals of this type, which may include, but are not limited to:

- Formological properties that transcend their associated sensory systems (e.g., magnitude, rhythm, rhyming, etc.)
- Form-meaning correspondences resulting in either idiosyncratic (not encoded in memory) or regularized (encoded in memory) units
- Classes of productive (open-class) and fixed (closed-class) schematized units
- The ability for units to be isolated (free) and act unto themselves (analytic), be dependent on other units (bound), or be combined to form novel internally structured units (synthetic)
- Strategies of combinatoriality within units (i.e., "morphological strategies" of affixation, reduplication, suppletion, compounding, blending)
- Establishment of relations between units to form abstract paradigmatic classes
- Combinatorial schemas allowing headedness and modification (X-bar "head-modifier" schema) applicable within and across units
- Combinatorial classes of categories (categorical schemas, like nouns, verbs, Initials, Peaks, word, affix, etc.)
- Establishment of novel or entrenched correspondences between conceptual domains (i.e., conceptual metaphors or conceptual blends)
- Semantic heuristics like *Agent First*, *Entities before Actions*, or *Topic-Comment*.

As these abstract properties arise across modalities' expressive systems, they appear to be good candidates for modality-general universals. Additional possibilities for universals may be the well-established "linguistic laws." For example, Zipf's Law classically observed a trade-off between the size of a lexical item and its usage frequency (Zipf 1935), though this broader observation of a relationship between size and frequency has extended across multiple aspects of the linguistic system (Piantadosi, Tily, and Gibson 2011, Torre et al. 2019). In addition, this same length-frequency trade-off has been observed across many structures in sign languages (Börstell, Hörberg, and Östling 2016) and visual languages (Cohn 2024). Another candidate would be the Mezereth-Altmann Law that the larger a construct (unit, phrase, etc.), the smaller its constituents (Altmann 1980, Menzerath 1928). In addition, observations of trade-offs between the complexity of units (morphology) and sequences (grammar) have been observed in various measurements of both spoken/written and visual languages (Bentz et al. 2022, Cohn 2024, Ehret 2018, Koplenig et al. 2017). All of these relationships point to ways that cognition constrains the manifestation of expressive systems in consistent ways across modalities.

Finally, we may extend the notion of universals to other aspects of domain-general processing, such as consistencies observed in the neural responses across various behaviors. As discussed previously, similar neural signatures have been observed to semantic (Kutas and Federmeier 2011) and grammatical processing (Cohn 2020b, Koelsch 2011a) across modalities. The degree to which these neural responses arise from the same or different neural tissue has often been taken as an indication for the cognitive "uniqueness" of expressive systems. However, if you accept that all expressions arise from a common architecture in the first place, it is less revelatory that "different behaviors" like speech, music, or visual narratives do or do not use the exact same neural tissue. The question should not be whether processing is or is not "like language" but rather what are the cognitive properties and neural processing of different behaviors, how do they relate to each other, and what does this tell us about the broader architecture of human expression?

All of this is to say that our notion of universals extends the diversity of the structures and mechanisms encoded in systems within and across modalities. In this sense, classification of different universals can be investigated and identified according to Marr's (1982) levels of cognition, for whether they reflect commonalities across modalities in terms of their computational, algorithmic, or implementational properties. As hinted above, reconceptualizing our communicative capacities into a holistic model warrants a reframing of the notions of modality-specificity and modality-generality, since all the domains under question belong to a shared architecture in the first place.

11.2.3 Innateness

The notion of universals relates to the common traits that cut across different systems, and as such is intertwined with the question of the innate properties of those systems. That is, what aspects of our communicative capacities are biologically endowed and which require exposure and practice to an external stimulus? Questions of innateness have been fundamental in discussions of language for over half a century (Elman, Bates, and Johnson 1996, Chomsky 1965, Christiansen and Chater 2016, Elman, Bates, and Johnson, 1996, Tomasello 2010, Lenneberg 1967, Pinker 1994). While many aspects of this debate will undoubtably persist, the Parallel Architecture—particularly as a multimodal faculty—provides a framework for reconceptualizing innateness (Jackendoff 2002). As foreshadowed in Chapter 1, the correspondences that give rise to *semia* are innate, while those for *omnia* require exposure and practice to external systems. We will elaborate on this below.

As discussed in Chapter 1, a core feature of the Parallel Architecture is that not all structures need to be fully engaged or developed at all times. Emergent states arise through the presence (or absence) of certain structures. For example, omnia systems express meaning with a modality using a complex grammar that allows for an extensive lexicon, while semia systems only use a simple combinatorial system rendering a more limited lexicon. In other words, the Parallel Architecture provides an allowance of *potentiality*, where development determines the maturity of the expressive systems, offering people a range of possibilities that manifest in different emergent states.

The view following from this potentiality is that certain core capacities are biologically endowed, while others require social development. Our innate capacities include each of our three natural modalities (vocal, bodily, and graphic) and their basic connections to conceptual structures using simple combinatorial schemas (i.e., one-unit, two-unit, and linear schemas). Because these correspondences between formologies and meaning are innate, so are their optimizations for signification, resulting in the *semiotic optimality* of graphic-iconicity, bodily-indexicality, and vocal-symbolicity, though all modalities maintain all possible types of signification. In other words, our capacity for semia systems is innate. We diagram this in Figure 11.4a.

Our definition of what is *innate* is thus informed by what persists in the absence of developing an external system, what Susan Goldin-Meadow (2003b) calls the *resilient* aspects of language. While dramatic cases of language deprivation support this view of semia as innate (discussed below), it should also be apparent because people who do not acquire a sign language (omnia) still maintain a basic ability to gesture (semia). For that matter, gestures persist as an instinctive behavior even for people who do acquire

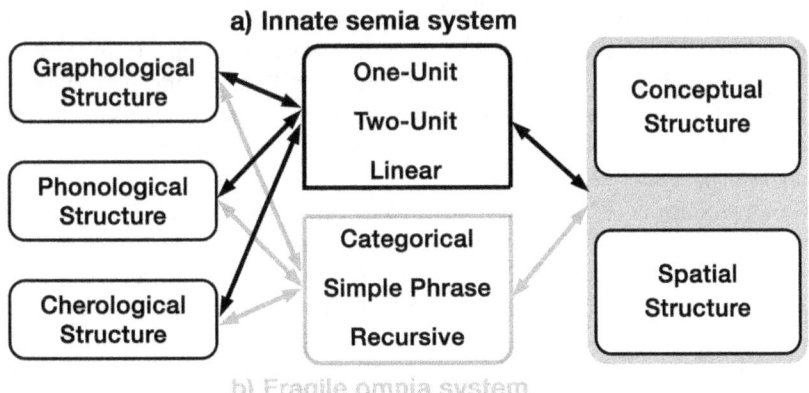

Figure 11.4 The Parallel Architecture with interfaces for a) innate correspondences resulting in semia and b) fragile correspondences resulting in omnia.

a sign language (Emmorey 2023, Liddell and Metzger 1998). This same relationship holds for visual languages: even if a person does not acquire a full-fledged visual lexicon and grammar, they still retain the basic ability to create graphic meanings (i.e., the status of "I can't draw" reflecting doodles and basic graphic patterns). In addition, people seem to default to communicative strategies characteristic of semia when they need to communicate with someone with whom they do not share an omnia system, such as when people are pushed to communicate only in gestures (Gershoff-Stowe and Goldin-Meadow 2002, Goldin-Meadow et al. 2008), or in picture-only sequences like emoji (Cohn, Engelen, and Schilperoord 2019, Cohn and Schilperoord 2023, Gawne and McCulloch 2019). These cases all reflect how the innate semia system provides a core meaning-making capacity regardless of whether more complex systems are acquired or not.

Further evidence for an innate semia system comes from cases where semia systems are the only ones available. In unfortunate cases of language deprivation, when a person is not exposed to an external omnia system, they are left with only a semia system, which may or may not be pushed to its furthest limits. For example, deaf children who do not have access to the vocal stimulus and are not provided stimulus of a sign language are known to invent homesigns, which are their own bodily semia systems that serve as a primary communicative system (Goldin-Meadow 2003b). In other cases, hearing children who are not exposed to a spoken language, as in cases of language deprivation, typically retain a basic ability for vocal semia, and when eventually are taught a spoken language have difficulty achieving full proficiency in the omnia system (Friedmann and Rusou 2015, Goldin-Meadow 2003b). Delayed exposure to an omnia in any modality can have long-lasting, detrimental effects on the development of the neurobiology related to language (Cheng et al. 2023).

Innate semia systems maintain correspondences between modalities and meaning that use simple combinatorial schemas, a lexicon with a limited number of items, which rely on semantic heuristics for sequencing (Agent First, Entities before Actions, etc.). These traits of semia systems are in line with what has been observed in the communicative capacities of other animals (Engesser and Townsend 2019, Fitch 2020, Ghirlanda, Lind, and Enquist 2017), which also maintain systems with multiple modalities that express meaning, but with limited combinatoriality and a constrained set of semantic categories (typically expressing topics related to their identities and relationships, environments, food, mating, threats, and others). Many animals make use of modalities which are unavailable or less developed in humans, such as producing and sensing electric shocks, meaningful smells, low-frequency sound waves, sonar, and many other diverse modalities. Like those in humans, these modalities typically combine in multimodal systems for their particular species. To the extent that research has discovered, animal communication is characterized by the use of multimodal semia, and this is consistent with the core communicative capacity of humans.

Given these alignments of multimodal semia systems across species, what seemingly makes humans different is the *potentiality* for omnia systems that extend beyond these semia systems. We posit that the schemas articulated by the Complexity Hierarchy reflect the innate capacities for human combinatoriality in their most abstract form. However, the activation of complex combinatoriality (categorical, phrase structures, and recursion) requires interaction with them in specific lexical items within a communicative system (i.e., syntactic, morphological, and/or narrative constructions, among others). As a result, omnia are only developed with exposure to and interaction with an external system that includes such lexical schemas. In other words, the abstract capacity for complex combinatoriality is innate, but needs to be "woken up" by interaction with specific representations that instantiate those complex combinatorial schemas.

The complex abstract schemas articulated within the Complexity Hierarchy reflect the human cognitive abilities for categorization of units along segmentation and chunking. These cognitive capacities are engaged by acquiring lexical representations, yet the basic processing abilities persist, and they allow for production or creation of new lexical schemas, whether within the same system (e.g., new constructions within a spoken language) or in a new system (e.g., acquiring a new language, no matter the modality). Nevertheless, while the potential for complex combinatoriality may remain, full proficiency in these systems may become more difficult as people age, particularly beyond their youthful sensitive learning period (Cheng et al. 2023, Friedmann and Rusou 2015, Newport, Bavelier, and Neville 2001). That is, mastering the complex grammar of various omnia becomes more challenging with age, in which case it may depend more on memorization, will be fed by the combinatoriality of already-acquired omnia systems (i.e., L1 interference), and may default to processing mechanisms characteristic of semia rather than full omnia (Pienemann and Lenzing 2020). This fallback to semia systems reflects "good enough" processing strategies (Ferreira and Patson 2007, Jackendoff and Wittenberg 2014).

Interaction with an omnia system does not just develop the combinatorial component on its own, but rather this combinatoriality is embedded within correspondences across structures. Because a lexicon encodes the correspondences between information about a formology, combinatorial schemas, and conceptual structure, lexical items span various sizes, from small units (like morphemes) to fixed sequences (like idioms or stock phrases) to abstract constructions (like syntactic schemas). Within omnia systems, lexical items may establish abstracted relationships (Jackendoff and Audring 2020), whether vertical (schemas embedded in inheritance hierarchies) or horizontal (relational "sister schemas"). The lexicon of an omnia thus contains fixed items and the relational categories that bind them, which altogether ultimately is the omnia system instantiated within cognition (i.e., the lexicon is the language). The establishment of such an omnia system allows for the scaffolding of a more extensive lexicon within that system (e.g., Vygotsky 1965), giving way to easier acquisition of additional lexical items (i.e., having a vocabulary allows you to more easily learn a larger vocabulary). Thus, acquiring an omnia system facilitates the growth of a lexicon beyond the limited capacities of a semia system.

Development of an omnia system—and all its structural complexities—requires social interaction, because this is where the omnia system is found. The innate potentiality of omnia needs to be engaged through exposure to and practice with an external omnia system produced by its users. Social interaction provides a feedback loop for acquisition and production of these lexical items, sponsoring growth from a semia system to an omnia system. Social interaction thus plays a crucial role in developing greater complexity of an omnia system, which has been observed both naturally when homesigners interact to develop a more robust sign language (Kegl 1994, Senghas 1995), and in laboratory settings through iterated learning paradigms (Christiansen and Chater 2016, Kirby, Griffiths, and Smith 2014, Smith 2018).

If social interaction is a crucial determiner for growth from a semia to an omnia, it's worth asking: why don't omnia in all modalities develop all the time? Given that our communicative faculty inherently has three parallel modalities, why do many people acquire full proficiency in spoken omnia, but not bodily or graphic omnia? Indeed, people frequently gesture in daily interactions, but these bodily semia do not necessarily develop into new sign languages regularly, nor do people's doodles always develop into mature visual languages.

We have two explanations for this. First, semia systems persist regardless of whether omnia are developed or acquired. Again, even proficient users of sign languages (omnia) may gesture (semia) (Emmorey 2023, Liddell and Metzger 1998). Thus, it is not that semia "turn into" omnia, so much as omnia can be constructed *on top* of the semia system.

Second, development of an omnia requires the communicative need and/or demand for such a system, a motivation for regularizing lexical items that subsequently constitute a complex system. In the absence of such motivation, one modality (such as speaking) may be "good enough" with semia systems persisting alongside it. This often occurs in speech-dominated communities. The byproduct of this situation is that speech then *appears* to be a central and primary system while the bodily and graphic modalities appear to be peripheral. However, such rankings via usage may be deceptive, as they do not reflect the properties of the communicative cognitive architecture. Rather, in communities already maintaining an existing omnia system, this core-periphery conception follows from the weighing of costs and benefits of acquiring or developing additional full omnia systems, and from social pressures pushing for adherence to the existing dominant omnia system. Evidence of encouraged conformity to the dominant vocal omnia is especially apparent in hearing societies when deaf individuals are pushed to speak or to receive implants to hear, rather than communities accepting wider inclusion of sign languages. Less dramatically, notions that textual books without pictures are the only "real books" also follow from a dominant vocal omnia perspective, pushing back against efforts to promote more pervasive use of visual languages outside of entertainment contexts.[1] It is worth noting that such core-periphery distinctions are less salient in communities where many or all modalities persist as omnia systems (Green 2014, Wilkins 2016).

To summarize, semia systems persist as humans' innate capacities for making basic correspondences between modalities and meaning. Omnia make use of innate, cognitive potentialities, but require social interaction to be acquired or created. Again, this innate system is reflected in the resilient properties that persist in the absence of an external system, while omnia reflect fragile properties—an unconstrained lexicon and complex combinatoriality—that require exposure to and acquisition of an external system (Goldin-Meadow 2003b). These fragile omnia systems are thus built on top of the core of the resilient, innate semia capacities, which is why semia persist even when omnia are acquired. This persistence leads to a prevalence in *Asymmetrical* combinatorial interactions between our resilient semia and any acquired omnia (as seen in co-speech gesture and many text-picture interactions).

In addition to the innate capacities and those acquired by exposure, some communicative abilities require explicit learning. In contemporary society, the communicative architecture has been modified to make correspondences between modalities in unnatural ways. Specifically, writing systems create cross-modal correspondences between speech sounds and graphics (and potentially, bodily movements and graphics). These synesthetic correspondences need to be explicitly learned in order to master literacy. Their unnatural properties are on display in the number of years that are required to be fully proficient in reading and writing: primary school alone is a dozen years. Compare this to our natural omnia which develop a foundation in only a few years through exposure and practice. That is, people must work intensely to extend speech beyond the vocal modality, because it is not an amodal capacity that is mutable for free.

An additional comparison between natural and unnatural capacities is whether they allow for receptive and productive proficiency. Passive exposure often results in asymmetrical proficiency between comprehension and production in a given system. Often, receptive proficiency exceeds people's productive proficiency. Most people are capable of understanding graphic omnia through exposure to pictures, but not everyone has the ability to produce pictures proficiently (i.e., many people "can't draw"). Similarly, many gain fluency in understanding second languages better than they can produce them, or can understand languages that they do not speak if they share enough structure with their native languages (Gooskens 2019). Compare this to writing systems, where receptive and productive proficiency appear more entwined through explicit learning, and such passive acquisition is less possible.

All of this is to say that synesthetic correspondences not only reflect non-innate aspects of the communicative architecture, but they reflect human *inventions* which impose new connections into the architecture in order to "draw sounds." Research has indeed suggested that writing systems recycle or repurpose parts of the brain devoted to other perceptual capacities (Hervais-Adelman et al. 2019). This recycling is different than the potentialities we observe for innate capacities which need to be "activated" or "woken up" by interaction with omnia (such as the neurobiology associated with complex combinatoriality). Rather, this neural recycling creates correspondences not innately prespecified by the system, but imposed on it by explicit learning of cultural inventions. Writing creates new, unnatural correspondences between natural modalities innately present within humans' multimodal architecture.

Additional cultural inventions include tool-based modalities such as the technology used to record or produce visual or auditory information. While natural modalities provide a channel to express mental representations, photographic, video, and auditory technology allows for the reproduction and creation of natural percepts for expressive means. On the one hand, these tool-based modalities simply provide another avenue for accessing the natural modalities, such as hearing recordings of speech or seeing video of signing. On the other hand, these tools can also be used productively, whether through analog means (e.g., taking photos) or digital creation (e.g., generating or altering photo-realistic images). In these cases, natural percepts (or *seemingly* natural percepts) make correspondences to our combinatorial and conceptual structures in similar ways as natural modalities. Yet, tool-based modalities like audio or video recording have only arisen in the past few hundred years, and provide cultural inventions with pathways to expression beyond innate, natural modalities.

Altogether, humans are endowed with an architecture that balances what is innate (semia) and what is activated through encoded cultural systems (omnia), along with the flexibility to invent and learn expressive means created through cultural development (synesthetic and tool-based modalities). Since these capacities are all encoded within a larger *multimodal* architecture, we might also ask: are multimodal interactions also innate? Do we need to acquire multimodality through lexical items? Are semia systems independent or do we have innate connections between modalities to begin with? Given that multimodality arises from modality, combinatorial, and conceptual interactions, are these within-structure interactions innate or do they come from usage? While we are not prepared to answer these questions in any definite way, it should be noted that an amodal assumption of language has no way to raise these questions, since an amodal model has no inclusion of differing modalities to interact.

11.2.4 Relativity and Permeability

Since all of our expressive modalities are incorporated into a common architecture, what does that mean for the relationships between semia and omnia of *different* modalities? For example, can the language that you speak or sign affect the language that you draw (or vice versa)? We call this **permeability**: the potential influences of one modality's patterning of information on another modality's patterns for similar concepts (Cohn 2016, 2024). For example, permeability characterizes the degree to which the language you speak affects the way that you draw, gesture, or sign, and vice versa. It can be directional (one modality being the source influencer for other target modalities) or be dispersed across systems with no apparent source/target relationships.

Often, the phenomenon of permeability has been subsumed within the notion of *linguistic relativity* (Sapir 1921, Slobin 1996, Whorf 1956), the idea that the structure of a language affects other aspects of cognition. If our expressive systems are viewed as independent of each other—such as speech being isolated from gestures or drawing—then the influence of one modality on another would indeed seem like a relativistic effect. In these cases, the structure of language would extend outside of its primary architecture to affect other interacting cognitive systems (perception, attention, navigation, spatial cognition, etc.). In other words, does the language you speak, sign, or draw affect your perception of or attention to objects or events, or how you navigate through the world?

Yet, with a multimodal Parallel Architecture, different modalities are *not* independent, but rather emerge from a holistic shared system. The mutual influence of modalities does not reach outside the language system, but reflects relationships persisting between elements within a common architecture. Because of this difference, we need to explicitly clarify between relationships within the same communicative

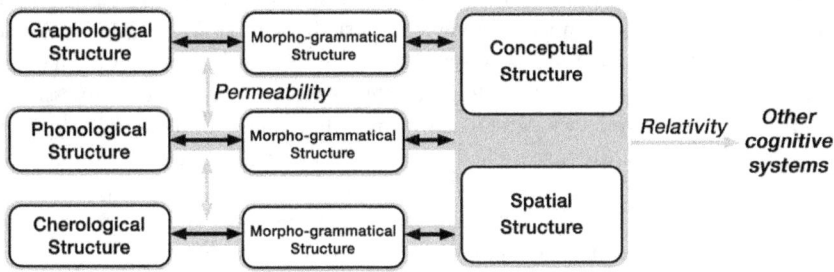

Figure 11.5 The Parallel Architecture with permeable relations between communicative systems, and relativistic relations of those systems to other cognitive systems.

architecture (permeability) from those that persist with additional cognitive systems (relativity). We illustrate this relationship in Figure 11.5.

Evidence of permeability abounds in the literature on relativity, though we can now identify them as distinctive. For example, in the spoken language of Aymarra, the past is lexicalized as in front and the future is behind, and correspondingly, speakers of Aymarra gesture toward the front when speaking about the past and gesture to the rear when speaking about the future (Núñez and Sweetser 2006). In Mandarin Chinese the past is described as upward and the future is downward, and gestures similarly correspond to these directions (Gu et al. 2017). Similarly, Australian Aboriginals who speak languages with absolute spatial systems have been shown to encode their allocentric conceptions of space in their gestures (Haviland 1993). These are all cases of permeability where the spoken language and gesture share a common framing of the concepts.

Examples of permeability also arise in relationships between spoken and visual languages. In line with the findings about gesture, Australian Aboriginals also maintain absolute space in their graphic systems produced in sand drawings, which maintain an aerial viewpoint locked into accurate cardinal directions (Green 2014, Wilkins 2016). In addition, the typological varieties of framing motion events in spoken languages have been shown to affect the depiction of path structures of motion events in the visual languages used in comics (Hacımusaoğlu and Cohn 2022, Tversky and Chow 2017). Similarly, the structuring of thematic roles in spoken languages may affect preferences for the spatial depiction of agents and patients in graphic representations (Chatterjee 2001). In these cases, the structure of spoken and graphic modalities maintains common framing of concepts.

These various examples show the permeability across the vocal, bodily, and graphic modalities found in different emergent relationships in the Parallel Architecture. Permeability arises between omnia and semia, such as in the semia of gestures that maintain the framing of temporal or spatial conceptualizations also found in the omnia of the spoken languages. Permeability is also observed between omnia, such as between spoken and visual languages (as in the allocentric spatial structure of sand drawings or the motion events shown in visual languages of comics).

We predict that omnia can more easily permeate semia than other omnia. This is in line with our discussion of innateness where we posit that semia provide a more resilient system with fewer conventionalized lexical times. There is greater possibility that the structuring provided by omnia would permeate the structuring of semia expressions, given that semia have fewer entrenched forms. This differs from the relationships between omnia, where conventionalized forms may conflict in their framing of concepts. A counterpoint may be for omnia that co-develop across modalities, such as where spoken and visual languages culturally develop alongside each other, and thus maintain common, permeable framing without directional influence.

The holistic nature of the multimodal Parallel Architecture allows us to explicitly model the influences across modalities (permeability), while intimating how these systems may further interact with other aspects of cognition (relativity). In this light, the notion of permeability arises as a consequence of the organization of the architecture, and as such, we should somewhat expect permeability across modalities. Nevertheless, though the multimodal Parallel Architecture warrants such relationships, the extent to which they persist is an empirical question.

11.3 Conclusion

Throughout this chapter we have explored the consequences of a multimodal model of the communicative faculty on diversity, universals, innateness, relativity, and permeability. To summarize, we find diversity between the lexicons encoded across structures of the Parallel Architecture (omnia, semia, sequentia, modalia). Diversity persists across cultures, registers, genres, and many other contexts that vary the structures of different systems. Universals are the common structures that persist across these diverse manifestations, whether arising as common structures within a modality (modality-specific universals) or across modalities (modality-general universals).

Within the Parallel Architecture, innate properties are considered as biologically endowed in human cognition, providing a cognitive toolkit with the potentiality to mature given interactions with external systems. What is truly innate in this architecture is what persists in the absence of development in concert with external systems—i.e., humans' capacity for semia is innate, arising from wired-in correspondences between formologies and conceptual structure. Developing omnia requires exposure to and interaction with an external system in order to make use of more complex structure (i.e., complex combinatoriality and an unlimited lexicon). Finally, the diverse lexicons encoded within and across modalities may establish relationships in how they frame information (permeability), while potentially affecting cognitive systems outside our communicative architecture (relativity).

Altogether, these distinctions arise as natural consequences of the structural organization of the multimodal Parallel Architecture. All of these notions are central to theories of language, and have been widely discussed and debated for decades. Our model provides a straightforward structural framework both for defining these notions and for explaining how they work.

12

Evolution of a Multimodal Language Faculty

The past decades have seen an increasing focus on the evolution of language, creating a field devoted to investigating what has long remained a mystery. Yet, we feel the need to invoke the title of Jackendoff (2010b), "Your theory of language evolution depends on your theory of language," by which he means that the way you theorize the evolution of language also depends on your conceptualization of what language is and how it is structured in the first place. In this book, we have offered an alternative to the predominant amodal views of linguistic structure—the multimodal Parallel Architecture—and as such, it indeed warrants a reconceptualization of language evolution by positing a fundamentally different view of the end-state of these evolutionary processes.

Most contemporary theories of language evolution maintain a view of vocal primacy, whereby speech is the core expressive capacity compared to "peripheral" capacities. This manifests in gesture-first theories of language evolution, where the modern presence of sign languages is explained by language starting in the bodily modality and then transferring to the "core" vocal modality (Armstrong 2002, Corballis 2002, Givón 1995, Hewes 1973, Tomasello 2010). In parallel to this view, other theories have posited that language evolution involved a progression through different types of semiotic reference, going from iconic and/or indexical to symbolic, with the "arbitrary linguistic sign" as the assumed end-state (Deacon 1997, Everett 2017). Finally, much focus has been given to the evolution of syntactic structure, whether it progressed through "protolanguages" as intermediate steps (Jackendoff 2002, Jackendoff and Wittenberg 2017, Planer and Sterelny 2021), or whether a recursive end-state came in one big jump (Berwick and Chomsky 2016).

While all of these domains are debated, an abiding assumption is a treatment of linguistic evolution as if it were like the famous painting of the *March of Progress*, which depicts modern humans as the apex of a series of linear evolutionary stages (discussed in Chapter 5). By analogy, models of linguistic evolution similarly maintain the idea of a contemporary unimodal, symbolic, and recursive "language"—particularly speech—as the apex of evolutionary stages which have since been shed. As described, the gesture-first hypothesis maintains that evolution began with gestures, but then ended up with the vocal modality as primary. The semiotic theory maintains that language ended up as symbolic, starting with and minimizing its iconicity and indexicality. Finally, syntactic theories posit that language ended up as recursive, leaving behind their simpler combinatorics.

The multimodal Parallel Architecture provides a different viewpoint on all of these theories of language evolution. To repeat what we have covered in previous chapters, 1) humans' expressive capacity is a multimodal system that maintains the vocal, bodily, and graphic formologies as parallel systems; 2) modalities use all types of semiotic reference, which operate as complementary types of signification with no inherent ranking; and 3) expressions use combinatorial schemas across various levels of complexity, from single-unit expressions to recursion. A consequence of this view is that the end-state of evolutionary processes is not a unimodal complex "language," but rather a multimodal system that affords omnia, semia, sequentia, and modalia.

Seen in this light, existing theories of language evolution typically place everything considered as "core" into their view of the modern human language faculty. Everything viewed as "periphery" is allocated to preceding evolutionary stages that have since been surpassed. If this core versus periphery view is rejected, as in the Multimodal Paradigm, it necessitates an alternative perspective of language evolution. We now turn to addressing each of these positions in detail, followed by a discussion of the demands of an evolutionary theory entailed by the Multimodal Paradigm.

12.1 Amending the Evolutionary End-State

We now address each of the major domains of theories of language evolution, which in fact mimic the inherent tripartite structure of the linguistic system in terms of modality, meaning, and grammar.

12.1.1 Modality Evolution

The idea that "language" began in the bodily modality and then transferred to the primary vocal modality has existed for over a century, but has seen a resurgence in research over the past several decades (Armstrong 2002, Corballis 2002, Givón 1995, Hewes 1973, Tomasello 2010). This view argues that the bodily modality provided easier communicative ability using humans' primary sensory capacity of vision, but that "language" shifted to the vocal modality in order to free up hands for use with tools and other actions, along with nighttime communication. While these views have become prominent, other *modality-transference* theories have placed the vocal modality first, perhaps motivated by singing (e.g., Masataka 2007, Mithen 2006, Vaneechoutte and Skoyles 1998), an idea also theorized by Darwin (1871).

These theories hold that, first, the vocal modality is primary and is thus the end-state of evolutionary processes, and, second, the bodily modality exists and thus needs to be accounted for. In the case of the gesture-first hypothesis, the bodily modality is ultimately viewed as peripheral, and is thus allocated to a prior evolutionary stage which is then surpassed. This view implicitly places the bodily modality in contemporary usage as a type of primitive communication, reinforcing its peripheral status.

There are several problems with theories of modality-transference. The most glaring issue is that all human modalities persist as contemporary linguistic capacities (McNeill 2012, Orzechowski, Wacewicz, and Żywiczyński 2016). The bodily modality remains present, whether it develops into a full sign language or is used only in bodily semia like gestures. The fact that modalities require exposure and practice to become omnia (like sign languages) while semia persist (like gestures) may create the illusion of transference and a core-periphery relationship, given the social dominance of the vocal modality. Regardless, the bodily modality is always present, which in the Multimodal Paradigm is the acknowledgment that modalities exist as parallel components within the language architecture, not as options for "language" to flow out of. As long as one rejects the core-periphery rankings of modalities, such parallelism should be easily recognizable.

In broader terms, the idea of modality-transference rests on assumptions of an amodal language faculty, reinforcing a peripheral treatment of modalities in general. If "language" is thought to transfer from one modality to another, then modalities are not included within the scope of the definition of "language." The evolving "language" in this view is actually describing the evolution of subcomponents of the language architecture, typically combinatorics and lexical development (i.e., conventionalization into types)—again maintaining the Saussurean Sign—but not properties of the formologies. As we have argued throughout, modalities constitute inherent component parts of the linguistic system, and cannot be separated from the notion of "language" evolving.

Finally, we note that in discussions of modalities, graphics are largely excluded from the scope of language evolution until the cultural developments of writing. While some work has speculated on modality-transference between speech and graphics (Miyagawa, Lesure, and Nóbrega 2018), graphics are largely considered in terms of concomitant intellectual capacities, where the ability to produce pictures is a proxy for expressive maturity of all modalities (Dehaene et al. 2022). In this view, the ability to speak is a prerequisite for producing the complexity of the peripheral graphic modality—i.e., a sentiment that if they could draw, they must have already had language—rather than incorporating graphic production into a complementary model of the evolution of the communicative architecture.

Following the Multimodal Paradigm, theories of language evolution need to account for the parallel existence of *all* modalities (de Boer 2017, McNeill 2012, Orzechowski, Wacewicz, and Żywiczyński 2016), and that for all three natural modalities (vocal, bodily, and graphic), semia are retained in the absence of full development of omnia. All modalities exist as complementary parts within an overarching system without any unimodal primacy, each of them serving their own expressive purpose and carrying their own affordances for meaning-making within the whole of communication.

12.1.2 Meaning Evolution

Theories that target the evolution of meaning-making stress the ultimate importance of reaching an arbitrary linguistic sign through stages corresponding to different types of semiotic signification. A primary theory here posits that language evolution progresses from iconic to indexical to symbolic signs (Deacon 1997). Alternative views have contested this specific progression by positing a different order of semiotic types, such as indexical signs preceding iconic signs on the way to symbolic signs

(Everett 2017). In all cases, these views maintain the idea of symbolic, arbitrary signs as a characteristic "design feature" of the linguistic end-state (Hockett 1960).

Theories of semiotic progression are predicated on conception of a Saussurean Sign that inherently packages signifier and signified into an inseparable but arbitrary relationship. As we have discussed repeatedly, signification here characterizes a type of signal rather than the ways that a signal makes reference to a meaning, as in Peircean semiotics. This is why most theories characterize evolution as progressing from "icons to indexes to symbols," rather than from iconic to indexical to symbolic signs. In addition, a conception of an inseparable form-meaning package also leads to a conflation of conventionality and symbolicity, pushing theories of language evolution to require symbolicity in order to posit conventionality, or taking all conventionality as evidence of symbolicity.

This assumption of a Saussurean Sign often arises because of a neglect of, or failure to engage with, the full complexity of Peircean semiotics. Because the prevailing Saussurean framework has grounded linguistic research, theories typically only adapt the part of Peirce's model that seems compatible with, and able to elaborate on, the structuralist notion of arbitrariness. That is, iconicity and indexicality are viewed as "adding to" the notion of arbitrariness (symbolicity). However, this leaves out crucial distinctions made by Peirce between the properties of signals (idiosyncratic, regularized) and the ways they interface with meaning (iconic, indexical, and symbolic), among others.

When acknowledging the greater nuance of the Peircean model, we arrive at the need for a theory that properly distinguishes between the evolution of 1) the properties of the signal and 2) the properties of how a signal interfaces with meaning. Theories of the signal need to characterize the evolutionary shift from idiosyncratic to regularized and conventional signals. This is essentially a property of typification and pattern recognition.

As we have repeatedly stated, regularization and conventionalization are often conflated with symbolicity, though they are orthogonal. This confusion can be resolved by viewing the relation between a signal and its meaning as a matter of *correspondence*, rather than viewing the meaning as inherent to the sign (that is, as a Saussurean Sign). The latter view necessarily leads to symbolicity, which is why it is often misunderstood as all conventionalization. Humans and other animals use all types of signification (iconicity, indexicality, and symbolicity), but what humans do particularly well is the creation of conventionalized signals. Scholars often refer to this as the use of "symbols," but in a Peircean sense the appropriate term would be the emergence of *legisigns*, which reflect typification of signals using any type of signification. It's less that humans are a "symbolic species" (e.g., Deacon 1997) than we are a "legisign species" that uses iconicity, indexicality, *and* symbolicity in complementary ways.

Indeed, research on the development of such conventionality of signals has proliferated in the study of language evolution in iterated learning paradigms (Christiansen and Chater 2016, Kirby, Griffiths, and Smith 2014, Smith 2018). However, in line with confusions about "symbols," this research often misinterprets patterns of regularization and conventionality as indicative of symbolicity, or as a shift from iconicity to symbolicity. Nevertheless, this work has provided insights into how signals become systematized over generations of exposure, which has further shown consistencies in these features across modalities.

In addition, theories of evolution should account for how signals provide access to meaning. The focus on the arbitrary sign creates another core-periphery treatment of signification types, with iconicity and indexicality again being ranked lower and thus placed as evolutionary precursors to the more important symbolicity. However, as we have argued throughout, all modalities do all types of signification, but modalities have affordances that optimize certain types.

From a holistic perspective, humans use different types of signification to create a richer communicative signal, whether that proliferation of signification occurs within one modality or through the combination of multiple modalities. It is not that symbolicity is functionally superior to iconicity and indexicality, but rather that they accomplish different things in how they convey meaning. Indeed, symbolicity is often inferior to iconicity and indexicality in certain types of meaning-making and in certain contexts (for example, conveying spatial relations). Again, as we argued with modality-transference, we take it as misguided to treat types of signification as competing with each other, rather than acknowledging their equal and parallel roles within the whole of communication.

12.1.3 Grammar Evolution

There are two broad views on the evolution of grammatical structure. First, Chomsky and his adherents maintain a view that syntax is characterized only by a recursive mechanism, and thus the evolution of this singular operation required a sudden adaptation (Berwick and Chomsky 2016). Opponents of this view have instead argued that grammar evolved gradually through various stages of increasingly complex "protolanguages" (Bickerton 1990, Givón 1995, Jackendoff 2002, Planer and Sterelny 2021). Indeed, one motivation for the Complexity Hierarchy was to characterize potential stages of the evolution of combinatorial structure (Jackendoff and Wittenberg 2017, Wittenberg and Jackendoff 2023).

We broadly endorse the view that combinatorial structure evolved incrementally through increasingly complex states. However, we need to amend this view with two caveats. First, recursion (and other levels of combinatorial complexity) is not limited to syntactic or grammatical structures, but rather these combinatorial schemas operate across all structures within the Parallel Architecture. This requires a theory that addresses the evolution of combinatoriality across all of these structures, whether motivated by a singular neurocognitive combinatorial structure or as separate structures.

Second, the view that recursive combinatoriality is *the* important thing to characterize, with other states only being "on the way" to recursion, misses that humans' contemporary communicative faculty has available, and persistently uses, simple combinatoriality (i.e., semia). Theories of evolution need to characterize how humans ended up with the contemporary end-state that allows both semia and omnia systems. By considering recursive combinatoriality as the sole contemporary state, other levels of combinatorial complexity have been designated as persisting "fossils" in our linguistic faculty (Jackendoff and Wittenberg 2017, Wittenberg and Jackendoff 2023). The notion of "protolanguage" indeed implies a *march of progress* that characterizes a whole system by stages of less complexity that have evolved to its contemporary state, leaving behind such "fossils." This is misleading, as the whole range of combinatorics characterized by the Complexity Hierarchy persist as fundamental co-existing parts of our broader communicative capacities. Again, this orientation designates elements viewed as peripheral into less-important earlier stages of evolution, rather than rejecting the core-periphery distinction in the first place.

12.2 Multimodal Evolution

In the prior sections, we have argued that primary theories of language evolution have mischaracterized the contemporary end-state of our communicative faculties, with debates largely persisting around what to do with seemingly peripheral structures. When we reject such core-periphery assumptions, we arrive at a different evolutionary target characterized by equal status of modalities, signification, and combinatorial structure. There has been a growing acknowledgment about the necessity of the evolution of a multimodal system (de Boer 2017, McNeill 2012, Orzechowski, Wacewicz, and Żywiczyński 2016), but the lack of a multimodal model of language limits options for characterizing the evolution of such a system. So, what do we need to account for in the evolution of a multimodal language faculty?

In line with our discussion earlier, it is helpful to explicitly reframe the question about what a study of language evolution should accomplish. Instead of asking how humans arrived at an amodal, yet vocally primary, symbolic, and recursive system, a multimodal orientation should pose the question of "How did humans arrive at a multimodal semia system that allows for additional omnia systems, with multiplicitous signification and combinatorial complexity?"

Addressing this point necessitates us to also ask, *why* would we arrive at a multimodal architecture? Theories that do not posit a multimodal architecture have comfortably ignored this question, simply assuming that the system arrives at an amodal or unimodal outcome (despite multimodality being apparent in most animals, including humans). Some work has posited that language evolved as a mechanism to allow for human thought (e.g., Hauser, Chomsky, and Fitch 2002), although we agree with the view that communicative intent provides a more plausible evolutionary pressure (e.g., Jackendoff 2002, Planer and Sterelny 2021). However, these overarching functions do not address why humans' communicative capacities have evolved *this* way in particular. As discussed in the last chapter, a multimodal system functionally benefits communication in terms of *multiplicity* and *utility*. We will not fully repeat these arguments, but multiplicity provides redundancy for the source of meaning, while utility provides a complementary access to meaning-making resulting in richer communication.

One of the challenges with studying language evolution is, as we have stressed, that "language" itself is a phenomenon that emerges through the interaction of its component parts. Often, when "language" is said to evolve, the discussion emphasizes

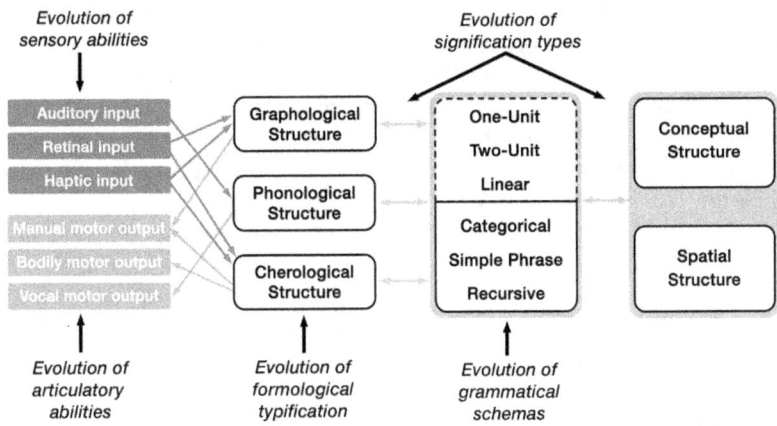

Figure 12.1 Various parts of the Parallel Architecture that require explaining in an evolutionary theory.

just one of its features (e.g., recursion, symbolicity), rather than addressing its numerous subcomponents. A full view of the evolution of humans' communicative faculties must then ask about each of its structures and their interactions. That is, we should not so much speak of the evolution of "language"—as if that were an indivisible capacity—so much as we should investigate the evolution of the component parts that make up what may or may not become language, depending on its development. We diagram these various demands to an evolutionary theory in Figure 12.1.

Following this, research on the evolution of a multimodal language faculty needs to address the following questions:

1) *How and why did humans' vocal, bodily, and graphic modalities evolve to be used for communication?*

If humans have a multimodal system with three natural modalities, why did these specific modalities arise for communication and not others? Why is it that only humans have the capacity to draw, but we share our ability to vocalize and use the body with other animals? Why didn't we create lexicons and grammars to communicate with odors or tastes? How did human anatomy evolve to allow for the expression of complex formemes in each of our modalities? How did humans develop the segmental and categorical features of formological structures in each of the natural modalities? How did humans develop the capacity for both regularized and conventionalized signals in addition to our idiosyncratic expressions?

2) *How and why did humans evolve different levels of combinatorial complexity?*

The question about the evolution of categorical and hierarchic segmental structure has been richly discussed across theories of language evolution, though mostly constrained by an amodal perspective. We add several additional questions: How did humans evolve to use signals in different combinatorial arrays? Why is exposure and practice required to attain complex combinatoriality, but not for resilient simple combinatoriality? What is the relationship between combinatorial complexity and each expressive modality? How did the same abstract combinatorial properties evolve to have different representations depending on their subcomponents in the multimodal architecture (i.e., combinatoriality within formology, grammar, conceptual structure) or their expressive systems (i.e., musical, syntactic, and narrative structures all use different types of categories)?

3) *How and why did humans evolve different interfaces between modalities and conceptual structures?*

How did modalities evolve to use all types of signification? How did modalities evolve to be optimized for certain types of signification? How do modalities differ in providing us access to and awareness of the contents of our thoughts?

4) *How and why did humans evolve to create interactions between modalities, which give way to interactions between grammars and conceptual structures?*

How did humans evolve to combine vocal, bodily, and/or graphic signals into singular composite expressions? How did humans evolve to use modalities simultaneously, rather than separately? How did humans evolve to allow for complementary signification when combining modalities?

Each of these questions persists independently of each other, but they also need to be addressed in relation to each other to account for how the full architecture of human communication evolved.

12.3 Human Uniqueness

Many approaches to language evolution like to point out the uniqueness of human linguistic capacities. Much focus in the study of the evolution of language has been placed on questions of combinatoriality, likely because this is so apparent as a unique feature of human communication compared to our evolutionary precursors. However, though researchers like to highlight language (re: speech) as a unique human capacity, other animals can vocalize and use their bodies to communicate (Cartmill and Byrne 2010, Fitch 2018). When it comes to human communication, what is really unique is our capacity to *draw*.

In discussions of the evolution of communication, humans' graphic capacities are often viewed as a proxy for intellectual development, with either the assumption that having a vocal language capacity was a prerequisite for producing graphics (like cave paintings), or that graphics are subsumed within a broader view of "artistic abilities" (whatever that means) that signal a Great Leap Forward in cognitive abilities including language. Only rarely is the capacity to produce pictures considered within overall theories of the evolution of our linguistic and communicative capacities. While we are not prepared to provide a full evolutionary theory of this full multimodal faculty, we are compelled to at least ponder the evolution of the unique human capacities of graphic production and complex combinatoriality alongside the vocal and bodily modalities.

An important reason to further consider the evolution of the graphic modality is that it is the only natural modality which has left consistent traces of its representations in the archaeological record. While the representations produced by the vocal and bodily modalities have little to no material remains, remnants of the graphic modality persist through both carvings and paintings. To the extent that our modalities are informative to each other, may have co-evolved with each other, and/or may signal modality-general capacities, this record provides important clues for understanding the evolution of the multimodal language faculty. If the complexities of the graphic capacity evolved alongside the vocal and bodily modalities, the archeological record related to graphics may be a source of data that signifies broader cognitive development of the whole system.

On this point, while much focus has been given to carvings and cave paintings, the origins of the graphic modality may not have come from such a temporally persistent material. One plausible origin for the graphic capacity comes from drawing in sand by imitating tracks of animals (Figure 12.2a), which functionally could have

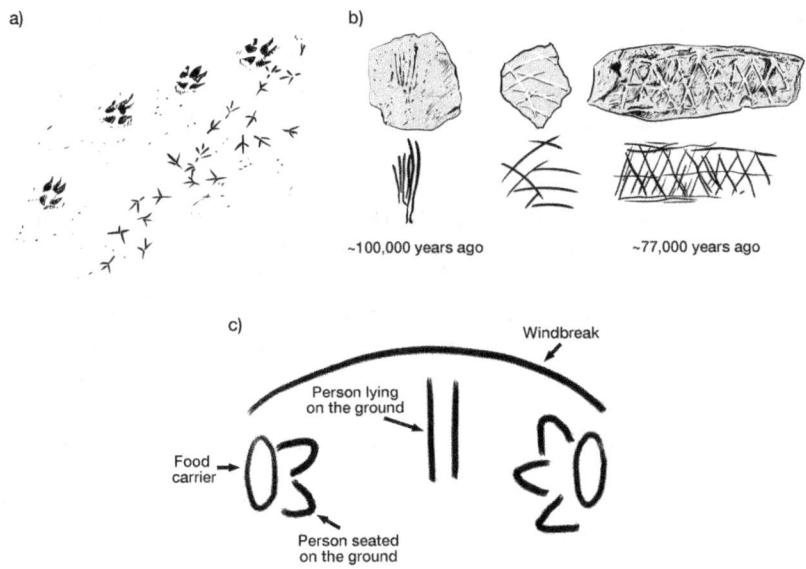

Figure 12.2 a) Graphemic qualities of animal tracks, b) etchings from ochre and shells up to 100,000 years ago (redrawn from figures in Henshilwood et al. 2002, Tylén et al. 2020), and c) a diagram of a sand drawing scene from Central Australian Aboriginals (Green 2014, Wilkins 2016).

arisen from and benefited hunting. Indeed, complex systems of sand drawing persist in contemporary Australian Aboriginal communities (Figure 12.2c) where they are conceptualized as "tracks" and these systems provide important counterpoints to many assumptions about drawings (Green 2014, Wilkins 2016). These sand drawings are rapidly fading, are highly abstracted yet still broadly iconic, are produced in real-time communicative contexts, and are produced in multimodal expressions alongside speech and gesture and/or sign languages (see Figure 12.2c for a schematized example).

In this light, when considering cave paintings and carvings, it is thus worth remembering several things. First, cave paintings may indeed be late in graphic production compared to more rapidly fading precedents like drawing in sand or drawing with other less durable materials. Second, cave paintings may have been created in multimodal contexts alongside vocal and bodily expressions where only the graphics persist. Third, drawings are created in time, and the order of this dynamic production script may be difficult to perceive in an otherwise static finished work. In other words, cave paintings may have been created as an unfurling sequential depiction alongside speaking and signing, but both the temporally created visual sequence and multimodality are now lost because all that remains is a single static depiction. Thus, even our persisting records of graphics may be incomplete.

In addition, we should clarify some points about the graphic modality that may contrast from naïve and "commonsense" notions of pictures. First, in line with our claims throughout this book, and with a growing literature acknowledging the linguistic structure of graphics (Arts and Schilperoord 2016, Cohn 2013b, Forceville 2016, 2020, Greenberg 2011, Willats 1997), we reject the broad assumptions that picture-making is related to the articulation of perception. Though this phenomenological idea about drawing persists because of the iconicity of graphics and because that's what drawing may "feel like," it is not an accurate reflection of cognitive capacities. Thus, we do not assume that articulating perception is the functional purpose for which pictures evolved. Instead, humans create pictures to communicate thoughts visually, just as we do with the vocal and bodily modalities. Secondly, many approaches to the evolution of graphics take all marks to be meaningful "symbols." However, we also do not assume that all marks are indicative of meaning. In some cases, mark-making may simply reflect the development of graphemes with no interfacing with meaning (i.e., they are modalia).

Nevertheless, the archaeological record does provide numerous insights about the process by which humans' graphic modality evolved. Deliberate mark-making has been observed on surfaces dating as far back as 250 to 350,000 years ago in Europe, and 500,000 in Asia (García-Diez and Ochoa 2019). These marks show incremental increases in their complexity and systematicity of configurations by around 77,000 years ago (Henshilwood et al. 2002), as in Figure 12.2b. Such consistent production of shapes has been interpreted as reflecting an evolving capacity for geometry in humans which is lacked by our primate cousins (Dehaene et al. 2022, Sablé-Meyer et al. 2021). When interpreted in terms of the marks themselves, and without the assumption of meaning-making, this progressive patterning can be interpreted as a process of *typification* to develop graphemes as basic productive shapes (Tylén et al. 2020). That is, they demonstrate the development of the modality itself, rather than what they may signify.

Consider a scenario where tracks provided the impetus for the development of drawing. First, tracks produced by animals provide highly repeated geometric patterns on the surface of the ground, which have properties of basic graphemes—i.e., lines, curves, dots, blobs, etc. (Figure 12.2a). Tracks themselves are idiosyncratic (each being different), but recognizing similar tracks as tied to a common foot requires seeing them as instances of a type. Doing so would necessitate the typification of marks, which in turn could lead to the emergence of abstracted graphemes. While this typification could be done in the service of establishing correspondences to meaning (i.e., "these consistent marks signify a type of foot"), this process could also persist solely in terms of recognizing patterning of graphics alone. In other words, tracks could be seen and imitated as graphic elements with no recognition of their relationship to feet. However, when that connection would be made—both as iconic of a foot and as indexical to the foot it came from—it could benefit hunting.

To summarize our speculation on this process, one of our primate ancestors first would see tracks on the ground. They would then recognize the consistency of those repeated marks. They would then draw similar marks into the dirt. This imitation becomes a cognitive act, because it uses (or develops) graphemes that are independent of what is seen in the world. To clarify this, the marks left by actual tracks are incidental shapes that occur because of the form of whatever makes an imprint. The creation of a shape with intentionality by a drawer is not incidental and is not based on the shape of an imprinting object. Rather, a produced region (line, blob) is a cognitive construct, which can be typified and repeated outside of this context. In addition, such a process could involve either pure imitation of the visual patterns alone, leading to creation of abstract graphemes, or it could have involved already recognizing the meaning of such imprints that were imitated. In this case, the recognition of graphemes would follow the attempted creation of a holistic form. Nevertheless, the presence of abstract marks alone on etchings and subsequent increases in their configurational complexity suggest against a view that graphics were created first holistically and then decomposed into graphemic parts.

Additional evidence comes from the graphic capacities ascribed to Neanderthals. Systematic marks have been attributed to Neanderthals, but debates persist about their capacities to produce patterned graphic configurations (Hoffmann et al. 2018, Slimak et al. 2018), and especially about their ability to create iconic depictions (García-Diez 2022). Anatomically modern humans have been said to have split from Neanderthals around 400,000 to 700,000 years ago, which suggests that the initial development of graphemes occurred with our shared ancestors. This places grapheme capacities to be far older than most evidence of systematic carvings, prior to the genetic separation from Neanderthals.

With this in mind, when did we start using those graphics to convey meaning? While patterned configurations of marks could be indicative of meaning, iconic depictions are the best indicators of marks that are referential. The oldest records of iconic depictions have been preserved in cave paintings dating from around 45,000 years ago found in Southeast Asia, while the oldest in Europe date to around 40,000 years ago (Aubert et al. 2019). The iconic depictions in European cave paintings have also been argued to be accompanied by regularized symbolic markings, already suggesting a full range of signification (Bacon et al. 2023). These paintings are all fairly complex and detailed in their iconicity, implying that they reflect an already robust system.

In addition, the migration of humans to Australia occurred around 65,000 years ago, and these humans would already have had such graphic capacities. Archeological evidence suggests fewer figurative prehistoric cave paintings in Australia (Bednarik 2006), despite modern Aboriginals' complex systems of sand drawings (Green 2014, Wilkins 2016). This perhaps suggests that early humans migrating into Australia were already producing an antecedent system of sand drawings as a primary graphic system preceding the widespread use of cave walls as a new canvas. Modern Australian sand drawings have a base lexicon of highly abstracted monomorphemic graphic signs that convey each concept with a single grapheme. For example, a U-shape depicts a person using iconic reference (Figure 12.2c), as it is said to represent a shape similar to the imprint that a sitting human leaves on the ground (Green 2014, Wilkins 2016). Such abstraction is in part caused by the ecological materiality of sand or dirt, which does not allow for much detail. If early humans used a comparably structured antecedent system of abstracted iconicity prior to migration to Australia, subsequent detailed iconicity could be developed along with the use of more sophisticated tools and surfaces. The systematic configurations observed in etchings may have reflected "playing" with graphemes to create more complex graphological relationships (for example, creating line junctions), and indeed modern children's drawing development includes a stage of scribbling comparable to the vocal babbling stage playing with their formology (Kindler and Darras 1997, Willats 1997, 2005). More complex graphic configurations would in turn allow for creating more complex iconic representations as we see in cave paintings.

All of this suggests that the evolution of iconic reference between the graphic modality and conceptual structures occurred far before 65,000 years ago, with an upper limit of around 400 to 700,000 years ago when human ancestors and Neanderthals split. At this point, we can now ask, how does this evolution of our graphic capacities relate to the broader development of a multimodal linguistic capacity? As we have stated before, our primate ancestors already had a capacity for simple vocal and bodily expression. Our graphic modality is then unique to humans, seemingly along with greater capacity for complex combinatoriality. Some researchers have also pointed to humans having the cognitive prerequisites necessary for language (e.g., combinatoriality, vocal ability) by 200,000 years ago based on archeological records about tool making, though humans did not necessarily use this cognitive toolkit in the absence of socioeconomic needs (Planer and Sterelny 2021). Altogether, this places graphic development directly within the speculated timeline for the evolution of vocal and bodily expressions.

All of this implies that somewhere after the divergence of homo sapiens and Neanderthals roughly 400–700,000 years ago, humans established an innate semia system with all three natural vocal, bodily, and graphic modalities along with basic correspondences to conceptual structure. Such a multimodal semia system is consistent with the communicative capacities of other animals, thereby placing humans' base faculties in line with other species (Engesser and Townsend 2019, Fitch 2020, Ghirlanda, Lind, and Enquist 2017). We again stress that this semia system persists even in modern humans. The question then becomes how did humans arrive at the potential for omnia systems on top of this semia system between 100 to 200,000 years ago? In other words, what was the evolutionary process that led a trimodal semia system with formological and conceptual structures to establish interfaces with complex combinatorial structures?

First, we agree with other approaches that posit combinatorial capacities first evolved outside the communicative system, such as for the hierarchic structure required of action planning (Arbib 2005, 2012, Planer and Sterelny 2021). This would contrast with the idea that combinatoriality evolved exclusively "within" the communicative system (i.e., developed solely for language). In this case, the evolution of communicative combinatoriality would characterize greater possibilities or options for interfacing between those existing hierarchic capacities and an innate semia system that already allowed for correspondences between formology and conceptual structure. In addition, if communicative combinatorial capacities shifted from origins related to action planning, it implies a process of abstraction away from the representations related to actions (e.g., Jackendoff 2007), to a format that is abstract enough to permeate across domains. Such abstraction is consistent with the schemas posited in the Complexity Hierarchy in Chapter 6 to reflect basic sequencing possibilities in cognition (Dehaene et al. 2015, Jackendoff and Wittenberg 2014). It remains an open question whether such abstraction occurred before or during the evolution of our combinatoriality as interfaced with our communicative capacities.

Second, we agree with theories of an incremental evolution of combinatoriality, whereby combinations of elements became increasingly more complex over time. However, this progression is not usefully characterized as going through different stages of "protolanguages" (Bickerton 1990, Givón 1995, Jackendoff 2002, Planer and Sterelny 2021), because that implies the evolution of an indivisible and unimodal system. Instead, given that the communicative architecture is composed of independent parts that each needed to be evolved, it follows that the evolution of combinatoriality pertains to the schematic elements within the Complexity Hierarchy (Dehaene et al. 2015, Jackendoff and Wittenberg 2014). This would apply across structures of the architecture (formology and grammar) and across modalities (vocal, bodily, and graphic), meaning that the evolution of the combinatoriality of all such structures needs to be accounted for.

How then did humans' modalities evolve to interface with complex combinatoriality? While we are not prepared to detail an incremental evolutionary process, we offer an account that focuses on the overall conditions of that evolution. A first possibility would be that one modality develops the interfaces to complex combinatorial structures first, followed by interfaces to other modalities. This is a modality-transference view (i.e., gesture-first), yet within the Parallel Architecture it could more appropriately be characterized as "interface-transference," as it would posit a new interface between a formology and combinatorial structure, rather than the transference of a unitary "linguistic capacity" between modalities. There are many "just so" stories throughout the literature about why the vocal or bodily modalities may have developed combinatoriality first (Armstrong 2002, Corballis 2002, Givón 1995, Hewes 1973, Masataka 2007, Mithen 2006, Planer and Sterelny 2021, Tomasello 2010, Vaneechoutte and Skoyles 1998). We could add our own "just so" story that complex combinatoriality evolved due to the graphic modality first, before transferring to the vocal and bodily modalities. Indeed, since the graphic modality and complex combinatoriality are both unique to humans, a possible scenario could be that they evolved in tandem, not the vocal or bodily modalities which were already there.

Nevertheless, given the multimodal nature of the communicative faculty, we find a more likely scenario to be the *coevolution* of modalities and complex combinatoriality. Indeed, not only are the graphic modality and complex combinatoriality new for homo sapiens, but so is the *integration* of different modalities into singular multimodal expressions. Primates rarely produce synchronized vocalizations and gestures (Cartmill, Beilock, and Goldin-Meadow 2012), and neurological research has suggested greater connectivity for multimodality in humans than other primates (Ardesch et al. 2019). It makes more sense for the coevolution of modalities' complexity considering they also evolved to be integrated with each other. Otherwise, one or all modalities would have needed to independently become complex, and then both to transfer that complexity to, and to integrate with, other modalities.

Coevolution would also be the most likely scenario given the functional benefits of *multiplicity* and *utility* that we outlined in Chapter 11. As we argued, multiple modalities allow for contextually appropriate use of different affordances of sensory signals. For example, vocal signals are good in the dark and when hands are full, bodily and graphic signals are good for staying quiet, bodily signals are good across distances, and others. In addition, a coevolution view is more amendable to the functional utility and complementary semiotic nature of our modalities. In other words, if modalities complement each other in their signification—for example symbolic speech and iconic gestures which both access a common growth point—it makes sense that they all evolved together to do this integration. Again, the evolutionary consequences of this holistic, complementary relationship between modalities would explain why humans evolved a system distinct from the independent treatment of multiple modalities as it occurs in other animals. This coevolution view diminishes the relevance of speculating which modality came first with no assumption of a core-periphery relationship, and satisfies the calls for a multimodal evolution (de Boer 2017, McNeill 2012, Orzechowski, Wacewicz, and Żywiczyński 2016).

12.4 Conclusion

Throughout this chapter we have reflected on the implications of a multimodal architecture for the evolution of humans' communicative faculty. As we have argued, models of language evolution need to more accurately account for the contemporary end-state of the communicative faculty, disregarding social distinctions between core and peripheral systems. It is inappropriate to situate everything that is considered as peripheral automatically into the evolutionary past, when they continue to persist as fundamental, non-peripheral parts of humans' contemporary cognition. While we have not provided a sketch of language evolution, we have hopefully outlined what is required of an evolutionary theory to fully account for the richness of the whole of human communication, along with the complexity of its architecture.

13

Toward a Multimodal Linguistics

Throughout this book, we have asked the question: *What theory of our language and communicative faculty can accommodate the complexity of multimodal expression?* To address this question, we proposed a multimodal architecture where both unimodal and multimodal expressions emerge out of a distributed system of parallel structures. Like all models of language and communication, this multimodal Parallel Architecture carries with it assumptions about the fundamental nature of human expression. In this case, not only does this model account for a wider range of phenomena than unimodal models are capable of, but it heralds a new paradigm for thinking about language, communication, and cognition more broadly.

Our multimodal model is a direct confrontation with traditional assumptions which emphasize the amodal and unimodal character of language, and privileges speech. Although many approaches recognize the necessity of addressing multimodality and its properties (e.g., Bateman, Wildfeuer, and Hiippala 2017, Clark 1996, Goldin-Meadow 2003b, Kress 2009, Kress and van Leeuwen 2001, Mayer 2009, McNeill 1992, Patel-Grosz et al. 2023), we argue that accounting for human expressive behaviors necessitates a Multimodal Paradigm that further reconfigures the basic assumptions about our linguistic and communicative capacities. These basic assumptions manifest directly from the properties of our model, and better reflect what people do in their basic expressive and communicative practices and the evidence gathered through decades of scientific research. This evidence has fundamental repercussions for thinking about language and communication that go against the amodal assumptions.

In order to move forward with a study of language and communication that accommodates the full range of human expressive potential, we must interrogate these basic amodal assumptions and their origins. Doing so will allow us to highlight their deficiencies and to clearly articulate the necessary alternatives provided by the Multimodal Paradigm. This chapter therefore examines these paradigmatic assumptions across the beliefs about language's modalities, the core versus peripheral nature of different behaviors, and the features of linguistic structure.

13.1 Amodal versus Multimodal

A fundamental assumption of theories throughout the past century is that *language is amodal*. This idea holds that, though the primacy of speech has gone undisputed, the true nature of language persists regardless of its channel of expression, and cognitively these modality-neutral properties may flow into different modalities indiscriminately. In this framing, "language" is in principle separated from its modalities. This amodal assumption is also wrapped up in the notion that linguistic representations are abstract symbols, and their arbitrariness allows them to be mutable across modalities. The focus on arbitrariness is inherited from Saussurean linguistics and structuralism, a point we will return to in a later section. Language also appears amodal because, though speech appears to be its primary pathway, it also appears in other modalities. For example, speech also manifests in writing (and secondarily, braille, semaphore, Morse code, etc.). By the same token, under this view, sign languages simply provide an alternative pathway for "language" in cases where speech is deprived.

Yet, this view of amodal representations does not explain why various modalities have particular characteristics that differ from each other based on the affordances of the modalities themselves. Indeed, conveying speech with writing has consequences: literacy changes the structure of the brain (Carreiras et al. 2009, Dehaene 2011, Wolf 2008), since it requires the adaptation of the vocal modality to the graphic modality, which has its own natural expressions. As argued in Chapter 2, instead of speech simply manifesting in writing because language is amodal, writing is a *synesthesia*, making it a cognitive adaptation from one natural modality (vocal) to another natural modality (graphics) to make an *un*natural correspondence. The distinctive properties of writing relative to speech arise out of this unnatural correspondence, where speech then takes on new affordances of the graphic modality.

In addition, if an amodal assumption of language is followed to its extremes, it would imply that sign languages operate exactly the same as speech, only occurring in the body. Indeed, this belief manifests in the attempts to convert speech into the body, such as with Manually Coded English, where all properties of English appear encoded as bodily gestures (Supalla 1991). Yet, research on sign language has demonstrated that it has unique characteristics unavailable in speech which rely on the affordances of the bodily modality (Emmorey 2023, Goldin-Meadow and Brentari 2017, Liddell 2003, Lillo-Martin and Gajewski 2014, Sandler 2017). Furthermore, direct conversions of speech into the bodily modality (e.g., Manually Coded English) are said to function unnaturally (Supalla 1991). Similar unnatural qualities arise in "ideographies" or "picture writing" where the graphic modality is pushed to function similarly to textual writing, rather than to use its own natural affordances (Cohn and Schilperoord 2023).

An amodal treatment also fails to explain why modalities retain meaning-making capacities even when they do not develop into full languages. For example, whether or not a person acquires a full sign language, they still likely can produce co-speech gestures. In addition, even without developing the ability to draw in a robust visual language, people still retain the capacity to doodle. If linguistic representations are fully amodal and merely find different pathways to appear, then such bodily and graphic semia would be expected to disappear when not engaged. These non-vocal modalities of the body and graphics are often considered only important when they are manifesting or interacting with speech, and otherwise are treated as peripheral. Yet, these semia—meaning-making systems with a basic structure—persist alongside modalities that do develop into full omnia.

This persistence of semia alongside omnia also has consequences unaddressed by theories of language evolution. As we have discussed in Chapter 12, a primary debate concerns whether "language" evolved first in the bodily modality and then transferred to the ultimately more primary vocal modality (Armstrong 2002, Corballis 2002, Givón 1995, Hewes 1973, Tomasello 2010). This framing of the debate reflects an amodal belief that "language" is separate from its modalities, and merely flows from one modality to the other. Thus, the main goal of these theories is to explain the evolution of how humans use amodal symbols in speech, not the full range of our actual human communicative capacities. Nevertheless, as has been pointed out, this framing does not account for why we retain the ability to gesture alongside speech, or why sign languages exist independently of speech (McNeill 2012). That is, theories of amodal language evolution fail to account for why semia persist alongside omnia, or for why we independently develop omnia in multiple modalities.

In addition, multimodality itself is a challenge for the amodal view of linguistic representations. How can we distribute amodal representations into multiple modalities at once, especially when their combination may create inferences unavailable in the surface of either modality? This also invokes the issue of why semia in one modality persist alongside, and indeed are entwined with, omnia in another modality, including in entrenched constructions (as discussed in Chapters 9 and 10).

The consequence of these observations is that language is indeed *not* amodal, but rather that all modalities persist alongside each other within a singular cognitive architecture. This manifests in the multimodal Parallel Architecture where the natural vocal, bodily, and graphic modalities all simultaneously correspond to combinatorial and conceptual structures. There is no flow of "language" into one modality or another, because modalities are an intrinsic component of languages, co-present and functional as part of a shared system within which "languages" are emergent activation states.

Given that humans' cognitive architecture begins with all modalities, exposure and practice determine whether they develop into full omnia across development or maintain as semia. We posit that innate correspondences persist between our natural formologies (phonology, cherology, and graphology) and conceptual structures regardless of whether a person acquires a system with a complex combinatorial structure and an extensive lexicon (i.e., omnia). Semia are our "resilient" and innate meaning-making system (Goldin-Meadow 2003b). That is, humans innately have the capacity to create simple expressions (single units, linear sequences) of sounds, bodily motions, and drawings. This trimodal semia system constitutes a baseline that places the human communicative faculty in line with those of many other animals.

Modalities can further develop as full omnia when a person is exposed to and practices with an omnia system. Thus, a person will develop a sign language if they receive the requisite exposure and practice with such an external system that provides them with a lexicon and combinatorial structure. Yet, even if a person does not learn a sign language, they retain their resilient ability to express meaning with gestures

(Goldin-Meadow 2003b). Similarly, if a person does not learn a full visual language (often reflected in the statement of "I can't draw"), they retain the ability to create basic drawings (Cohn 2012).

The amodal perspective can thus be seen as a byproduct of having a cognitive system with multiple modalities persisting in parallel that each can be developed to different degrees of complexity. If one maintains a belief that language has a unimodal manifestation—along with privileging one of those modalities—then omnia emerging in different modalities will be interpreted as an amodal system flowing out of different options. Thus, the idea of language as amodal is a misperception of viewing a multimodal system through the lens of language being unimodal.

13.2 Core versus Periphery

A second persisting assumption is that language (often implicitly spoken and written) is the core expressive system while other modalities remain relegated to the periphery. We see this distinction in phrasings like "verbal" and "non-verbal" behavior, as if all behaviors that are not "verbal" are exceptional and not distinctive enough to be named on their own. The peripheral status of the bodily and graphic modalities becomes especially apparent in the ways they are treated. Despite the clear integration of gestures with spoken expressions, arguments persist about whether gestures belong as "part of" the language system (Ladewig 2020). In addition, sign languages are often considered as a type of communication used when the "primary" speech system is unavailable, despite sign languages also being used prevalently among hearing individuals in various communities.

In addition, the study of visual languages and graphic communication is often not even considered by the broader sciences of language and cognition outside of studies of perception, maintaining the assumption that graphics only reflect basic percepts. This idea is simply false (Cohn 2013b, Greenberg 2011, Gombrich 1961, Wilkins 2016, Willats 1997, Wilson 1988, 1999). Questions like whether a picture can negate, lie, or argue (often with the answer being "no") serve as ammunition for the core-periphery viewpoint, despite these traits all occurring in the graphic modality (Giora et al. 2009, Oversteegen and Schilperoord 2014). In an amodal view, modalities merely provide options for output of certain structures, and if those structures do not manifest in familiar ways as the "core" system, then the modality appears to be "peripheral."

All of this renders a view that speech alone provides our core communicative capacity, while other modalities merely persist in a supportive, auxiliary way—often assumed to be universal—outside this core vocal system. We see these assumptions persisting in the misperception that there is only one sign language or one visual language, rather than many crosslinguistic varieties. It also arises in the belief that our bodily and graphic expressions are universally transparent, merely being pantomime (bodily) or fully reflecting perception (graphics).

One immediate consequence of placing speech as the core is that lexically encoded form-meaning mappings would primarily or even exclusively be available in the vocal modality, unless some impairment "pushes it" into an alternative modality. Yet, both the bodily and graphic modalities encode systematic lexical items of their own, independent of speech. In the bodily modality, sign languages have lexicons on par with any other omnia (de Vos and Pfau 2015, Liddell 2003), while bodily semia have encoded forms both in isolation as gestural emblems and as co-speech gestures (Gawne and Cooperrider 2022, McNeill 1992). Graphic communication also uses extensive visual lexicons of fixed form-meaning correspondences at varying levels of complexity (Cohn 2013b, 2024, Forceville 2011, McCloud 1993, Schilperoord 2013, Schilperoord and Cohn 2023, Weissman et al. 2023, Wilkins 2016, Wilson 1988, 1999).

In addition, as demonstrated throughout this book, all of our modalities integrate in multimodal interactions, including the encoding of systematic multimodal lexical items. Gestures have long been recognized as combining with speech in conventionalized and predictable patterns at a fundamental level (Clark 1996, Fricke 2013, Kendon 1988, Ladewig 2020, McNeill 1992). In addition, systematic combinations of text and image also persist as multimodal constructions across a range of media. This should immediately become apparent when interacting on social media where multimodal "memes" proliferate, which are almost all examples of productive multimodal lexical items (Bateman, Wildfeuer, and Hiippala 2017, Dancygier and Vandelanotte 2017, Schilperoord and Cohn 2023).

Furthermore, neurocognitive research has shown that similar processing persists across all modalities. Consistent neural responses have long been observed to the semantic processing of speech, sign, writing, gestures, drawings, pictures, sounds, and all other meaning-making domains (Kutas and Federmeier 2011, Ralph et al. 2016). In addition, the matrix schema of one modality can modulate the semantic processing of substitutions (Federmeier and Kutas 2001, Ganis, Kutas, and Sereno 1996, Manfredi, Cohn, and Kutas 2017, Nigam, Hoffman, and Simons 1992, Weissman, Cohn, and Tanner under review). Similarly, manipulating the combinatorial structure of music and visual sequences evokes neural responses similar to those produced by manipulating the grammar of written/spoken languages (Cohn 2020b, Koelsch 2011a, Patel 2003), implying at least partial overlap in processing despite differing representations. The brain does not make distinctions between core and periphery in terms of modalities.

Observations like these cannot be accounted for by a core versus peripheral distinction. Alternatively, the Multimodal Paradigm posits that all of our natural modalities (vocal, bodily, and graphic) persist with equal status alongside each other, reflecting the observations that modalities use consistent structural principles and cognitive mechanisms. Rather than holding relative rankings, different behaviors manifest as emergent states from a single holistic architecture, whether as semia, sequentia, or omnia, and whether as unimodal or multimodal expressions.

As described above, exposure and practice across a developmental trajectory determine which parts of this holistic Parallel Architecture manifest into omnia compared to those that persist as semia. The developmental trajectory of omnia across modalities appears to maintain similar characteristics, starting with a period of playing with the modality itself (babbling, scribbling), then consolidating basic patterns and units, progressing through more complex utterances (Cohn 2012, 2020a, Goldin-Meadow 2003b, Willats 2005). This trajectory for all modalities is most optimized within a sensitive learning period which apexes around puberty, after which fluency can only be attained through more conscious efforts (Cohn 2012, Goldin-Meadow 2003b). If an omnia system is not developed, then that modality persists as a resilient semia.

The Multimodal Paradigm also provides an explanation for *why* we have multiple modalities in the first place, which is not forthcoming in an amodal core versus peripheral view. As discussed, modalities provide multiplicity as various options for meaning-making. Multiple modalities with equal status provide different avenues for communication subject to both environmental conditions (darkness, having a full mouth, needing to keep quiet, etc.), while also providing ways to compensate in permanent or situational impairment.

Differences across modalities also allow utility as complementary semiotic functioning that makes use of their different affordances. This function is lost in arguments that modalities should operate in the exact same ways, such as that in order to hold a worthy status, pictures need to be able to negate, lie, or argue in the *same manner* as speech. Indeed, pictures do not have words like "no" or "not," but that does not mean that they cannot be used to evoke negation, lie, or argue. They just do so in ways that are distinctive to the affordances of those modalities (Giora et al. 2009, Oversteegen and Schilperoord 2014), which are every bit as natural to the graphic modality as lexicalized negation words may be to the vocal modality. In addition, we should not expect modalities to operate as fully redundant systems, since that would eliminate any advantage to having multiple complementary modalities in the first place.

Just because most people have not achieved fluency in sign languages or have not reached proficiency in drawing a visual language does not mean that these systems are peripheral or that they do not maintain the same level of complexity as speech. As argued above, the conception of bodily and graphic modalities being "peripheral" may have arisen out the degree to which they are developed into full omnia, which is conditioned upon by their cultural and ecological contexts. These distinctions, however, are not cognitive, and thus they should not shape our conception of the cognitive architecture for communicative systems.

13.3 Unique Design Features

An additional key assumption is that "language" uses unique structural principles and cognitive systems. This view posits that the representational systems involved in language (re: speech), and its concomitant cognitive architecture, are unlike those found in other species or other human behaviors (e.g., Hauser, Chomsky, and Fitch 2002). Assumptions of language's exceptionalism have a long history, including Hockett's (1960) listing of "design features" of language which described traits supposedly unique to language and exclusionary of other systems (and which have most all been shown to be inaccurate). The most persistent dogmas are that, first, linguistic signs are fundamentally *arbitrary*, which has been handed down from structuralism (de Saussure 1972 [1916]), and, second, that only language is structured with *recursive* combinatoriality, especially syntax (Chomsky 1995, Hauser, Chomsky, and Fitch 2002).

The core positioning of particular structural features as criteria for behaviors being considered "linguistic" has consequences for their classification. In this perspective, any lack of sufficient arbitrariness designates a behavior to the periphery in its value. In addition, under this perspective, if an argument is to be made for something to be considered as "language," then it must be claimed to also be arbitrary, whether or not this is an accurate description of its features. This overemphasis occurred in early research on sign language, where claims of arbitrariness were required to justify its linguistic status (Goldin-Meadow and Brentari 2017, Lillo-Martin and Gajewski 2014).

However, substantial research has shown that arbitrariness is not a unique design feature of language. Speech uses a broad range of signification beyond arbitrariness, including iconicity and indexicality (Clark 1996, Dingemanse et al. 2015, Ferrara and Hodge 2018), and the bodily and graphic modalities also use arbitrary signs, while additionally maintaining this full range of signification (Liddell 2003, McNeill 1992). Thus, speech uses both arbitrary and non-arbitrary signification, while we also find arbitrariness in modalities other than speech. We will discuss further consequences of the Saussurean Sign below.

Emphasizing recursion also has consequences on the consideration of the structure of speech and other behaviors. Because recursion has been associated with syntax specifically, it has been emphasized as the primary important feature of language, a position that has been called "syntactico-centrism" (Culicover and Jackendoff 2005, Jackendoff 2002). Syntactic recursion has thus taken a primary position within the study of the structure and processing of language, and to discussion of how it has evolved (Berwick and Chomsky 2016, Jackendoff 2002, 2010b, Jackendoff and Wittenberg 2017, Planer and Sterelny 2021). Nevertheless, many full-fledged languages do not use recursion in their syntactic structures (Jackendoff and Wittenberg 2014), while at the same time recursive combinatoriality proliferates across cognitive behaviors and expressive modalities. Recursion appears both in individual and sequential pictures (Cohn 2020b, Willats 1997), and in non-meaningful expressions in music (Jackendoff and Lerdahl 2006). Recursion has also been well-documented in other cognitive behaviors like perception, memory, and event structure (Jackendoff 2011, Marr 1982, Võ 2021, Zacks and Tversky 2001).

Altogether, using linguistic features like arbitrariness and recursion as criteria for "uniqueness" or "linguistic status" of behaviors may lead to inaccurate classification in the face of more obvious traits. For example, emphasis on arbitrariness would lead to the dismissal of the structure of drawing as a core aspect of human communication, since pictures are primarily iconic in their signification. Yet, drawing is perhaps the most unique of human behaviors, given that, to create meaning, other animals do vocalize and move their bodies, but they do not draw. All of this is to say that design features make poor criteria for evaluating human behaviors. Rather, it is more important to simply observe and accurately account for the variety of structures that persist across human behaviors, whatever they may be, and to acknowledge that all our expressive behaviors have value in the first place.

13.4 Expressive Signs

As hinted in the last section, a final amodal assumption comes from the Saussurean Sign, which has shaped the way that language and communication has been theorized for over a hundred years. This conception of expressive units assumes that form and meaning constitute an inseparable package characterized by arbitrariness, thus conflating the nature of the sign (its modality) with the way it signifies (the interface between modality and meaning). The orientation of the Saussurean Sign as the unit of expression has led to assumptions about the architecture of language and for the signification of units.

13.4.1 Language Architectures

Most theories of language begin with shared assumptions that the system includes components of a modality, grammar, and meaning, along with a lexicon. However, if we assume that form (modality) and meaning create indivisible units, as in the Saussurean Sign, then it leads to theories that must accommodate these units within the linguistic architecture. For example, the lexicon under this conception would consist of an inventory of these passive units (i.e., a "bag of words"), and the rest of the architecture of the linguistic system explains how these units are organized.

Throughout the 20th century, models of the language architecture have attempted to account for the source of organization of these indivisible linguistic units (Harris 2021, Huck and Goldsmith 1995). The tradition of generative grammar focuses exclusively on the building of syntactic structures from which all meaning is derived, except those parts that are already in these indivisible lexical units (Chomsky 1965, 1995). Within the tradition of cognitive grammar (and its predecessor, generative semantics), all emphasis is put on the meaning itself, plus its connection to sounds (modality), constituting a Saussurean Sign, reserving for the grammar some negotiating role between these poles of form and meaning (Lakoff 1971, Langacker 1987, McCawley 1995).

Although these views differ widely in their valuation of the components of the linguistic architecture, both principally incorporate the Saussurean Sign as a fundamental unit, whether implicitly or explicitly. Both of these perspectives maintain the holism of the linguistic unit, while also designating the organizational, combinatorial, and generative structures to a particular component within the system, whether that is syntax or semantics. Such an indivisible form-meaning unit therefore results in either syntactic- or semantic-centrism.

The conception of expressive units as indivisible form-meaning pairs also has consequences for multimodality. First, if there is only a single source of combinatoriality for organizing units within an architecture, it makes it unclear how units across modalities may be combined. Does the grammar or semantic system of speech then also structure its combination with gestures? Second, by maintaining the conception of holism of these units, entire expressive behaviors seem indivisible, such that speech, gestures, drawings, etc. all appear to be their own distinctive behaviors without sharing common componential structures. Again, if these behaviors are viewed as independent, it raises challenges for the cognitive structure of their combinations.

Under this view, would expressions in each modality have their own independent combinatorial systems, and if so, how do they combine in such intimate ways? For substitution (like *I* ♥ *NY*), does that mean a singular generative system is pulling from lexicons of different modalities?

We believe that these debates about linguistic structure, and the problems with how they account for both unimodal and multimodal expressions, stem from maintaining the Saussurean Sign as a foundational unit. Though the Parallel Architecture maintains the same components of the linguistic system as other models, its distribution of these components undermines this assumed foundational unit (Jackendoff 2002, Jackendoff and Audring 2020). Rather than indivisible forms traveling through structures of organization, the Parallel Architecture instead distributes the structure of the units across its subcomponents, all of which use combinatoriality. The lexicon in this case is not a repository of passive items separate from combinatorial structures, but consists of units that are composed of pieces of structure interfaced across each component of the architecture. In essence, the architecture *is* the lexicon.

By incorporating the lexicon as interfaces across components of the architecture, it accommodates units of varying sizes, granularity, and complexity. It allows for both encoded and novel units from different modalities, reflecting semia and omnia particular to each modality. In addition, it affords encoding and creating horizontal combinations of modalities resulting in multimodal lexical items. This means that multimodality is not the combination of indivisible signs from different modalities, like speech *plus* gesture or writing *plus* pictures, which may or may not happen to share common encoding of meaning in their form-meaning pairs. Rather, multimodal expressions reflect emergent states from a distributed architecture where different modalities may co-index shared conceptual structures.

13.4.2 Modalities and Meaning

The view that form (modality) and meaning create indivisible units also leads to theories that must accommodate the processing of meaning in these units. If the nature of the meaning is reflected in the nature of the form, then different brain areas and cognitive mechanisms should persist for the encoding of these different meaningful expressions, i.e., different brain areas for visual and verbal meanings. This perspective is intuitive given that it reflects our phenomenology of modalities as different types of sensory experiences. We find this view most prominently reflected in "dual-coding models" of the processing of visual and verbal meaning-making (Paivio 1986), reinforcing modular views of cognition (Fodor 1983). In these models, visual and verbal stimuli are taken to be processed by different cognitive resources. Such an approach assumes that the nature of the stimulus (i.e., its sensory and formological features) persists in the characteristics of its cognitively instantiated meaning—visual stimuli have visual meanings and verbal stimuli have verbal meanings—and therefore needs to be processed as such.

Dual-route models remain influential and pervasive both within and outside academic scholarship. However, cognitive neuroscience research over the past several decades has largely converged on a view that, though modalities may engage sensory-specific resources, semantic memory itself is "supramodal," indiscriminate of specific modalities (Calzavarini 2023, Kuhnke et al. 2023, Kutas and Federmeier 2011, Ralph et al. 2016, Xu et al. 2009). This is not to say that semantic memory is "amodal," but rather that the nature of meaning is different than the nature of sensory signals in the first place. Thus, if form and meaning are not inextricably tied, various forms can tap into a network of distributed meanings in multiplicitous ways. The unique meaning-making capacities of each modality are not encoded as such, but rather follow from the affordances of those modalities and the ways that they signify.

Following from this, indivisible form-meaning units lead to the perception that expressive behaviors are independent, each having their own distinct representations and encoded meanings. If multimodality is then the interaction between these indivisible behaviors, their separately encoded meanings need some additional mechanism to link together across separately formatted representations. Thus, not only do these dual-route models necessitate independent structures for the encoding of each modality's meaning, but they also require structures for their integration. If you reject the inseparability of form and meaning units, these entailments mandating separate structures disappear, and a supramodal semantic memory suffices to connect in distributed ways to different modalities. Indeed, as we have argued throughout this book, the view maintained by dual-route models does not hold up—nor does the notion of the semiotic sign from which they derive—both on theoretical and empirical grounds.

13.4.3 Signification

The Saussurean Sign also creates assumptions about the relationship between form and meaning itself. "Arbitrariness" is often taken to describe properties of the form, i.e., the sounds of a word are arbitrary for its meaning. This focus gives the appearance of arbitrariness being a property of the formology, rather than a property of the *relationship* between a formology and meaning. Similar notions have extended to iconicity, where the patterns of sound, the body, or graphics are then assumed to carry iconic features (e.g., Sandler 2017), rather than iconicity reflecting a type of aligned correspondence between the properties of a formology and its meaning.

In addition, because arbitrariness relies on conventionality for its signification, conventionality (i.e., the regularity of the form) has been overextended to characterize how forms relate to meaning (i.e., symbolicity). As was overtly stated by Peirce, though symbolicity may rely on conventionality (i.e., legisigns), all types of signification can be conventional. Yet, because conventionality and symbolicity are conflated in the Saussurean Sign, conventional signals with iconicity and indexicality are inelegantly explained. As we have discussed, conventional signals with iconic reference proliferate, such as in ideophones of speech, signs in sign languages, or in many graphic representations from simple stick figures to complex scenic templates. A consequence of conflating conventionality and symbolicity is that these conventional iconic phenomena need to be accounted for by "fixes" like that symbolicity and iconicity lie on a continuum or spectrum (e.g., Greenberg 2021, Saraceni 2003, Waugh 1993).

In addition, this conflation also leads to claims that conventionalization is evidence of symbolicity. This arises in many iterated learning experiments, where the consolidation of forms into regularized patterns is interpreted as the development of symbols (Christiansen and Chater 2016, Kirby, Griffiths, and Smith 2014, Smith 2018). This same sentiment persists in observations about prehistoric graphics, where patterning of graphic representations is taken to be evidence for early symbolic thinking (Dehaene et al. 2022, Sablé-Meyer et al. 2021). Again, this work conflates conventionality and regularity (properties of a modality), for the ways that those signals may correspond to meaning.

The regularization of forms in a modality does not tell us about whether it conveys meaning. Indeed, even in speech we have regularized strings of phonemes that have no correspondence to meaning, like *sha-la-la*, *bee-bop-a-lu-bop*, and *twee-dee-dee*. We have called these phenomena *modalia* in Chapter 1. A Saussurean view would be more or less forced to assume this regularity as a type of symbol, or not a sign at all. Technically, the sensory signals from *all* modalities are arbitrary, since sounds, bodily movements, and graphics all inherently contain no meaningful properties. They are merely sensory experiences. It is only through the correspondence of those sensory signals to conceptual structure that we recognize them as meaningful, and it is this correspondence that can be characterized as a type of signification (iconicity, indexicality, symbolicity).

Because the Saussurean Sign collapses form and meaning into a single unit, it allows no elaboration on the characteristics of each of those components. In contrast, Peircean semiotics acknowledges different classes of how forms manifest (*representamen* or *sign vehicle*), how meanings are encoded (*object*), the relationship between them (*signification* or *the ground*), and the resulting compositional integration of meaning (*interpretant*). Within Peircean semiotics, each of these components is broken down into particular subparts. However, most linguistics has ignored this full model, instead recasting the types of signification in terms of the Saussurean Sign as a description of the signal itself. As a result, whereas Peircean semiotics views iconicity, indexicality, and symbolicity as the interfaces between form and meaning, the traditional view recasts them as types of forms which display properties of meaning: icons, indexes, and symbols.

As we have argued in Chapter 2, following Peirce, expressions of modalities have different regularities. Idiosyncratic signals are novel and not systematized (Peirce: sinsigns). Regularized signals are those that maintain consistency and patterning (legisigns) displaying conventionality. The process of regularization captures the development of a signal from being idiosyncratic (sinsign) to conventional (legisign), no matter their type(s) of meaning-making. As we argued in Chapter 4, these signals can maintain different correspondences to Conceptual Structure, so that conventionalized forms can evoke meaning through iconicity, indexicality, *and* symbolicity. For example, the visual form of the Apple computer logo is highly conventionalized, but maintains iconicity (signifying an apple), indexicality (signifying that someone has taken a bite out of it), and symbolicity (signifying a company). Thus, while symbolicity may rely on conventionality for its meaning-making, they are not the same thing.

The Peircean orientation of distributed properties of form and meaning is directly in line with the Parallel Architecture and its notion of correspondences. Following

Jackendoff's original architecture, we have argued that multiple modalities encode properties of their forms, and conceptual structures also encode and derive meaning. Thus, in line with Peirce, form and meaning are separate, but they maintain consistent patterns of interfacing, and the nature of those interfaces are types of reference (iconicity, indexicality, and symbolicity). When these correspondences between form and meaning are regularized and stored in memory, we have a lexical item.

Because of this distributed view, all modalities allow for all types of signification. Our vocal, bodily, and graphic modalities all can express signals that employ iconicity, indexicality, or symbolicity. Nevertheless, each of our modalities may afford particular mappings to meaning. Because of its capacity for depiction, the graphic modality well affords iconicity. Because the body can situate a speaker relative to other things, the bodily modality well affords indexicality. Finally, because of its dissociation from depiction and indication, the vocal modality well affords symbolicity. These optimizations have often been taken as absolutes, like that sounds *are* symbols or pictures *are* icons, rather than as tendencies motivated by affordances of forms. The advantage of this multiplicity of signification, and its optimization within particular modalities, is that they allow a communicator to combine modalities in complementary ways that maximize signification for providing a richer access to meaning. This complementary nature of signification across modalities arises inherently through the multimodal Parallel Architecture.

13.5 What Have We Done?

In the previous sections, we have argued that the dominant theories of the language sciences for at least the last 100 years have shaped our basic assumptions about the character of communication more broadly. To reiterate, though language is viewed as amodal and can flow into different modalities, speech is maintained as the core system while others remain peripheral. Linguistic units are viewed as indivisible pairings of form and meaning which share an arbitrary nature, and because they are indivisible, any proposal for the architecture of language must accommodate units of this particular type. This arbitrariness is one of several potential unique design features that define language in contrast to other systems, validating its core status.

Though an amodal notion of language has been dominant for the last century, we have illustrated how its assumptions do not reflect actual human behavior or cognition, and therefore restrict our theories about the nature of those behaviors. In place of this amodal conception of language, we have put forth a Multimodal Paradigm that does justice to the full range of human expression. This paradigm acknowledges that multimodality is our default method of communication, and modalities are maintained in parallel with an equal status, with each modality providing its own distinctive affordances. Both unimodal and multimodal expressions arise out of emergent interactions between structures of modalities, grammar, and meaning, and these emergent behaviors share and overlap in their common cognitive resources. The correspondences between form and meaning allow for multiple types of signification in all modalities, though the affordances of modalities may allow for optimization

Table 13.1 Contrasting assumptions between the amodal and multimodal conceptions of language.

Amodal	Multimodal
Language is amodal and flows into different modalities.	All modalities equally persist in parallel within a unitary expressive system.
Language (re: speech) is primarily unimodal and supplemented by and/or transfers to other modalities.	Human expression is multimodal by default, and transference between modalities requires establishing synesthetic mappings.
Language (re: speech) is the core expressive system and other modalities are peripheral.	All modalities maintain equal status within a holistic cognitive system.
Language is an autonomous system.	All our communicative behaviors arise out of emergent interactive states from shared components within a holistic architecture.
Modalities are different output options for a singular language system.	All modalities persist in parallel as resilient semia, and acquisition determines which parts of the system also develop into omnia.
Language uses unique design features.	Similar structural principles and cognitive mechanisms persist across expressive systems.
The form of expressions contributes little to the substance of their meaning.	Expressions are bound to the affordances of their modalities.
Signification of meaning is conflated with the signal of a modality (such as arbitrariness).	Signification arises through different types of correspondences between a modality and meaning.
Arbitrariness (symbolicity) is the pinnacle of linguistic reference, while other signification types are supplementary.	All significations persist across all modalities, and complement each other to create richer meaning-making.

of signification, complementing each other to produce a richer access to meaning. Table 13.1 summarizes these contrasts.

It is worth highlighting that the Multimodal Paradigm itself is guided by a more general comparative principle. Humans only have one brain, and multiple behaviors all emerge from that brain, which may not compartmentalize its cognition neatly according to the behaviors that manifest from it. As a result, we posit the **Principle of Equivalence** (Cohn 2013b, 2024):

Given modality-specific constraints, the mind/brain treats all expressive capacities in similar ways.

This principle follows in two parts, one about the similarities across behaviors and the other about the differences. First, because behaviors arise from a singular brain, we should expect that similar structures persist across modalities, and that similar neural responses arise in their processing. We have reviewed much of these similarities throughout this book. However, we should not believe that all behaviors operate in identical ways, but their differences should follow from the affordances of their modalities. For example, the vocal modality uses an inherent duration and emerges with a singular stream of sound, compared to the graphic modality which allows for persisting representations that can be engaged in a simultaneous, non-linear way. These traits of the signal will naturally lead to various affordances, including how that modality may express meaning and how it allows us to be aware of our own thoughts.

Under the Principle of Equivalence, we should not ask about the exclusivity of processing related to different behaviors, but rather to what degree is there similarity or difference in the structures and resources underlying different behaviors. In this endeavor comparisons can be made at numerous levels of cognition. Marr (1982) famously distinguished between levels of the representational properties of a system, its algorithmic mechanisms, and its neural implementation. We can thus compare behaviors and modalities across all of these levels, and similarities and differences may acceptably arise at different levels. For example, different behaviors may share in their representational and algorithmic properties, but differ in their exact neural implementation, or vice versa. It may be possible to find such similarities between behaviors in some or all of Marr's levels of cognition. However, doing so bestows them no relative value or status. Whether the combinatorial structures of speech, music, and visual narratives originate from the same or different brain areas does not mitigate their similarities in representational structure, nor does it say anything about their value as behaviors. Rather, in research as well, we should seek a baseline equivalence for studying and considering our various modalities and behaviors.

13.6 What's Next?

If we are to shift our views from an amodal to a Multimodal Paradigm, what does this mean for how we treat and study language, communication, and their cognition? With a multimodal view, the same fundamental questions persist but with a better perspective on what the system is that they address. We think that questions asked by Jackendoff (2002) still act as the guidelines for research, but can now be posed to a broader framework of what language is:

1. What elements does a speaker/signer/drawer store in memory, and in what form?
2. How are these elements combined or processed online to create or comprehend novel (multimodal) utterances?
3. How are these elements acquired?
4. How did these elements evolve?

The first question, about what we store in memory, can now be broadened to involve multiple modalities and their combinations. This question ultimately relates to the *lexicon*. In contrast to the view that the lexicon is a "bag of words," we follow the constructionist view that lexical items come in various sizes and complexity (Fillmore 1988, Goldberg 1995, Jackendoff and Audring 2020). In addition, by incorporating multiple modalities into a single model, this notion of a lexicon allows for fixed correspondences between the vocal, bodily, and graphic modalities. This yields lexical items both for semia, like gestural emblems (thumbs up, waving hello/goodbye) and graphic emblems (like stick figures and emoji), and for stored omnia in sign languages and visual languages. In addition, the holistic nature of the multimodal Parallel Architecture yields lexical items that are encoded across multiple modalities, such as we find in the Verb-Image Construction, two-unit constructions, signage, meme templates, and many other combinations that are stored as **multimodal lexical items**.

The second question, about how we produce and comprehend utterances, now can take two forms, both in the study of unimodal processing of multiple modalities and of multimodal processing. The psychological study of language and its processing has long examined production and comprehension in both the vocal and the bodily modalities (Levelt 2013), and research on co-speech gesture already has a rich history (Goldin-Meadow 2003b, a, Kendon 1972, McNeill 1992). By comparison, under the assumption that the iconicity of pictures makes them have no representational structure akin to other languages, the study of the graphic modality has largely been couched in the field of perception research. Yet, psycholinguistics has also long studied the integration and/or comparison of pictures and words (e.g., picture-word priming, visual world paradigms, etc.), just without acknowledging the modality status of pictures. The multimodal Parallel Architecture provides a grounding for an equal treatment of the graphic modality within the study of language and cognition, and prior work can now be interpreted through this holistic framework, which also yields new questions to be investigated.

The third question, about acquisition, can now be understood in terms of the development of both individual and multiple modalities, and the relationships between them. Acquisition of systems within the vocal, bodily, and graphic modalities all progress through stages of increasing complexity, crucially occurring within a sensitive learning period that apexes around puberty (Cohn 2012, Goldin-Meadow 2003b, Lenneberg 1967). This yields questions of whether there are common stages in acquisition across all modalities. For example, the development of speech starts with a babbling stage, which is also reflected in the bodily modality (i.e., manual babbling), and in the scribbling stage of the graphic modality. This implies that development begins with a stage of playing with the structure of the modality, before using it to evoke meaning (if it is not already). Whether similar characteristics exist in the development across modalities is a question requiring further research, as is a focus on multimodality beyond just unimodal development (van der Klis, Adriaans, and Kager 2023). Our model also allows for a distinction in the development of semia versus omnia. For example, research has already examined how development differs for gestures or home signs compared to sign language (Goldin-Meadow 2003b), yet comparisons of graphic development have largely not yet distinguished between children's progress when exposed to and imitating visual vocabularies compared to when they do not (Cohn 2012, Willats 2005, Wilson 1988).

Finally, the fourth question relates to how these elements evolved. As we described in Chapter 12, a shift to a multimodal understanding of language and communication necessitates changing what is believed to have evolved in the first place. The multimodal Parallel Architecture provides a different hypothesis on the assumed end-state of evolution. We contend that our evolution should not be conceived of as a "march of progress" toward an amodal symbolic system which uses recursive combinatoriality and preferentially manifests in unimodal vocal expressions. Rather, our end-state is a multimodal system by default, with proliferation of all three types of signification (iconicity, indexicality, symbolicity). Multiple modalities inherently persist in parallel, creating a core resilient semia system with innate correspondences to conceptual structures. Omnia can then be built on top of this resilient system with cultural development of robust lexicons and complex combinatorial structures. This view of the evolutionary end-state warrants a different conception of how such a system evolved, and for how such a system relates to those of other species.

These fundamental questions persist for the study of our communicative systems no matter the paradigm. However, new questions arise when considering a Multimodal Paradigm, which are either unaddressed or put to the periphery in amodal models. These include, but are not limited to:

- How do languages (omnia) persist both separately and together in different modalities?
- How do omnia and semia interact with each other within and across modalities?
- How do the combinatorial structures of one modality involve units of another modality (substitution)?
- How do the affordances of modalities provide varying access to meanings, both conceptual and spatial?
- How do different types of signification (iconicity, indexicality, and symbolicity) interact within and across modalities to contribute to the whole of meaning?
- How can multimodal patterns be entrenched in memory with constructional properties?
- What is the nature of a multimodal lexicon?
- How do semia and omnia in different modalities develop relative to the constraints imposed by their ecological environment, including the tools used in their production and reception?
- Why do we retain the ability to create meaning in semia, whether or not those modalities develop as omnia? (e.g., whether or not people learn a sign language, they create bodily semia of gestures)
- Why do people use semia in interactions with omnia?
- What is the role of social interaction in the development of omnia beyond semia?
- Given that semia persist alongside omnia, what has been the relationship of semia and omnia in evolution?
- Can the patterns of modalities influence or "permeate" each other?
- What architectural and cognitive properties persist across all modalities?

- To what extent do the component structures and mechanisms of different expressive behaviors share their neural implementation?

The multimodal Parallel Architecture provides a framework for asking and answering all of these questions, which we believe are fundamental to what we actually do in communication. In addition, the Multimodal Paradigm allows us to posit them in the first place. We contend that any model of language that seeks to characterize the full range of expressions in and across human languages must acknowledge the relevance of these questions, and be able to answer them.

For example, brain research often asks which neural areas may be associated with "language" versus those of other behaviors, which is essentially asking to what degree their external manifestation is isomorphic to their neural instantiation. However, under the Multimodal Paradigm, the null hypothesis would be that multiple behaviors belong to a common system, and the question then becomes to what extent the neural instantiation of their *components* may overlap. Indeed, substantial research for decades (if not centuries) has already provided insights on a multimodal view of our communicative capacities (e.g., Bateman, Wildfeuer, and Hiippala 2017, Clark 1996, Goldin-Meadow 2003b, Kress 2009, Kress and van Leeuwen 2001, Levelt 2013, Mascarenhas et al. 2023, Mayer 2009, McNeill 1992, Patel-Grosz, et al. 2023). Yet, much of this research has not explored the implications for a broader architecture or how multimodality challenges prevailing assumptions about language.

While the Multimodal Paradigm provides an alternative framework for addressing issues related to the structure, cognition, development, and evolution of our communicative capacities, it can also change how we conceive of modalities and how we use them more broadly. Consider how a multimodal viewpoint of expression might change our ideas of creativity and artistry. The peripheral status assigned to the graphic modality is an important reason why the graphic modality in Western culture is intrinsically tied to artistry. Our capacity to draw is viewed as "creating art," rather than reflecting a fundamental component of our basic communicative capacities which is equal to our other modalities.

Indeed, acknowledgement of a Multimodal Paradigm allows us to recognize the widespread discrimination between modalities that currently exists. The speech-centric focus of society has pervasive and serious consequences on people's lives, such as how deaf individuals are often pushed to speak or get implants to conform to a dominant speaking society (leading to possibilities of language deprivation), rather than encouraging the broader populace to all sign alongside their speech. From the view of a holistic multimodal architecture, people who do not learn a sign language are just as lacking in the development of a modality into an omnia as people who do not learn a spoken language.

Similar sentiments extend to the graphic modality. Education privileges decades of focus on learning to write (which is of course very useful), but make almost no mandatory educational requirements to acquire visual languages for proficiency in drawing. This discrimination also appears in more subtle ways, such as the separate shelving in bookstores (such that they still exist) of books that have pictures versus those that do not. This division persists in views of children's reading habits, where many believe that books with pictures, including comics or graphic novels aimed at adults, are "simpler" than books with only text (they are not), and the expectation that children should eventually "outgrow" books with pictures ("you're too old to read comics now"). Such sentiments carry over to the denigration of these works in educational contexts, despite research showing their benefits. All of these assumptions are confounded if we substitute a speech-centric, core versus periphery treatment of modalities, with a view of all of our modalities belonging to a common, shared architecture.

These divisions are reflected in the way we talk about them, even in simple questions, like the asymmetry of asking "what do you speak in?" with the answer of *a spoken language*, compared to "what do you draw in?" with the answer of *a visual language*. The categories used to describe behaviors make them appear distinct and independent. Yet, such categories are not shaped by cognition, but by cultural predispositions and biases. Speaking, signing, and drawing may appear to be independent and highly varying systems when viewed from the outside, and cultural predispositions have engendered us to treat them as distinct, but that does not mean such an orientation is maintained within our cognitive architecture.

The categories we use—no matter which modality they manifest in—both enlighten and restrict, by being inclusive of some things and exclusive of others. The Multimodal Paradigm attempts in many ways to transcend these categories by characterizing the building blocks of all such systems, and thereby illustrating where these categorizations emerge. In other words, we simply continue what is the overall orientation to the study of cognition in the first place: We recognize that what we produce in our behaviors—and the cultural assumptions that we build about these behaviors—may not reflect what is actually occurring in our cognition.

The study of language and communication has always been driven by our desire to achieve a deeper understanding of who and what we are. Therefore, asking these fundamental questions about how we as human beings express ourselves, about the structure and cognition that underlies this expressive instinct, and about its relationship to other species, necessitates an understanding sensitive to the full, multimodal richness of human communication.

Notes

Chapter 2

1. We might imagine a blurring of the line of intentionality in the case of actors, who effectively use the body for emotions and actions which are in themselves at least semi-controlled and intentional. Essentially, they attempt to control the production of what would normally be non-communicative expressions. Or at least, the good actors do this ... a violating case comes from people who "look like they are acting" which means they do not mask their intentionality to look unintentional.
2. A corroborating piece of evidence is that we can have abstract drawings or paintings (and meaningless vocables or bodily motions), which are graphic representations that play with the graphic modality but deny comprehenders correspondence to conceptual structure. On the other hand, you cannot have abstract photographs in the same sense (or a photograph *of an abstract painting*!). Sometimes photography may capture information with percepts that cannot easily be recognized, but it cannot be "abstract" in the same sense of playing with the primitives of the modality to invite or evoke correspondences to conceptual structure.
3. We view odors themselves as sensory experiences, but tool-mediated odors might be classed for the type of phenomena that they involve. For example, perfumes may relate to odors the way that photos relate to visual perceptions. We can imagine cases where a type of odor can be classed as a "modality" when control is exerted over its production and contexts, such as in "smell-o-vision" when odors are intentionally manipulated while an audience watches a movie. An equivalent might be foods and cuisines in relation to taste. Nevertheless, if these would be classed as "modalities" rather than simply "sensory systems," they would still be categorized as "non-conceptual" because the sensory experiences are manifestations of themselves, rather than the sensory systems connecting to conceptual structures. That is, despite exhibiting complexly crafted flavors through tool use and combinatorics (i.e., a recipe), ratatouille is not a signifier for a "meaning" other than its own sensory experience and the associations that a person might carry for that particular flavor or dish.
4. In this light, the "boring" part of writing is the actual cross-sensory mapping—i.e., hearing sounds by seeing graphics—while the "unique" instances of color-grapheme synesthesia are actually more structurally boring—i.e., linking one aspect of visuals to another.

Chapter 3

1. Across tools that serve the purpose of indexical mediation, differences may arise in the perceived embodiment of the tools. Gestures themselves are of course embodied, as part of the bodily modality. Pointing sticks are experienced as somewhat embodied, serving as an instrumental extension to, or substitute for, a pointing gesture. There is a direct physical relationship between a hand holding a stick and its interaction with a static representation. In contrast, laser pointers lack this direct physical relationship, becoming indicators on a static surface, but disembodied from the person doing the mediating gesture (here that gesture simply being a hand movement holding a pointer).
2. Though Root and Adjacent Awareness are discussed here as binary features, it is worth considering a few edge cases. In the case of whispering, a Public carrier may be limited in the number of adjacents that can access it. A similar case arises in Private carriers which depict telepathy, where the thoughts of one (or several) limited characters are shared, but is not broadcast to more adjacents. One possible way to account for these constrained cases is that all awareness "flows" on something like an "awareness vector" to access the contents of the carrier. The tail is thus the primary awareness vector for the root, with "adjacent vectors" arising for all possible adjacents in a scene. Another possibility is for adjacent awareness to have some "scope" in a "proximity space" that then modulates the range of which adjacents can access the carrier's contents. An example of such proximity space for adjacent vectors might be in comics where an animal talks frequently, but is understood only by their owner.

Chapter 4

1. Modality differences and concreteness are often conflated in many cognitive neuroscience studies. Imagine a study that presents various words (like "dog") and pictures (like a drawing of a dog) to participants and finds distinct brain areas are activated. If we assume the form and meaning to be conflated (as in a Saussurean Sign), then we might interpret such results as implying that distinct brain areas correspond to "verbal meanings" and "visual meanings." However, the English word "dog" uses an arbitrary signal to convey an abstracted meaning, while leaving the networked concepts as implicitly co-activated (type of dog, body parts of dogs, etc.). Meanwhile, a drawing uses resemblance with that object to show the more concrete meanings that are inaccessible to the word, while leaving the more abstracted category as co-activated. So, are the activated areas then just corresponding to semantic features reflective of the signification and concreteness/abstractness afforded by those signals, rather than reflecting something about the signals themselves? Truly controlled studies comparing modalities would thus need to also control for the relative concreteness and signification of expressions afforded across all modalities.
2. These primitives also belong to further super-categories of Situation (Event, State), Material Entity (Object, Group, Aggregate, Substances), and Space (Place, Path). The argument here is that these sub-categories share primary features that make them subordinate to their super-categories. We here focus on the basic-level primitives while remaining cognizant of the larger classes to which they belong.

3   This is not to say that metaphoric mappings across domains are not possible within Conceptual Semantics (Jackendoff and Aaron 1991). As we will see, many such mappings do arise. However, many phenomena that are called "metaphors" are disparate concepts tapping into shared semantic features, like for example a metaphor of TIME IS SPACE, whereby spatial and temporal (or situational) categories simply share common features (Jackendoff 2010a).

4   Another difference pertains to the current accessibility status referred to here in both modalities. Whereas many vocal languages use articles (*the, a*) to that end, visual languages rely on the immediate context. Given these differences, we leave out correspondences to the definite articles in our formalization of Conceptual Structure.

5   Lakoff and Johnson (1980) would call this an "image metaphor." We retain here Peirce's terminology because it is embedded within the larger notion of signification, and there is potential for confusion between imagetic iconicity, metaphoric iconicity, and image metaphors as terms.

Chapter 5

1   This notion of $CS_{Integrated}$ also reflects what Peirce calls the "Interpretant" compared to the encoded semantics of the "Object" of $CS_{Expression}$.

Chapter 6

1   While we simplify our interpretation here, it is worth pointing out that the graphics themselves in instruction manuals often do not fully show the manifested events, but instead only show the preparations for those events. Panel 2 of Figure 6.7 technically shows a preparation for the completed event of putting the mask on. This completion is implied by the arrow, which is similar to the motion lines that we analyzed in Figure 4.3d, only showing the moving object at the source and implying the goal (as opposed to motion lines which show the goal and imply the source). Thus, with these "future lines" the panel shows a preparation but implies its completion.

2   Even the term "nominalization" here implies a directionality and preference to the levels of combinatoriality involved. The term implies that the verb forms are primary, while the noun forms are derived. We follow a theoretical framework that rejects the notion of such derivation (Jackendoff 1977, Jackendoff and Audring 2020). The Complexity Hierarchy and its mapping of segmental levels to different strata within Conceptual Structure clarify this issue.

3   It is also worth considering that the delineation of morphology and syntax comes with biases from the languages spoken by linguists who have created these categories. Contemporary linguistics has mostly grown from work by European and American scholars, whose languages maintain fairly isolable word units that become sequenced, which served as the base for comparison with non-European languages (Goldsmith and Laks 2019, Levelt 2013). In our terms, such systems represent particular traits of segmental complexity, but they are not the only (or "prototypical") ways that languages operate. This is not to mention that such classifications have also been centered around structures within the vocal modality specifically, and thus are taken

as the prototypical form to which other modalities are assumed to operate if they are to be considered as having "linguistic" properties at all (e.g., Hockett 1960).

4   We might speculate whether there is a level of "optimization" for how any given system creates correspondences between meaning and combinatorial and segmental levels. A system constrained to simple units across simple arrays (like linear schemas) would make demands on working memory to keep track of units, while also requiring substantial inferencing for relating those units. At the same time, a system using complex units across complex arrays would be harder to process and harder to learn. The trade-offs observed typologically for particular systems across modalities may provide evidence that systems strive for an optimal balance for the allocation of complexity across units and arrays for the expression of meaning.

Chapter 10

1   It is worth noting that the encoding of the heart with a conceptual predicate has broader implications. Imagine a situation where one person writes "What are your feelings for me?" and the reply is just a heart shape. The encoded conceptual predicate of LOVE(X,Y) explains why this is a coherent response, because it can be understood as contextually filled by LOVE(*I, YOU*) where the arguments are inferred by context. In other words, the heart here functions elliptically. By extension, if one person asks "What wine do you drink?" and the reply is an emoji with red wine (🍷), the elliptical response carries an argument for the function of DRINK(X).

Chapter 11

1   This same core-periphery issue related to dominance also persists within the same modality. For example, minority spoken languages may face discrimination within contexts of another more dominant spoken language. These are the same social issues at play that we see between modalities, but here persisting in a tension between spoken omnia systems. Thus, these issues of how semia may or may not become omnia must interact with more general issues of human social and societal dynamics.

References

Aglioti, Salvatore M., Paola Cesari, Michela Romani, and Cosimo Urgesi. 2008. "Action anticipation and motor resonance in elite basketball players." *Nature Neuroscience* 11 (9):1109–16. doi: 10.1038/nn.2182.

Altmann, Gabriel. 1980. "Prolegomena to Menzerath's law." *Glottometrika* 2 (2):1–10.

Arbib, Michael A. 2005. "From monkey-like action recognition to human language: An evolutionary framework for neurolinguistics." *Behavioral and Brain Sciences* 28 (2):105–24. doi: 10.1017/S0140525X05000038.

Arbib, Michael A. 2012. *How the Brain Got Language: The Mirror System Hypothesis*. Vol. 16. Oxford, UK: Oxford University Press.

Ardesch, Dirk Jan, Lianne H. Scholtens, Longchuan Li, Todd M. Preuss, James K. Rilling, and Martijn P. van den Heuvel. 2019. "Evolutionary expansion of connectivity between multimodal association areas in the human brain compared with chimpanzees." *Proceedings of the National Academy of Sciences* 116 (14):7101–6. doi: 10.1073/pnas.1818512116.

Armstrong, David F. 2002. *Original Signs: Gesture, Sign, and the Sources of Language*. Washington, DC: Gallaudet University Press.

Aronoff, Mark, Irit Meir, and Wendy Sandler. 2005. "The paradox of sign language morphology." *Language* 81 (2):301.

Arts, Anja, and Joost Schilperoord. 2016. "Visual optimal innovation." In *Multimodality and Performance*, edited by Carla Fernandes, 61–81. Newcastle upon Tyne, UK: Cambridge Scholars Publishing.

Asher, Nicholas, and Alex Lascarides. 2003. *Logics of Conversation*. Cambridge: Cambridge University Press.

Aubert, Maxime, Rustan Lebe, Adhi Agus Oktaviana, Muhammad Tang, Basran Burhan, Hamrullah, Andi Jusdi, Abdullah, Budianto Hakim, Jian-xin Zhao, I. Made Geria, Priyatno Hadi Sulistyarto, Ratno Sardi, and Adam Brumm. 2019. "Earliest hunting scene in prehistoric art." *Nature* 576 (7787):442–5. doi: 10.1038/s41586-019-1806-y.

Backus, Ad. 2015. "A usage-based approach to code-switching: The need for reconciling structure and function." In *Code-switching between Structural and Sociolinguistic Perspectives*, edited by Gerald Stell and Kofi Yakpo, 19–38. Berlin: De Gruyter.

Bacon, Bennett, Azadeh Khatiri, James Palmer, Tony Freeth, Paul Pettitt, and Robert Kentridge. 2023. "An upper Palaeolithic proto-writing system and phenological calendar." *Cambridge Archaeological Journal*:1–19. doi: 10.1017/S0959774322000415.

Baggio, Giosuè. 2018. *Meaning in the Brain*. Cambridge, MA: MIT Press.

Barber, Horacio A., Leun J. Otten, Stavroula-Thaleia Kousta, and Gabriella Vigliocco. 2013. "Concreteness in word processing: ERP and behavioral effects in a lexical decision task." *Brain and Language* 125 (1):47–53. doi: 10.1016/j.bandl.2013.01.005.

Barsalou, Lawrence W. 2008. "Grounded cognition." *Annual Review of Psychology* 59 (1):617–45. doi: 10.1146/annurev.psych.59.103006.093639.

Bateman, John A. 2012. "The decomposability of semiotic modes." In *Multimodal Studies*, edited by Kay L. O'Halloran and Bradley A. Smith, 37–58. New York: Routledge.

Bateman, John A. 2014. *Text and Image: A Critical Introduction to the Visual/Verbal Divide*. New York: Routledge.
Bateman, John A. 2018. "Peircean semiotics and multimodality: Towards a new synthesis." *Multimodal Communication* 7 (1). doi: 10.1515/mc-2017-0021.
Bateman, John A., Francisco O. D. Veloso, Janina Wildfeuer, Felix HiuLaam Cheung, and Nancy Songdan Guo. 2016. "An open multilevel classification scheme for the visual layout of comics and graphic novels: Motivation and design." *Digital Scholarship in the Humanities* 32 (3):476–510. doi: 10.1093/llc/fqw024.
Bateman, John A., and Janina Wildfeuer. 2014. "A multimodal discourse theory of visual narrative." *Journal of Pragmatics* 74:180–208. doi: 10.1016/j.pragma.2014.10.001.
Bateman, John A., Janina Wildfeuer, and Tuomo Hiippala. 2017. *Multimodality: Foundations, Research and Analysis–A Problem-oriented Introduction*. Berlin: Walter de Gruyter GmbH & Co KG.
Bednarik, Robert G. 2006. "The known cave art of South Australia." *Cave Art Research* 6:1–14.
Bentz, Christian, Ximena Gutierrez-Vasques, Olga Sozinova, and Tanja Samardžić. 2022. "Complexity trade-offs and equi-complexity in natural languages: A meta-analysis." *Linguistics Vanguard*. doi: 10.1515/lingvan-2021-0054.
Berman, Greta. 1999. "Synesthesia and the arts." *Leonardo* 32 (1):15–22. doi: 10.1162/002409499552957.
Berwick, Robert C., and Noam Chomsky. 2016. *Why Only Us: Language and Evolution*. Cambridge: MIT press.
Bickerton, Derek. 1990. *Language and Species*. Chicago: University of Chicago Press.
Biederman, Irving. 1987. "Recognition-by-components: A theory of human image understanding." *Psychological Review* 94:115–47.
Bliss, Charles Kasiel. 1965. *Semantography (Blissymbolics): A Logical Writing for an Illogical World*. Sydney: Semantography (Blissymbolics) Publications.
Boeckx, Cedric, Anna Martinez-Alvarez, and Evelina Leivada. 2014. "The functional neuroanatomy of serial order in language." *Journal of Neurolinguistics* 32:1–15. doi: 10.1016/j.jneuroling.2014.07.001.
Bolinger, Dwight. 1989. *Intonation and Its Uses: Melody in Grammar and Discourse*. Stanford: Stanford University Press.
Booij, Geert. 2010. *Construction Morphology*. Oxford: Oxford University Press.
Börstell, Carl, Thomas Hörberg, and Robert Östling. 2016. "Distribution and duration of signs and parts of speech in Swedish sign language." *Sign Language & Linguistics* 19 (2):143–96.
Bransford, John D., and Marcia K. Johnson. 1972. "Contextual prerequisites for understanding: Some investigations of comprehension and recall." *Journal of Verbal Learning and Verbal Behavior* 11 (6):717–26.
Brentari, Diane. 2011. "Sign language phonology." In *The Handbook of Phonological Theory*, edited by John Goldsmith, Jason Riggle, and Alan C. L. Yu, 691–721. West Sussex, UK: Wiley-Blackwell.
Brentari, Diane, and Laurinda Crossley. 2002. "Prosody on the hands and face: Evidence from American sign language." *Sign Language & Linguistics* 5 (2):105–30. doi: 10.1075/sll.5.2.03bre.
Brewer, William F. 1985. "The story schema: Universal and culture-specific properties." In *Literacy, Language, and Learning*, edited by David R. Olson, Nancy Torrance, and Angela Hildyard, 167–94. Cambridge: Cambridge University Press.
Brumm, Adam, Agus Oktaviana Adhi, Basran Burhan, Budianto Hakim, Rustan Lebe, Jian-xin Zhao, Hadi Sulistyarto Priyatno, Marlon Ririmasse, Shinatria Adhityatama,

Iwan Sumantri, and Maxime Aubert. 2021. "Oldest cave art found in Sulawesi." *Science Advances* 7 (3):eabd4648. doi: 10.1126/sciadv.abd4648.

Calzavarini, Fabrizio. 2023. "Rethinking modality-specificity in the cognitive neuroscience of concrete word meaning: a position paper." *Language, Cognition and Neuroscience*:1–23. doi: 10.1080/23273798.2023.2173789.

Carreiras, Manuel, Mohamed L. Seghier, Silvia Baquero, Adelina Estévez, Alfonso Lozano, Joseph T. Devlin, and Cathy J. Price. 2009. "An anatomical signature for literacy." *Nature* 461 (7266):983–6. doi: 10.1038/nature08461.

Cartmill, Erica A., Sian Beilock, and Susan Goldin-Meadow. 2012. "A word in the hand: action, gesture and mental representation in humans and non-human primates." *Philosophical Transactions of the Royal Society B: Biological Sciences* 367 (1585):129–43.

Cartmill, Erica A., and Richard W. Byrne. 2010. "Semantics of primate gestures: Intentional meanings of orangutan gestures." *Animal Cognition* 13 (6):793–804. doi: 10.1007/s10071-010-0328-7.

Casati, Roberto, and Alessandro Pignocchi. 2008. "Communication advantages of line drawings." In *Cognición & Lenguaje: Estudios en homenaje a José Luis Guijarro Morales*, edited by María Luisa Mora Millán, 75–97. Servicio de Publicaciones de la Universidad de Cádiz.

Chafe, Wallace. 1994. *Discourse, Consciousness, and Time: The Flow and Displacement of Conscious Experience in Speaking and Writing*. Chicago, IL: University of Chicago Press.

Charnavel, Isabelle. 2019. "Steps toward a Universal Grammar of dance: Local grouping structure in basic human movement perception." *Frontiers in Psychology* 10. doi: 10.3389/fpsyg.2019.01364.

Chatterjee, Anjan. 2001. "Language and space: Some interactions." *Trends in Cognitive Sciences* 5 (2):55–61.

Cheng, Qi, Austin Roth, Eric Halgren, Denise Klein, Jen-Kai Chen, and Rachel I. Mayberry. 2023. "Restricted language access during childhood affects adult brain structure in selective language regions." *Proceedings of the National Academy of Sciences* 120 (7):e2215423120. doi: 10.1073/pnas.2215423120.

Chomsky, Noam. 1956. "Three models for the description of language." *IRE Transactions on Information Theory* 2:113–24.

Chomsky, Noam. 1957. *Syntactic Structures*. The Hague: Mouton.

Chomsky, Noam. 1965. *Aspects of the Theory of Syntax*. Cambridge, MA: MIT Press.

Chomsky, Noam. 1968. *Language and Mind*. New York: Harcourt, Brace, Jovanovitch.

Chomsky, Noam. 1970. "Remarks on nominalization." In *Readings in English Transformational Grammar*, edited by R. Jacobs and P. Rosenbaum, 184–221. Waltham, MA: Ginn.

Chomsky, Noam. 1986. *Knowledge of Language: Its Nature, Origin, and Use*. New York, NY: Praeger.

Chomsky, Noam. 1995. *The Minimalist Program*. Cambridge, MA: MIT Press.

Christiansen, Morten H., and Nick Chater. 2016. *Creating Language: Integrating Evolution, Acquisition, and Processing*. Cambridge, MA: MIT Press.

Cienki, Alan, and Cornelia Müller. 2008. *Metaphor and Gesture*. Vol. 3. Amsterdam: John Benjamins Publishing Company.

Clark, Andy, and David Chalmers. 1998. "The extended mind." *Analysis* 58 (1):7–19. doi: 10.1093/analys/58.1.7.

Clark, Herbert H. 1996. *Using Language*. Cambridge, UK: Cambridge University Press.

Clark, Herbert H. 2016. "Depicting as a method of communication." *Psychological Review* 123 (3):324–47. doi: 10.1037/rev0000026.

Clark, Richard E., and Gavriel Salomon. 1986. "Media in teaching." *Handbook of research on teaching* 3:464–78.

Coderre, Emily L., and Neil Cohn. 2023. "Individual differences in the neural dynamics of visual narrative comprehension." *Psychonomic Bulletin & Review*.

Coderre, Emily L., Neil Cohn, Sally K. Slipher, Mariya Chernenok, Kerry Ledoux, and Barry Gordon. 2018. "Visual and linguistic narrative comprehension in autism spectrum disorders: Neural evidence for modality-independent impairments." *Brain and Language* 186:44–59.

Coderre, Emily L., Elizabeth O'Donnell, Emme O'Rourke, and Neil Cohn. 2020. "Predictability modulates the N400 in non-verbal narrative processing." *Scientific Reports* 10:10326. doi: 10.1038/s41598-020-66814-z.

Cohn, Neil. 2012. "Explaining 'I can't draw': Parallels between the structure and development of language and drawing." *Human Development* 55 (4):167–92. doi: 10.1159/000341842.

Cohn, Neil. 2013a. "Beyond speech balloons and thought bubbles: The integration of text and image." *Semiotica* 2013 (197):35–63. doi: 10.1515/sem-2013-0079.

Cohn, Neil. 2013b. *The visual language of comics: Introduction to the structure and cognition of sequential images*. London, UK: Bloomsbury.

Cohn, Neil. 2013c. "Visual narrative structure." *Cognitive Science* 37 (3):413–52. doi: 10.1111/cogs.12016.

Cohn, Neil. 2014a. "Framing 'I can't draw': The influence of cultural frames on the development of drawing." *Culture & Psychology* 20 (1):102–17. doi: 10.1177/1354067x13515936.

Cohn, Neil. 2014b. "You're a good structure, Charlie Brown: The distribution of narrative categories in comic strips." *Cognitive Science* 38 (7):1317–59. doi: 10.1111/cogs.12116.

Cohn, Neil. 2015a. "How to analyze visual narratives: A tutorial in Visual Narrative Grammar." www.visuallanguagelab.com/P/VNG_Tutorial.pdf.

Cohn, Neil. 2015b. "Narrative conjunction's junction function: The interface of narrative grammar and semantics in sequential images." *Journal of Pragmatics* 88:105–32. doi: 10.1016/j.pragma.2015.09.001.

Cohn, Neil. 2016. "Linguistic relativity and conceptual permeability in visual narratives: New distinctions in the relationship between language(s) and thought." In *The Visual Narrative Reader*, edited by Neil Cohn, 315–40. London: Bloomsbury.

Cohn, Neil. 2018a. "Combinatorial morphology in visual languages." In *The Construction of Words: Advances in Construction Morphology*, edited by Geert Booij, 175–99. London: Springer.

Cohn, Neil. 2018b. "In defense of a 'grammar' in the visual language of comics." *Journal of Pragmatics* 127:1–19. doi: 10.1016/j.pragma.2018.01.002.

Cohn, Neil. 2019. "Being explicit about the implicit: Inference generating techniques in visual narrative." *Language and Cognition* 11 (1):66–97. doi: 10.1017/langcog.2019.6.

Cohn, Neil. 2020a. *Who Understands Comics? Questioning the Universality of Visual Language Comprehension*. London: Bloomsbury.

Cohn, Neil. 2020b. "Your brain on comics: A cognitive model of visual narrative comprehension." *Topics in Cognitive Science* 12 (1):352–86. doi: 10.1111/tops.12421.

Cohn, Neil. 2024. *The Patterns of Comics: Visual Languages of Comics from Asia, Europe, and North America*. London: Bloomsbury.

Cohn, Neil, Jan Engelen, and Joost Schilperoord. 2019. "The grammar of emoji? Constraints on communicative pictorial sequencing." *Cognitive Research: Principles and Implications* 4 (1):33. doi: 10.1186/s41235-019-0177-0.

Cohn, Neil, and Tom Foulsham. 2020. "Zooming in on the cognitive neuroscience of visual narrative." *Brain and Cognition* 146:105634. doi: 10.1016/j.bandc.2020.105634.

Cohn, Neil, and Tom Foulsham. 2022. "Meaning above (and in) the head: Combinatorial visual morphology from comics and emoji." *Memory & Cognition*. doi: 10.3758/s13421-022-01294-2.

Cohn, Neil, and Marta Kutas. 2017. "What's your neural function, visual narrative conjunction? Grammar, meaning, and fluency in sequential image processing." *Cognitive Research: Principles and Implications* 2 (27):1–13. doi: 10.1186/s41235-017-0064-5.

Cohn, Neil, Beena Murthy, and Tom Foulsham. 2016. "Meaning above the head: Combinatorial constraints on the visual vocabulary of comics." *Journal of Cognitive Psychology* 28 (5):559–74. doi: 10.1080/20445911.2016.1179314.

Cohn, Neil, and Martin Paczynski. 2013. "Prediction, events, and the advantage of Agents: The processing of semantic roles in visual narrative." *Cognitive Psychology* 67 (3):73–97. doi: 10.1016/j.cogpsych.2013.07.002.

Cohn, Neil, Martin Paczynski, Ray Jackendoff, Phillip J. Holcomb, and Gina R. Kuperberg. 2012. "(Pea)nuts and bolts of visual narrative: Structure and meaning in sequential image comprehension." *Cognitive Psychology* 65 (1):1–38. doi: 10.1016/j.cogpsych.2012.01.003.

Cohn, Neil, Martin Paczynski, and Marta Kutas. 2017. "Not so secret agents: Event-related potentials to semantic roles in visual event comprehension." *Brain and Cognition* 119:1–9. doi: 10.1016/j.bandc.2017.09.001.

Cohn, Neil, Tim Roijackers, Robin Schaap, and Jan Engelen. 2018. "Are emoji a poor substitute for words? Sentence processing with emoji substitutions." In *40th Annual Conference of the Cognitive Science Society*, edited by T.T. Rogers, M. Rau, X. Zhu, and C. W. Kalish, 1524–9. Austin, TX: Cognitive Science Society.

Cohn, Neil, and Joost Schilperoord. 2022. "Remarks on multimodality: Grammatical interactions in the parallel architecture." *Frontiers in Artificial Intelligence* 4:1–21. doi: 10.3389/frai.2021.778060.

Cohn, Neil, and Joost Schilperoord. 2023. "Visual languages and the problems with ideographies: A commentary on Morin" *Behavioral and Brain Science*.

Cohn, Neil, Lincy van Middelaar, Tom Foulsham, and Joost Schilperoord. forthcoming. "Anaphoric distance dependencies in visual narrative structure and processing."

Cooperrider, Kensy, James Slotta, and Rafael Núñez. 2018. "The preference for pointing With the hand is not universal." *Cognitive Science* 42 (4):1375–90. doi: 10.1111/cogs.12585.

Coopmans, Cas W., and Neil Cohn. 2022. "An electrophysiological investigation of co-referential processes in visual narrative comprehension." *Neuropsychologia* 172:108253. doi: 10.1016/j.neuropsychologia.2022.108253.

Coopmans, Cas W., Helen de Hoop, Karthikeya Kaushik, Peter Hagoort, and Andrea E. Martin. 2021. "Hierarchy in language interpretation: Evidence from behavioural experiments and computational modelling." *Language, Cognition and Neuroscience*:1–20. doi: 10.1080/23273798.2021.1980595.

Corballis, Michael. 1991. *The Lopsided Ape: Evolution of the Generative Mind*. Oxford: Oxford University Press.

Corballis, Michael C. 2002. *From Hand to Mouth*. Princeton: Princeton University Press.
Coulmas, Florian. 1989. *The Writing Systems of the World*. Malden, MA: Blackwell Publishers Inc.
Cramer, Henriette, Paloma de Juan, and Joel Tetreault. 2016. "Sender-intended functions of emojis in US messaging." Proceedings of the 18th International Conference on Human-Computer Interaction with Mobile Devices and Services, Florence, Italy.
Croft, William. 2003. *Typology and Universals*. 2nd ed. Cambridge, UK: Cambridge Univesity Press.
Culicover, Peter W., and Ray Jackendoff. 2005. *Simpler Syntax*. Oxford: Oxford University Press.
Cutting, James E. 2016. "Narrative theory and the dynamics of popular movies." *Psychonomic Bulletin & Review* 23 (6):1713–43. doi: 10.3758/s13423-016-1051-4.
Częstochowska, Justyna, Kristina Gligorić, Maxime Peyrard, Yann Mentha, Michał Bień, Andrea Grütter, Anita Auer, Aris Xanthos, and Robert West. 2022. "On the context-free ambiguity of emoji." *Proceedings of the International AAAI Conference on Web and Social Media* 16 (1):1388–92. doi: 10.1609/icwsm.v16i1.19393.
Dancygier, Barbara, and Lieven Vandelanotte. 2017. "Internet memes as multimodal constructions." *Cognitive Linguistics* 28 (3):565. doi: 10.1515/cog-2017-0074.
Danesi, Marcel. 2016. *The Semiotics of Emoji: The Rise of Visual Language in the Age of the Internet*. London: Bloomsbury.
Darwin, Charles. 1871. *The Descent of Man and Selection in Relation to Sex*. London: John Murray.
Davis, Jessica, and Howard Gardner. 1992. "The cognitive revolution: Its consequences for the understanding and education of the child as artist." In *The Arts, Education, and Aesthetic Knowing: Ninety-first Yearbook of the National Society for the Study of Education*, edited by B. Reimer and R.A. Smith, 92–123. Chicago: University of Chicago Press.
de Boer, Bart. 2017. "Evolution of speech and evolution of language." *Psychonomic Bulletin & Review* 24 (1):158–62. doi: 10.3758/s13423-016-1130-6.
de Saussure, Ferdinand. 1972 [1916]. *Course in General Linguistics*. Translated by Roy Harris. Chicago, IL: Open Court Classics. Original edition, 1916.
de Vos, Connie, and Roland Pfau. 2015. "Sign language typology: The contribution of rural sign languages." *Annual Review of Linguistics* 1 (1):265–88. doi: 10.1146/annurev-linguist-030514-124958.
Deacon, Terrance. 1997. *The Symbolic Species: The Co-evolution of Language and the Brain*. New York, NY: WW Norton and Co.
Dehaene, Stanislas. 2011. "The massive impact of literacy on the brain and its consequences for education." In *Human neuroplasticity and education*, edited by Antonio M. Battro, Stanislas Dehaene, and Wolf J. Singer, 19–32. Vatican City, Vatican: The Pontifical Academy of Sciences.
Dehaene, Stanislas, Fosca Al Roumi, Yair Lakretz, Samuel Planton, and Mathias Sablé-Meyer. 2022. "Symbols and mental programs: A hypothesis about human singularity." *Trends in Cognitive Sciences*. doi: 10.1016/j.tics.2022.06.010.
Dehaene, Stanislas, Florent Meyniel, Catherine Wacongne, Liping Wang, and Christophe Pallier. 2015. "The neural representation of sequences: From transition probabilities to algebraic patterns and linguistic trees." *Neuron* 88 (1):2–19. doi: 10.1016/j.neuron.2015.09.019.
Delong, Katherine A., Thomas P. Urbach, and Marta Kutas. 2005. "Probabilistic word pre-activation during language comprehension inferred from electrical brain activity." *Nature Neuroscience* 8 (8):1117–21.

Dingemanse, Mark. 2017. "On the margins of language: Ideophones, interjections and dependencies in linguistic theory." In *Dependencies in Language: On the Causal Ontology of Linguistic Systems*, edited by N.J. Enfield, 195–202. Berlin: Language Science Press.

Dingemanse, Mark, Damián E. Blasi, Gary Lupyan, Morten H. Christiansen, and Padraic Monaghan. 2015. "Arbitrariness, iconicity, and systematicity in language." *Trends in Cognitive Sciences* 19 (10):603–15. doi: 10.1016/j.tics.2015.07.013.

Edwards, Terra, and Diane Brentari. 2020. "Feeling phonology: The conventionalization of phonology in protactile communities in the United States." *Language* 96 (4):819–40.

Ehret, Katharina. 2018. "Kolmogorov complexity as a universal measure of language complexity." In *Proceedings of the First Shared Task on Measuring Language Complexity: Workshop on "Measuring Language Complexity,"* edited by Aleksandrs Berdicevskis and Christian Bentz, 8–14. Torun, Poland: EvoLang XII.

Elman, Jeffrey L., Elizabeth A. Bates, and Mark H. Johnson. 1996. *Rethinking Innateness: A Connectionist Perspective on Development*. Vol. 10. Cambridge: MIT Press.

Emmorey, Karen. 2001. *Language, Cognition, and the Brain: Insights from Sign Language Research*. Mahwah, NJ: Psychology Press.

Emmorey, Karen. 2021. "New perspectives on the neurobiology of sign languages." *Frontiers in Communication* 6. doi: 10.3389/fcomm.2021.748430.

Emmorey, Karen. 2023. "Ten things you should know about sign languages." *Current Directions in Psychological Science* 0 (0):1–8. doi: 10.1177/09637214231173071.

Emmorey, Karen, Helsa B. Borinstein, Robin Thompson, and Tamar H. Gollan. 2008. "Bimodal bilingualism." *Bilingualism: Language and Cognition* 11 (01):43–61. doi: 10.1017/S1366728907003203.

Emmorey, Karen, Kurt Winsler, Katherine J. Midgley, Jonathan Grainger, and Phillip J. Holcomb. 2020. "Neurophysiological correlates of frequency, concreteness, and iconicity in American sign language." *Neurobiology of Language* 1 (2):249–67. doi: 10.1162/nol_a_00012.

Engesser, Sabrina, and Simon W. Townsend. 2019. "Combinatoriality in the vocal systems of nonhuman animals." *Wiley Interdisciplinary Reviews: Cognitive Science* 10 (4):e1493. doi: 10.1002/wcs.1493.

Evans, Nicholas, and Stephen C. Levinson. 2009. "The myth of language universals: Language diversity and its importance for cognitive science." *Behavioral and Brain Sciences* 32 (5):429–48. doi: 10.1017/S0140525X0999094X.

Everett, Daniel. 2017. *How Language Began: The Story of Humanity's Greatest Invention*. London, UK: Profile Books.

Ewen, Colin J., and Harry van der Hulst. 2001. *The Phonological Structure of Words: An Introduction*. Cambridge, UK: Cambridge University Press.

Fadiga, Luciano, Laila Craighero, and Alessandro D'Ausilio. 2009. "Broca's area in language, action, and music." *Annals of the New York Academy of Sciences* 1169:448–58. doi: 10.1111/j.1749-6632.2009.04582.x.

Fan, Judith E., Wilma A. Bainbridge, Rebecca Chamberlain, and Jeffrey D. Wammes. 2023. "Drawing as a versatile cognitive tool." *Nature Reviews Psychology*. doi: 10.1038/s44159-023-00212-w.

Fauconnier, Gilles, and Mark Turner. 1998. "Conceptual integration networks." *Cognitive Science* 22 (2):133–87.

Fazio, Patrik, Anna Cantagallo, Laila Craighero, Alessandro D'Ausilio, Alice C. Roy, Thierry Pozzo, Ferdinando Calzolari, Enrico Granieri, and Luciano Fadiga. 2009. "Encoding of human action in Broca's area." *Brain* 132 (7):1980–8. doi: 10.1093/brain/awp118.

Federmeier, Kara D., and Marta Kutas. 2001. "Meaning and modality: Influences of context, semantic memory organization, and perceptual predictability on picture processing." *Journal of Experimental Psychology: Learning, Memory, & Cognition* 27 (1):202–24.

Fedorenko, Evelina, and Idan A. Blank. 2020. "Broca's area is not a natural kind." *Trends in Cognitive Sciences* 24 (4):270–84. doi: 10.1016/j.tics.2020.01.001.

Fenlon, Jordan, Kearsy Cormier, and Diane Brentari. 2017. "The phonology of sign languages." In *The Routledge Handbook of Phonological Theory*, edited by S. J. Hannahs and Anna R. K. Bosch, 453–75. London, UK: Routledge.

Ferrara, Lindsay, and Gabrielle Hodge. 2018. "Language as description, indication, and depiction." *Frontiers in Psychology* 9:1–15. doi: 10.3389/fpsyg.2018.00716.

Ferrari, Enrique. 2023. "The study of emoji linguistic behaviour: an examination of the theses raised (and not raised) in the academic literature." *Communication and Society* 36 (2):115–28.

Ferreira, Fernanda, and Nikole D. Patson. 2007. "The 'good enough' approach to language comprehension." *Language and Linguistics Compass* 1 (1-2):71–83. doi: 10.1111/j.1749-818X.2007.00007.x.

Fillmore, Charles J. 1988. "The mechanisms of 'construction grammar.'" Annual Meeting of the Berkeley Linguistics Society.

Fitch, W Tecumseh, and Mauricio D Martins. 2014. "Hierarchical processing in music, language, and action: Lashley revisited." *Annals of the New York Academy of Sciences* 1316 (1):87–104.

Fitch, W. Tecumseh. 2014. "Toward a computational framework for cognitive biology: Unifying approaches from cognitive neuroscience and comparative cognition." *Physics of Life Reviews* 11 (3):329–64. doi: 10.1016/j.plrev.2014.04.005.

Fitch, W. Tecumseh. 2018. "The biology and evolution of speech: A comparative analysis." *Annual Review of Linguistics* 4 (1):255–79. doi: 10.1146/annurev-linguistics-011817-045748.

Fitch, W. Tecumseh. 2020. "Animal cognition and the evolution of human language: Why we cannot focus solely on communication." *Philosophical Transactions of the Royal Society B* 375 (1789):20190046.

Fodor, Jerry A. 1983. *The Modularity of Mind*. Cambridge, MA: MIT press.

Forceville, Charles. 2009. "Non-verbal and multimodal metaphor in a cognitivist framework: Agendas for research." In *Multimodal Metaphor*, edited by Charles Forceville and Eduardo Urios-Aparisi, 19–35.

Forceville, Charles. 2011. "Pictorial runes in *Tintin and the Picaros*." *Journal of Pragmatics* 43 (3):875–90.

Forceville, Charles. 2016. "Conceptual metaphor theory, blending theory, and other cognitivist perspectives on comics." In *The Visual Narrative Reader*, edited by Neil Cohn, 89–114. London: Bloomsbury.

Forceville, Charles. 2020. *Visual and Multimodal Communication: Applying the Relevance Principle*. Oxford, UK: Oxford University Press.

Forceville, Charles. 2021. "Multimodality." In *The Routledge Handbook of Cognitive Linguistics*, edited by Xu Wen and John R. Taylor, 676–87. London, UK: Routledge.

Forceville, Charles, and Eduardo Urios-Aparisi. 2009. *Multimodal Metaphor*. New York: Mouton De Gruyter.

Ford, Paul, Dave Collins, Richard Bailey, Áine MacNamara, Gemma Pearce, and Martin Toms. 2012. "Participant development in sport and physical activity: The impact of biological maturation." *European Journal of Sport Science* 12 (6):515–26. doi: 10.1080/17461391.2011.577241.

Frederiksen, Anne Therese, and Rachel I. Mayberry. 2022. "Pronoun production and comprehension in American Sign Language: The interaction of space, grammar, and semantics." *Language, Cognition and Neuroscience* 37 (1):80–102. doi: 10.1080/23273798.2021.1968013.

Freytag, Gustav. 1894. *Technique of the Drama*. Chicago: S.C. Griggs & Company.

Fricke, Ellen. 2013. "Towards a unified grammar of gesture and speech: A multimodal approach." In *Body-Language-Communication. An International Handbook on Multimodality in Human Interaction*, edited by Cornelia Müller, Alan Cieni, Ellen Fricke, Silva Ladewig, David McNeill, and Sedinha Tessendorf, 733–54. Berlin, Boston: De Gruyter Mouton.

Friedmann, Naama, and Dana Rusou. 2015. "Critical period for first language: The crucial role of language input during the first year of life." *Current Opinion in Neurobiology* 35:27–34. doi: 10.1016/j.conb.2015.06.003.

Ganis, Giorgio, Marta Kutas, and Martin I. Sereno. 1996. "The search for 'common sense': An electrophysiological study of the comprehension of words and pictures in reading." *Journal of Cognitive Neuroscience* 8:89–106.

García-Diez, Marcos. 2022. "Chapter 13—'Art': Neanderthal symbolic graphic behaviour." In *Updating Neanderthals*, edited by Francesca Romagnoli, Florent Rivals, and Stefano Benazzi, 251–60. London, UK: Academic Press.

García-Diez, Marcos, and Blanca Ochoa. 2019. "Art origins: The emergence of graphic symbolism." In *Encyclopedia of Global Archaeology*, 1–19. Cham: Springer International Publishing.

Gawne, Lauren, and Kensy Cooperrider. 2022. "Emblems: Gestures at the interface." *psyarxiv.com*.

Gawne, Lauren, and Gretchen McCulloch. 2019. "Emoji as digital gestures." *Language@Internet* 17 (2). doi: urn:nbn:de:0009-7-48882.

Gentner, Dedre. 1983. "Structure-mapping: A theoretical framework for analogy." *Cognitive Science* 7 (2):155–70. doi: 10.1016/S0364-0213(83)80009-3.

Gernsbacher, Morton Ann. 1990. *Language Comprehension as Structure Building*. Hillsdale, NJ: Lawrence Earlbaum.

Gershoff-Stowe, Lisa, and Susan Goldin-Meadow. 2002. "Is there a natural order for expressing semantic relations?" *Cognitive Psychology* 45:375–412.

Ghirlanda, Stefano, Johan Lind, and Magnus Enquist. 2017. "Memory for stimulus sequences: a divide between humans and other animals?" *Royal Society Open Science* 4 (6):161011. doi: 10.1098/rsos.161011.

Gibson, James J. 2014 [1979]. *The Ecological Approach to Visual Perception: Classic Edition*. New York: Psychology Press. Original edition, 1979.

Ginns, Paul. 2006. "Integrating information: A meta-analysis of the spatial contiguity and temporal contiguity effects." *Learning and Instruction* 16 (6):511–25. doi: 10.1016/j.learninstruc.2006.10.001.

Giora, Rachel, Ofer Fein, Ann Kronrod, Idit Elnatan, Noa Shuval, and Adi Zur. 2004. "Weapons of mass distraction: Optimal innovation and pleasure ratings." *Metaphor and Symbol* 19 (2):115–41. doi: 10.1207/s15327868ms1902_2.

Giora, Rachel, Vered Heruti, Nili Metuki, and Ofer Fein. 2009. "'When we say no we mean no': Interpreting negation in vision and language." *Journal of Pragmatics* 41 (11):2222–39. doi: 10.1016/j.pragma.2008.09.041.

Givón, Talmy. 1995. *Functionalism and Grammar*. Amsterdam: John Benjamins.
Goldberg, Adele E. 1995. *Constructions: A Construction Grammar Approach to Argument Structure*. Chicago, IL: University of Chicago Press.
Goldberg, Adele E., and Ray Jackendoff. 2004. "The English resultative as a family of constructions." *Language* 80 (3):532–68.
Goldin-Meadow, Susan. 2003a. *Hearing Gesture: How Our Hands Help Us Think*. Cambridge: Harvard University Press.
Goldin-Meadow, Susan. 2003b. *The Resiliance of Language: What Gesture Creation in Deaf Children Can Tell Us about How All Children Learn Language*. New York and Hove: Psychology Press.
Goldin-Meadow, Susan, and Diane Brentari. 2017. "Gesture, sign, and language: The coming of age of sign language and gesture studies." *Behavioral and Brain Sciences* 40:e46.
Goldin-Meadow, Susan, Wing Chee So, Asli Özyürek, and Carolyn Mylander. 2008. "The natural order of events: How speakers of different languages represent events nonverbally." *Proceedings of the National Academy of Sciences* 105 (27):9163–8.
Goldrick, Matthew, Michael Putnam, and Lara Schwarz. 2016. "Coactivation in bilingual grammars: A computational account of code mixing." *Bilingualism: Language and Cognition* 19 (5):857–76. doi: 10.1017/S1366728915000802.
Goldsmith, John. 1976. "Autosegmental Phonology." PhD Dissertation, Linguistics, MIT.
Goldsmith, John A., and Bernard Laks. 2019. *Battle in the Mind Fields*. Chicago: University of Chicago Press.
Gombrich, Ernst Hans. 1961. *Art and Illusion: A Study in the Psychology of Pictorial Representation*. New York: Pantheon Books.
Gooskens, Charlotte. 2019. "Receptive Multilingualism." In *Multidisciplinary Perspectives on Multilingualism*, edited by Montanari Simona and Quay Suzanne, 149–74. Berlin, Boston: De Gruyter Mouton.
Graziano, Maria, Elena Nicoladis, and Paula Marentette. 2020. "How referential gestures align with speech: Evidence from monolingual and bilingual speakers." *Language Learning* 70 (1):266–304. doi: 10.1111/lang.12376.
Green, Jennifer. 2014. *Drawn from the Ground: Sound, Sign and Inscription in Central Australian Sand Stories*. Cambridge, UK: Cambridge University Press.
Greenberg, Gabriel. 2011. "The semiotic spectrum." Doctoral Dissertation, Philosophy, Rutgers The State University of New Jersey-New Brunswick.
Greenberg, Gabriel. 2021. The Iconic-Symbolic Spectrum. UCLA.
Greenberg, Joseph H. 1966. "Some universals of grammar with particular reference to the order of meaningful elements." In *Universals of Grammar*, edited by Joseph H. Greenberg, 73–113. Cambridge, MA: MIT Press.
Grosz, Patrick, Elsi Kaiser, and Francesco Pierini. 2021. "Discourse anaphoricity and first-person indexicality in emoji resolution." In *Proceedings of Sinn und Bedeutung 25*, edited by Patrick Grosz, L. Martí, H. Pearson, Y. Sudo, and S. Zobel, 340–57. London, UK: University College London and Queen Mary University of London.
Grushkin, Donald A. 2017. "Writing signed languages: What for? What form?" *American Annals of the Deaf* 161 (5):509–27.
Gu, Yan, Lisette Mol, Marieke Hoetjes, and Marc Swerts. 2017. "Conceptual and lexical effects on gestures: The case of vertical spatial metaphors for time in Chinese." *Language, Cognition and Neuroscience* 32 (8):1048–63. doi: 10.1080/23273798.2017.1283425.

Guest, Ann Hutchinson. 1989. *Choreographics: A Comparison of Dance Notation Systems from the Fifteenth Century to the Present*. London: Routledge.

Habets, Boukje, Sotaro Kita, Zeshu Shao, Asli Özyurek, and Peter Hagoort. 2011. "The role of synchrony and ambiguity in speech–gesture integration during comprehension." *Journal of Cognitive Neuroscience* 23 (8):1845–54. doi: 10.1162/jocn.2010.21462.

Hacımusaoğlu, Irmak, and Neil Cohn. 2022. "Linguistic typology of motion events in visual narratives." *Cognitive Semiotics* 15 (2): 197–222. https://doi.org/10.1515/cogsem-2022-2013.

Hagoort, Peter. 2014. "Nodes and networks in the neural architecture for language: Broca's region and beyond." *Current Opinion in Neurobiology* 28:136–41. doi: 10.1016/j.conb.2014.07.013.

Hagoort, Peter. 2017. "The core and beyond in the language-ready brain." *Neuroscience & Biobehavioral Reviews* 81:194–204. doi: 10.1016/j.neubiorev.2017.01.048.

Hagoort, Peter, Colin M. Brown, and J. Groothusen. 1993. "The syntactic positive shift (SPS) as an ERP measure of syntactic processing." *Language and Cognitive Processes* 8 (4):439–83. doi: 10.1080/01690969308407585.

Hagoort, Peter, and Peter Indefrey. 2014. "The neurobiology of language beyond single words." *Annual Review of Neuroscience* 37 (1):347–62. doi: 10.1146/annurev-neuro-071013-013847.

Hall, Matthew L., Victor S. Ferreira, and Rachel I. Mayberry. 2014. "Investigating constituent order change with elicited pantomime: A functional account of SVO emergence." *Cognitive Science* 38 (5):943–72. doi: 10.1111/cogs.12105.

Hall, Matthew L., Rachel I. Mayberry, and Victor S. Ferreira. 2013. "Cognitive constraints on constituent order: Evidence from elicited pantomime." *Cognition* 129 (1):1–17. doi: 10.1016/j.cognition.2013.05.004.

Harris, Randy Allen. 1993. *The Linguistics Wars*. New York, NY: Oxford University Press.

Harris, Randy Allen. 2021. *The Linguistics Wars: Chomsky, Lakoff, and the Battle Over Deep Structure*. New York, NY: Oxford University Press.

Haspelmath, Martin. 2017. "The indeterminacy of word segmentation and the nature of morphology and syntax." *Folia Linguistica* 51 (s1000):31–80. doi: 10.1515/flin-2017-1005.

Haspelmath, Martin. 2018. "The last word on polysynthesis: A review article." *Linguistic Typology* 22 (2):307–26.

Hauser, Marc D., Noam Chomsky, and W. Tecumseh Fitch. 2002. "The faculty of language: What is it, who has it, and how did it evolve?" *Science* 298:1569–79.

Haviland, John. 1993. "Anchoring, iconicity, and orientation in Guugu Yimithirr pointing gestures." *Journal of Linguistic Anthropology* 3 (1):3–45.

Henshilwood, Christopher, S., Francesco d'Errico, Royden Yates, Zenobia Jacobs, Chantal Tribolo, A. T. Duller Geoff, Norbert Mercier, C. Sealy Judith, Helene Valladas, Ian Watts, and G. Wintle Ann. 2002. "Emergence of modern human behavior: Middle Stone Age engravings from South Africa." *Science* 295 (5558):1278–80. doi: 10.1126/science.1067575.

Hervais-Adelman, Alexis, Uttam Kumar, Ramesh K. Mishra, Viveka N. Tripathi, Anupam Guleria, Jay P. Singh, Frank Eisner, and Falk Huettig. 2019. "Learning to read recycles visual cortical networks without destruction." *Science Advances* 5 (9):eaax0262. doi: 10.1126/sciadv.aax0262.

Hewes, Gordon W. 1973. "Primate communication and the gestural origin of language." *Current anthropology* 14 (1–2):5–24.

Hintz, Florian, Yung Han Khoe, Antje Strauß, Adam Johannes Alfredo Psomakas, and Judith Holler. 2023. "Electrophysiological evidence for the enhancement of gesture-speech integration by linguistic predictability during multimodal discourse comprehension." *Cognitive, Affective, & Behavioral Neuroscience* 23 (2):340–53. doi: 10.3758/s13415-023-01074-8.

Hobbs, J.R. 1985. *On the Coherence and Structure of Discourse*. Stanford, CA: CSLI Technical Report 85-37.

Hockett, Charles F. 1960. "Logical considerations in the study of animal communication." In *Animal Sounds and Communication*, edited by W.E. Lanyon and W.N. Tavolga, 392–430. Washington, DC: American Institute of Biological Sciences, Symposium Series Number 7. Original edition, 1960.

Hoffmann, D. L., C. D. Standish, M. García-Diez, P. B. Pettitt, J. A. Milton, J. Zilhão, J. J. Alcolea-González, P. Cantalejo-Duarte, H. Collado, R. de Balbín, M. Lorblanchet, J. Ramos-Muñoz, G. Ch Weniger, and A. W. G. Pike. 2018. "U-Th dating of carbonate crusts reveals Neandertal origin of Iberian cave art." *Science* 359 (6378):912–15. doi: 10.1126/science.aap7778.

Holler, Judith, and Stephen C. Levinson. 2019. "Multimodal language processing in human communication." *Trends in Cognitive Sciences* 23 (8):639–52. doi: 10.1016/j.tics.2019.05.006.

Homann, Lauren A., Brady R. T. Roberts, Sara Ahmed, and Myra A. Fernandes. 2022. "Are emojis processed visuo-spatially or verbally? Evidence for dual codes." *Visual Cognition*:1–13. doi: 10.1080/13506285.2022.2050871.

Huck, Geoffrey J., and John A Goldsmith. 1995. *Ideology and Linguistic Theory: Noam Chomsky and the Deep Structure Debates*. Vol. 10. London: Routledge.

Huettig, Falk, Jenny Audring, and Ray Jackendoff. 2022. "A parallel architecture perspective on pre-activation and prediction in language processing." *Cognition* 224 (4):105050. doi: 10.1016/j.cognition.2022.105050.

Huff, Markus, Dina Rosenfelder, Maria Oberbeck, Martin Merkt, Frank Papenmeier, and Tino G. K. Meitz. 2020. "Cross-codal integration of bridging-event information in narrative understanding." *Memory & Cognition*. doi: 10.3758/s13421-020-01039-z.

Jackendoff, Ray. 1977. *X-Bar Syntax: A Study of Phrase Structure*. Cambridge, MA: MIT Press.

Jackendoff, Ray. 1983. *Semantics and Cognition*. Cambridge, MA: MIT Press.

Jackendoff, Ray. 1987. *Consciousness and the Computational Mind*. Cambridge, MA: MIT Press.

Jackendoff, Ray. 1990. *Semantic Structures*. Cambridge, MA: MIT Press.

Jackendoff, Ray. 2002. *Foundations of Language: Brain, Meaning, Grammar, Evolution*. Oxford: Oxford University Press.

Jackendoff, Ray. 2007. *Language, Consciousness, Culture: Essays on Mental Structure (Jean Nicod Lectures)*. Cambridge, MA: MIT Press.

Jackendoff, Ray. 2009a. "Compounding in the parallel architecture and conceptual semantics." In *Oxford Handbook of Compounding*, edited by R. Lieber and P. Stekauer, 105–28. Oxford: Oxford University.

Jackendoff, Ray. 2009b. "Parallels and nonparallels between language and music." *Music Perception: An Interdisciplinary Journal* 26 (3):195–204.

Jackendoff, Ray. 2010a. *Meaning and the Lexicon: The Parallel Architecture 1975-2010*. Oxford: Oxford University Press.

Jackendoff, Ray. 2010b. "Your theory of language evolution depends on your theory of language." In *The Evolution of Human Language: Biolinguistic Perspectives*, edited by Richard K. Larson, Viviane Déprez, and Hiroko Yamakido, 63–72. Cambridge, UK: Cambridge University Press.

Jackendoff, Ray. 2011. "What is the human language faculty?: Two views." *Language* 87 (3):586–624.

Jackendoff, Ray, and David Aaron. 1991. "Review: *More Than Cool Reason: A Field Guide to Poetic Metaphor* by George Lakoff & Mark Turner." *Language* 67 (2):320–38.

Jackendoff, Ray, and Jenny Audring. 2020. *The Texture of the Lexicon: Relational Morphology and the Parallel Architecture*. Oxford, UK: Oxford University Press.

Jackendoff, Ray, and Fred Lerdahl. 2006. "The capacity for music: What is it, and what's special about it?" *Cognition* 100:33–72.

Jackendoff, Ray, and Eva Wittenberg. 2014. "What you can say without syntax: A hierarchy of grammatical complexity." In *Measuring Linguistic Complexity*, edited by Frederick Newmeyer and L. Preston, 65–82. Oxford: Oxford University Press.

Jackendoff, Ray, and Eva Wittenberg. 2017. "Linear grammar as a possible stepping-stone in the evolution of language." *Psychonomic Bulletin & Review* 24 (1):219–24. doi: 10.3758/s13423-016-1073-y.

Jesse, Alexandra, and Elizabeth K Johnson. 2012. "Prosodic temporal alignment of co-speech gestures to speech facilitates referent resolution." *Journal of Experimental Psychology: Human Perception and Performance* 38 (6):1567.

Johnson, Mark. 2013. *The Body in the Mind: The Bodily Basis of Meaning, Imagination, and Reason*. Chicago, IL: University of Chicago press.

Kaminishi, Ikumi. 2006. *Explaining Pictures: Buddhist Propaganda and Etoki Storytelling in Japan*. Honolulu, HI: University of Hawaii Press.

Kaplan, Ronald M., and Joan Bresnan. 1981. *Lexical-functional Grammar: A Formal System for Grammatical Representation*. Cambridge, MA: Massachusetts Institute of Technology, Center For Cognitive Science.

Kegl, Judy Anne. 1994. The Nicaraguan sign language project: An overview." *Signpost* 7:24–31.

Kegl, Judy Anne. 2020. "Human Language, Unique Features of." In *The International Encyclopedia of Linguistic Anthropology*, edited by James Stanlaw, 1–4. Hoboken, NJ: John Wiley & Sons, Inc.

Kemmerer, David. 2012. "The cross-linguistic prevalence of SOV and SVO word orders reflects the sequential and hierarchical representation of action in Broca's area." *Language and Linguistics Compass* 6 (1):50–66.

Kendon, Adam. 1972. "Some relationships between body motion and speech." In *Studies in Dyadic Communication*, edited by A. W. Siegman and B. Pope, 177–210. New York: Pergamon Press.

Kendon, Adam. 1988. "How gestures can become like words." In *Cross-cultural Perspectives in Nonverbal Communication.*, edited by F. Poyatos, 131–141. Ashland, OH: Hogrefe & Huber Publishers.

Kennedy, John M. 1982. "Metaphor in Pictures." *Perception* 11 (5):589–605.

Kiefer, Markus, Philipp Kuhnke, and Gesa Hartwigsen. 2023. "Distinguishing modality-specificity at the representational and input level: A commentary on Calzavarini (2023)." *Language, Cognition and Neuroscience*:1–5. doi: 10.1080/23273798.2023.2209928.

Kindler, Anna M., and Bernard Darras. 1997. "Map of Artistic Development." In *Child Development in Art*, edited by Anna M. Kindler, 17–44. Virginia: National Art Education Association.

Kirby, Simon, Tom Griffiths, and Kenny Smith. 2014. "Iterated learning and the evolution of language." *Current Opinion in Neurobiology* 28:108–14. doi: 10.1016/j.conb.2014.07.014.

Kita, Sotaro. 2009. "Cross-cultural variation of speech-accompanying gesture: A review." *Language and Cognitive Processes* 24 (2):145–67. doi: 10.1080/01690960802586188.

Klomberg, Bien, and Neil Cohn. 2022. "Picture perfect Peaks: Comprehension of inferential techniques in visual narratives." *Language and Cognition* 14 (4):596–621. doi: 10.1017/langcog.2022.19.

Klomberg, Bien, Irmak Hacımusaoğlu, Lenneke Lichtenberg, Joost Schilperoord, and Neil Cohn. 2023. "Continuity, co-reference, and inference in visual sequencing." *Glossa: A Journal of General Linguistics* 8 (1). doi: 10.16995/glossa.9982.

Klomberg, Bien, Joost Schilperoord, and Neil Cohn. 2024. "Constructing Domains in Visual Narratives: Structural Patterns of Incongruity Resolution." *Journal of Comparative Literature and Aesthetics: Advances in Neuroaesthetics* 47 (1).

Koechlin, Etienne, and Thomas Jubault. 2006. "Broca's area and the hierarchical organization of human behavior." *Neuron* 50:963–74.

Koelsch, Stefan. 2011a. "Toward a neural basis of music perception—A review and updated model." *Frontiers in Psychology* 2 (110):1–20.

Koelsch, Stefan. 2011b. "Towards a neural basis of processing musical semantics." *Physics of Life Reviews* 8 (2):89–105. doi: 10.1016/j.plrev.2011.04.004.

Kootstra, Gerrit Jan. 2015. "A psycholinguistic perspective on code-switching: Lexical, structural, and socio-interactive processes." In *Code-switching between Structural and Sociolinguistic Perspectives*, edited by Gerald Stell and Kofi Yakpo, 39–64. Berlin, München, Boston: De Gruyter.

Koplenig, Alexander, Peter Meyer, Sascha Wolfer, and Carolin Müller-Spitzer. 2017. "The statistical trade-off between word order and word structure—Large-scale evidence for the principle of least effort." *PLOS ONE* 12 (3):e0173614. doi: 10.1371/journal.pone.0173614.

Krampen, Martin. 1984. "Children's drawings as compositions of graphemes: A cross-cultural comparison." *Visual Arts Research* 10 (1):7–12.

Kress, Gunther. 2009. *Multimodality: A Social Semiotic Approach to Contemporary Communication*. New York: Routledge.

Kress, Gunther, and Theo van Leeuwen. 1996. *Reading Images: The Grammar of Visual Design*. London: Routledge.

Kress, Gunther, and Theo van Leeuwen. 2001. *Multimodal Discourse: The Modes and Media of Contemporary Communication*. London: Oxford Press.

Kuhnke, Philipp, Marie C. Beaupain, Johannes Arola, Markus Kiefer, and Gesa Hartwigsen. 2023. "Meta-analytic evidence for a novel hierarchical model of conceptual processing." *Neuroscience & Biobehavioral Reviews* 144:104994. doi: 10.1016/j.neubiorev.2022.104994.

Kunzle, David. 1973. *The History of the Comic Strip*. Vol. 1. Berkeley: University of California Press.

Kuperberg, Gina R. 2021. "Tea with milk? A hierarchical generative framework of sequential event comprehension." *Topics in Cognitive Science* 13 (1):256–98. doi: 10.1111/tops.12518.

Kutas, Marta, and Kara D. Federmeier. 2011. "Thirty years and counting: Finding meaning in the N400 component of the event-related brain potential (ERP)." *Annual Review of Psychology* 62 (1):621–47. doi: 10.1146/annurev.psych.093008.131123.

Kutas, Marta, and Steven A. Hillyard. 1980. "Reading senseless sentences: Brain potential reflect semantic incongruity." *Science* 207:203–5.

Kutas, Marta, and Steven A. Hillyard. 1984. "Brain potentials during reading reflect word expectancy and semantic association." *Nature* 307:161–3.

Labov, William. 1973. "The boundaries of words and their meanings." In *New Ways of Analyzing Variation in English*, edited by Charles-James N. Bailey and Roger W. Shuy, 340–71. Washington, DC: Georgetown University Press.

Labov, William, and J. Waletzky. 1967. "Narrative analysis: Oral versions of personal experience." In *Essays on the Verbal and Visual Arts*, edited by J. Helm, 12–44. Seattle: University of Washington Press.

Ladewig, Silva. 2020. *Integrating Gestures: The Dimension of Multimodality in Cognitive Grammar*. Berlin: Walter de Gruyter GmbH & Co KG.

Lakoff, George. 1964. "Structural complexity in fairy tales." Department of Linguistics, Indiana University.

Lakoff, George. 1971. "On generative semantics." In *Semantics: An Interdisciplinary Reader in Philosophy, Linguistics and Psychology*, edited by Danny D. Steinberg and Leon A. Jakobovits, 232–96. Cambridge: Cambridge University Press.

Lakoff, George. 1987a. "Image metaphors." *Metaphor and Symbolic Activity* 2 (3):219–22. doi: 10.1207/s15327868ms0203_4.

Lakoff, George. 1987b. *Women, Fire, and Dangerous Things: What Categories Reveal about the Mind*. Chicago, IL: University of Chicago Press.

Lakoff, George, and Mark Johnson. 1980. *Metaphors We Live By*. Chicago, IL: University of Chicago Press.

Landau, Barbara. 2017. "Update on 'What' and 'Where' in spatial language: A new division of labor for spatial terms." *Cognitive Science* 41 (S2):321–50. doi: 10.1111/cogs.12410.

Landau, Barbara, and Ray Jackendoff. 1993. "'What' and 'where' in spatial language and spatial cognition." *Behavioral and Brain Sciences* 16 (2):217–38. doi: 10.1017/S0140525X00029733.

Langacker, Ronald W. 1987. *Foundations of Cognitive Grammar*. Palo Alto: Stanford University Press.

Lashley, Karl Spencer. 1951. *The Problem of Serial Order in Behavior*. Vol. 21. Oxford: Bobbs-Merrill.

Laubrock, Jochen, Sven Hohenstein, and Matthias Kümmerer. 2018. "Attention to comics: Cognitive processing during the reading of graphic literature." In *Empirical Comics Research: Digital, Multimodal, and Cognitive Methods*, edited by Alexander Dunst, Jochen Laubrock and Janina Wildfeuer, 239–63. New York: Routledge.

Lenneberg, Eric H. 1967. *Biological Foundations of Language*. New York: Wiley.

Lerdahl, Fred, and Ray Jackendoff. 1982. *A Generative Theory of Tonal Music*. Cambridge, MA: MIT Press.

Levelt, Willem J. M. 2013. *A History of Psycholinguistics: The Pre-Chomskyan Era*. Oxford: Oxford University Press.

Liddell, Scott K. 2003. *Grammar, Gesture, and Meaning in American Sign Language*. Cambridge: Cambridge University Press.

Liddell, Scott K., and Melanie Metzger. 1998. "Gesture in sign language discourse." *Journal of Pragmatics* 30 (6):657–97. doi: 10.1016/S0378-2166(98)00061-7.

Lillo-Martin, Diane C., and Jon Gajewski. 2014. "One grammar or two? Sign languages and the nature of human language." *WIREs Cognitive Science* 5 (4):387–401. doi: 10.1002/wcs.1297.

Lillo-Martin, Diane, and Jonathan Henner. 2021. "Acquisition of sign languages." *Annual Review of Linguistics* 7 (1):395–419. doi: 10.1146/annurev-linguistics-043020-092357.

Logi, Lorenzo, and Michele Zappavigna. 2021. "A social semiotic perspective on emoji: How emoji and language interact to make meaning in digital messages." *New Media & Society* 0 (0):14614448211032965. doi: 10.1177/14614448211032965.

Long, Bria, Judith E Fan, and Michael C Frank. 2018. "Drawings as a window into developmental changes in object representations." Proceedings of the 40th Annual Conference of the Cognitive Science Society.

Loschky, Lester C., Joseph Magliano, Adam M. Larson, and Tim J. Smith. 2020. "The Scene Perception & Event Comprehension Theory (SPECT) applied to visual narratives." *Topics in Cognitive Science* 12 (1):311–51. doi: 10.1111/tops.12455.

Luetke-Stahlman, Barbara, and Wanda O Milburn. 1996. "A history of seeing essential English (SEE I)." *American Annals of the Deaf* 141 (1):29–33.

Macnamara, John. 1978. *How Do We Talk about What We See*. Montreal: McGill University. Unpublished mimeo, Department of Psychology.

Maess, Burkhard, Stefan Koelsch, Thomas C. Gunter, and Angela D. Friederici. 2001. "Musical syntax is processed in Broca's area: An MEG study." *Nature Neuroscience* 4 (5):540–5.

Mair, Victor H. 2019. *Painting and Performance: Chinese Picture Recitation and Its Indian Genesis*. Honolulu, HI: University of Hawaii Press.

Mandler, Jean M. 2004. *The Foundations of Mind: Origins of Conceptual Thought*. New York: Oxford University Press.

Mandler, Jean M. 2010. "The spatial foundations of the conceptual system." *Language and Cognition* 2 (1):21–44.

Mandler, Jean M., and Nancy S. Johnson. 1977. "Remembrance of things parsed: Story structure and recall." *Cognitive Psychology* 9:111–51.

Manfredi, Mirella, Neil Cohn, and Marta Kutas. 2017. "When a hit sounds like a kiss: an electrophysiological exploration of semantic processing in visual narrative." *Brain and Language* 169:28–38. doi: 10.1016/j.bandl.2017.02.001.

Mann, William C., and Sandra A. Thompson. 1987. *Rhetorical Structure Theory: A Theory of Text Organization*. Marina del Rey, CA: Information Sciences Institute.

Marr, David. 1982. *Vision*. San Francisco, CA: Freeman.

Marschark, Marc. 1994. "Gesture and sign." *Applied Psycholinguistics* 15 (2):209–36. doi: 10.1017/S0142716400005336.

Marslen-Wilson, William D., and Lorraine Komisarjevsky Tyler. 1980. "The temporal structure of spoken language understanding." *Cognition* 8:1–71.

Martinec, Radan, and Andrew Salway. 2005. "A system for image–text relations in new (and old) media." *Visual Communication* 4 (3):337–71. doi: 10.1177/1470357205055928.

Marx, Elena, and Eva Wittenberg. 2022. "Event structure predicts temporal interpretation of English and German past-under-past relative clauses." Proceedings of the 44th Annual Conference of the Cognitive Science Society.

Masataka, Nobuo. 2007. "Music, evolution and language." *Developmental Science* 10 (1):35–9. doi: 10.1111/j.1467-7687.2007.00561.x.

Matchin, William, and Gregory Hickok. 2019. "The cortical organization of syntax." *Cerebral Cortex* 00:1–18. doi: 10.1093/cercor/bhz180.

Mayberry, Rachel I., Jen-Kai Chen, Pamela Witcher, and Denise Klein. 2011. "Age of acquisition effects on the functional organization of language in the adult brain." *Brain and Language* 119 (1):16–29. doi: 10.1016/j.bandl.2011.05.007.

Mayer, Richard E. 2009. *Multimedia Learning*. 2nd ed. Cambridge, UK: Cambridge University Press.

McCawley, James D. 1995. "Generative semantics." In *Concise History of the Language Sciences*, edited by E. F. K. Koerner and R. E. Asher, 343–8. Amsterdam: Pergamon.

McCloud, Scott. 1993. *Understanding Comics: The Invisible Art*. New York, NY: Harper Collins.

McCulloch, Gretchen, and Lauren Gawne. 2018. "Emoji grammar as beat gestures." In *Proceedings of the 1st International Workshop on Emoji Understanding and Applications in Social Media (Emoji2018)*, edited by S. Wijeratne, E. Kiciman, H. Saggion, and A. Sheth, 1–4. Stanford, CA: http://ceur-ws.org.

McGurk, Harry, and John Macdonald. 1976. "Hearing lips and seeing voices." *Nature* 264 (5588):746–8. doi: 10.1038/264746a0.

McNeill, David. 1992. *Hand and Mind: What Gestures Reveal about Thought*. Chicago, IL: University of Chicago Press.

McNeill, David. 2012. *How Language Began: Gesture and Speech in Human Evolution*. Cambridge, UK: Cambridge University Press.

Meir, Irit, Mark Aronoff, Carl Börstell, So-One Hwang, Deniz Ilkbasaran, Itamar Kastner, Ryan Lepic, Adi Lifshitz Ben-Basat, Carol Padden, and Wendy Sandler. 2017. "The effect of being human and the basis of grammatical word order: Insights from novel communication systems and young sign languages." *Cognition* 158:189–207. doi: 10.1016/j.cognition.2016.10.011.

Meir, Irit, Mark Aronoff, Wendy Sandler, and Carol Padden. 2010. "Sign languages and compounding." In *Cross-Disciplinary Issues in Compounding*, edited by Sergio Scalise and Irene Vogel, 301–22. Amsterdam, The Netherlands: John Benjamins.

Meir, Irit, Wendy Sandler, Carol Padden, and Mark Aronoff. 2010. "Emerging sign languages." In *Oxford Handbook of Deaf Studies, Language, and Education*, edited by Marc Marschark and Patricia Elizabeth Spencer, 267–80. Oxford: Oxford University Press.

Menzerath, Paul. 1928. "Über einige phonetische Probleme." Actes du premier Congres international de linguistes.

Mithen, Steven J. 2006. *The Singing Neanderthals: The Origins of Music, Language, Mind, and Body*. Cambridge, MA: Harvard University Press.

Miyagawa, Shigeru, Cora Lesure, and Vitor A. Nóbrega. 2018. "Cross-modality information transfer: A hypothesis about the relationship among prehistoric cave paintings, symbolic thinking, and the emergence of language." *Frontiers in Psychology* 9. doi: 10.3389/fpsyg.2018.00115.

Molotiu, Andrei. 2009. *Abstract Comics: The Anthology: 1967–2009*. Seattle, WA: Fantagraphics Books.

Morin, Olivier. 2022. "The puzzle of ideography." *Behavioral and Brain Sciences*:1–69. doi: 10.1017/S0140525X22002801.

Muysken, Pieter. 2020. "Code-switching and grammatical theory." In *The bilingualism reader*, 280–97. New York: Routledge.

Myers-Scotton, Carol. 1997. *Duelling Languages: Grammatical Structure in Codeswitching*. Oxford, UK: Oxford University Press.

Myers-Scotton, Carol. 2002. *Contact Linguistics: Bilingual Encounters and Grammatical Outcomes*. Oxford, UK: Oxford University Press.

Naidu, Viswanatha, Jordan Zlatev, Vasanta Duggirala, Joost Van De Weijer, Simon Devylder, and Johan Blomberg. 2018. "Holistic spatial semantics and post-Talmian motion event typology: A case study of Thai and Telugu." *Cognitive Semiotics* 11 (2). doi: 10.1515/cogsem-2018-2002.

Nakazawa, Jun. 2005. "Development of manga (comic book) literacy in children." In *Applied Developmental Psychology: Theory, Practice, and Research from Japan*, edited by David W. Shwalb, Jun Nakazawa, and Barbara J. Shwalb, 23–42. Greenwich, CT: Information Age Publishing.

Nespor, Marina, and Wendy Sandler. 1999. "Prosody in Israeli sign language." *Language and speech* 42 (2–3):143–76.

Neville, Helen J., Janet L. Nicol, Andrew Barss, Kenneth I. Forster, and Merrill F. Garrett. 1991. "Syntactically based sentence processing classes: Evidence from event-related brain potentials." *Journal of Cognitive Neuroscience* 3 (2):151–65.

Newport, Elissa L., Daphne Bavelier, and Helen J Neville. 2001. "Critical thinking about critical periods: Perspectives on a critical period for language acquisition." In *Language, Brain and Cognitive Development: Essays in Honor of Jacques Mehler*, edited by Emmanuel Dupoux, 481–502. Cambridge: MIT Press.

Nieuwland, Mante S., Dale J. Barr, Federica Bartolozzi, Simon Busch-Moreno, Emily Darley, David I. Donaldson, Heather J. Ferguson, Xiao Fu, Evelien Heyselaar, Falk Huettig, E. Matthew Husband, Aine Ito, Nina Kazanina, Vita Kogan, Zdenko Kohút, Eugenia Kulakova, Diane Mézière, Stephen Politzer-Ahles, Guillaume Rousselet, Shirley-Ann Rueschemeyer, Katrien Segaert, Jyrki Tuomainen, and Sarah Von Grebmer Zu Wolfsthurn. 2020. "Dissociable effects of prediction and integration during language comprehension: Evidence from a large-scale study using brain potentials." *Philosophical Transactions of the Royal Society B: Biological Sciences* 375 (1791):20180522. doi: 10.1098/rstb.2018.0522.

Nigam, A., J. Hoffman, and R. Simons. 1992. "N400 to Semantically Anomalous Pictures and Words." *Journal of Cognitive Neuroscience* 4 (1):15–22. doi: 10.1162/jocn.1992.4.1.15.

Núñez, Rafael, and Eve Sweetser 2006. "With the future behind them: Convergent evidence from Aymara language and gesture in the crosslinguistic comparison of spatial construals of time." *Cognitive Science* 30:1–49.

Olivier, Fernand. 1974. Le "dessin enfantin est-il une écriture?" *Enfance* 27 (3):183–216.

Orzechowski, Sylwester, Sławomir Wacewicz, and Przemysław Żywiczyński. 2016. "The problem of 'modality transition' in gestural primacy hypothesis in language evolution: Towards multimodal hypotheses." *Studia Semiotyczne—English Supplement Volume XXVIII*:112.

Osterhout, Lee, and Phil Holcomb. 1992. "Event-related potentials elicited by syntactic anomaly." *Journal of Memory and Language* 31:758–806.

Oversteegen, Eleonore, and Joost Schilperoord. 2014. "Can pictures say no or not? Negation and denial in the visual mode." *Journal of Pragmatics* 67:89–106. doi: 10.1016/j.pragma.2014.03.009.

Pa, Judy, Stephen M. Wilson, Herbert Pickell, Ursula Bellugi, and Gregory Hickok. 2008. "Neural organization of linguistic short-term memory is sensory modality–dependent: Evidence from signed and spoken language." *Journal of Cognitive Neuroscience* 20 (12):2198–210. doi: 10.1162/jocn.2008.20154.

Paggio, Patrizia, and Alice Ping Ping Tse. 2022. "Are emoji processed like words? An eye-tracking study." *Cognitive Science* 46 (2):e13099.

Painter, Claire, James R. Martin, and Len Unsworth. 2012. *Reading Visual Narratives: Image Analysis of Children's Picture Books*. London: Equi-nox.

Paivio, A. 1986. *Mental Representations: A Dual Coding Approach*. New York: Oxford University Press.

Palmer, Stephen. 1992. "Common region: A new principle of perceptual grouping." *Cognitive Psychology* 24 (3):436–47.

Palmer, Stephen, and Irvin Rock. 1994. "Rethinking perceptual organization: The role of uniform connectedness." *Psychonomic Bulletin & Review* 1:29–55.

Panesi, Sabrina, and Sergio Morra. 2021. "Executive function, language, and the toddler's discovery of representational drawing." *Frontiers in Psychology* 12 (1926). doi: 10.3389/fpsyg.2021.659569.

Papafragou, Anna, and Yue Ji. 2023. "Events and objects are similar cognitive entities." *Cognitive Psychology* 143:101573. doi: 10.1016/j.cogpsych.2023.101573.

Patel, Aniruddh D. 2003. "Language, music, syntax and the brain." *Nature Neuroscience* 6 (7):674–81. doi: 10.1038/nn1082.

Patel, Aniruddh D. 2008. *Music, Language, and the Brain*. Oxford, UK: Oxford University Press.

Patel-Grosz, Pritty, Patrick Georg Grosz, Tejaswinee Kelkar, and Alexander Refsum Jensenius. 2022. "Steps towards a semantics of dance." *Journal of Semantics* 39 (4):693–748. doi: 10.1093/jos/ffac009.

Patel-Grosz, Pritty, Salvador Mascarenhas, Emmanuel Chemla, and Philippe Schlenker. 2023. "Super linguistics: An introduction." *Linguistics & Philosophy* 46: 627–92.

Peeters, David, Emiel Krahmer, and Alfons Maes. 2021. "A conceptual framework for the study of demonstrative reference." *Psychonomic Bulletin & Review* 28 (2):409–33. doi: 10.3758/s13423-020-01822-8.

Peirce, Charles Sanders. 1940. "Logic as semiotic: The theory of signs." In *The Philosophy of Peirce: Selected Writings*, edited by Justus Buchler, 98–119. London: Kenga Paul, Trench, Trubner & Co. Ltd.

Penhune, Virginia B. 2011. "Sensitive periods in human development: Evidence from musical training." *Cortex* 47 (9):1126–37. doi: 10.1016/j.cortex.2011.05.010.

Perlman, Marcus, and Greg Woodin. 2021. "A complete real-world theory of language should explain how iconicity remains a stable property of linguistic systems." *Journal of Cognition* 4 (1):1–4. doi: 10.5334/joc.166.

Petersen, Robert S. 2011. *Comics, Manga, and Graphic Novels: A History of Graphic Narratives*. Santa Barbara, CA: ABC-CLIO.

Peterson, Mary A. 2001. "Object perception." In *Blackwell Handbook of Sensation and Perception*, edited by E. Bruce Goldstein, 168–203. Malden, MA: Blackwell Publishing Ltd.

Piantadosi, Steven T., Harry Tily, and Edward Gibson. 2011. "Word lengths are optimized for efficient communication." *Proceedings of the National Academy of Sciences* 108 (9):3526. doi: 10.1073/pnas.1012551108.

Pienemann, Manfred, and Anke Lenzing. 2020. "Processability Theory 1." In *Theories in second language acquisition*, 162–91. New York, NY: Routledge.

Pimienta, Julian. 2022. "Attachment to manga (Japanese comics): Conceptualizing the behavioral components of manga attachment and exploring attachment differences between avid, moderate, and occasional manga readers." *The Journal of Anime and Manga Studies* 3:174–226.

Pinker, Steven. 1994. *The Language Instinct: How the Mind Creates Language*. New York: HarperCollins.

Pinker, Steven, and Ray Jackendoff. 2005. "The faculty of language: What's special about it?" *Cognition* 95 (2):201–36. doi: 10.1016/j.cognition.2004.08.004.

Planer, Ronald, and Kim Sterelny. 2021. *From Signal to Symbol: The Evolution of Language*. Cambridge: MIT Press.

Plug, Ilona, M. Van den Bergh, Joost Schilperoord, Neil Cohn, and Renske van Enschot. In prep. "Butterflies and bananas: An experimental study into the effects of (a)symmetry and context on topic assignment in juxtapositions."

Pollard, Carl, and Ivan A. Sag. 1994. *Head-driven Phrase Structure Grammar*. Chicago: University of Chicago Press.

Pontecorvo, Elana, Michael Higgins, Joshua Mora, Amy M. Lieberman, Jennie Pyers, and Naomi K. Caselli. 2023. "Learning a sign language does not hinder acquisition of a spoken language." *Journal of Speech, Language, and Hearing Research* 66 (4): 1291–308. doi: 10.1044/2022_JSLHR-22-00505.

Potter, Mary C., Judith F Kroll, Betsy Yachzel, Elisabeth Carpenter, and Janet Sherman. 1986. "Pictures in sentences: Understanding without words." *Journal of Experimental Psychology: General* 115 (3):281. doi: 10.1037/0096-3445.115.3.281.

Pratha, Nimish K., Natalie Avunjian, and Neil Cohn. 2016. "Pow, punch, pika, and chu: The structure of sound effects in genres of American comics and Japanese manga." *Multimodal Communication* 5 (2):93–109.

Prinz, Jesse. 2017. "The intermediate level theory of consciousness." In *The Blackwell Companion to Consciousness*, edited by Susan Schneider and Max Velmans, 257–71. West Sussex, UK: Wiley-Blackwell.

Pustejovsky, James. 1991. "The Generative Lexicon." *Computational Linguistics* 17:409–41.

Pustejovsky, James. 1995. *The Generative Lexicon*. Cambridge, MA: MIT Press.

Pyers, Jennie E., Rachel Magid, Tamar H. Gollan, and Karen Emmorey. 2021. "Gesture helps, only if you need it: Inhibiting gesture reduces tip-of-the-tongue resolution for those with weak short-term memory." *Cognitive Science* 45 (1):e12914. doi: 10.1111/cogs.12914.

Ralph, Matthew A. Lambon, Elizabeth Jefferies, Karalyn Patterson, and Timothy T. Rogers. 2016. "The neural and computational bases of semantic cognition." *Nature Reviews Neuroscience* 18:42. doi: 10.1038/nrn.2016.150.

Rasenberg, Marlou, Asli Özyürek, and Mark Dingemanse. 2020. "Alignment in multimodal interaction: An integrative framework." *Cognitive Science* 44 (11):e12911. doi: 10.1111/cogs.12911.

Raviv, Limor, Antje Meyer, and Shiri Lev-Ari. 2019. "Larger communities create more systematic languages." *Proceedings of the Royal Society B: Biological Sciences* 286 (1907):20191262. doi: 10.1098/rspb.2019.1262.

Read, H. 1958. *Education through Art*. 3rd ed. New York: Pantheon Books.

Robertson, David A. 2000. "Functional neuroanatomy of narrative comprehension." In *Doctoral Doctoral dissertation, Psychology*. Madison: University of Wisconsin.

Rosch, Eleanor, Carolyn B. Mervis, Wayne D. Gray, David M. Johnson, and Penny Boyes-Braem. 1976. "Basic objects in natural categories." *Cognitive Psychology* 8 (3):382–439. doi: 10.1016/0010-0285(76)90013-X.

Rosenblatt, Elizabeth, and Ellen Winner. 1988. "The art of children's drawing." *Journal of Aesthetic Education* 22 (1):3–15.

Royce, Terry D. 2007. "Intersemiotic complementarity: A framework for multimodal discourse analysis." In *New Directions in the Analysis of Multimodal Discourse*, edited by Terry D. Royce and Wendy L. Bowcher, 63–109. Mahweh, NJ: Lawrence Erlbaum Associates, Inc.

Rumelhart, David E. 1975. "Notes on a schema for stories." In *Representation and understanding*, edited by Daniel Bobrow and Allan Collins, 211–36. New York, NY: Academic Press.

Sablé-Meyer, Mathias, Joël Fagot, Serge Caparos, Timo van Kerkoerle, Marie Amalric, and Stanislas Dehaene. 2021. "Sensitivity to geometric shape regularity in humans and baboons: A putative signature of human singularity." *Proceedings of the National Academy of Sciences* 118 (16):e2023123118. doi: 10.1073/pnas.2023123118.

Sadock, Jerrold M. 1991. *Autolexical Syntax: A Theory of Parallel Grammatical Representations.* Chicago, IL: University of Chicago Press.
Sandler, Wendy. 2010. "Prosody and syntax in sign languages." *Transactions of the Philological Society* 108 (3):298–328. doi: 10.1111/j.1467-968X.2010.01242.x.
Sandler, Wendy. 2017. "The Challenge of Sign Language Phonology." *Annual Review of Linguistics* 3 (1):43–63. doi: 10.1146/annurev-linguistics-011516-034122.
Sapir, Edward. 1921. *Language: An Introduction to the Study of Speech.* New York: Harcourt, BRace and Company, Inc.
Saraceni, Mario. 2003. *The Language of Comics.* New York, NY: Routeledge.
Schank, R. C., and R. Abelson. 1977. *Scripts, Plans, Goals and Understanding.* Hillsdale, NJ: Lawrence Earlbaum Associates.
Scheffler, Tatjana, Lasse Brandt, Marie de la Fuente, and Ivan Nenchev. 2022. "The processing of emoji-word substitutions: A self-paced-reading study." *Computers in Human Behavior* 127: 107076. doi: 10.1016/j.chb.2021.107076.
Schilperoord, Joost. 2013. "Raising the issue: A mental-space approach to Iwo Jima-inspired editorial cartoons." *Metaphor and Symbol* 28 (3):185–212. doi: 10.1080/10926488.2013.768513.
Schilperoord, Joost. 2017. "Ways with pictures: Visual incongruities and metaphor." In *Visual Metaphor; Structure and Process,* edited by Gerard Steen. Amsterdam: John Benjamins Publishing Company.
Schilperoord, Joost, and Neil Cohn. 2022. "Before: Unimodal linguistics, After: Multimodal linguistics: An exploration of the *Before-After* construction." *Cognitive Semantics* 8 (1): 109–40. doi: 10.1163/23526416-bja10025.
Schilperoord, Joost, and Neil Cohn. 2023. "Let there be… visual optimal innovations: Making visual meaning through Michelangelo's The Creation of Adam." *Visual Communication* 22 (4): 650–70. doi: 10.1177/14703572211004994.
Schilperoord, Joost, Vanja de Groot, and Nic van Son. 2005. "Nonverbatim captioning in Dutch television programs: A text linguistic approach." *The Journal of Deaf Studies and Deaf Education* 10 (4): 402–16. doi: 10.1093/deafed/eni038.
Schilperoord, Joost, and Lisanne van Weelden. 2018. "Rhetorical shadows: The conceptual representation of incongruent shadows." *Spatial Cognition & Computation* 18 (2): 97–114. doi: 10.1080/13875868.2017.1298113.
Schilperoord, Joost, and Arie Verhagen. 2006. "Grammar and language production: Where do function words come from?" In *Cognitive Linguistics Investigations: Across Languages, Fields and Philosophical Boundaries,* edited by June Lunjenbroers, 139–69. Amsterdam: John Benjamins.
Schlenker, Philippe, Marion Bonnet, Jonathan Lamberton, Jason Lamberton, Emmanuel Chemla, Mirko Santoro, and Carlo Geraci. 2022. "Iconic syntax: Sign language classifier predicates and gesture sequences." *Linguistics and Philosophy.* doi: lingbuzz/006060.
Schubert, Thomas W. 2005. "Your highness: Vertical positions as perceptual symbols of power." *Journal of Personality and Social Psychology* 89 (1):1.
Selkirk, Elisabeth O. 1984. *Phonology and Syntax: The Relationship between Sound and Structure.* Cambridge: MIT Press.
Senghas, Ann. 1995. "The development of Nicaraguan sign language via the language acquisition process." *Proceedings of Boston University Conference on Language Development* 19:543–52.
Sitnikova, Tatiana, Phillip J. Holcomb, and Gina R. Kuperberg. 2008. "Two neurocognitive mechanisms of semantic integration during the comprehension of visual real-world events." *Journal of Cognitive Neuroscience* 20 (11):1–21.

Skirgård, Hedvig, Hannah J. Haynie, Damián E. Blasi, Harald Hammarström, Jeremy Collins, Jay J. Latarche, Jakob Lesage, Tobias Weber, Alena Witzlack-Makarevich, Sam Passmore, Angela Chira, Luke Maurits, Russell Dinnage, Michael Dunn, Ger Reesink, Ruth Singer, Claire Bowern, Patience Epps, Jane Hill, Outi Vesakoski, Martine Robbeets, Noor Karolin Abbas, Daniel Auer, Nancy A. Bakker, Giulia Barbos, Robert D. Borges, Swintha Danielsen, Luise Dorenbusch, Ella Dorn, John Elliott, Giada Falcone, Jana Fischer, Yustinus Ghanggo Ate, Hannah Gibson, Hans-Philipp Göbel, Jemima A. Goodall, Victoria Gruner, Andrew Harvey, Rebekah Hayes, Leonard Heer, Roberto E. Herrera Miranda, Nataliia Hübler, Biu Huntington-Rainey, Jessica K. Ivani, Marilen Johns, Erika Just, Eri Kashima, Carolina Kipf, Janina V. Klingenberg, Nikita König, Aikaterina Koti, Richard G. A. Kowalik, Olga Krasnoukhova, Nora L. M. Lindvall, Mandy Lorenzen, Hannah Lutzenberger, Tânia R. A. Martins, Celia Mata German, Suzanne van der Meer, Jaime Montoya Samamé, Michael Müller, Saliha Muradoglu, Kelsey Neely, Johanna Nickel, Miina Norvik, Cheryl Akinyi Oluoch, Jesse Peacock, India O. C. Pearey, Naomi Peck, Stephanie Petit, Sören Pieper, Mariana Poblete, Daniel Prestipino, Linda Raabe, Amna Raja, Janis Reimringer, Sydney C. Rey, Julia Rizaew, Eloisa Ruppert, Kim K. Salmon, Jill Sammet, Rhiannon Schembri, Lars Schlabbach, Frederick W. P. Schmidt, Amalia Skilton, Wikaliler Daniel Smith, Hilário de Sousa, Kristin Sverredal, Daniel Valle, Javier Vera, Judith Voß, Tim Witte, Henry Wu, Stephanie Yam, Jingting Ye, Maisie Yong, Tessa Yuditha, Roberto Zariquiey, Robert Forkel, Nicholas Evans, Stephen C. Levinson, Martin Haspelmath, Simon J. Greenhill, Quentin D. Atkinson, and Russell D. Gray. 2023. "Grambank reveals the importance of genealogical constraints on linguistic diversity and highlights the impact of language loss." *Science Advances* 9 (16):eadg6175. doi: 10.1126/sciadv.adg6175.

Slimak, Ludovic, Jan Fietzke, Jean-Michel Geneste, and Roberto Ontañón. 2018. "Comment on 'U-Th dating of carbonate crusts reveals Neandertal origin of Iberian cave art.'" *Science* 361 (6408):eaau1371. doi: 10.1126/science.aau1371.

Slobin, Dan I. 1996. "From 'thought and language' to 'thinking for speaking.'" *Rethinking linguistic relativity* 17:70–96.

Smirnova, Anastasia. 2021. "Variation in linguistic complexity and its cognitive underpinning." Proceedings of the Annual Meeting of the Cognitive Science Society, UC Merced.

Smith, Kenneth. 2003. "The transmission of language: Models of biological and cultural evolution." Doctoral Dissertation, Theoretical and Applied Linguistics, University of Edinburgh.

Smith, Kenny. 2018. "The cognitive prerequisites for language: Insights from iterated learning." *Current Opinion in Behavioral Sciences* 21:154–60. doi: 10.1016/j.cobeha.2018.05.003.

Sproat, Richard. 2000. *A Computational Theory of Writing Systems*. Cambridge, UK: Cambridge University Press.

St. George, Marie, Suzanne Mannes, and James E. Hoffinan. 1994. "Global semantic expectancy and language comprehension." *Journal of Cognitive Neuroscience* 6 (1):70–83. doi: 10.1162/jocn.1994.6.1.70.

Stadler, Waltraud, Veit S. Kraft, Roee Be'er, Joachim Hermsdörfer, and Masami Ishihara. 2021. "Shared representations in athletes: Segmenting action sequences from taekwondo reveals implicit agreement." *Frontiers in Psychology* 12. doi: 10.3389/fpsyg.2021.733896.

Stokoe, William. 1960. "Sign language structure: An outline of the visual communication systems of the American deaf." In *Studies in Linguistics Occasional Paper 8*. University of Buffalo.

Supalla, Samuel. 1991. "Manually coded English: The modality question in signed language development." In *Theoretical Issues in Sign Language Research. Volume 2: Psychology*, edited by Susan D. Fischer and Patricia Siple, 85–109. Chicago: University of Chicago Press.

Supalla, Samuel, Cecile McKee, and J.H. Cripps. 2014. *An Overview on the ASL-phabet*. Tucson, AZ: Gloss Institute.

Sutton, Valerie. 1995. *Lessons in Sign Writing*. La Jolla, CA: The Deaf Action Committee.

Szawerna, Michał. 2017. *Metaphoricity of Conventionalized Diegetic Images in Comics: A Study in Multimodal Cognitive Linguistics, Łódź Studies in Language 54*. Frankfurt am Main: Peter Lang Publishing.

Talmy, Leonard. 1985. "Lexicalization patterns: Semantic structure in lexical forms." In *Language Typology and Syntactic Description: Vol. 3. Grammatical categories and the lexicon*, edited by T. Shopen, 36–149. Cambridge: Cambridge University Press.

Talmy, Leonard. 2000a. *Toward a Cognitive Semantics*. Vol. 1. Cambridge, MA: MIT Press.

Talmy, Leonard. 2000b. *Toward a Cognitive Semantics*. Vol. 2. Cambridge, MA: MIT Press.

Tanner, Darren, Maria Goldshtein, and Benjamin Weissman. 2018. "Individual differences in the real-time neural dynamics of language comprehension." In *Psychology of Learning and Motivation*, edited by Kara D. Federmeier and Duane G. Watson, 299–335. Cambridge, MA: Academic Press.

Tasić, Miloš, and Dušan Stamenković. 2015. "The interplay of words and images in expressing multimodal metaphors in comics." *Procedia—Social and Behavioral Sciences* 212:117–22. doi: 10.1016/j.sbspro.2015.11.308.

Tieu, Lyn, Philippe Schlenker, and Emmanuel Chemla. 2019. "Linguistic inferences without words." *Proceedings of the National Academy of Sciences* 116 (20):9796–801. doi: 10.1073/pnas.1821018116.

Tiippana, Kaisa. 2014. "What is the McGurk effect?" *Frontiers in Psychology* 5. doi: 10.3389/fpsyg.2014.00725.

Tomasello, Michael. 2010. *Origins of Human Communication*. Cambridge: MIT press.

Torre, Iván G., Bartolo Luque, Lucas Lacasa, Christopher T Kello, and Antoni Hernández-Fernández. 2019. "On the physical origin of linguistic laws and lognormality in speech." *Royal Society open science* 6 (8):191023.

Trainor, Laurel J. 2005. "Are there critical periods for musical development?" *Developmental Psychobiology* 46 (3):262–78. doi: 10.1002/dev.20059.

Tversky, Barbara, and Tracy Chow. 2017. "Language and culture in visual narratives." *Cognitive Semiotics* 10 (2):77–89. doi: 10.1515/cogsem-2017-0008.

Tylén, Kristian, Riccardo Fusaroli, Sergio Rojo, Katrin Heimann, Nicolas Fay, N. Johannsen Niels, Felix Riede, and Marlize Lombard. 2020. "The evolution of early symbolic behavior in Homo sapiens." *Proceedings of the National Academy of Sciences* 117 (9):4578–84. doi: 10.1073/pnas.1910880117.

Uddén, Julia, Mauricio de Jesus Dias Martins, Willem Zuidema, and W. Tecumseh Fitch. 2020. "Hierarchical structure in sequence processing: How to measure it and determine its neural implementation." *Topics in Cognitive Science* 12 (3):910–24. doi: 10.1111/tops.12442.

Umiker-Sebeok, Donna Jean, and Thomas Albert Sebeok. 1987. *Monastic Sign Languages*. New York: Mouton de Gruyter.

van Berkum, Jos J. A. 2012. "The electrophysiology of discourse and conversation." In *The Cambridge Handbook of Psycholinguistics*, edited by Michael J. Spivey, M. Joanisse, and Ken McRae. Cambridge: Cambridge University Press.

van Berkum, Jos J. A., Colin Brown, Pienie Zwitserlood, Valesca Kooijman, and Peter Hagoort. 2005. "Anticipating upcoming words in discourse: Evidence from ERPs and reading times." *Journal of Experimental Psychology: Learning, Memory, and Cognition* 31 (3):443–67.

van den Hoven, Paul, and Joost Schilperoord. 2017. "Perspective by incongruity: Visual argumentative meaning in editorial cartoons." In *Multimodal Argumentation and Rhetoric in Media Genres*, edited by Assimakis Tseronis and Charles Forceville, 136–63. Amsterdam: John Benjamins Publishing Company.

van der Hulst, Harry. in prep. "The phonology of drawing."

van der Klis, Anika, Frans Adriaans, and René Kager. 2023. "Infants' behaviours elicit different verbal, nonverbal, and multimodal responses from caregivers during early play." *Infant Behavior and Development* 71:101828. doi: 10.1016/j.infbeh.2023.101828.

Van Petten, Cyma, and Marta Kutas. 1991. "Influences of semantic and syntactic context on open—and closed-class words." *Memory and Cognition* 19:95–112.

Vandeghinste, Vincent, Ineke Schuurman Leen Sevens, and Frank Van Eynde. 2015. "Translating text into pictographs." *Natural Language Engineering* 23 (2):217–44. doi: 10.1017/S135132491500039X.

Vaneechoutte, Mario, and John R Skoyles. 1998. "The memetic origin of language: Modern humans as musical primates." *Journal of Memetics-Evolutionary Models of Information Transmission* 2 (2):84–117.

Varela, Francisco J., Evan Thompson, and Eleanor Rosch. 1991. *The Embodied Mind: Cognitive Science and Human Experience*. Cambridge, MA: MIT press.

Verhagen, Arie. 2005. *Constructions of Intersubjectivity: Discourse, Syntax, and Cognition*. New York, NY: Oxford University Press.

Võ, Melissa Le-Hoa. 2021. "The meaning and structure of scenes." *Vision Research* 181:10–20. doi: 10.1016/j.visres.2020.11.003.

Vygotsky, Lev S. 1965. *Thought and Language*. Translated by E. Hanfmann and G. Vakar. Cambridge: MIT press.

Waugh, Linda R. 1993. "Against arbitrariness: Imitation and motivation revived, with consequences for textual meaning." *Diacritics* 23 (2):71–87. doi: 10.2307/465317.

Wedel, Michel, and Rik Pieters. 2017. "A review of eye-tracking research in marketing." In *Review of Marketing Research*, edited by Naresh K. Malhotra, 123–47. Armonk, NY: M.E. Sharpe.

Weissman, Benjamin, Neil Cohn, and Darren Tanner. under review. "Predictable words and emoji: Neural correlates of verbal and pictorial lexical prediction in sentence processing".

Weissman, Benjamin, Jan Engelen, Elise Baas, and Neil Cohn. 2023. "The Lexicon of Emoji? Conventionality Modulates Processing of Emoji." *Cognitive Science* 47 (4):e13275. doi: 10.1111/cogs.13275.

Weissman, Benjamin, Jan Engelen, Lena Thamsen, and Neil Cohn. in prep. "Emoji and the affordances of pictorial composition."

Weissman, Benjamin, and Darren Tanner. 2018. "A strong wink between verbal and emoji-based irony: How the brain processes ironic emojis during language comprehension." *PLoS ONE* 13 (8):e0201727.

Whorf, Benjamin Lee. 1956. "The relation of habitual thought and behavior to language." In *Language, Thought, and Reality: Selected Writings of Benjamin Lee*

Whorf, edited by John B. Carroll, 134–59. Cambridge, MA: MIT Press. Original edition, 1956.

Wilbur, Ronnie B., M. Marschark, and P. Spencer. 2003. *Modality and the Structure of Language: Sign Languages versus Signed Systems*. Oxford: Oxford University Press.

Wilkins, David P. 2003. "Why pointing with the index finger is not a universal (in sociocultural and semiotic terms)." In *Pointing: Where Language, Culture, and Cognition Meet*, edited by Sotaro Kita, 171–215. Mahwah, NJ: Erlbaum.

Wilkins, David P. 2016. "Alternative representations of space: Arrernte narratives in sand." In *The Visual Narrative Reader*, edited by Neil Cohn, 252–81. London: Bloomsbury. Original edition, 1997. Proceedings of the CLS Opening Academic Year '97 '98, edited by M. Biemans and J. van de Weijer, 133-164. Nijmegen: Nijmegen/Tilburg Center for Language Studies.

Willats, John. 1997. *Art and Representation: New Principles in the Analysis of Pictures*. Princeton: Princeton University Press.

Willats, John. 2005. *Making Sense of Children's Drawings*. Mahwah, NJ: Lawrence Erlbaum.

Willems, Roel M., Aslı Özyürek, and Peter Hagoort. 2008. "Seeing and hearing meaning: ERP and fMRI evidence of word versus picture integration into a sentence context." *Journal of Cognitive Neuroscience* 20 (7):1235–49. doi: 10.1162/jocn.2008.20085 %M 18284352.

Willoughby, Louisa, Shimako Iwasaki, Meredith Bartlett, and Howard Manns. 2018. "Tactile sign languages." *Handbook of Pragmatics* 21:239–58.

Willoughby, Louisa, Howard Manns, Shimako Iwasaki, and Meredith Bartlett. 2020. "From seeing to feeling: How do deafblind people adapt visual sign languages?" In *Dynamics of Language Changes: Looking Within and ACROSS Languages*, edited by Keith Allan, 235–52. Singapore: Springer Singapore.

Wilson, Brent. 1988. "The artistic tower of Babel: Inextricable links between culture and graphic development." In *Discerning Art: Concepts and Issues*, edited by George W. Hardiman and Theodore Zernich, 488–506. Champaign, IL: Stipes Publishing Company.

Wilson, Brent. 1999. "Becoming Japanese: Manga, children's drawings, and the construction of national character." *Visual Arts Research* 25 (2):48–60.

Wilson, Brent. 2016. "What happened and what happened next: Kids' visual narratives across cultures." In *The Visual Narrative Reader*, edited by Neil Cohn, 185–227. London: Bloomsbury.

Wilson, Brent, and Marjorie Wilson. 2009. *Teaching Children to Draw: A Guide for Teachers and Parents*. Second ed. Worcester, MA: Davis Publications, Inc.

Winter, Bodo, Gary Lupyan, Lynn K. Perry, Mark Dingemanse, and Marcus Perlman. 2023. "Iconicity ratings for 14,000+ English words." *Behavior Research Methods*. doi: 10.3758/s13428-023-02112-6.

Wittenberg, Eva, and Ray Jackendoff. 2023. "The co-evolution of pragmatics and grammatical complexity." In *Evolutionary Pragmatics*, edited by B. Geuts and R. Moore. Oxford: Oxford University Press.

Wolf, Maryanne. 2008. *Proust and the Squid: The Story and Science of the Reading Brain*. New York: Harper Perennial.

Woodin, Greg, Bodo Winter, Marcus Perlman, Jeannette Littlemore, and Teenie Matlock. 2020. "'Tiny numbers' are actually tiny: Evidence from gestures in the TV News Archive." *PLOS ONE* 15 (11):e0242142. doi: 10.1371/journal.pone.0242142.

Wu, Ying Choon, and Seana Coulson. 2005. "Meaningful gestures: Electrophysiological indices of iconic gesture comprehension." *Psychophysiology* 42 (6):654–67. doi: 10.1111/j.1469-8986.2005.00356.x.

Xu, Jiang, Patrick J Gannon, Karen Emmorey, Jason F Smith, and Allen R Braun. 2009. "Symbolic gestures and spoken language are processed by a common neural system." *Proceedings of the National Academy of Sciences* 106 (49):20664–9.

Zaccarella, E., and A. D. Friederici. 2017. "The neurobiological nature of syntactic hierarchies." *Neuroscience & Biobehavioral Reviews* 81:205–12. doi: 10.1016/j.neubiorev.2016.07.038.

Zacks, Jeffrey M., and Barbara Tversky. 2001. "Event structure in perception and conception." *Psychological Bulletin* 127 (1):3–21.

Zhao, Fang, and Nina Mahrt. 2018. "Influences of comics expertise and comics types in comics reading." *International Journal of Innovation and Research in Educational Sciences* 5 (2):218–24.

Zipf, George K. 1935. *The Psychobiology of Language*. Oxford, England: Houghton-Mifflin.

Zuidema, Willem, and Arie Verhagen. 2010. "What are the unique design features of language? Formal tools for comparative claims." *Adaptive Behavior* 18 (1):48–65. doi: 10.1177/1059712309350973.

Zwaan, Rolf A., and Gabriel A. Radvansky. 1998. "Situation models in language comprehension and memory." *Psychological Bulletin* 123 (2):162–85.

Index

absent coreference 114, 116–17, 126, 133–42, 189, 208, 209, 246, 247
absentia 23
abstract art 23, 24
activity constraint 123, 163
Adjacent Awareness 83–5, 296
adjoined interfaces 79, 81–9, 135, 143, 208, 215
affix 29, 30, 82–4, 101, 111, 125, 153, 156–8, 166, 169, 171, 175, 178, 201, 240, 247, 253
affordances 33, 35, 36, 41, 42, 45–7, 59, 63, 64, 95, 101, 110, 111, 116, 127–30, 140, 142, 147, 168, 177, 179, 197, 201, 202, 205, 228, 231, 247–8, 252, 265, 267, 276, 278, 282, 286, 288–92
aligned coindexation 105, 106, 109–11, 119, 128, 286
aligned units 75–7
allocation 35, 185, 187–94, 198, 207, 216, 223, 225, 226, 230–41, 298
  independent 185, 187, 188–9, 194, 198, 207–24
  substitutive 185, 187, 189–94, 198, 207, 216, 223, 224–41
ambiguity, grammatical 12, 15, 25, 108, 170, 173, 174
amodal assumption of language 4–6, 9, 15, 17, 19, 25–7, 30–4, 36, 41, 93, 205, 225, 245, 247, 249, 250, 259, 260, 263, 265, 268, 270, 277–90, 292
analytic morphology 176, 178, 253
arbitrariness 4, 5, 7, 14–16, 18, 31, 32, 36, 49, 62, 101–2, 109–11, 182, 248, 263, 265–7, 278, 282–4, 286–9, 296
array 54, 148–70, 175–9, 182–3, 186, 187, 190–2, 198–202, 212–20, 226, 238, 240, 270, 298
assemblage structure (graphology) 57, 59
asymmetrical grammatical interaction 185–7, 192–4, 214–20, 223, 230–1, 233–5, 238, 240, 249, 259

Australian Aboriginals 10, 77, 261, 271, 274
auxiliary domain 120, 124–6, 139

background knowledge 120–1, 125, 138–40, 161, 229
balanced semantic weight 113–16
Bateman, John xv, 10, 30, 41, 44, 59, 103, 110, 113, 117, 142, 277, 281, 293
beat gestures 71, 76
beat modality interfacing 76, 77, 79, 88
Before-After Construction 154–6, 202, 211–2
binding, see conceptual binding
blending, see conceptual blending
blindness 6, 52
bodily modality 4–6, 18–27, 31–4, 41, 44–7, 50–4, 59–63, 65–7, 69, 73, 75, 78, 99–101, 104–10, 129, 132, 138, 140, 152, 154, 168, 177, 180, 189, 194, 197, 199–201, 204, 232, 235, 246–52, 255–9, 263–5, 270–82, 287, 288, 291, 292, 295, 296
bound morpheme 29, 83, 156, 157, 169, 240
Braille 4, 41, 42, 45, 64, 278
Brainwaves 16, 17, 93
Broca's area 16
bundling 35, 75, 78, 80–2, 85–9, 216, 220, 222

carriers 81–9, 127–9, 133–5, 187, 208, 212, 213, 220, 223, 296
  non-sentient 85
  private 85, 134, 296
  public 84, 296
  satellite 81–7, 127, 133–5
categorical schema 148, 149, 164–8, 185–92, 198, 201, 202, 238, 253, 257, 269
cave paintings 10, 46, 59, 64, 270–4
cheremes 47, 52, 61, 66

cherology 26, 27, 41, 47, 52–4, 61, 66, 204, 248, 279
Chomsky, Noam 3, 4, 6, 7, 15, 19, 26, 147, 166, 169, 252, 254, 263, 267, 268, 282, 283, 284
co-durative interfaces 73, 75–9, 81, 88, 89, 207, 215
co-speech gesture 4, 7, 10, 12, 17, 18, 21, 24–7, 30, 31, 34, 36, 41, 42, 69, 71, 75–81, 89, 93, 96, 104, 107–8, 115, 116, 127–32, 137–40, 151–2, 154, 187, 189, 192–4, 207–11, 214–16, 225, 226, 230–5, 238, 241, 246–8, 251, 255, 256, 258–61, 276, 278, 279–81, 285, 291, 296
codeswitching 6, 35, 192, 194, 232, 236, 238, 241
coercion 190, 229
cognitive grammar 284
cognitive toolkit 252, 262, 274
coindexation 105–11, 116, 119, 159
color-grapheme synesthesia 72, 295
combinatorial types, see Complexity Hierarchy
combinatoriality 15, 19, 20–3, 34–5, 67, 110, 147–83, 185, 201–2, 205, 214, 218, 223, 253, 256–9, 262, 267, 270, 271, 274–6, 283–5, 292, 297
Comparison Construction 154–6
complete coreference 114–16, 126–9, 133, 189, 208–10, 222, 247, 272, 297
complex combinatoriality 20–3, 34, 35, 147–52, 158, 164, 175, 179, 185, 201, 202, 214, 218, 223, 256–9, 262, 267, 270, 271, 274–6, 285, 292, 297
Complexity Hierarchy 35, 147–83, 185, 198, 201, 252, 256, 257, 267–9, 275, 297
compositional structure (graphology) 58, 59
conceptual binding 35, 81, 97, 98, 101, 108, 128, 129, 140, 153, 156, 159, 160, 163, 165, 181, 190, 192, 211, 213, 227, 234
conceptual blending 24, 110, 116, 121, 208, 253
conceptual integration 24, 35, 75, 77, 87, 88, 89, 93, 113, 116, 117, 121, 124, 126, 128, 133, 142–3, 163, 189, 213, 215, 219, 234, 276, 280, 286, 287, 291

conceptual metaphor 7, 18, 24, 84, 96, 106, 109, 110, 116, 121, 125, 126, 139, 140, 215, 253, 297
Conceptual Semantics 95–7, 115, 117, 142, 297
Conceptual Structure 19–22, 24, 25, 27, 29, 31, 33, 35, 41–3, 48–50, 56, 58, 60–7, 84, 89, 93–111, 113–42, 147–56, 160, 161, 166–8, 170–2, 174–7, 179–83, 189–92, 194, 197, 199, 201–4, 207, 208, 211–13, 215, 218–22, 227, 229, 230–6, 239, 240, 247–9, 252–5, 257, 260–3, 270, 274, 275, 279, 285, 287, 288, 292, 295, 297
Conjunction 171, 174, 238
construction grammar 28
constructions 11, 12, 15, 27–30, 35, 75, 98, 138, 154–8, 166, 170, 171, 180, 181, 189, 190, 202, 203, 211–13, 223, 225–30, 233–6, 240, 241, 247, 249, 251, 257, 279, 281, 291, 292
continuity constraint 121–3, 163, 211
conventionality 14, 49, 102, 109, 182, 200, 248, 266, 286, 287
core versus periphery 4, 17, 31, 205, 225, 249, 258, 263–8, 276, 277, 279–82, 288–94, 298
coreference 13, 35, 114–42, 163, 189, 194, 207–9, 211, 212, 215, 216, 218, 220, 222
  graphic 121–6
  multimodal 126–42
  vocal 117–21
coreference schemas 115, 116, 119, 129, 130, 132, 133
coreference types
  absent 114, 116–17, 126, 133–42, 189, 208, 209, 246, 247
  complete 114–16, 126–9, 133, 189, 208–10, 222, 247, 272, 297
  included 126, 130–3, 189
  partial 126, 131–3, 189
cross-modal 30, 34, 68, 70, 71, 88, 89
cross-sensory 35, 68, 70–2, 295

dance 22–4, 52, 60, 61, 63, 66, 175, 251
deaf 6, 8, 21, 25, 31, 33, 52, 154, 161, 177, 178, 204, 224, 246, 256, 258, 293

deaf community 6, 31, 161, 204, 246, 293
deafblind 6, 52
Dehaene, Stanislas 9, 19, 25, 62, 149, 158, 265, 272, 275, 278, 287
design features of language 3, 4, 14–16, 18, 32, 248, 282–3, 288, 289
diagrammatic iconicity 105, 106, 223, 237, 238
diversity, linguistic 3, 4, 5, 13, 37, 245, 249–54, 262
drawing 10, 13, 21, 22, 26, 30, 34, 41, 42, 44, 46, 54, 59, 61, 63, 65, 69, 71, 75, 77, 79, 100, 105, 123, 175, 177, 197, 202, 204, 223, 247, 251, 260, 261, 271, 272–4, 279–84, 293–6
drawing development 10, 13, 21, 274, 281, 293
dual-coding models 285
duration/durativity (formological feature) 35, 45, 46, 53, 66, 68–75, 77, 79, 88, 197, 216, 231, 238, 290
   co-durative 73, 75–9, 81, 88, 89, 207, 215
   mixed durative 73, 77–9, 81, 88, 89, 109, 207
   non-durative 54, 71, 73, 77–89, 207, 215, 239

emergent interfaces 79, 82–9, 134, 135, 143, 187
emergent states in the Parallel Architecture 19–23, 27, 30, 31, 32, 35, 197–205, 207, 208, 214, 223, 245, 255, 261, 279, 281, 285, 288, 289
Emmorey, Karen 5, 6, 7, 16, 25, 31, 94, 187, 192, 194, 232, 235, 256, 258, 278
emoji 10, 21, 64, 113, 114, 135–9, 152, 156, 157, 159–61, 163, 168, 179, 186–92, 201, 202, 207, 214–16, 225, 226, 231, 236, 239, 240, 249, 256, 291, 298
Equivalence, see Principle of Equivalence
evolution 6, 15, 36, 43, 123–5, 263–76, 279, 292, 293
   of grammar 267–8, 269, 270, 274–6
   of language 6, 15, 263–76, 279, 292

   of modalities 264–5, 269, 271–3, 275
   of semantics 265–7, 270, 272–6
external compositional structure (graphology) 58, 59

figura (formology) 56–8
Forceville, Charles 12, 24, 30, 41, 142, 272, 281
formemes 47, 54, 55, 60, 65–70, 74, 269
formology 26, 27, 29, 30–4, 37, 42, 47, 48, 50, 53, 54, 56, 60, 65–8, 70, 74, 89, 101–2, 106, 109, 177, 180, 182, 197, 210, 253, 255, 257, 262, 264–5, 269, 270, 274–5, 285–6
fragile systems 8, 13, 20–2, 34, 255, 258
Framing Plane 86–7
free morpheme 83, 101, 153, 157, 158, 169, 175, 205, 240, 253

generative grammar 15, 284, 285
generative semantics 284
gesture 4, 6, 7, 10, 12, 17, 18, 21, 24–7, 30, 31, 34, 36, 41, 42, 44–6, 50, 52, 60, 67, 69, 71, 73, 75–9, 81, 88, 89, 93–6, 104–10, 115, 116, 127–32, 137–40, 151, 152, 154, 177, 186–9, 192–4, 199, 200, 207, 208, 210, 211, 214–16, 225, 226, 230–2, 234, 235, 238, 241, 246–51, 255–65, 272, 275, 276, 278, 279, 280, 281, 284, 285, 291, 292, 296
gesture-first evolution 6, 263, 264, 275
Goldin-Meadow, Susan xv, 5, 7, 8, 14, 20, 21, 25, 31, 33, 50, 78, 89, 105, 110, 152, 154, 160, 161, 199, 201, 255, 256, 258, 276, 278–80, 282, 283
Goldsmith, John 3, 4, 15, 18, 19, 50, 166, 203, 284, 297
grammar 5, 12, 13, 15, 19–24, 27–31, 34–6, 63, 73, 82, 89, 97, 101, 107, 110, 118, 138, 143, 145, 147–83, 185–94, 197, 198, 203, 204, 207, 220, 222, 226, 229, 232–8, 245, 251, 254–7, 264, 267–70, 275, 281, 284, 288
grammar interactions 35, 185–94, 207–41
   allocation 35, 185, 187–94, 198, 207, 216, 223, 225, 226, 230–41, 298
   symmetry 35, 185–7, 189, 191–4, 198, 207–25, 230–5, 238, 249, 259

grammatical categories 12, 25, 64, 149–51, 163, 164–6, 168, 176, 180, 182, 185, 188, 191, 192, 198, 201, 202, 229, 234–6, 238
graphemes 47, 52, 54–9, 61, 64, 66, 69, 70, 71, 85, 100, 101, 223, 272–4
graphic modality 4, 18–27, 31–4, 41, 44–7, 50, 54–66, 71, 72, 75, 77–9, 81–5, 89, 93, 99–105, 108–11, 117, 121, 127, 130, 133, 141, 147, 152, 154–7, 159, 161, 168, 171, 174–81, 192, 197, 199, 201–4, 223, 225–8, 232–6, 239, 247–52, 255, 256–9, 265, 270–82, 286–95, 297
graphic planes 86–8
    Framing Plane 86–7
    Representational Plane 86–7
graphic systems, see also visual language 9, 10, 13, 14, 50, 105, 234, 261
graphology 26–30, 47, 54, 59, 64, 66, 69–71, 101, 203, 279
ground, the 102, 287

handshape (cherology) 5, 45, 47, 52, 62, 63, 76, 232
head-modifier schema 154, 169, 180
heart shape 10–2, 28–30, 87, 109, 125, 156, 157, 175, 178, 189, 218, 225, 227–9, 239, 247, 298
heuristics, semantic 8, 154, 160, 164, 253, 256
Hockett, Charles 3, 4, 14, 46, 110, 111, 248, 266, 282, 298
homesign 7, 8, 21, 25, 26, 34, 154, 161, 201, 246, 256, 258
human uniqueness 16, 254, 270–6, 282–3

I ♥ NY 10, 29, 30, 36, 189, 225, 227, 228, 230, 240, 285
Iconicity 5, 14, 15, 17, 32, 49, 50, 62, 103–6, 108–11, 116, 119, 180, 181, 197, 247, 248, 255, 263, 266, 267, 272, 274, 283, 286, 287, 288, 291, 292, 297
    diagrammatic 105, 106, 223, 237, 238
    iconicity schema 106
    imagetic 105, 106, 297
    metaphoric 106, 297

ideophones 15, 21, 35, 104, 150, 194, 198, 199, 218, 235, 239, 241, 247, 286
idiosyncratic signs (see also sinsign) 21–4, 47–9, 102–5, 110, 180, 182, 197, 199–201, 204, 207, 223, 253, 266, 269, 273, 287
imagetic iconicity 105, 106, 297
imbalanced semantic weight 113–16, 189
included coreference 126, 130, 131, 133, 189
independent allocation 185, 187, 188–9, 194, 198, 207–24
independent modality interfaces 76, 78
    co-durative independent 76, 78
    mixed durative independent 79
    non-durative independent 79–81, 84–9
indexical mediation 78, 79, 88, 296
indexicality 5, 14, 32, 50, 81, 82, 84, 106–11, 127, 129, 180–2, 197, 247, 248, 255, 263, 266, 267, 283, 286–8, 292
    indexicality schema 108
inherent interfaces 79, 85–6, 89, 135, 142, 210
innateness 7–9, 33–6, 50, 96, 245, 249, 252, 254–60, 262, 274, 275, 279, 292
instruction manuals 59, 160, 162, 164, 202, 237, 297
intentionality 42, 52, 273, 295
interface rules 102
intermediate level hypothesis 89
internal compositional structure (graphology) 58, 59
interpretant 102, 287, 297
intonation (phonology) 51, 52, 54, 59, 165
irony 138
iterated learning 258, 266, 287

Jackendoff, Ray xiv, xv, 3, 4, 6, 7, 15–20, 22, 25–30, 35, 43, 60, 75, 89, 93, 95–100, 102, 117–20, 133, 135, 138, 147–50, 153, 160, 164, 165, 169, 171, 175, 176, 178, 181, 192, 199, 203, 218, 219, 232, 235, 236, 238, 252, 255, 257, 263, 267, 268, 275, 283, 285, 288, 290, 291, 297
junctions (graphological) 55–7, 274

Kress, Gunther 30, 41, 113, 142, 277, 293

Lakoff, George 3, 6, 24, 100, 106, 110, 116, 121, 136, 138, 175, 284, 297
language, assumptions of 3–5, 31–4, 263–8, 277–90
language, definition of 17–19, 23–6, 249–51, 263–8
left inferior frontal gyrus, see also Broca's area 16
legisign 47, 102, 109, 180, 182, 266, 286, 287
Lerdahl, Fred 15, 22, 25, 60, 175, 283
lexical items 12–14, 24, 27, 29, 30, 48, 75, 100, 101, 108, 117–21, 141, 176, 191, 205, 208, 209, 212, 213, 223, 224, 229, 238, 254, 257–60, 281, 285, 288, 291
lexicon 5, 8, 13, 15, 20–4, 27, 29, 36, 48, 141, 151, 152, 189, 199–201, 204, 210, 234–8, 249, 251, 255–8, 262, 269, 274, 279, 281, 284, 285, 291
linear schema 148, 149, 158–65, 168, 171, 173, 177–80, 186, 191, 198, 199, 212–14, 218, 238, 255, 298
linguistic relativity, see relativity (see also permeability)
linguistics 9, 14, 41, 159, 171, 241, 249, 277–94, 297
long-term memory 228, 251

macromorph 178
Manually Coded English 5, 63, 168, 278
march of progress (evolutionary theories) 263, 268, 292
March of Progress (picture) 123–5, 263
Marr, David 16, 96, 100, 175, 176, 254, 261, 283, 290
martial arts 22, 24
matrix schema (substitution) 189–92, 194, 226, 227, 229, 232, 234–6, 238–40, 281
McGurk effect 69, 70, 72
Memory 17, 19, 24, 25, 43, 48, 75, 93, 94, 100, 115, 128, 148, 149, 164, 168–72, 180, 197–9, 224, 228, 249, 251, 253, 283, 286, 288, 290, 292, 298
metaphor 7, 18, 24, 84, 96, 106, 109, 110, 121, 125, 126, 139, 140, 215, 253, 297

metaphoric iconicity 106, 297
metrical structure 51, 57, 59–61, 175
   graphology 57, 59
   phonology 51
Mezereth-Altmann Law 254
micromorph 177, 178
mixed durative interfaces 73, 77–9, 81, 88, 89, 109, 207
modalia 19, 20, 23–7, 30–1, 37, 49, 198, 245, 251, 262, 264, 272, 287
modality, definition and properties of 5, 6, 18–37, 41–89, 94–7
   natural modalities 33, 35, 44, 46, 47, 50, 54, 60–6, 71–2, 78, 105, 110, 150, 156, 168, 179, 180, 185, 197, 199, 201, 204, 223, 241, 255, 258–60, 265, 269, 271, 274, 278, 279, 281, 282
   natural non-conceptual modalities 60–1, 66
   synesthetic modalities 61–6, 72, 168, 199, 223, 259, 260, 289
   tool mediated modalities 44, 50, 64–6, 72, 77, 78, 156, 157, 204, 295
modality interfaces 71, 73–89, 117, 129, 140, 142, 143, 188, 197, 234, 270, 275
modality-generality 47, 65, 65, 67, 148, 252, 253, 254, 262, 271
modality-specificity 26, 27, 47, 73, 93, 94, 252, 254, 262, 289
modality-transference theories 264, 265, 275
monomorph 29, 30, 83, 84, 101, 150, 152, 156–8, 177, 178, 208, 212, 227, 229, 232, 240, 274
morphology 15, 20, 28, 35, 58, 63, 83, 87, 101, 121, 135, 157, 169, 170, 175–8, 183, 197, 198, 228, 236, 240, 254, 297
morphology-grammar trade-off 179, 254, 298
motion events 99, 100, 156, 261
motion lines 12, 63, 87, 99, 100–3, 105, 108, 109, 111, 121, 125, 157, 175, 178, 218, 223, 297
multi-mapping 34, 67
multimodal interactions 6, 10, 12, 17, 24, 26, 27, 30–6, 41, 72–5, 89, 94, 113–19, 126–43, 171, 185–94, 207–34, 238–41, 249, 260, 270, 281

multimodal lexical items 14, 29, 30, 75, 141, 208, 209, 212, 213, 223, 224, 229, 238, 257, 260, 281, 285, 288, 291
multimodal optimal innovations 140, 141
Multimodal Paradigm 31–4, 36, 67, 225, 250, 264–6, 277, 281, 282, 288–94
Multimodal Parallel Architecture 27, 28, 30–6, 41, 42, 48, 60, 67, 73, 100, 102, 114, 143, 182, 188, 197, 198, 199, 201–5, 207, 214, 215, 220–4, 230, 234, 238, 245–55, 258, 260–5, 267, 269, 275, 277, 279, 281, 285, 287–9, 291–3
multimodal semantic interactions 113–17, 126–42
multiplicity 36, 245–9, 268, 276, 282, 288
multisensory 34, 45, 67–70
music 15–18, 22–6, 42, 43, 46, 60, 61, 66, 77, 175, 251, 252, 254, 270, 281, 283, 290

N400 16, 17, 93, 94, 226
narrative categories 163, 166–9, 174
narrative grammar 167, 168, 172–5, 179, 187, 192, 220, 233, 238
natural modalities 33, 35, 44, 46, 47, 50, 54, 60–6, 71–2, 78, 105, 110, 150, 156, 168, 179, 180, 185, 197, 199, 201, 204, 223, 241, 255, 258–60, 265, 269, 271, 274, 278, 279, 281, 282
natural non-conceptual modalities 60–1, 66
Neanderthals 273, 274
neurocognition of language 8, 9, 16–17, 19, 93–5, 149
non-durative interfaces 79–81, 84–9
  adjoined 79, 81–9, 135, 143, 208, 215
  emergent 79, 82–9, 134, 135, 143, 187
  independent 79–81, 84–9
  inherent 79, 85–6, 89, 135, 142, 210
non-sentient carriers 85

object (Peircean) 102, 287, 297
omnia 19–27, 30, 31, 34–6, 149, 150, 164, 165, 169, 185, 198–205, 207, 232, 234–8, 245, 246, 249–51, 255–62, 264–8, 274, 279–82, 285, 289, 291–3, 298

one-unit schema 148–52, 171, 178, 179, 186, 187, 189, 191, 194, 198–201, 215, 235, 255
onomatopoeia, see also ideophones 104, 150, 151, 187, 192, 194, 225, 232–6
ontological semantics 96, 168, 175–9, 182
optimal innovations 118, 119, 121, 124, 140, 141, 223
  multimodal 140, 141
  visual 124–5, 141
  vocal 118–19, 141, 223
ordered linear schema 149, 158–65, 173, 191, 199, 202, 213, 216

P600 17
Parallel Architecture 19, 20, 27–36, 41, 42, 42, 48, 49, 60, 67, 73, 97, 100–3, 109, 114, 143, 182, 188, 197, 198–205, 207, 208, 214, 215, 220–4, 230, 234, 238, 245–7, 249, 251–3, 255, 258–65, 267, 269, 275, 277, 279, 281, 285, 287–9, 291–3
partial coreference 126, 131–3, 189
parts of speech, see also grammatical categories 165, 235
Peirce, Charles Sanders 14, 35, 47–9, 102, 103, 105, 108–10, 180, 182, 200, 266, 286–8, 297
perception (sensory input) 43–6, 48, 56, 58, 64–8, 70–2, 73, 74, 89, 103, 175, 248, 259, 295
permeability 260–2
persisting modality interfacing 76–9, 88, 138, 215, 216, 231
phonemes 47–52, 55, 60, 61, 64, 66, 69–71, 104, 287
phonology 4, 6, 10, 15, 16, 19, 26, 27, 29, 30, 42, 47, 49–52, 55, 60, 66, 70, 71, 103, 104, 108, 131, 156, 203, 279
photography 16, 41, 58, 64, 65, 66, 82, 108, 156, 204, 208, 259, 260, 295
phrase structure 8, 15, 148, 149, 164–5, 168, 169, 170, 180, 185, 186, 198, 202, 257
place of articulation (cherology) 52–3
polysynthetic morphology 156, 178, 180, 240

predicates, conceptual 84, 96–9, 115–17, 121, 123, 129, 141, 150–3, 157, 158, 175–80, 182, 212, 213, 227, 229, 230, 232, 236, 239, 240, 266, 298
primitives 5, 19, 42, 44–5, 47, 50–2, 54, 60, 61, 64–6, 68, 70, 72, 73, 74, 295
 formological 47, 50–2, 54, 60, 61, 64–6, 68–70, 72, 74
 sensory 42, 44–5, 50, 60, 64, 68, 70, 72, 73, 74
Principle of Equivalence 289, 290
private carriers 85, 134, 296
production 5, 10, 13, 16, 42–6, 52, 54, 60, 65–8, 70, 73, 74, 77, 93, 104, 115, 154, 172, 220, 222, 238, 257, 259, 265, 271, 272, 291, 292, 295
production (sensory output) 42, 43–6, 52, 54, 60, 65–8, 70, 73, 74, 77, 93, 104, 220
Productive Heart Construction 227–9
projection 103, 105
prosody (phonology) 51, 54, 71, 75–6, 127, 165, 177
protolanguage 263, 267, 268, 275
prototypical correspondences between grammar and meaning 167, 168, 175–80, 190, 227, 239
public carriers 84, 296

rebus writing 62, 156, 157, 168, 225
recursion 12, 14–16, 25, 36, 56, 148, 149, 169–75, 178, 179, 186, 198, 202, 253, 257, 263, 264, 267–9, 283, 292
reference types, see also signification 14, 101–3, 108–11, 264, 266, 288, 289
region (graphology) 29, 52, 55–8, 100, 108, 154, 155, 175, 208, 212, 273
region structure (graphology) 56–8
regularity of signs (see also conventionality, legisigns) 48, 49, 109, 110, 180, 182, 205, 286, 287
relational iconicity, see diagrammatic iconicity
relativity 36, 249, 260–2
replica 48, 49, 51, 180
representamen 102, 287
Representational Plane 86–7

resilient systems 8, 13, 21, 22, 33, 50, 255, 258, 259, 262, 270, 279, 282, 289, 292
Root Awareness 83–5, 89, 296

safety manuals 159–63, 202, 213
sand drawings 10, 59, 77, 204, 261, 271, 272, 274
Sapir-Whorf hypothesis, see relativity
satellite carriers 81–7, 127, 133–5
Saussure, Ferdinand de 4, 101, 110, 278, 283
Saussurean Sign 14, 49, 101–3, 109, 182, 265, 266, 278, 283–7, 296
semantic features 81, 84, 94–6, 129, 197, 296
semantic memory 17, 19, 24, 25, 43, 93, 94, 115, 197, 286
semantic weight 113–14, 189, 216, 217
semantics 4, 7–9, 11, 15, 19, 21, 81, 82, 84, 93–111, 113–43, 156, 162, 167, 168, 175, 176, 178, 189, 191, 215, 220, 226, 230, 234, 239, 284, 297
semia 19–27, 30–6, 149, 150, 158, 164, 185, 198–205, 207, 232, 235, 236, 238, 245, 246, 249, 251, 255–62, 264–8, 274, 275, 278, 281, 282, 285, 289, 291, 292, 298
Semiotic Optimality Principle 111, 248
semiotics 14, 21, 32, 35, 47, 102, 110, 111, 180, 181–2, 248, 255, 263–6, 276, 282, 286, 287
 of grammar 180–2
 of meaning 101–11
 of modalities 47–50
sensory primitives 42, 44–5, 50, 60, 64, 68, 70, 72, 73, 74
sensory stimulus 43–6, 50, 51, 60, 66, 68–71, 74, 93, 285
sensory systems 42–50, 61, 65–73, 94, 246, 253, 295
sequence, see also ordered linear array 158
sequentia 19, 20, 22–7, 30, 31, 33, 35, 37, 52, 60, 61, 150, 198, 245, 251, 262, 264, 281
set, see also unordered linear sequence 158
sign language 4–8, 10, 14, 16–18, 20, 21, 24–7, 34, 44, 45, 50, 52, 53, 60, 62, 63, 69, 104, 105, 110, 154, 161, 192,

194, 201, 203, 204, 223, 232, 235, 246, 248, 250–2, 254–6, 258, 263, 265, 272, 278–83, 286, 291–3
sign vehicle 102, 287
signage 85, 160, 201, 202, 213, 291
signification 14, 15, 32, 35, 95, 101–11, 128, 180–2, 197, 247–9, 255, 264–8, 270, 274, 276, 283, 284, 286–9, 292, 296, 297
simple combinatoriality 21, 23, 148–64, 179, 185, 201, 202, 214, 223, 256, 267, 270, 274
simple phrase schema 164, 165, 168–70, 198
sinsign 47, 102, 180, 200, 287
sister schemas 29, 119, 121, 176, 210, 257
spatial correspondence (modality) 79, 188, 189, 194, 234
Spatial Structure 48, 56–8, 96, 100–11, 123, 128, 130, 131, 136, 138, 140, 152, 157, 175, 197, 261
Speech 3–10, 12–14, 16, 18, 24–7, 30–2, 36, 41–7, 50, 51, 60–4, 67, 69, 73, 75–9, 81, 83, 84, 86, 87, 89, 93, 96, 100, 108, 115, 127, 128, 130–2, 138, 139, 150–3, 160, 156, 166, 168, 171–3, 176, 178, 183, 187, 189, 192, 193, 197, 198, 201, 203, 207, 208, 214, 216, 218, 223, 225, 230–5, 238, 239, 241, 246–9, 251, 254, 258–60, 263, 265, 270, 272, 276–94
stress (phonology) 51, 52, 59, 67, 127
structuralism 278, 282
substitution schema 190–2, 226
substitutive allocation (substitution) 35, 185, 187–94, 207, 216, 223, 225–41
   constraints on 238–40
   multimodal 189–94, 225–35
   unimodal 194, 235–8
supramodal semantic hub 17, 19, 25, 94, 95, 197, 286
symbolicity 32, 50, 103, 108, 109, 111, 116, 180, 197, 247, 248, 255, 266, 267, 269, 286–9, 292
symbolicity schema 109
symmetrical complex relations 186, 187, 192, 193, 220–5, 233, 234, 249
symmetrical grammatical interaction 185–7, 191–4, 208–25, 233–5, 249, 259

symmetrical simple relations 186, 191, 208–14
symmetry, grammatical 35, 185–7, 189, 191–4, 198, 207–25, 230–5, 238, 249, 259
synchronous modality interfacing 75, 76, 88, 89, 215, 215, 231, 232
synesthesia 62, 70–2, 278, 295
synesthetic modalities 61–6, 72, 168, 199, 223, 259, 260, 289
syntax 4, 12, 15, 16, 18–20, 25, 35, 54, 96, 101, 156, 166–77, 182, 183, 192, 198, 203, 225, 227, 229, 230, 236, 267, 283, 284, 297

tabula (graphology) 56, 58, 59
temporal correspondence 46, 73, 75, 78, 79, 88, 215
text-image relationships 10, 26, 79, 81, 82, 86, 115, 128, 131–7, 216, 218, 231, 251
That Deaf Guy 177, 178, 224
tokens 23, 48, 51, 102, 109, 122, 123, 149, 156, 166, 168, 169, 180, 197, 198, 278
tool mediated modalities 44, 50, 64–6, 72, 77, 78, 156, 157, 204, 295
translatability 33, 85, 127, 168, 174
translation 174, 187, 222
two-unit schema 148, 149, 152–8, 164, 171, 186, 191, 198–202, 212, 255, 291
types 48, 49, 180, 265
typification 169, 180, 266, 272, 273

Unification 19, 107, 115, 149, 189, 190, 229, 234, 236
unimodality 4, 5, 24, 26, 27, 30, 31, 32, 35, 36, 41, 69, 73, 89, 94, 113, 115–17, 120, 126, 133, 133, 140–2, 185, 194, 197–205, 212, 219, 235, 236, 238, 241, 245, 246, 249, 251, 263–5, 268, 275, 277, 280, 281, 285, 288, 289, 291, 292
unimodality, assumption of 4, 5, 31, 32, 36, 245, 246, 249, 263, 264, 275, 277, 280, 289
unique features of language, see design features of language
universality 166, 252

universals 6, 13, 36, 63, 166, 170, 245, 249, 251–4, 262, 280
  modality-general universals 252–3, 262
  modality-specific universals 252, 262
unordered linear schema 158–65, 202, 213, 216
upfix 29, 87, 121, 125, 126, 157
utility 36, 133, 245, 247–9, 268, 276, 282

van der Hulst, Harry 26, 50
Verb-Image Construction 11, 228–30, 236, 240, 291
visual language 12–14, 21, 24, 27, 50, 63, 110, 172, 179, 203, 204, 221, 234, 236, 246, 250–2, 254, 256, 258, 261, 262, 278, 280, 282, 291, 293, 294, 297
visual morphology 83, 121, 157, 228
visual optimal innovations 124–5, 141
vocal modality 18, 20, 21, 26, 33, 50, 54, 60, 69, 71, 104, 107, 111, 132, 177, 180, 199, 203, 205, 235, 246–8, 259, 262, 264, 265, 278–82, 288, 290, 297

Wernicke's area 16
Willats, John 12, 13, 15, 19, 21, 47, 54, 56, 57, 100, 103, 105, 175, 272, 274, 280, 281, 283, 292
Wittenberg, Eva 15, 19, 35, 147, 148, 150, 153, 160, 164, 165, 171, 181, 199, 257, 263, 267, 268, 275, 283
working memory 149, 249, 298
writing 4, 8–10, 12, 14, 17, 24, 26, 27, 30, 41, 54, 61–6, 69–71, 89, 113, 129, 142, 168, 199, 203, 208, 215, 221, 223, 225, 259, 265, 278, 281, 285, 295
writing systems 9, 10, 54, 61–4, 70, 71, 203, 259

X-bar schema, see also head-modifier schema 97, 169, 253

Zipf's Law 254

www.ingramcontent.com/pod-product-compliance
Lightning Source LLC
Chambersburg PA
CBHW071759300426
44116CB00009B/1139